Animals and Women

Animals and Women

Feminist Theoretical Explorations

Edited by

Carol J. Adams

and

Josephine Donovan

Duke University Press
Durham and London 1995

© 1995 Duke University Press
All rights reserved
Printed in the United States of America on acid-free paper ∞
Designed by Sylvia Steiner
Typeset in Trump by Keystone Typesetting, Inc.
Library of Congress Cataloging-in-Publication Data appear
on the last printed page of this book.

hy do I care so much?
Why, in order to change attitudes and actions in the labs,
do I subject myself repeatedly to the personal nightmare
of visiting these places . . . ?
The answer is simple. . . . It is time to repay something of the debt
I owe the chimpanzees.

—Jane Goodall (1993)

This book is dedicated to all
the nonhuman creatures who have touched our lives,
in partial repayment of our debt to them.

Contents

Contents

Acknowledgments

This anthology has benefited considerably from the active involvement of Susanne Kappeler over the years that it was being assembled. She played an important role in commenting on the essays, and thus in the shaping of the anthology as it exists. We thank her for her ongoing commitment to this project and for the personal support she offered. We are grateful to Patricia Lamb Feuerstein and Marti Kheel for the use of the Feminists for Animal Rights bibliography, which we built upon in compiling the bibliography of feminist approaches to animal issues. We also wish to express our thanks to Marilyn Emerick, Batya Bauman, Joan Dunayer, and the *Animals' Agenda* for their help in preparing the bibliography. We would like to acknowledge Bruce Buchanan, Greta Gaard, Steve Kellman, Stanley Fish, Jane Tompkins, Rachel Toor, and Katherine Malin for their contributions to the production of this book. The editors would also like to express their appreciation to one another for making the process of collaboration such an enriching and stimulating experience.

Introduction

Why should feminists be concerned about the treatment of animals? Why should there be a *feminist* perspective on the status of animals? This collection of articles begins to answer these questions.

It could be argued that theorizing about animals is inevitable for feminism. Historically, the ideological justification for women's alleged inferiority has been made by appropriating them to animals: from Aristotle on, women's bodies have been seen to intrude upon their rationality. Since rationality has been construed by most Western theorists as the defining requirement for membership in the moral community, women—along with nonwhite men and animals—were long excluded. Until the twentieth century this "animality" precluded women's being granted the rights of public citizenship.

At least three responses to this historical alignment of women and animals have appeared in feminist theory. The first approach is perhaps the most familiar. It argues that women are not like animals, but are distinctly human. In *The Second Sex*, Simone de Beauvoir contended that women need to move beyond the physical, material level of existence and to engage in masculine transcendence, thus rejecting their "animal" aspects. Liberal feminists have similarly conceived women's liberation as requiring a denial of women's "animality" and an affirmation of their rationality. From Mary Wollstonecraft in *A Vindication of the Rights of Woman* to contemporary theorists, liberal feminists have stressed that women are intellects and have rational minds—*like* men and *unlike* animals. It may be that this emphasis on severing the woman-animal identification was a necessary phase in the transformation of cultural ideology about women.

More recently, however, some feminists have argued against rejecting the woman-nature connection. They maintain that what Rosemary Radford Ruether called "the male ideology of transcendent dualism" is at the root of both the oppression of women and the exploitation of nature, including animals (Ruether 1974, 195). Similarly, in *Beyond Power* (1985), Marilyn French saw the domination of women as a result of the Western masculine denial of the human-animal connection. "Patriarchy," she argued, "is an ideology founded on the assumption that man is distinct from the animals and superior to [them]. The reason for this superiority is man's contact with a higher power/knowledge called god, reason, or control. The reason for man's existence is to shed all animal residue and realize his 'divine' nature, the part that *seems* unlike any part owned by animals—mind, spirit, or control" (341). Feminist philosopher Elizabeth Spelman coined the term *somatophobia* to denote the equating of women, children, animals, and "the natural" with one another and with the despised body. Somatophobia refers to the hostility to the body that is a characteristic of Western philosophy and its emphasis on reason (Spelman 1982, 120, 127). Spelman explains that somatophobia, a legacy of the soul/body distinction, is often enacted in unequal relationships, such as men to women, masters to slaves, fathers to children, humans to animals (127). Feminists need to recognize somatophobia, Spelman argues, to see the context for women's oppression and the relationship it has with other forms of oppression.

The insights of Ruether, French, and Spelman suggest a second approach to the question of the historical connection between women and animals. This approach holds that feminist theory must engage itself with the status and treatment of the other animals. This position rejects a narrowly construed liberal feminism that pursues rights and opportunities only for women. Instead, it proposes a broader feminism, a radical cultural feminism, which provides an analysis of oppression and offers a vision of liberation that extends well beyond the liberal equation, incorporating within it other life-forms besides human beings. This is the approach represented in this anthology. We believe that feminism is a transformative philosophy that embraces the amelioration of life on earth for all life-forms, for all natural entities. We believe that all oppressions are interconnected: no one creature will be free until all are free—from abuse, degradation, exploitation, pollution, and commercialization. Women and animals have shared these oppressions historically, and until the mentality of domination is ended in all its forms, these afflictions will continue.

A third approach (one that is very widespread) asserts that feminist theory has nothing to do with animals. It may make this assertion implicitly, by failing to engage directly with any issues concerning animals. The premise here is that silence about oppression has no theoretical implications—that is, that silence can be value neutral. But in reality there is no neutral place from which to observe evil. To observe in silence is to be complicit. Thus we have two choices before the evil of animal abuse: either we participate in their oppression or we challenge it.

Sometimes advocates of this approach explicitly oppose the idea that there should or can be a feminist perspective on animals' oppression. Thus, in periodicals as diverse as *Signs, Women's Review of Books*, and *Fur Age Weekly*, we can encounter explicit feminist rejections of feminist theorizing about animals. Moreover, some feminists complain that feminist attention to issues involving animals diverts women from attention to the pressing human needs of violence against women, homelessness, and health crises such as AIDS and breast cancer. We are asked: How can we justify such diversions? How can we devote our attention to animals when there is so much human suffering?

We cannot allow the biases of such questions to go unchallenged. The presumption that these efforts are opposed to each other arises from the dualistic premise that humans' and animals' needs are in conflict. It also implies that human needs are paramount, reinforcing a status hierarchy that has favored neither women nor other animals. It is a haunting repetition of the traditional trivializing of women's issues. We could respond by saying that these efforts are not in opposition to one another. That is, we can, for instance, challenge homelessness *and* be vegetarian, work against violence against women while refusing to wear fur or leather. Should we have to justify concern for animals by indicating that human beings are not neglected? Just as feminists were charged with man-hating when we began to channel our energies and our theorizing to women's needs and experiences, animal activists now stand accused of people-hating. Such charges reveal anxiety about the moral content of the activism as well as ignorance about the underlying and interconnected roots of oppression.

We could respond that many efforts on behalf of animals will qualitatively improve humans' living conditions as well, which is likely to be the case. But such an argument reduces an analysis of interspecies oppression to a human-centered perspective. Yes, in terms of reducing environmental degradation, challenging the maldistribution of food because of the squandering of food resources in the production of "meat," and preventing human diseases associated with eating animals, such as heart disease and certain forms of cancer, it is true that it is in humans' interest to be attentive to and to challenge animal exploitation. But these responses concede to an insidious anthropocentrism while trying to dislodge it.

It is not our goal to assimilate animals into feminist theory only to the point where it furthers women's issues. This may be one consequence of the feminist theoretical explorations represented here because of the historical association of women and animals. But we wish to propose a vision that goes beyond anthropocentric theory. We believe it is important that feminist theory accede to this broader perspective for the good not just of women, but also of animals and indeed of life on earth.

It also makes for sounder theory. In this collection, for example, Lynda Birke demonstrates how problematic it is that feminism has relied on overgeneralized and inaccurate ideas of "animals," as well as "humans," in rejecting biological determinism for women. Maria Comninou explains how the conjoining of animals' issues and women's issues exposes the patriarchal biases of recent court decisions; she shows, for instance, how the term "harassment" is treated differently depending upon whether it is women or (predominantly male) hunters being harassed; so too, does the freedom of speech issue find different advocates depending upon whose speech is being infringed: animal rights activists or pornographers. Similarly, Carol Adams's article argues for the importance for both the human and animal victims of recognizing the abuse and use of animals by men who batter, while Marian Scholtmeijer strives to unite the interests and powers of women and nonhuman animals by seeking, in works of fiction, interspecies terms of resistance to dominant ideological constructions.

In challenging the human-biased premises of feminist theory, we challenge all human-biased theorizing, including that found in environmental theory. Articles by Linda Vance and Karen Davis expose its anthropocentrism, and indicate how this anthropocentrism is fed by sexism. Just as the imputed animality of women precluded our inclusion in the political community, so a great deal of exploitation and abuse of animals is legitimized by feminizing them. This is especially the case, as Karen Davis notes, with farm animals, and, as Marti Kheel explains, with wild animals who are sexualized in the hunt. Conversely, as Joan Dunayer argues, speciesism underlies much linguistic sexism.

Some feminists hostile to animal rights base this hostility on a concern that animal rights offers an ideological platform for granting rights to human fetuses based on issues of sentience. Gary Francione points to a new way of looking at the abortion/animal abuse equation by comparing the context of an abused animal (home or laboratory) rather than comparing the fetus and the animal per se.

Many women in the Western tradition have an ethical history that is rooted in culturally prescribed practices of caring. Part of this history is an active concern about animals. The great majority of activists in the nineteenth-century antivivisection and anticruelty movements were women, as today, it is estimated, 70 to 80 percent of animal rights movement adherents are women. To us this suggests a fourth approach to the question of the interconnections between women and animals, one in which women exert leadership in the animal advocacy movement out of a sense of ethical responsibility, deriving from our historical praxis of care. In the collection *Beyond Animal Rights: A Feminist Caring Ethic for the Treatment of Animals* (1996), we propose a new direction in "animal rights" theory, one rooted in women's caring traditions.

Several articles consider this tradition and ethical position. Diane Antonio selected *Canis lupus* as the subject of her inquiry about ethical caring due to the imminent extinction of wolves, whom she sees as sharing with women a peculiar history of violent mistreatment by human males. Brian Luke asserts that contrary to the assumptions of prevailing patriarchal animal rights theory, humans' caring connection with animals goes very deep; animal liberation, he argues, is less a matter of taming ourselves—imposing controls on naturally antisocial tendencies—and more a matter of going feral—breaking free from institutionalized constraints on our compassion.

Virginia Woolf's essay on the Plumage Bill reflects the complexities that can arise in the encounter between feminism and animal protectionism. While Woolf was herself clearly a proponent of animal welfare, the attacks on women by advocates of the Plumage Bill piqued her ire, provoking her to write her first feminist polemic, which paved the way for *A Room of One's Own* and *Three Guineas*. Reginald Abbott's article analyzes Woolf's essay in its historical context. Her essay follows as an appendix.

We have assembled this collection to further explorations of the theoretical connections between feminism and animal advocacy, as well as between women and animals. In the process of gathering these essays we discovered that certain areas need further research and theoretical attention. We found, for example, that ecofeminists and deep ecology theorists in general had paid little attention to domesticated animals and the evils of factory farming. One major reason for this, as Karen Davis suggests, is that farm animals are feminized and therefore trivialized in our cultural iconography. Wild animals—and the natural world in general—remain perceived as masculine, and therefore wild animals are seen as having higher status. To be concerned about chickens' welfare is to be concerned about the most trivial of the lowly, at least so most people (including most feminists) would maintain. Here we see an important intersection between sexism and speciesism that merits the feminist exploration Davis brings to the issue. We would like to see more feminist analysis of the status of domesticated animals.

The historical and cultural ascription of masculinity to the (American) wilderness or to the natural world also needs to be examined further. Why is it, for example, that so many wildlife documentaries turn into a nearly pornographic parade of carnivorous violence? Such representations give a warped view of the natural world, where the vast majority of creatures are not carnivorous—do not kill and eat one another—and where caring, cooperation, and symbiosis are more prevalent than the "red in tooth and claw" behavior repeatedly served up in the media. We suggest that such messages work to reinscribe male-supremacist ideologies, both in promoting a view of nature as dominated by aggressive and violent males, and in sanctioning human male behavior that follows this model. It is designed, we believe, to arouse fear in women and to promote their sense of needing men's protection. As Lynda Birke observes, such narratives are "politics by other means" (borrowing a phrase from Donna Haraway). Here again further feminist research and theorizing about media narratives' construction of women and animals are needed.

We also noticed some specific theoretical gaps. More thinking needs to be done about the intersections of race, nation, class, and species, which Susanne Kappeler explores in her essay in this volume. More anthropological explorations would be useful. Is there a primary, prehistoric connection between the domestication and commodification of animals and what Friedrich Engels called "the world historical defeat of the female sex"? And much more historical work is required. For example, we need more archival research on the historical connections between women and vegetarianism. There are interesting historical ties between the nineteenth-century antivivisection/anticruelty movements and the temperance movement—undoubtedly because of the linkage between women and animals as objects of human male domestic violence, a nexus that continues today, as Carol Adams's article indicates.

In the meantime, we conclude the introduction to this pioneering volume by reasserting our underlying philosophy. We support the radical feminist thesis that the male pattern of female subordination and degradation, which is nearly universal in human societies, is prototypical for many other forms of abuse, although we also wonder whether that original pattern of domination was not itself preceded by and modeled upon the domination of animals by humans. In any event, we believe that women, as themselves victims of objectification and exploitation, must not abandon other victims of such treatment in their rush to be accepted as "persons" entitled to equal rights. Women must not deny their historical linkage with animals but rather remain faithful to them, bonded as we are not just by centuries of similar abuse but also by the knowledge that they—like us, often objectified as Other—are subjects worthy of the care, the respect, even the reverence, that the sacredness of consciousness deserves. Such an assertion of subjectivity is necessarily subversive of domination in all its forms.

It is clear that one of the main sources of the continuing atrocious abuse of animals by humans is an attitude that allows their reification or objectification. That ontology conveniently allows their commodification for mass-produced slaughter and their mechanization for laboratory experimentation. In fact, the reduction of animals to "its" is at the root of most animal abuse. The attribution of deadness to what is alive, conscious, and sensitive involves a psychology of denial that conveniently facilitates the interests of the powerful. Such denial unquestionably has allowed the great human atrocities of the century to occur, and such denial continues to allow unspeakable animal suffering to proceed as a commonplace norm.

For feminists to engage in this kind of denial, to support and participate in the oppression of the less powerful, is not only hypocritical; it is, we believe, a profound betrayal of our deepest commitments.

Josephine Donovan
Carol J. Adams

Note

Because readers are still uncomfortable with substitute terms, we use the term *animal* in this introduction to refer to animals other than humans. Many contributors do likewise.

References

Donovan, Josephine, and Carol J. Adams. 1996. *Beyond Animal Rights: A Feminist Caring Ethic for the Treatment of Animals*. New York: Continuum.

French, Marilyn. 1985. *Beyond Power*. New York: Summit.

Ruether, Rosemary Radford. 1975. *New Heaven/New Earth: Sexist Ideologies and Human Liberation*. New York: Seabury.

Spelman, Elizabeth. 1982. Woman as Body: Ancient and Contemporary Views. *Feminist Studies* 8 (1):109–31.

The Goodall quote used as epigraph is from Dale Peterson and Jane Goodall, *Visions of Caliban: On Chimpanzees and People* (Boston: Houghton Mifflin, 1993), 281.

Part I

Sexism/Speciesism:
Interlocking Oppressions

I

Joan Dunayer

Sexist Words,
Speciesist Roots

Through massive and sustained exploitation, humans inflict enormous suffering on other animals. Humans generally justify their exploitation of other species by categorizing "animals" as inferior and therefore rightfully subjugated while categorizing humans as superior and naturally entitled to dominate. So inveterate and universal is the false dichotomy of animal vs. human—and so powerfully evocative—that symbolically associating women with "animal" assists in their oppression. Applying images of denigrated nonhuman species to women labels women inferior and available for abuse; attaching images of the aggrandized human species to men designates them superior and entitled to exploit. Language is a powerful agent in assigning the imagery of animal vs. human. Feminists have long objected to "animal" pejoratives for women and the pseudogenerics *man* and *mankind*. These linguistic habits are rooted in speciesism, the assumption that other animals are inferior to humans and do not warrant equal consideration and respect.[1]

Nonhuman-animal pejoratives frequently target women: *catty, shrew, dumb bunny, cow, bitch, old crow, queen bee, sow.* In *An Intelligent Woman's Guide to Dirty Words*, Ruth Todasco (1973) identifies "Woman as Animal" as a major category of "patriarchal epithets" (27). What attitudes and practices have prompted these epithets?

Viewed through speciesism, a nonhuman animal acquires a negative image. When metaphor then imposes that image on women, they share its negativity. Terming a woman a "dog" carries the sexist implication that women have a special obligation to be attractive, since the label refers to physical appearance only when applied to females. And so, using *dog* against any woman indirectly insults all women. The affront to all dogs, however, is direct. Denied individual identities, they merge into Ugly. Without this disdainful view of dogs, *dog* would not offend. Similarly *social butterfly*, being female specific, assigns gender to fickleness and frivolity. The phrase would confer very different traits if the butterfly's flight from flower to flower were perceived as life-sustaining rather than trivial. Reserved for women, *dumb bunny* links femaleness to mindlessness. But the expression rests on the speciesist assumption that rabbits are stupid.

In addition to speciesist attitudes, speciesist practices underlie nonhuman-animal metaphors that disparage women. Most such metaphors, philosopher Robert Baker (1975) notes, refer to domesticated animals like the chicken, cow, and dog—those bred for service to humans.[2]

Comparison to chickens, linguist Alleen Pace Nilsen (1977) observes, spans a woman's life: "a young girl is a *chick*. When she gets old enough she marries and soon begins feeling *cooped up*. To relieve the boredom she goes to *hen parties* and *cackles* with her friends. Eventually she has her *brood*, begins to *henpeck* her husband, and finally turns into an *old biddy*" (29). Nilsen's analysis, however, does not delve beneath the metaphors' sexist use, to their origins in hens' exploitation. Comparing women to hens communicates scorn because hens are exploited as mere bodies—for their egg-laying capacity or flesh. In viewing the actual chick, the egg or "poultry" producer anticipates her exploitation as hen. Analogously the sexist male desires to exploit the human "chick" as a female body, for sexual pleasure. The hen's exploiter values only her physical service, dismissing her experiential world as unimportant or nonexistent. *Hen party* empties women's experiences of all substance or significance; like hens, women have no worth apart from their function within the exploiter's world. The hen ("biddy") who offers neither desirable flesh nor continued profitable egg production is regarded as "spent"—and discarded. No longer sexually attractive or able to reproduce, the human "old biddy" too has outlived her usefulness. If hens were not held captive and treated as nothing more than bodies, their lives would not supply symbols for the lives of stifled and physically exploited women.[3]

Hens' current oppression far outstrips the oppression from which the metaphors arose. Over 99 percent of U.S. chickens spend their lives in crowded confinement (see Appleby, Hughes, and Elson 1992, 31–33; Bell 1992; Coats 1989, 81–82; North and Bell 1990, 456). The laying hen is crammed, usually with three to five other birds, into a wire cage so small that she cannot spread her wings (see Appleby, Hughes, and Elson 1992, 30; Coats 1989, 90–92; Johnson 1991, 26–27, 122).[4] "Broiler" chickens (bred for their flesh) are crowded, by the tens of thousands, onto the floor of a confinement unit. By slaughter time they barely have room to move (see Acker and Cunningham 1991, 635–36; Coats 1989, 87; North and Bell 1990, 456–58).[5] Laying hens rarely live beyond two years, "broilers" two months (see Appleby, Hughes, and Elson 1992, 30–31; Austic and Nesheim 1990, 287–88; North and Bell 1990, 453, 475).[6] The imprisoned hen cannot develop social bonds, raise a brood, or become an "old biddy." The hen's defaced image derives from her victimization.

As a term for a woman, *cow* is, in anthropologist John Halverson's words, "thoroughly derogatory" (1976, 515), characterizing the woman as fat and dull. Why does metaphorical reference to the cow connote these traits while reference to the bull does not? Exploitation of the cow for her milk has created a gender-specific image. Kept perpetually pregnant and/or lactating, with swollen belly or swollen udder, the "dairy cow" is seen as fat. Confined to a stall, denied the active role of nurturing and protecting a calf—so that milking becomes something done *to* her rather than *by* her—she is seen as passive and dull. The cow then becomes emblematic of these traits, which metaphor can attach to women. Like the laying hen, the dairy cow is exploited *as female body.* Since the cow's exploitation focuses on her uniquely female capacities to produce milk and "replacement" offspring, it readily evokes thoughts of femaleness more generally. Bearing with it a context of exploitation, the cow's image easily transfers to women.

Approximately eight months of each year, today's dairy cow is both pregnant and lactating. During each ten-month lactation period, machines drain her of ten times the milk her calf would suckle (see Acker and Cunningham 1991, 111; Coats 1989, 51; Mason and Singer 1990, 11). In the U.S. the largest feedlot dairy operations each hold thousands of cows, year round, in crowded dirt lots. Fed from troughs, these cows never see pasture (see Bath et al. 1985, 303; Coats 1989, 52; Herrick 1990).[7] Free-stall systems confine cows—frequently, throughout the year—to a crowded barn and adjacent dirt or concrete yard (see Bath et al. 1985, 365–66; Coats 1989, 52–53; Fox 1984, 106, 108).[8] Tie-stall operations keep each cow chained by the neck in a narrow stall, often for months at a time (see Bath et al. 1985, 361–65; Mason and Singer 1990, 12). When a cow's milk yield permanently declines, she is slaughtered. *Cow* verbally abuses women by identifying them with the abused cow.[9]

In the language of dog breeders, *bitch* denotes a female dog able to produce a litter. As pejorative, the term has remained female specific. But why should calling a woman a "bitch" impute malice and selfishness? Given that most dogs are loving and eager to please, the metaphor's sharp contempt seems puzzling. Breeders, however, have always treated the female dog with contempt—as a means to a useful, profitable, or prestigious litter.

Among recommended methods for breeding bulldogs, the American Kennel Club's official magazine includes "holding the bitch in the proper position"—"by her legs" or "by straps"—and "assist[ing]" the male in "penetration" (Schor 1989, 140). Breeders subject the bulldog bitch to this ordeal because, through inbreeding, they have afflicted her breed with characteristics that preclude natural mating: a low front and high rear (see Schor 1989). Also bred to be brachycephalic (flat-faced) (see American Kennel Club 1992, 486–88),[10] bulldogs suffer chronic breathing difficulty from pathologically short and twisted air passages. Often an overlong soft palate further obstructs breathing (see Fox 1965, 62). Recently a veterinary newsletter reported on a bulldog "placed on her back" for artificial insemination even though her breathing was especially labored. "Her breathing continued to be labored. When the bitch began to struggle," she was restrained (New Claims 1991, 1). Her breathing worsened. Still the forced insemination continued. Struggling to breathe, she died. Familiarity with the numerous ways in which breeders have disabled dogs through inbreeding and treated them like commodities dispels any mystery as to why *bitch* carries contempt (see Dunayer and Dunayer 1990; Wolfensohn 1981).[11]

Comparisons between women and domesticated animals are offensive, Baker (1975) concludes, because they "reflect a conception of women as mindless servants" (56). But the metaphors' offending components—"mindless" and "servants"—derive from speciesist attitudes and practices. Without speciesism, domesticated animals would not be regarded as mindless; without speciesism, they would not be forced into servitude. Exploiting the hen for her eggs, the cow for her milk, and the bitch for her ability to produce litters invites demeaning female-specific metaphors.

The exploitation of domesticated animals, such as chickens, also leads to negative images of *other* animals—predators who threaten that exploitation, like the fox. A woman termed a "vixen" is resented, and somewhat feared, as scolding, malicious, or domineering, especially toward a man. She threatens a man's self-esteem and sense of security, intruding into his perceived domain. In the days when "poultry" were kept in coops or yards, the actual vixen was much resented, and feared, as an intruder. Being a predator, she often crossed human-drawn boundaries to kill chickens or other fowl whom humans consider their property. Quick-witted and fleet, she frequently evaded capture, repeatedly "outfoxing" the human oppressor. Having no male-specific equivalent, the pejorative *vixen* expresses sexist resentment toward the contentious woman, but it derives from speciesist resentment toward the predatory fox.

The vixen as prey conjures a very different image, which forms the basis for *foxy lady.* In this case the expression's origins lie in humans' exploitation and abuse of foxes themselves. Hunters and trappers view the fox as an object of pursuit—a future trophy or pelt. To the extent that the vixen eludes capture, she piques their desire to possess her and arouses their admiration. Even as she frustrates their goal, she prolongs their "sport" and proves "worthy" of pursuit. Hence, the ambivalence of *foxy lady.* A man who labels a woman "foxy" admires her as stylish and attractive yet sees her largely as a sex object worth possessing. Overwhelmingly, hunters and trappers are male (see Novak et al. 1987, 60; U.S. Fish and Wildlife Service 1993, 36). Their skin-deep view of those they pursue easily extends from nonhuman animals to women. "The major connection between *man* and fox is that of predator and prey," Baker (1975) reasons. "If women are conceived of as foxes, then they are conceived of as prey that it is fun to hunt" (53). Although Baker condemns the conception of women as foxes and the resulting conception of women as prey, he fails to condemn the necessary link between the two—the conception of *foxes* as prey. The speciesist practices of hunting and trapping enable the sexist equation woman = prey: if woman = fox *and* fox = prey, then woman = prey.

In the U.S., fur "farming" and trapping abuse more foxes than any other practices—killing hundreds of thousands each year (see Clifton 1991, Novak et al. 1987, 1018). "Farmed" foxes live confined to small wire cages and usually die from anal electrocution (see Clifton 1991; de Kok 1989). Most foxes trapped in the wild are caught in the excruciating steel-jaw leghold trap (see *Close-Up Report* 1992; Gerstell 1985, 37–40). Any woman who wears a fox coat wraps herself in the remains of some eleven to eighteen foxes who suffered intensely (see Fur Is Dead 1990; *The Shame of Fur* 1988). She also invites continued sexist comparisons between women and nonhuman victims. In *Rape of the Wild* (1989), ecofeminists Andrée Collard and Joyce Contrucci remark that women who wear fur unwittingly adopt the "identity of prey" and so participate in their own degradation (55, n. 34).

Likening women to nonhuman animals undermines respect for women because nonhuman animals generally receive even less respect—far less. In most (if not all) contemporary human societies, the status of nonhuman animals is much lower than women's. In the U.S., for example, an overall absence of legal protection for nonhuman animals permits their massive institutionalized exploitation and abuse (see Francione 1994; Galvin 1985). They are bred for show, for sale, for servitude. They are imprisoned in aquariums and zoos, forced to perform in nightclubs and circuses, terrorized and injured at rodeos and fairs. Each year, by the millions they are vivisected (see Singer 1990, 36–37; U.S. Congress 1986, 49–66), killed for their fur (see Fox 1990, 116; Novak et al. 1987, 1092), murdered for "sport" (see Satchell 1990; Van Voorhees et al. 1992, 10); by the billions they go from intensive confinement to slaughter (see *Catfish Production* 1995, 8, 10; *Livestock Slaughter* 1995, 1; *Poultry Slaughter* 1995, 15–16).

While only some nonhuman-animal pejoratives denigrate women, *all* denigrate nonhuman animals. Numerous nonhuman-animal terms act as invective solely or largely against men and boys: *shark, skunk, lap dog, toad, weasel, snake, jackass, worm.* The male-specific *wolf* and *cur* parallel the female-specific *vixen* and *bitch. Cock of the walk* and *bullheaded* correspond to *mother hen* and *stupid cow. Dumb ox* equates to *dumb bunny.* And *old buzzard* and *goat* resemble *old biddy* and *crow.* Nonhuman-animal terms also serve as racist epithets, as when blacks are called "monkeys" or "gorillas." Often, invoking another animal as insult doesn't target any human group: *sheepish, birdbrain, crazy as a loon.* In such cases the comparison's fundamental speciesism stands alone. Whether or not a person is avaricious, labeling them a "vulture" exhibits prejudice against no group except vultures.

Although some expressions that compare humans to other animals are complimentary (*busy as a bee, eagle-eyed, brave as a lion*), the vast majority offend. Anthropologist Edmund Leach (1964) categorizes "animal" metaphors as "obscenity," along with "dirty words" (largely of "sex and excretion") and "blasphemy and profanity" (28). While Halverson (1976) rejects Leach's categorization, he agrees that "animal" metaphors are overwhelmingly negative. What's more, Halverson identifies their most universal component as "the basic distinction human *v.* animal" (515). This distinction is the essence of speciesism.

Linguistic practice, like other human practices, is even more deeply speciesist than sexist. Humans, after all, have a verbal monopoly. Our language necessarily reflects a human-centered viewpoint more completely than a male-centered one. Considered in relation to the plight of nonhuman animals, Adrienne Rich's words of feminist insight express a terrible absolute: "this is the oppressor's language" (1971, 16, 18).

Speciesist language has far from trivial consequences. Although nonhuman animals cannot discern the contempt in the words that disparage them, this contempt legitimates their oppression. Like sexist language, speciesist language fosters exploitation and abuse. As feminist philosopher Stephanie Ross (1981) has stated with regard to women, "oppression does not require the awareness or co-operation of its victims" (199).

Every negative image of another species helps keep that species oppressed. Most such images are gross distortions. Nonhuman animals rarely possess the character traits that pejoratives assign to them. In reality the imputed traits are negative *human* traits. Wolves do not philander like the human "wolf." Most are steadfastly monogamous (see Fox 1971, 121; Mech 1991, 89, 91). Chickens are not "chicken." Throughout the centuries, observers have reported the hen's fierceness in defending her chicks and the rooster's courage in protecting the flock (see Robbins 1987, 49; Smith and Daniel 1975, 65–66, 137, 159, 162, 212, 324). (In today's factory prisons, of course, chickens can no longer display their bravery.) Pigs do not "make pigs of themselves." Unlike many other animals (including humans), they show no tendency to overeat (see Hedgepeth 1978, 71; Pond, Maner, and Harris 1991, 11). Pigs are not filthy. Whenever possible, they avoid fouling their living area (see Baxter 1984, 234–37; Hedgepeth 1978, 96). If unable to bathe in water, they will wallow in mud to cool themselves. Lacking functional sweat glands, they cannot instead "sweat like a pig" (see Baxter 1984, 35, 209; Hedgepeth 1978, 66). Rats[12] are not "rats." While ingeniously resourceful, they do not use their quick intelligence to betray their familiars. Rat societies, in which serious fighting is an anomaly, exemplify peace and cooperation (see Barnett 1975, 262; Hart 1982, 108; Hendrickson 1983, 39, 80, 93–94). Moreover, rats care for the helpless in their communities, such as the orphaned young and those too old to fend for themselves (see Calhoun 1962, 257; Hendrickson 1983, 15, 80, 93–94).[13]

Why the lies, then? Why the contempt? With contemptuous words, humans establish and maintain emotional distance from other animals.[14] This distance permits abuse without commensurate guilt. Humans blame their nonhuman victims. Physically unable to fly away, having no prior experience of predators from which to learn fear, dodos were massacred by humans, who labeled them fools. Humans load mules with heavy packs, force them to carry these loads up the most precipitous slopes in the harshest weather, and excoriate them as "stubborn" because they are not always eager to oblige. Having compelled captive seals to perform demeaning and unnatural acts, humans use the sneering phrase *trained seal* for a person who demonstrates mindless obedience. Pigs, as Leach (1964) remarks, bear an especially heavy "load of abuse" (50): "we rear pigs for the sole purpose of killing and eating them, and this is rather a shameful thing, a shame which quickly attaches to the pig itself" (51). Today most U.S. pigs experience lifelong confinement (see Baker 1993; Mason and Singer 1990, 8).[15] Ordinarily those kept until they reach slaughter weight are restricted to crowded wire cages, then crowded pens. Those kept longer, for breeding, remain confined to individual stalls so narrow that they cannot turn around (see Coats 1989, 36–46; *Factory Farming* 1987, 45–52; Fox 1984, 41–68; Johnson 1991, 34–35). By the time they go to slaughter, many pigs are crippled (see Coats 1989, 46; Hill 1990; Pursel et al. 1989, 1285).[16] Naturally inquisitive and sociable, with a great capacity for affection and joy, pigs suffer intensely from imprisonment. Using *pig* as a pejorative lends acceptability to their massive abuse.

Expressions such as *male chauvinist pig* display the same species-

Animals & Women

ism as *stupid cow*. Particularly amiable and sensitive, pigs possess none of the sexist's ugly character traits. Affection, cooperation, and protection of others characterize natural pig society, which is matriarchal. Boars rarely show aggression, even toward other adult males, and are especially gentle with the young. A boar mates with a sow only if she is sexually receptive—after much mutual nuzzling, rubbing, and affable grunting (see Hedgepeth 1978, 94–95, 137; Serpell 1986, 5–6). Intended to castigate men for their assumption of superiority to women, *male chauvinist pig* conveys the speaker's own assumption of superiority, to pigs. Referring to sexism, Ross (1981) notes that "many women adopt the very attitudes which are oppressing them" (199). Those attitudes include speciesism.

When a woman responds to mistreatment by protesting "I'm a human being!" or "I want to be treated with respect, not like some animal," what is she suggesting about the acceptable ways of treating other animals? Perhaps because comparisons between women and nonhuman animals so often entail sexism, many women are anxious to distance themselves from other animals. Feminists, especially, recognize that negative "animal" imagery has advanced women's oppression. However, if our treatment and view of other animals became caring, respectful, and just, nonhuman-animal metaphors would quickly lose all power to demean. Few women have confronted how closely they mirror patriarchal oppressors when they too participate in other species' denigration. Women who avoid acknowledging that they are animals closely resemble men who prefer to ignore that women are human.

When used to denote other species only, *animal* falsely removes humans from animalkind.[17] In parallel, through their male imagery, the pseudogenerics *man* and *mankind* effectively exclude women from humankind. By reserving *animal* for *other* animals, humans deny their kinship with nonhuman animals, abjuring membership in all groups larger than species—such as primatekind, mammalkind, and animalkind (see Clark 1988). This use of *animal* reflects the speciesist belief that humans fundamentally differ from all nonhuman animals and are inherently superior. More subtly, *man* and *mankind* too reflect speciesism. Their power to lower women's status rests on the premise that those outside our species do not merit equal consideration and respect. Linguistically ousting women from humankind has force because lack of membership in the human species condemns an individual, however thinking and feeling, to inferior status. Parakeets, bats, goldfish, mice, octopi, whales, orangutans—these and other nonhuman animals do not lack sensitivity. They do, however, lack legal rights—because they don't happen to be human (see Daws 1983; Francione 1993; Galvin 1985; Midgley 1985). If the cutoff for perceived dignity and worth, and for the right to be free from exploitation and abuse, were not the border between human and nonhuman, the suggestion that women are somehow less human than men would have no political force. "Man's" glorification is the flip side of "animals'" denigration. The sexism of *man* and *mankind* works by way of speciesism.

Throughout our language's history, men—being politically dominant—have exercised far more control than women over public discourse. Men's disproportionate influence has permitted them to largely determine "accepted" English usage (see Bodine 1975; Spender 1985, 147–51). Patriarchal men would not have linguistically appropriated humanness unless it represented superiority and privilege to their speciesist minds. "A picture of humanity as consisting of males," says feminist philosopher Marilyn Frye (1975), is inseparable from a "tendency to romanticize and aggrandize the human species and to derive from one's rosy picture of it a sense of one's individual specialness and superiority" (72). Men's appropriation of humanness, she proposes, "is at bottom a version of a self-elevating identification with Humanity" (71).[18]

Linguistic markers embody "man's" apotheosis. Frequent capitalization literally elevates Man above other animals, whose names remain lowercase. As *The Oxford English Dictionary* notes, singular form without a definite article further distinguishes *Man* from "other generic names of animals" (Simpson and Weiner 1989, 9:284), which are either plural or preceded by *the*. We say "giraffes, oysters, and cockatoos" or "the giraffe, the oyster, and the cockatoo"—not "Giraffe, Oyster, and Cockatoo." Functioning as a "quasi-proper name," *Man* personifies our species (Simpson and Weiner 1989, 9:284), endowing humans (male humans, at least) with some shared character, spiritual essence, or history of experience through which they become One. By implication there exists some ineffable, enduring quality Man-ness, but no Cat-ness, Swordfish-ness, or Monarch Butterfly-ness. Unique personification suggests that only humans transcend immediate, individual existence—that nonhuman animals never empathize with others, identify with a group, communicate experience, or remember the past and anticipate the future.

The word *human* is not differentiated from other animal names by the peculiarities of form that distinguish *Man*. We say "humans" or "the human" just as we say "lobsters" or "the lobster." Humans and lobsters get parallel linguistic treatment. As "humans" we are simply one of innumerable species. Nonspeciesist in its form, *human* is semantically nonsexist as well. Singled out by its form, *Man* divides all beings into two contrasting categories: members of our species and nonmembers. At the same time, it semantically assigns men to the first category, women to the second.

Standard definitions of *man* and *mankind* clearly convey the sense of species superiority on which the use of these pseudogenerics relies. In the 1992 *American Heritage Dictionary*, the entries for *man* include this self-congratulatory description:

> a member of the only extant species, *Homo sapiens*, distinguished by a highly developed brain, the capacity for abstract reasoning, and the ability to communicate by means of organized speech and record information in a variety of symbolic systems. (1090)

The definition exaggerates human uniqueness. Many nonhuman animals have "a highly developed brain." Many have "the capacity for abstract reasoning." And some have "the ability to communicate by means of organized speech." In English, Alex the African gray parrot identifies and describes objects, requests toys and food, and expresses such emotions as frustration, regret, and love (see Griffin 1992, 169–74; Linden 1993; Pearce 1987, 273–75).[19] Parrots do not merely "parrot." No doubt, members of numerous species would show "organized speech" if they possessed the necessary vocal apparatus. Instead Washoe the chimpanzee, Koko the gorilla, and other nonhuman primates have learned to communicate in American Sign Language (see Griffin 1992, 218–32; Kowalski 1991, 10–12).[20] Further, Kanzi the pygmy chimpanzee understands much spoken English and communicates by means of abstract visual symbols—demonstrating comprehension of "a variety of symbolic systems" (see Griffin 1992, 221–32; Lewin 1991; Linden 1993). Apes do not merely "ape."

Nonhuman animals like Alex, Washoe, Koko, and Kanzi have learned to use languages devised by humans. How would humans fare if expected to learn another species' method of communication—say, that of the bottle-nosed dolphin? Even if other species did lack the capacity for some typically human type of language and reasoning, why should this capacity be the criterion for superiority? Because it is the one that *we* possess? In the same self-serving and otherwise arbitrary manner, an individual might pronounce "I have great physical strength, so physical strength signifies superiority."

What if the definition of *man* were more truthful?

A member of the only extant species, *Homo presumptuous,* distinguished by a highly developed narcissism, the capacity for routine institutionalized cruelty, and the ability to communicate endless self-justification by means of organized religion and to record prejudices as if they were fact within a variety of speciesist, sexist, and otherwise oppressive systems.

Men would then shun *man* and *mankind* and eagerly substitute *humankind*—or *womankind*—for the species. Instead of monopolizing species membership, and its attendant glory, they would urge full (or exclusive) membership for women, who could then bear the blame.

Having defined *man* as "the men and women who uphold patriarchal values" (19), Collard and Contrucci (1989) identify what "man" regards as "his greatest glory: his passage from ape to human" (34). Alert to the link between speciesism and sexism, these feminists reverse the standard self-aggrandizing definition of our species, exposing humans' negative traits, connecting our history of devastation and cruelty to those with the mentality of dominance, and saying to "man": "Now, recognize the massive destruction and suffering you have caused!"

Patriarchal men have depicted themselves as "more human" than women because they have viewed *human* as signifying everything superior and deserving, everything that supposedly separates humans from "animals." "Our view of man," philosopher Mary Midgley (1978) argues in *Beast and Man,* "has been built up on a supposed contrast between man and animals" (25).[21]

Through the false opposition human vs. animal, humans maintain a fantasy world in which chimpanzees, snails, barracudas, and tree frogs are somehow more alike than chimpanzees and humans (see Clark 1988).[22] The evolutionary bush on which humans occupy one of myriad branches is reduced to a single stalk, with nonhuman animals mired at its roots and humans blossoming at its tip. In reality, species do not evolve toward greater humanness but toward greater adaptiveness in their particular ecological niche. Nor is species something stable and fixed (see Clark 1988; Dawkins 1993). The human species, like all others, continues to undergo variation. In capacities and tendencies humans vary across a vast range (see Midgley 1978, 58), which overlaps with the ranges spanned by other species. For example, many nonhuman animals possess more rationality and altruism than many humans. Who can name a single character trait or ability shared by *all* humans but by no other animals?

Human superiority is as much a lie as male superiority. Gorillas are stronger yet gentler than humans, cheetahs swifter and more graceful, dolphins more playful and exuberant. Bees who perceive ultraviolet light and dance a message of angle and distance; fish who simultaneously see forward, above, below, and behind while swimming through endlessly varied tropical color; birds who navigate over hemispheres, sensing the earth's magnetic field and soaring in rhythm with the rest of their flock; sea turtles who, over decades, experience vast stretches of ocean—what wisdom and vision are theirs? Other animals have other ways of knowing.

Our individual worlds are only as wide as our empathy. Why identify with only one species when we can be so much larger? Animal encompasses human. When human society moves beyond speciesism—to membership in animalkind—"animal" imagery will no longer demean women or assist in their oppression, but will represent their liberation. When we finally cross the species boundary that keeps other animals oppressed, we will have crossed the boundary that circumscribes our lives.

Notes

1. The relationship between speciesism and sexism is not unidirectional. Just as speciesism contributes to women's oppression, sexism contributes to the oppression of nonhuman animals. For example, sexism permits concern for nonhuman animals to be dismissed as "effeminate" or as "female sentimentality." A number of feminists have detailed ways in which sexism and speciesism are mutually reinforcing (see, for example, Adams 1990, 1994; Collard with Contrucci 1989).

2. "I believe the sexual subjugation of women, as it is practiced in all the known civilizations of the world, was modeled after the domestication of animals," writes feminist Elizabeth Fisher in *Woman's Creation* (1979, 190). The exploitation of women for breeding and labor, she observes, followed long after enslavement of nonhuman animals (190, 197). Fisher sees an enduring "connection between dependence on animals and an inferior position for women" (194). Addressing oppression in general, social historian Keith Thomas (1983) presents strong evidence that the domestication of nonhuman animals "became the archetypal pattern for other kinds of social subordination" (46).

3. Negative images created by speciesist practices and wielded against

women are not restricted to images of living and nonhuman animals. As Carol Adams discusses in *The Sexual Politics of Meat* (1990, 39–62), "meat" images born of butchering are also commonly applied to women (also see Corea 1984). For example, the pornographic film industry calls women new to the business "fresh meat" (see Corea 1984, 37).

4. In 1993 I visited a "state-of-the-art" Maryland egg-production facility. Four windowless warehouses imprisoned a total of half a million hens, squeezed nine to a cage. Row after row, four tiers of cages extended into the distance, disappearing into the dimly lit haze. From manure pits directly below, huge mounds of excrement saturated the air with eye-stinging ammonia. Cagemates shared a single water nipple and were forced to climb over one another to reach the food trough in front of their cage. In bursts the birds gave frantic cries, worlds away from the soft clucking of contented hens. With a dazed look, they stared outward—as if into empty darkness. As of 1 March 1995, the U.S. egg industry's captive laying hens numbered approximately 244 million (see *Chickens and Eggs* 1995, 5).

5. Most "broiler" operations allot each chicken floor space of only 0.7 to 0.8 square feet (see Acker and Cunningham 1991, 636; North and Bell 1990, 458). As expressed by the *Commercial Chicken Production Manual* (North and Bell 1990), "the question has always been and continues to be: What is the least amount of floor space necessary per bird to produce the greatest return on investment?" (456).

6. In the U.S. in 1994, the number of chickens slaughtered for their flesh exceeded 7.2 billion (see *Poultry Slaughter* 1995, 15).

7. The textbook *Dairy Cattle* states that cows on California's large feedlot dairy operations are denied access to pasture and "are fed stored feeds year round" (Bath et al. 1985, 303). What's more, an industry researcher recently remarked that "most" U.S. dairy operations have now "evolved from pasture grazing" to "feeding out of storage" (Howard Larsen, quoted in Don't Send 1990).

8. Dairy-industry publications acknowledge the existence of "numerous total confinement, free-stall operations" (Bath et al. 1985, 365–66), many of which keep cows on concrete "throughout their productive lifetimes" (*Guide* 1988, 28).

9. As of 1 January 1995, the U.S. dairy industry was exploiting over 9.5 million milking cows (see *Cattle* 1995, 1).

10. *The Complete Dog Book* (American Kennel Club 1992) contains the American Kennel Club's official standards for AKC-recognized dog breeds. Each standard specifies a particular "conformation" (structural arrangement of body parts). The bulldog standard decrees, among other features, an "extremely short" face and a nose "set back deeply between the eyes" (487).

11. On average, each breed of "purebred" dog harbors over a dozen genetic defects (see Padgett 1988); most purebred dogs suffer from at least one such defect (see McKeown et al. 1988).

12. In keeping with popular usage, *rat* here refers to the single rat species predominant in Europe and the U.S.—the Norway rat, also called the brown rat,

common rat, and (pejoratively) sewer rat. Nearly all domesticated rats belong to this species, including the docile albinos routinely burned, poisoned, maimed, electrically shocked, and otherwise caused to suffer in vivisection.

13. Over the years, seventeen rats have been my adopted friends. All were highly sensitive to their surroundings, loved to explore, and revealed a wide range of emotions. Rufus, I'll always remember, reacted to his first piece of cantaloupe with a somersault of joy. The ten rats I knew since they were pups enjoyed being petted. Some of them liked perching on my shoulder or sitting in my lap and would, if I sat on the floor, scurry to me from across the room. Five brothers who were full-grown when I adopted them regularly cuddled, and sometimes play-wrestled, with each other. When I talked to them, they responded with a look of friendly curiosity—an attentive expression different from the determined one with which they investigated their room or the tentatively accepting one they showed when petted. Vegan and Nori (both male) were already adults when brought, as a pair, to a humane society. For some time after I adopted them, they remained wary of humans; yet, even when handled, they never showed aggression. Eventually they welcomed being petted. Although their cage extended eight feet, they usually stayed side by side, snuggling. Vegan—the older and larger—was very protective of Nori, who was blind. Once, my cat China peered inquisitively into their cage while only Nori was near the front. I saw Vegan, startled, rush forward. Pushing Nori behind him, Vegan positioned himself as a shield. His eyes glittering, he confronted China directly. Rebuffed, China left the room. When Vegan died two years later, Nori drastically changed, becoming lethargic and withdrawn. For the rest of his life, he visibly mourned Vegan. Humans' gross misunderstanding and relentless persecution of rats causes me particularly sharp anger and grief.

14. Through metaphors that convey false images of other species, Adams (1990) notes, humans distance themselves from those species (see 64–65).

15. In the May 1993 issue of *Feed Situation and Outlook Report*, a U.S. Department of Agriculture economist concedes, "Most hogs are now raised in confinement" (Baker 1993, 12).

16. Approximately 96 million pigs were slaughtered in the U.S. in 1994 (see *Livestock Slaughter* 1995, 3).

17. *The American Heritage Dictionary* (1992) provides these conflicting definitions of *animal*: "a multicellular organism of the kingdom Animalia" and "an animal organism other than a human being" (72).

18. Writing before the word *speciesism* gained currency, Frye (1975) termed humans' assumption of superiority "humanism" (72).

19. Since the 1970s, Irene Pepperberg of the University of Arizona has studied Alex's ability to learn English. In a 1993 *Time* magazine article, Eugene Linden relates: "When the parrot, who lives with Pepperberg, became sick a few years ago, she had to take him to a vet and leave him overnight in a strange place for the first time in his life. As she headed for the door she heard Alex calling in his plaintive child's voice, 'Come here. I love you. I'm sorry. Wanna go back'" (59).

20. Asked when gorillas die, Koko reportedly responded with the gestures for "trouble" and "old." Asked how gorillas feel when they die—Happy? Sad? Afraid?—she answered, "Sleep" (see Kowalski 1991, 11–12).

21. For example, Aristotle—a founding father of Western patriarchy—defined humanity as animality's opposite and claimed humanity for men, leaving women in between as a psychological buffer zone (see Brown 1988, 55–56).

22. In our ancestry and genetic composition, we are not merely *like* apes; we *are* apes. Conventionally the classification "apes" includes two chimpanzee species (common chimpanzees and pygmy chimpanzees), gorillas, orang-utans, and gibbons—but excludes humans. According to evolutionary biologist Richard Dawkins (1993), this classification misleads. The African apes (chimpanzees and gorillas) share a more recent common ancestor with humans than with Asian apes (orangutans and gibbons). Therefore, Dawkins explains, no natural ape category includes African *and* Asian apes yet excludes humans. Physiologist Jared Diamond (1993) agrees: "The traditional distinction between 'apes' (defined as chimps, gorillas, etc.) and humans misrepresents the facts" (95). DNA studies, he points out, have revealed that both chimpanzee species share a higher percentage of their genes with humans (about 98.4 percent) than with gorillas (about 97.7 percent). How, then, can "African ape" include chimpanzees and gorillas but not humans? The DNA evidence, Diamond says, indicates that humans are most accurately classified as a third species of chimpanzee.

References

Acker, Duane, and Merle Cunningham. 1991. *Animal Science and Industry.* 4th ed. Englewood Cliffs, N.J.: Prentice-Hall.

Adams, Carol J. 1990. *The Sexual Politics of Meat: A Feminist-Vegetarian Critical Theory.* New York: Continuum.

——. 1994. *Neither Man nor Beast: Feminism and the Defense of Animals.* New York: Continuum.

The American Heritage Dictionary of the English Language. 3rd ed. 1992. Boston: Houghton Mifflin.

American Kennel Club. 1992. *The Complete Dog Book.* 18th ed. New York: Howell Book House.

Appleby, Michael C., Barry O. Hughes, and H. Arnold Elson. 1992. *Poultry Production Systems: Behaviour, Management, and Welfare.* Wallingford, England: C.A.B. International.

Austic, Richard E., and Malden C. Nesheim. 1990. *Poultry Production.* 13th ed. Philadelphia: Lea & Febiger.

Baker, Allen. 1993. Feed and Residual Use in 1993/94 Projected to Rise 1 Percent. *Feed Situation and Outlook Report,* May, 12.

Baker, Robert. 1975. "Pricks" and "Chicks": A Plea for "Persons." In *Philosophy and Sex,* ed. Robert Baker and Frederick Elliston, 45–64. Buffalo, N.Y.: Prometheus Books.

Barnett, Samuel A. 1975. *The Rat: A Study in Behavior.* 2nd ed. Chicago: University of Chicago Press.

Bath, Donald L., Frank N. Dickinson, H. Allen Tucker, and Robert D. Appleman. 1985. *Dairy Cattle: Principles, Practices, Problems, Profits.* 3rd ed. Philadelphia: Lea & Febiger.

Baxter, Seaton. 1984. *Intensive Pig Production: Environmental Management and Design.* London: Granada.

Bell, Donald. 1992. Egg Industry Technology Today. *Poultry Digest,* January, 10, 12, 14, 16.

Bodine, Ann. 1975. Androcentrism in Prescriptive Grammar: Singular "They," Sex-Indefinite "He," and "He or She." *Language in Society* 4(2):129–46.

Brown, Wendy. 1988. *Manhood and Politics: A Feminist Reading in Political Theory.* Totowa, N.J.: Rowman & Littlefield.

Calhoun, John B. 1962. *The Ecology and Sociology of the Norway Rat,* Public Health Service Publication No. 1008. Washington, D.C.: U.S. Department of Health, Education, and Welfare.

Catfish Production. 1995. Washington, D.C.: National Agricultural Statistics Service, U.S. Department of Agriculture, February.

Cattle. 1995. Washington, D.C.: National Agricultural Statistics Service, U.S. Department of Agriculture, February.

Chickens and Eggs. 1995. Washington, D.C.: National Agricultural Statistics Service, U.S. Department of Agriculture, March.

Clark, Stephen R. L. 1988. Is Humanity a Natural Kind? In *What Is an Animal?* ed. Tim Ingold, 17–34. London: Unwin Hyman.

Clifton, Merritt. 1991. Fur Farms: Where the Sun Doesn't Shine. *The Animals' Agenda,* November, 12–15.

Close-Up Report: Fight Fur Now! [pamphlet]. 1992. Washington, D.C.: Humane Society of the United States.

Coats, C. David. 1989. *Old MacDonald's Factory Farm: The Myth of the Traditional Farm and the Shocking Truth about Animal Suffering in Today's Agribusiness.* New York: Continuum.

Collard, Andrée, with Joyce Contrucci. 1989. *Rape of the Wild: Man's Violence against Animals and the Earth.* Bloomington: Indiana University Press.

Corea, Genoveffa [Gena]. 1984. Dominance and Control: How Our Culture Sees Women, Nature, and Animals. *The Animals' Agenda,* May/June, 20–21, 37.

Dawkins, Richard. 1993. Gaps in the Mind. In *The Great Ape Project: Equality beyond Humanity,* ed. Paola Cavalieri and Peter Singer, 80–87. New York: St. Martin's Press.

Daws, Gavan. 1983. "Animal Liberation" as Crime: The Hawaii Dolphin Case. In *Ethics and Animals,* ed. Harlan B. Miller and William H. Williams, 361–71. Clifton, N.J.: Humana Press.

Sexist Words, Speciesist Roots

de Kok, Wim. 1989. Prisoners of Vanity. *The Animals' Voice*, November/December, 20–23.

Diamond, Jared. 1993. The Third Chimpanzee. In *The Great Ape Project: Equality beyond Humanity*, ed. Paola Cavalieri and Peter Singer, 88–101. New York: St. Martin's Press.

Don't Send Dairy Cows to Pasture. 1990. *Successful Farming*, May/June, A1.

Dunayer, Joan, and Eric Dunayer. 1990. The Customized Companion Dog. *The Animals' Agenda*, November, 12–14.

Factory Farming: The Experiment That Failed. 1987. Washington, D.C.: Animal Welfare Institute.

Fisher, Elizabeth. 1979. *Woman's Creation: Sexual Evolution and the Shaping of Society.* Garden City, N.Y.: Anchor Press.

Fox, Michael W. 1965. *Canine Behavior.* Springfield, Ill.: Charles C. Thomas.

———. 1971. *Behaviour of Wolves, Dogs and Related Canids.* New York: Harper & Row.

———. 1984. *Farm Animals: Husbandry, Behavior, and Veterinary Practice.* Baltimore, Md.: University Park Press.

———. 1990. *Inhumane Society: The American Way of Exploiting Animals.* New York: St. Martin's Press.

Francione, Gary L. 1993. Personhood, Property, and Legal Competence. In *The Great Ape Project: Equality beyond Humanity*, ed. Paola Cavalieri and Peter Singer, 248–57. New York: St. Martin's Press.

———. 1994. Animals, Property, and Legal Welfarism: "Unnecessary" Suffering and the "Humane" Treatment of Animals. *Rutgers Law Review* 46(2):721–70.

Frye, Marilyn. 1975. Male Chauvinism: A Conceptual Analysis. In *Philosophy and Sex*, ed. Robert Baker and Frederick Elliston, 65–79. Buffalo, N.Y.: Prometheus Books.

Fur Is Dead. 1990. *PETA Annual Review* [People for the Ethical Treatment of Animals], 12–13.

Galvin, Roger W. 1985. What Rights for Animals? A Modest Proposal. *Pace Environmental Law Review* 2:245–54.

Gerstell, Richard. 1985. *The Steel Trap in North America: The Illustrated Story of Its Design, Production, and Use with Furbearing and Predatory Animals, from Its Colorful Past to the Present Controversy.* Harrisburg, Pa.: Stackpole Books.

Griffin, Donald R. 1992. *Animal Minds.* Chicago: University of Chicago Press.

Guide for the Care and Use of Agricultural Animals in Agricultural Research and Teaching. 1988. Champaign, Ill.: Consortium for Developing a Guide for the Care and Use of Agricultural Animals in Agricultural Research and Teaching.

Halverson, John. 1976. Animal Categories and Terms of Abuse. *Man* 11(4):505–16.

Hart, Martin [Maarten]. 1982. *Rats.* Trans. Arnold Pomerans. London: Allison & Busby. Original work published 1973.

Hedgepeth, William. 1978. *The Hog Book.* New York: Doubleday.

Hendrickson, Robert. 1983. *More Cunning than Man: A Social History of Rats and Men.* New York: Stein & Day.

Herrick, John B. 1990. Production Medicine Versus "Sick Cow Treatment." *Journal of the American Veterinary Medical Association* 196(10):1587–88.

Hill, Michael A. 1990. Economic Relevance, Diagnosis, and Countermeasures for Degenerative Joint Disease (Osteoarthrosis) and Dyschondroplasia (Osteochondrosis) in Pigs. *Journal of the American Veterinary Medical Association* 197(2):254–59.

Johnson, Andrew. 1991. *Factory Farming.* Oxford: Basil Blackwell.

Kowalski, Gary. 1991. *The Souls of Animals.* Walpole, N.H.: Stillpoint.

Leach, Edmund. 1964. Anthropological Aspects of Language: Animal Categories and Verbal Abuse. In *New Directions in the Study of Language,* ed. Eric H. Lenneberg, 23–63. Cambridge, Mass.: MIT Press.

Lewin, Roger. 1991. Look Who's Talking Now. *New Scientist,* 27 April, 49–52.

Linden, Eugene. 1993. Can Animals Think? *Time,* 22 March, 54–61.

Livestock Slaughter: 1994 Summary. 1995. Washington, D.C.: National Agricultural Statistics Service, U.S. Department of Agriculture, March.

Mason, Jim, and Peter Singer. 1990. *Animal Factories.* 2nd ed. New York: Harmony Books.

McKeown, D. B., U. A. Luescher, K. R. S. Fisher, and M. A. Machum. 1988. The Purebred Dog Industry—Will the Next 100 Years See Its Demise? *Dogs in Canada,* October, 30–32.

Mech, L. David. 1991. *The Way of the Wolf.* Stillwater, Minn.: Voyageur Press.

Midgley, Mary. 1978. *Beast and Man: The Roots of Human Nature.* Ithaca, N.Y.: Cornell University Press.

———. 1985. Persons and Non-Persons. In *In Defence of Animals,* ed. Peter Singer, 52–62. Oxford: Basil Blackwell.

New Claims Reveal the Endless Potential for Human Injury. 1991. *Professional Liability: The AVMA Trust Report,* September, 1.

Nilsen, Alleen Pace. 1977. Sexism as Shown through the English Vocabulary. In *Sexism and Language,* ed. Alleen Pace Nilsen, Haig Bosmajian, H. Lee Gershuny, and Julia P. Stanley, 27–41. Urbana, Ill.: National Council of Teachers of English.

North, Mack O., and Donald D. Bell. 1990. *Commercial Chicken Production Manual.* 4th ed. New York: Van Nostrand Reinhold.

Novak, Milan, James A. Baker, Martyn E. Obbard, and Bruce Malloch. 1987. *Wild Furbearer Management and Conservation in North America.* Ontario, Canada: Ontario Trappers Association and Ontario Ministry of Natural Resources.

Padgett, George A. 1988. Genetics: Specifically Regarding Cataracts. *The Kennel Doctor,* June, 4–6.

Pearce, John M. 1987. *An Introduction to Animal Cognition.* Hillsdale, N.J.: Lawrence Erlbaum Associates.

Pond, Wilson G., Jerome H. Maner, and Dewey L. Harris. 1991. *Pork Production Systems: Efficient Use of Swine and Feed Resources.* New York: Van Nostrand Reinhold.

Poultry Slaughter. 1995. Washington, D.C.: National Agricultural Statistics Service, U.S. Department of Agriculture, April.

Pursel, Vernon G., Carl A. Pinkert, Kurt F. Miller, Douglas J. Bolt, Roger G. Campbell, Richard D. Palmiter, Ralph L. Brinster, and Robert E. Hammer. 1989. Genetic Engineering of Livestock. *Science,* 16 June, 1281–88.

Rich, Adrienne. 1971. The Burning of Paper Instead of Children. In *The Will to Change: Poems 1968–1970,* 15–18. New York: W. W. Norton.

Robbins, John. 1987. *Diet for a New America.* Walpole, N.H.: Stillpoint.

Ross, Stephanie. 1981. How Words Hurt: Attitudes, Metaphor and Oppression. In *Sexist Language: A Modern Philosophical Analysis,* ed. Mary Vetterling-Braggin, 194–216. Totowa, N.J.: Rowman & Littlefield.

Satchell, Michael. 1990. The American Hunter under Fire. *U.S. News & World Report,* 5 February, 30–31, 33–36.

Schor, Saul D. 1989. Bulldogs: Breeding Instructions. *Pure-Bred Dogs— American Kennel Gazette,* December, 139–40.

Serpell, James. 1986. *In the Company of Animals: A Study of Human-Animal Relationships.* Oxford: Basil Blackwell.

The Shame of Fur [booklet]. 1988. Washington, D.C.: Humane Society of the United States.

Simpson, J. A., and E. S. C. Weiner, eds. 1989. *The Oxford English Dictionary.* 2nd ed. Oxford: Clarendon Press.

Singer, Peter. 1990. *Animal Liberation.* 2nd ed. New York: New York Review of Books.

Smith, Page, and Charles Daniel. 1975. *The Chicken Book.* Boston: Little, Brown.

Spender, Dale. 1985. *Man Made Language.* 2nd ed. London: Routledge & Kegan Paul.

Thomas, Keith. 1983. *Man and the Natural World: Changing Attitudes in England 1500–1800.* London: Allen Lane.

Todasco, Ruth, ed. 1973. *An Intelligent Woman's Guide to Dirty Words: English Words and Phrases Reflecting Sexist Attitudes toward Women in Patriarchal Society, Arranged According to Usage and Idea.* Chicago: Loop Center YWCA.

U.S. Congress, Office of Technology Assessment. 1986. *Alternatives to Animal Use in Research, Testing, and Education.* Washington, D.C.: U.S. Government Printing Office.

U.S. Fish and Wildlife Service and U.S. Bureau of the Census. 1993. *1991 National Survey of Fishing, Hunting, and Wildlife-Associated Recreation.* Washington, D.C.: U.S. Government Printing Office.

Van Voorhees, David A., John F. Witzig, Maury F. Osborn, Mark C. Holliday, and Ronald J. Essig. 1992. *Marine Recreational Fishery Statistics Survey, Atlantic and Gulf Coasts, 1990–1991.* Silver Spring, Md.: National Marine Fisheries Service, U.S. Department of Commerce.

Wolfensohn, Simon. 1981. The Things We Do to Dogs. *New Scientist,* 14 May, 404–7.

2

Lynda Birke

Exploring the Boundaries: Feminism, Animals, and Science

My concern in this essay is twofold. First, I want to explore how feminism—as a movement dedicated to social change—either has ignored issues to do with animals or has itself relied on particular ideas of "animals" (and of "humans") that might be challenged. Secondly, I want to do this in relationship to the rapidly burgeoning literature on feminism and science; despite the fact that large areas of the natural sciences are *about* animals, this literature has barely considered them. One reason for this, Barbara Noske has suggested, is that contemporary feminism is only superficially critical of science: it takes at face value at least some of science's premises about human relationships to nature. In particular, she says "feminists have uncritically embraced the subject-object division between humans and animals, an attitude inherited from Western scientific tradition as a whole. . . . Objectifying portrayals of animals continue to be accepted as true" (1989, 114).

Exploring connections between two areas of thought—in this case, feminism and how we perceive animals—could take us in many different directions. Here, my primary concern is to look at these connections in relation to science. I begin by considering one area that is of considerable importance to feminist thinking—the rejection of biological determinism/essentialism—and note how this depends upon making particular assumptions about animals. This is both an issue of general concern to feminism and one of specific concern in that it raises questions for feminist analyses of science. The second part of this essay focuses more specifically on animals and their place in science, in terms of how they are used in the laboratory, for example, or observed in the wild—as well as how scientists write about them.

But first a note on writing about these issues and personal politics. It is no longer enough in feminism to talk simply and naively about "women" as women. My own experience is not only as a woman, but is also situated in my experiences of being white, of being middle-class, of growing up in postwar London, of being a lesbian. Each of those categories has its own political and ethical frameworks, and has shaped my experience. Sometimes these overlap—they are, after all, embedded in the same structures of power and domination. Sometimes, they do not (as a lesbian, for example, I am part of an oppressed minority; as white/middle-class, I am part of the dominant culture). The issues are complex and are often located simultaneously in different ethical and political spaces. So too are many of the issues concerning animals. I'm vegetarian, because I choose not to eat animals; yet I have done things "in the dominant culture" that some people feel exploit animals (like working in science). Although I write about the issues in largely academic style (that is my training), these kinds of contradictions, the different ethical spaces, will inevitably weave in and out of my thinking, both as a feminist and as someone concerned about animals.

Feminism and the Human-Animal Relationship

To what extent do these things matter to feminism? One response to exploring issues relating to feminism and animals (and science) is "What has that got to do with women?" One of the strengths of feminist thought is that it is never "just" about women: it is a critical discourse that tends to ask uncomfortable questions about everything. To ask questions about how our theorizing relates to what we understand of the natural world is as much a part of our remit as anything else.

Feminists have certainly made some links between their concerns and concerns around animals; in the nineteenth century, this took the form of feminist involvement in antivivisectionist campaigns (Elston 1987). For these feminists, there were clear parallels in the ways that women and animals were treated by science. Today, the links have been made mainly in relation to a broader environmentalist politics (e.g., Benney 1983; Slicer 1991).

In feminist critiques of science, analysis of issues to do with animals has been patchy. Field studies of animals, particularly primates, have been the focus of Donna Haraway's work for many years (1979–1989); in that, she has traced the ways in which the narratives of primatology have been located in wider politics around race and gender (Haraway 1989a).

Outside her work, however, feminist literature on science has paid little heed to animals—including the animals within laboratory research. Despite the emphasis in feminist critiques on the ideological power of science, we have paid insufficient attention to the structures of power that enable scientists to justify the way animals are treated. To give one example, in a discussion of feminist method, Sandra Harding notes the sexist bias of science in the way that scientists typically ignore females: "it is a problem that biologists prescribe that cosmetics be tested only on male rats on the grounds that the estrous cycle unduly complicates experiments on female rats" (1989, 18). That is indeed a problem: but so is the assumption that rats should be used to test cosmetics at all.

The "animal question" does, however, raise several questions for feminist critiques of science. Feminists have criticized particularly the content of science, for example, in critiques of biological determinism (e.g., Hubbard 1990; Fausto-Sterling 1985). Yet that content is founded upon the use of animals by science, for how else has the knowledge about, say, hormones or brain function been acquired except through the use of animals? Other critics have emphasized the process and practice of science (e.g., Longino 1989); within at least some parts of the biological sciences, learning to do experiments on animals *is* the practice. And the science that we criticize (and make use of, in relation to women's health issues, for instance) is built up on knowledge gained from experiments on animals.

Perhaps one reason why feminists have not been quick to debate the ethics of animal use in science has to do with our unease about talking about animal issues at all. There is an emerging social and political concern about animals, as there is about the environment; yet feminism seems almost to have ignored the former. Not seeing it as relevant may, it seems to me, come from two related sources: first, there is the danger of women being seen as "closer" to animals or nature once we have tried to connect feminist politics to any concerned with animal issues. And to be "closer to animals" in our culture is to be denigrated.

Secondly, the denigration follows from the way the dominant culture defines the human (or male) self *against* others—including nature. Whatever is other in these definitions becomes less valued. Such separation of nonhuman animals from ourselves (either humans generally or women specifically) derives from the humanist/ rationalist traditions of the Enlightenment, in which the human world is sharply divided off from the nonhuman, and "lacks essential connections to them" (Plumwood 1991, 19). To some extent, Western feminism has bought into this separation, and it is only recently that feminist theorizing has begun to question that tradition seriously (in, for example, writing about ecofeminism).[1]

Where feminist writing has addressed issues to do with animals, it has tended to adopt a "commonsense" view of them. This is what Lynch (1988) called the "naturalistic" animal—the image we associate with wild animals, or perhaps with certain kinds of domesticated ones: it is a familiar, everyday kind of image of an animal (and different from at least some of the images of "animal" that are implicit in science, as I indicate below). There is something of a paradox here: on the one hand, much feminist writing relies on the assumption that humans are separate from other animals (a belief in evolutionary discontinuity). That is, embedded in feminist writing is the notion that our critical questions are bounded firmly by what is essentially human: nonhuman species do not enter our theoretical frameworks. On the other hand, a position of continuity, of similarity to other animals, is evident in other feminist writings—in ecofeminism, for instance, or in some feminist fiction that stresses the links between women and animals (e.g., Corrigan and Hoppe 1990, Zahava 1988).

The tension between discontinuity and continuity in our writing may, of course, reflect different positions within feminism, but it may also indicate an ambivalence that Ritvo (1991) has noted in the wider culture. She refers to evidence suggesting that "when people

Feminism, Animals, and Science

are not trying to deny that humans and animals belong to the same moral and intellectual continuum, they automatically assume that they do" (70). That assumption, she points out, permeates many scientific studies of animals in the late twentieth century as much as it does popular culture.

The place of animals in science is largely as objects of inquiry. But there are several ways in which animals fulfill that role. First, they may serve the function of being thought of as a mirror to human society, particularly those species that are closest to humanity. Not only does this role depend upon interpretations of animal societies that are deeply embedded in particular assumptions about human behavior, but it also depends upon seeing animal societies as somehow "out there," independent of human culture. Yet, as Donna Haraway has noted of Western studies of African primates, "baboons and people had coexisted and interacted on large areas of the African continent throughout hominid evolutionary history" (1989b, 297). Primatology is "politics by other means"; it is deeply imbued with the politics of gender, class, and race (also see Haraway 1989a).

One reason why feminist theorizing has paid little heed to "the animal question" is our resistance to seeing humans as animals. Partly, feminist resistance has to do with a refusal to be reduced to the level of the "beast within," the "animal" or dark side of ourselves. For feminists, it has seemed necessary to repudiate any connections between women and nature, to see them as regressive: women are fully human, feminists have rightly insisted, and to be human means to be preeminent over animals (see Plumwood 1990). To be aligned with nature (either "out there" or as nature within) is to be diminished, to lose free will; not surprisingly, feminists have resisted this move (Birke 1991a, 1994).

Partly, too, setting humans apart from other animals has been implicitly part of our opposition to biological determinism. In doing so, we have objected to the ways in which biologically determinist arguments have been used to justify women's oppression; we have also emphasized the myriad ways in which gender can be seen to be socially and culturally constructed.

Yet this emphasis on social construction has its drawbacks. For example, it has left little space for bodies and their functions: it is almost as if our bodies were not part of our selves. Instead, the body becomes "a blank page for social inscriptions including those of biological discourse" (Haraway 1991, 197). Emphasizing social construction has also cut us off from the rest of the animal kingdom, thus reinforcing the view that humans are not animals. In criticizing biological determinism, feminists have objected to the idea that human behavior and capabilities are the product of some underlying biological urge. We have also objected to the ready extrapolation from animals to humans, which is characteristic of so much biological determinism.

In these objections, however, the behavior of animals is not seen as problematic. Thus, we might object to the notion that human gender differences are determined uniquely by hormonal effects on the brain, or to the idea that there exists a "homosexual brain." But there is usually much less objection to such ideas being applied to other species.

The behavior of all nonhuman species, by contrast, is relegated to the catch-all category of biology. So, everything about animals—including their behavior—is biological, while for humans it is only our physiology that might be so labeled (that is, feminists are unlikely to object to the idea that ovarian hormones bring about changes in the lining of the uterus, but are highly critical of any suggestion that such hormones might have anything to do with brains or behavior).

Feminist beliefs about our gender-specific behavior, then, rest on a belief in evolutionary discontinuity—that humans are fundamentally different from other species. In doing so, they make certain assumptions about what constitutes "the biological." I want to examine two consequences of these assumptions. One is that the human/animal distinction rests on a notion of "animal nature" that is overgeneralizing and often untenable; the second is that if determinism is a problem for how we interpret our own behavior, then surely it should also raise questions for how we interpret the behavior of other species. It matters, I would argue, that some scientists talk blithely of creating, for example, a "homosexual rat" (Dorner 1976; for critiques, see Birke 1982, Fausto-Sterling 1993); and it matters both because that talk feeds into determinist ideas applied to ourselves and because it is crudely simplistic about the behavior of animals. Whether we like it or not, there is a reciprocal relationship between the two knowledges, of humans and of animals—each structures the other, and does so within particular political frameworks.

Culturally, we have made much of separating ourselves from "other animals." As the influence of organized religion began to wane in the early modern period, so theological explanations of our relationship to other animals lost their power (Thomas 1983). One response to this shift was to seek to define "human uniqueness" ever

Feminism, Animals, and Science

more closely, to emphasize our special characteristics—language, tool use, cognitive skills. The boundaries shift from time to time, as each characteristic is called into question and shown to exist in some form in other species; but they still serve to demarcate, to draw the line firmly between "humans" and "other animals."[1]

Yet whatever are these "other animals"? What is the "animal nature" that they allegedly have? The trouble is that I cannot recognize any particular kind of animal in these pronouncements: there simply is no one animal nature against which we can compare our wonderful human achievements. Each species, including ourselves, is more or less adapted to the environment in which it finds itself: and each is different. Humans are indeed unique, but so are dogs, ostriches, and parrots, or anything else.

What is important here is not to establish how special each species is, but to emphasize *how* we make use of the argument. It is not usually specific species against which we compare ourselves, but a vague notion of "other animals." This serves as a rhetorical device, a generalization that serves to elevate our own status, and as a corollary to reduce that of the "others." That is, we seek constantly to find new ways of shoring up the boundaries, and of attaching ethical significance to them. This is how we can justify using animals for our own ends in science and elsewhere. And feminists have gone along with that distinction in our emphasis on social constructionism. It seems paradoxical that at a time when feminist theory is moving beyond dualisms of gender it should do so by building analysis on yet another dichotomy: humans versus "other" animals.

The tendency to universalize "other animals" is apparent not only in feminist theory (even if it is largely implicit there). It also, I believe, underlies the work of many of those who advocate animal rights. That is, in speaking of "animal rights" they seem to generalize across a great many (or all) animal species. One inevitable consequence has been that opponents will seize on the notion of granting rights to, say, a worm and poke fun at it.

Now some generalization is necessary if there is to be any discussion of what we might mean if we are to extend notions of justice to nonhumans; this position is clearly useful to stand against trenchant beliefs in human superiority and exploitation of other animals. Yet it can be criticized for its universality. To counterpose ourselves to "other animals" is to universalize on both counts: which humans are we talking about? And which animals? Would we always want to grant "rights" to all species, or only to some in some circumstances?

What kinds of behavior, capabilities, and social organizations are lumped in the category of "other animals"?

The second problem resulting from our assumption that somehow animals are nothing but biology is that their behavior is interpreted as determined, as fixed. Partly, of course, this itself depends upon the reductionist logic of science, for that is precisely how the behavior of those animals tends to be studied in the first place. If, for example, scientists observe that there are sex differences (sic; that is what they typically are called in relation to animals) in the behavior of animals, then they are likely to assume that the origin of such differences lies *internal* to the animals—that they are caused by some physiological event or process.

Yet why make that assumption? If we can point to variation as a result of social influences in ourselves, why not in other animals? We know very little in practice about how differences emerge in animals out of their social interactions/experience. Within a large litter of animals, whatever happens to one pup may have repercussions on others: thus, if a scientist alters the hormones of one, there will be effects on the rest. The hormones, in short, are affecting a social system, not an individual (Birke 1986; Moore 1984).

Assuming that animals are "hardwired," driven by some physiological imperative, itself plays back into the very biological determinism that we so criticize.[3] Once animals are seen as hardwired, rather than flexible, then it is easy to extrapolate such assumptions to humans: the suggestion that there is a homosexual brain is one example of this sideways step. Such determinist ideas, moreover, seriously underestimate the complexity of development in any species. Rather, we need to emphasize that animal development is fluid and experiential, instead of "depicting animals as rigid brain-driven organisms impervious to their surroundings" (Fausto-Sterling 1993).[4]

Animals in Science

One reason, of course, why our understanding of how animals develop behaviorally is limited is that the formal study of animal behavior has operated within a strictly scientific mode. What this has meant is, first, that scientists employ a reductionist approach. It is much more straightforward to design an experiment looking at simple variables (altering hormone levels in an infant animal, for example, then seeing what happens to its adult behavior), than to design one allowing for the interplay of many complex variables.

Feminism, Animals, and Science

Secondly, it has meant that individuals have been studied largely as exemplars of particular species; within that framework, animals are denied emotions or feelings, as scientists insist on avoiding anthropomorphism (see Rollin 1989). In most studies of animal behavior it is groups that are important. In field studies, the focus is often on the social group and its dynamics; in the laboratory, what usually is studied is animals as representative groups (comparing, say, twenty animals receiving hormone treatment to twenty animals not so treated).

To transform the study of animal behavior (ethology), to make it less reductionist, would require—among other things—creating a firmer dialogue between scientists and others who work with animals—animal trainers, farmers, caretakers. These people often have a deep, intuitive understanding of the animals with whom they work; but it is a knowledge gained from working with individuals, knowing their idiosyncrasies and sustaining a dialogue with those animals, rather than from standing outside and studying animals in groups. (Personally, I suspect that I know at least as much about those species or individuals with whom I live—and therefore interact—as I do about any species I have studied "scientifically.") This knowledge typically is denied by the formal practice of science— which in turn raises many questions about who constructs knowledge and in what context.

Yet, ironically, it is also developments in ethology that have helped to provide justification for those who wish to challenge the human/animal boundary. Contemporary ethology has two main roots. One strand, particularly in Europe, was part of a natural history tradition, which focused on the lives of wild animals. The other root (more evident in North America) derived from behaviorism, with its emphasis on experimental studies of how animals learn. Behaviorism, in its turn, was a reaction at the end of the nineteenth century against the use of mentalist constructs (which could not, by definition, be studied scientifically; see Rollin 1989). So, for much of this century, experimental studies of animal behavior explicitly denied any kind of "mind" to animals (and only begrudgingly, if at all, allowed it to humans).[5]

In recent years, however, the tide has turned, and a renewed interest in "animal minds" has developed. Cognitive ethology, to give it a name, has revealed a wealth of ways in which nonhuman animals use complex mental concepts, or have consciousness (Griffin 1992); ways in which they might have a moral sense (Davis 1989); ways

Animals & Women

in which they can "lie" and so manipulate the behavior of others (Cheyney and Seyfarth 1990).

The parallel strands of field studies of wild animals and experimental, laboratory studies reflect a deeper tension in the history of biology. On the one hand, biology is partly about natural history, incorporating studies of the behavior and life history of a species. This tradition tends to produce accounts of animals based on description or on small-scale experiments in the wild—accounts that fit reasonably well with "commonsense" views of "naturalistic" animals (however much those views of what a "wild" animal is are themselves constructions). For that reason at least, there is little public opposition to such studies.[6] In this tradition, animals become exemplars of species as molded by natural selection.

On the other hand, biology also has a tradition of experimentalism, which often has been in tension with the naturalistic tradition (in, for example, the history of embryology; see Coleman 1977). Here, animals are only partly exemplars of species (and the contingencies of natural selection are of secondary theoretical importance); more often they are considered to be exemplars of "animal models" for human conditions.

In the experimentalist traditions, animals become a tool, part of the apparatus of science. They become the "analytic animal"—in other words, they undergo a transformation, through experimental procedures, into data (Lynch 1988). The relationship of the scientist to these "data" is, inevitably, different from that of the scientist who observes "naturalistic" animals in the wild.

Observing the behavior of wild animals allows them, partly, to be subjects. Primates, particularly, are seen as individual subjects with whom the primatologist may interact (see Haraway 1989a). But for most species, being in the laboratory means to be constituted as objects, as part of the apparatus of science. "Laboratory animals" are a collectivity, depersonalized;[7] they are studied en masse. Yet here, too, they serve the function of being the mirror of nature. Research involving rats is justified—to funding agencies and the wider public— on the grounds that they have a physiology similar to our own—the "animal model" for cancer, cardiovascular disease, or whatever.

There is undoubtedly considerable public concern about what happens to animals in laboratories. Public opposition seems, moreover, to be growing (Rowan 1989). Partly, this may be a response to efforts by antivivisectionist organizations (their focus on cosmetics testing and its effects on the market is one example). Partly, too, it may reflect a wider antagonism to science (Jasper and Nelkin 1992), based both on emotional reactions to cruelty to animals and on a growing recognition that science is far from being as value free and objective as it would claim to be (see also Keller 1985; Harding 1992).

Whatever its causes, opposition to the use of animals shares two important features with the science that uses them. First, both protagonists rely on "scientific facts" to support their case (the corollary of this is that those taking the opposite view must be ill-informed, or not accepting the truth). Secondly, both supporters and opposers of animal research rely on particular—but not identical—ideological constructions of "the animal."

Of course, whatever notion of "animal" we use, it is always a construction (just as "woman" is a construction). Historically, ideas about animals and their role(s) in relation to (Western) society have inevitably changed as the needs and priorities of human society have changed—in conjunction with the agricultural revolution in Europe, for instance (Thomas 1983). Harriet Ritvo (1987) has described, too, how ideas about animals were developed to mirror the beliefs underpinning British imperialism in the eighteenth to nineteenth centuries. And not only were the ideas being constructed but so were the animals themselves, literally being constructed through selective breeding programs (Russell 1986) to produce, for instance, "aristocratic" breeds of horses or dogs.

The debate about animals in science similarly evokes particular constructions of "laboratory animals." Antivivisectionist imagery relies on images of cuddly or cute animals being subjected to potentially painful procedures (such as an injection into the abdomen) or highly emotive ones (such as having electrodes inserted into the brain).[8] These are animals of everyday experience, of commonsense, the cuddly bunny rabbits, just like our pets.

Defenders of research also implicitly rely on this view of animals—for example, the Research Defence Society in Britain produces publicity materials that stress that nearly all experiments are done on rats and mice. Rats are not pets, nor are they the kind of animal that sells wildlife films; as such, they have little emotional currency and do not appeal to us in the way that images of cuddly, pet-like animals do. It is not, on the whole, the idea of experimentation performed on rats and mice that upsets people, but that performed on primates, fluffy rabbits and cats, and dogs—species whose role as complementary to us is assured.

Within science itself, animals are also constructed through specialist breeding programs. Most laboratory strains of purpose-bred animals were developed in the late nineteenth to early twentieth centuries. Breeding stock derived at that time from animals bred by lay "fanciers" (e.g., Paterson 1957), who also contributed much knowledge of breeding and inheritance; but science required uniformity[9]—the "fancy" varieties were "less satisfactory" for lab use (Wright 1922)—so efforts were made to create standardized breeds. In that sense, laboratory animals were literally constructed to fulfill a specific role in science.

Asking Feminist Questions

In this section, I want to explore two related issues: first, how animals are seen in science, and how this might link to the kinds of questions feminists ask about science; and secondly, where women scientists are located in relation to these questions.

The ways in which animals are seen within science and its practice reflect both the wider culture (of which science is part) and the specific approaches of science. The Judeo-Christian tradition teaches us that man (sic) has dominion over nature; accordingly, our culture assumes that animals are there for our use and have lower moral standing than people (Passmore 1974).

Science is also quintessentially about the pursuit of objectivity, about the belief that the scientific observer can stand outside nature, as feminists have often noted (e.g., Keller 1985). If nature is "out there," for our use, then we can pretend that we can stand outside it and observe. Feminists have criticized this stance; objectivity is part of the stereotypic masculinity of scientific practice (Keller 1985) and requires what Ruth Hubbard has called "context stripping." Feminist critics, on the contrary, emphasize the inseparability of subjectivity and objectivity in how we know the world (Hubbard 1990).

A corollary of that ideology of objectivity is that it denies feelings, including the possibility of feelings of sympathy toward the object(s) of study—be they nonhumans, the environment generally, or women. This denial is evident in the way that science is written—the use of particular words, the use of the passive voice. These help to create the "missing agent": this is most clearly the scientist, but it may also be the laboratory animal whose life became data. There is no person involved in the passive voice, merely a procedure or perhaps "an inability to assay" (in this case, the animal died in vain: it cannot become data if someone messed up the subsequent assay; see Lynch 1988).

The writing, moreover, is itself constructed in ways that diminish the significance of the animal. Gross (1990) suggests that the widespread use of the passive voice in scientific papers "is a routine means for making physical objects and events the subjects of scientific sentences" (73). Phrases such as "the animals were injected" are typical. Here, the animals are indeed the subject of the verb: but they do not become "subjects" in the more philosophical sense. What the passive voice does is to remove the scientist from the sentence, so reducing the emotional impact on the reader of what is done to the animal.[10]

Gross (1990) emphasizes the construction of scientific papers as fictionalized, idealized accounts in which "style . . . is not a window on reality, but the vehicle of an ideology that systematically misdescribes experimental and observational events" (84). Lynch (1988) similarly contrasts the idealized account of the written records, with what he terms "laboratory shop talk." Conversation, unlike written records, typically makes reference to "what can go wrong." It can also make reference to a more empathic feeling for the animals; Wieder (1980) has described, for example, how scientists working with chimpanzees may make reference to the cognitive abilities of the animals in conversation, but this awareness is lost in written accounts. If the written accounts of science reflect a seemingly objective ideology, conversations among scientists are much more ambivalent. On one hand, scientists may use language clearly reminiscent of the "air of bravado." So what if an animal dies, I was once told, "there's more where that came from." Lynch recalls the crude language and repartee accompanying scientists' repeated attempts to inject a rat successfully. Yet, on the other hand, scientists also express feelings about the animals and acknowledge the need for empathy and "good handling" (Lynch 1988), even though open discussion of these feelings is not encouraged. Indeed, Arluke (1992) found that even talking about having interviewed scientists who expressed unease met with resistance in scientific circles.

Another topic about which discussion is discouraged within science is culling. Culling, in the laboratory, is routine practice in the management of laboratory breeding stock; without regular culls, the population would become unwieldy. These are issues that receive far less public outcry than, say, the culling of seals, although they have in common the death of the animal. Nor does it evoke outcry in the way that certain experimental procedures do. What seems to matter in terms of public concern is suffering. Little is said about the animals that die because they are superfluous.

Unease about the practices of science does find its way into written accounts—the use of the word "sacrifice," for example, to describe killing (Arluke 1988)—but it is much more evident in conversation. In interviews, scientists are generally at pains to be seen as caring, emphasizing ways in which they draw the line—at particular techniques, at using particular species, or at the use of animals for testing cosmetics, for instance (Birke and Michael 1992a, 1992b). Culling, however, is rarely mentioned by scientists—although it is an issue repeatedly referred to by technicians, the people who have to do it (from unpublished interviews; see also Arluke 1990).

There are two things to note here. First, compassion and caring are attitudes that may be spoken of as desirable in scientific work with animals, even if this is not part of the written discourse of science (nor of its overt ideology in scientific training). These are admissions that—sometimes—scientists do not adhere to the expected certainties, to the distancing expected of them as scientists. Those who care for the animals (technicians or caretakers) are, of course, more able to express concern, often seeing themselves as "buffers" between the scientist and the animal—and these caretakers include more women. Interestingly, an article published in 1947 suggested that "the right technical assistant (preferably female)" was "by far the most important feature in the management of any rat colony" (McGaughey, Thompson, and Chitty 1947, 111).

Secondly, scientists express these feelings by distancing themselves from nefarious "others." It is others—scientists in other countries, the cosmetics industry, other laboratories; other users of animals, such as farmers—who fail to maintain ethical standards. In such a discourse, what the speakers themselves do is relatively unproblematic—not necessarily in the sense of laboratory techniques themselves, but in relation to thinking ethically. What comes across in interviews is that the scientists see themselves as making ethical decisions: it is the "others" who fail to do so, or do so poorly.

Otherness is a familiar theme in feminist writing. Zuleyma Tang Halpin suggests, for example, that concern for animals begins to threaten patriarchal science because it calls into question beliefs about the "otherness" of the subject matter of science. For Halpin, compassion and respect for animals are important concerns for feminist critiques of science, concerns that might themselves help to change the face of science. Once the scientist begins to "feel for his or her research animal, the self versus other duality begins to break down" (Halpin 1989, 282–83).

Ironically, the boundaries of otherness are also being blurred by developments within science itself (see Haraway 1991). Whatever we are born with may potentially be changed: people walk around with machine parts (pacemakers, say), or are attached to machines for periods of time (such as dialysis machines). Surgeons transplant organs from other individuals—even, in the notorious " 'Baby Fae' case," of a baboon heart transplant from other species. And scientists can now create organisms that contain genes, sections of DNA, from other organisms.[11] What does all this do to our apparent need to think of animals as "others" in order to justify our use of them? And what does this do to feminist reliance on keeping ourselves apart from the animal world?

For women in science, taking on the role of scientist means acquiring certain traits that might be stereotyped in our culture as unfeminine. One message, for example, that is implicit in scientific training is that emotions should not "get in the way" (Halpin 1989). To become a scientist requires becoming desensitized to emotional involvement with the animals that might be used. But to sympathize with the animals is, on the other hand, considered suspiciously feminine within the culture of science (Birke 1991b). Miriam Rothschild, for example, has described the process she went through in becoming a scientist, noting that other zoologists of her acquaintance feared being dubbed "unmanly" if they showed compassion to their animals (Rothschild 1986, 50). There is undoubtedly a premium placed on developing an air of bravado—the kid who doesn't throw up when asked to do a dissection, the student who has what it takes to pith the frog.[12]

Now I do not want to suggest that sympathy and compassion are essentially female qualities—nor even that they cannot be found in science. But they are stereotypically part of the construction of the feminine in our culture, and it is for just that reason that, like Rothschild, I have heard them repudiated in the labs. Yet of course they can be found. As Keller notes, relating how her biography of Barbara McClintock was received by the scientific world, scientists often believe that empathy, at least, is intrinsic to doing good science (1989, 37). Moreover, these qualities are less often reviled by technicians—people who work in science but are not central to the construction of its ideology.

For women, including feminists, working in science, the problems of how we relate to nature are acute. In the dominant culture, various "others" are similarly situated—nonwhite people, women, nonhuman animals. Yet a woman working in science has to accept its precepts, its beliefs that nature is out there, other to herself. In this sense, she must try to be "in two places at once": she is both the "other" and (ambiguously) part of the science to which nature is seen as other.

She must also accept that scientific research uses animals. If she dislikes that, for moral and/or political reasons, then she can either get out of science altogether or try to avoid doing nasty things to animals. Neither of these options, of course, actually changes the fact that much of the training she has received in science was itself based on findings from animals. Still, it does mean she can live more in accord with her principles.

But where does that leave those who stay in the game? I have no intention of suggesting that these women are necessarily lacking in principles. In my experience, what motivates them is the desire to do good through science; this potential for good is the principle they live by, and which they see as balanced against the possibility of suffering by animals. I may choose to tip that balance toward the animals; many tip it the other way. Some of the letters written by women scientists to *Labyrinth*, the Philadelphia women's newspaper, in response to an animal rights article illustrate this point. One writer felt, for example, that feminists should "think of all the good that such research has done for women at very little cost to the rest of the animal kingdom." She believes, therefore, that "animal rights and . . . feminism are not only unrelated, but are in many ways antithetical" (Ottenheimer 1990).

I would contest all those claims. Some new developments in biomedicine may have the potential for good—but they have been developed within a society in which women (and others) are oppressed, a society that places more value on obtaining cheap oil from the Middle East than on the lives of the people or animals killed by the weapons it creates. Feminists have often been critical of the ways in which women's interests have not been paramount in the development of various interventions in reproduction, for example. As for the "very little cost," I will merely point out that, in my rather small country, 3.24 million scientific procedures on animals were begun under license in 1991.[13] Worldwide, the number of animals used is staggering. Perhaps most are anesthetized for painful procedures: but many may not be, and nearly all lose their lives.

These are, I believe, issues for feminism. *Even if* we accept that science can produce good things for women (and it can); *even if* we accept that doing science is fun for those who do it (it is—which is why I did it in the first place), we still must accept that there is a price to pay. Feminist critiques of science have emphasized how it is often women (or lesbians, or nonwhite people) who pay the cost. What we must now add is that it is also animals.

It is not, moreover, an issue only for those who write critically about science. What the letter writers to *Labyrinth* are addressing is not only the question of the moral principles involved in using animals (although it is certainly partly that); their responses also relate indirectly to the question of how feminists should do research. What is, or might be, feminist praxis in the sciences—particularly if that science involves animals? For these scientists, feminist praxis centers on the possible outcomes of the research (in health care, say); for others (including me), feminist praxis in biology would have to take much more account of the subjectivity and possible suffering of the animals. We have barely begun to address these difficult debates.

Feminist writing about science, too, needs to pay more attention not only to the ethics of using animals in science, but also to the broader questions of how we use the *idea* of animals, what they represent for us. Let me offer a couple of suggestions.

First, we could look at ways in which "animals" are represented in science—not only our view of them as "mirrors" of nature, as examples of biological determinism, but also the images we have of these animals, and how they relate to other feminist work. When feminist writers evoke images of women as experimented upon (in relation to reproductive technology, for instance), there is similarity to the image of the animal-as-artifact in the lab, the analytic animal. How are these images constructed, and what is their meaning?

As a second approach, we could examine in more detail how we use the concept(s) of "others" in writing about science. Even though I am a scientist, when the feminist critic in me takes over, she often looks at scientists "from the outside"—as others. Yet I am on the inside, too. Scientists, moreover, are both apart from and included within the general public. Many of the beliefs they state in interviews align them with the wider public: this is one source of their ambivalence about animals.

In addition, we could examine more closely the construction of animals as others: in what circumstances, and to what extent, do we counterpose them as others? And who is the "us" to whom they are other? How do those boundaries relate to feminist theory? And what happens to our ideas about ourselves when those boundaries are threatened or blurred? These are all questions that need further thinking about and developing within feminist theory.

The wider relationships between feminist politics and issues concerning animals are not straightforward. For a start, animal rights does not map in any simple way onto the political dimensions that we tend to use. So, while some view it as having connections with left-wing politics (e.g., Noske 1989), others have linked animal rights to the extreme right (e.g., Henshaw 1989).

Yet both have something to learn from the other. From the animal side, what can be learned is how better to locate animal concerns in relation to wider politics. One reason why some critics have, in somewhat knee-jerk fashion, accused the animal supporters of being right wing (or even fascist) is that the latter *have* sometimes seemed to ignore other issues. It is unfortunately true that, in Britain, some members of animal rights groups have taken part in racist activities on the grounds of attacking cruelty to animals. Now it may be true that animals suffer less if they are stunned before killing, so that animals killed according to certain religious practices are likely to suffer. But that cannot justify (for example) anti-Semitic attacks. No human culture is free of animal suffering; and slaughterhouses that stun are hardly repositories of kindness and compassion. We need to find ways of expressing concern about what happens to the animals that do not express some kind of cultural imperialism.

For feminism, I suggest, what can be learned is to question not only boundaries of difference *within* humans (or between women), but also to question the boundaries of what constitutes humanness. What is it that we are afraid of when we flee from any suggestion of our own connections with other kinds of animals? It is not enough to say glibly that it is "biological determinism" that we wish to avoid if we continue to shore up such determinism by assuming that it applies to nonhuman animals.

What I want to emphasize here is how contradictory some of these issues are, how ethically and politically complex. In that sense,

Feminism, Animals, and Science

writing about animal rights could usefully pay more heed to debates in feminist theory, with their emphases on cultural difference and their questioning of boundaries (in relation to gender and race, for example). But feminism, too, needs to look at how it uses concepts of boundaries and otherness, at what assumptions it makes about "biology," animals, and the environment, about how those assumptions impact upon other politics. For me, arguably the most central contradiction in feminist thinking about science and animals is how a critical discourse that celebrates difference and fracturing of simple dichotomies rests firmly and unquestioningly on such a dichotomy. Whatever "animals" are, they are more than just whatever it is we wish to transcend.

Notes

I am very grateful to the editors of this volume, and to Ruth Hubbard, Anne Fausto-Sterling, Susanne Kappeler, and Mike Michael, for taking the trouble to read and comment on an earlier draft of this essay. Its spirit is also utterly dependent on the love and support of the various nonhumans with whom I am privileged to live.

1. See, for example, the *Hypatia* special issue on ecological feminism (1991, vol. 6, no. 1).

2. An interesting exception to this generalization comes from Nazi ideology (Arluke and Sax 1992), in which the boundaries were drawn in such a way that some humans were "less than" human, and some animals acquired a status equivalent to that of (Aryan) humans.

3. This is not to suggest that the behavior of all species of animals is flexible. Many species seem to have a relatively fixed behavioral repertoire. But vertebrates at any rate (and certainly mammals and birds) do appear to be much more flexible than we have tended to think hitherto. My point here is to emphasize that we should never assume fixity a priori.

4. Apart from the fact that determinist approaches are inadequate for explaining animal behavior, they also raise ethical questions. A great many animals are being used in laboratories to test hypotheses regarding human behavior and its determination, based on inappropriate assumptions— inappropriate, that is, with regard both to humans and to the animals concerned. This raises the ethical question of whether we can justify using animals as models for humans if the model is inappropriate.

5. In this sense, behaviorism was founded on an assumption of evolutionary continuity: all animals obeyed the same laws of learning. Behaviorism, however, still supported the mind/body dichotomy, largely by denying mind altogether.

6. Unless, of course, these studies threaten endangered species. Even so, the

furor is often less than that created by using animals in laboratories. That the concern is less, however, does not mean that studies of animals in the wild do not raise ethical issues. Many do, and these are now being addressed (e.g., Cuthill 1992).

7. Even the title "lab animals" is a bit of a misnomer, since very few actually *live* in the laboratory. Rather, they live in specialized animal houses. Of those bred in any one institutional animal house, relatively few actually enter laboratories.

8. To talk about the images in this way is not to imply that the procedures are not potentially painful or likely to induce suffering. It is not my intention here to belittle the message of those images, but simply to underline what *kind* of images of animals they rely on.

9. It is interesting to speculate why this is so. Genetic uniformity may have seemed important at a time when research into genetics and breeding was given new impetus by the rediscovery of Mendel's work in 1900. It is not, however, entirely clear that genetic uniformity does promote physiological or behavioral uniformity—nor is it clear why these qualities should be desired rather than variations being studied in their own right. Hubbard (1990) notes that genetics is about change and variation, *not* about uniformity—yet it is treated as though the latter is the case.

10. The passive voice has another effect. It requires that the reader, subliminally, supply an image of the person doing the injection or other procedure, and both stereotypically and statistically, that image is likely to be male. So, women readers are situated outside the activities being described.

11. This includes transgenic animals; these are usually agricultural animals into whom a human gene has been transposed. The animal is used as a cheap, living pharmaceutical factory. This practice undoubtedly raises ethical questions in terms of the potential for abuse of the animal; more specifically, the favored "system for expression" is likely to be mammary glands—so the ethical questions will focus on female animals and their offspring.

12. I have to confess to having failed this test of the scientist-in-making. Twenty-something years later, the feminist in me cringes at my strategy for avoiding pithing frogs in my third-year neurophysiology practicals: I got one of the men to do it. That doesn't change the fate for the frog: I simply avoided doing it myself.

13. Experiments using animals in Britain are regulated by the Home Office, under the Animals (Scientific Procedures) Act of 1986. Statistics are gathered for scientific procedures; but, as the act forbids the reuse of animals except under special circumstances, that number is assumed to correspond roughly to the number of animals.

References

Arluke, A. 1988. Sacrificial Symbolism in Animal Experimentation: Object or Pet? *Anthrozoos* 2:97–116.

———. 1990. Uneasiness Among Laboratory Technicians. *Laboratory Animal* 19:20–39.

———. 1992. Trapped in a Guilt Cage. *New Scientist* 4 (April):33–35.

Arluke, A., and B. Sax. 1992. Understanding Nazi Animal Protection and the Holocaust. *Anthrozoos* 5:6–31.

Benney, N. 1983. All of One Flesh: The Rights of Animals. In *Reclaim the Earth*, ed. L. Caldecott and S. Leland, 141–51. London: The Women's Press.

Birke, L. I. A. 1982. Is Homosexuality Hormonally Determined? *Journal of Homosexuality* 6:35–49.

———. 1986. *Women, Feminism and Biology: The Feminist Challenge.* Brighton, England: Wheatsheaf.

———. 1991a. Science, Feminism and Animal Natures: I. Extending the Boundaries. *Women's Studies International Forum* 14:443–49.

———. 1991b. Science, Feminism and Animal Natures: II. Feminist Critiques and the Place of Animals in Science. *Women's Studies International Forum* 14:451–58.

———. 1994. *Feminism, Animals, and Science: The Naming of the Shrew.* Buckingham, England: Open University Press.

Birke, L., and M. Michael. 1992a. The Researcher's Dilemma. *New Scientist*, 4 April, 25–28.

———. 1992b. Views from Behind the Barricade. *New Scientist*, 4 April, 29–32.

Cheyney, D. L., and R. M. Seyfarth. 1990. *How Monkeys See the World.* Chicago: University of Chicago Press.

Coleman, W. 1977. *Biology in the Nineteenth Century: Problems of Form, Function, and Transformation.* Cambridge: Cambridge University Press.

Corrigan, T., and S. Hoppe, eds. 1990. *And a Deer's Ear, Eagle's Song and Bear's Grace: Animals and Women.* Pittsburgh, Pa.: Cleis Press.

Cuthill, I. 1992. Field Experiments in Animal Behaviour: Methods and Ethics. In *Ethics in Research on Animal Behaviour*, ed. M. S. Dawkins and M. Gosling, 57–64. London: Academic Press (for the Association for the Study of Animal Behaviour/Animal Behavior Society).

Davis, H. 1989. Theoretical Note on the Moral Development of Rats (*Rattus norvegicus*). *Journal of Comparative Psychology* 103:88–90.

Dorner, G. 1976. *Hormones and Brain Differentiation.* Amsterdam: Elsevier.

Elston, M. A. 1987. Women and Antivivisection in Victorian England. In *Vivisection in Historical Perspective*, ed. N. Rupke, 259–94. London: Croom Helm.

Fausto-Sterling, A. 1993. Animal Models for the Development of Human Sexuality: A Critical Evaluation. Unpublished manuscript. Also forthcoming in *Journal of Homosexuality* (special issue on biology).

———. 1985. *Myths of Gender.* New York: Basic Books.

Griffin, D. R. 1992. *Animal Minds.* Chicago: University of Chicago Press.

Gross, A. G. 1990. *The Rhetoric of Science.* Cambridge: Harvard University Press.

Halpin, Z. T. 1989. Scientific Objectivity and the Concept of "the Other." *Women's Studies International Forum* 12:285–94.

Harding, S., 1989. Is There a Feminist Method? In *Feminism and Science,* ed. N. Tuana, 17–32. Bloomington: Indiana University Press.

———. 1991. *Whose Science? Whose Knowledge? Thinking from Women's Lives.* Buckingham, England: Open University Press.

Haraway, D. 1989a. *Primate Visions: Gender, Race and Nature in the World of Modern Science.* London: Routledge.

———. 1989b. Monkeys, Aliens, and Women: Love, Science and Politics at the Intersection of Feminist Theory and Colonial Discourse. *Women's Studies International Forum* 12:295–312.

———. 1991. *Simians, Cyborgs and Women: The Reinvention of Nature.* London: Free Association Books.

Henshaw, D. 1989. *Animal Warfare: The Story of the Animal Liberation Front.* London: Fontana.

Hubbard, R. 1990. *The Politics of Women's Biology.* New Brunswick, N.J.: Rutgers University Press.

Jasper, J., and D. Nelkin. 1992. *The Animal Rights Crusade.* New York: Free Press.

Keller, E. F. 1985. *Reflections on Gender and Science.* New Haven: Yale University Press.

———. 1989. The Gender/Science System: Or, Is Sex to Gender as Nature is to Science? In *Feminism and Science,* ed. Nancy Tuana, 33–44. Bloomington: University of Indiana Press.

Longino, H. 1989. Can There Be a Feminist Science? In *Feminism and Science,* ed. N. Tuana, 45–57. Bloomington: Indiana University Press.

Lynch, M. E. 1988. Sacrifice and the Transformation of the Animal Body into a Scientific Object: Laboratory Culture and Ritual Practice in the Neurosciences. *Social Studies of Science* 18:265–89.

McGaughey, C. A., H. V. Thompson, and D. Chitty. 1947. The Norway Rat. In *The UFAW Handbook on the Care and Management of Laboratory Animals,* Universities Federation for Animal Welfare, ed. A. N. Worden. London: Bailliere Tindall.

Moore, C. L. 1984. Maternal Contributions to the Development of Masculine Sexual Behavior in Laboratory Rats. *Developmental Psychobiology* 17:347–56.

Noske, B. 1989. *Humans and Other Animals.* London: Pluto Press.

Ottenheimer, D. 1990. Letter to the editor. *Labyrinth,* April.

Passmore, J. 1974. *Man's Responsibility for Nature.* London: Gerald Duckworth & Co.

Paterson, J. S. 1957. The Guinea-Pig or Cavy. In *The UFAW Handbook on the Care and Management of Laboratory Animals*, 2d ed., Universities Federation for Animal Welfare, ed. A. N. Worden and W. Lane-Petter. London: Bailliere Tindall.

Plumwood, V. 1990. Women, Humanity and Nature. In *Socialism, Feminism and Philosophy*, ed. S. Sayers and P. Osborne, 211–34. London: Routledge.

——. 1991. Nature, Self, and Gender: Feminism, Environmental Philosophy and the Critique of Rationalism. *Hypatia* 6 (special issue on ecological feminism):3–27.

Ritvo, H. 1987. *The Animal Estate: The English and Other Creatures in the Victorian Age*. Harmondsworth, England: Penguin.

——. 1991. The Animal Connection. In *The Boundaries of Humanity: Humans, Animals, Machines*, ed. J. J. Sheehan and M. Sosna, 68–84. Berkeley: University of California Press.

Rollin, B. 1989. *The Unheeded Cry: Animal Consciousness, Animal Pain, and Science*. Oxford: Oxford University Press.

Rothschild, M. 1986. *Animals and Man: The Romanes Lecture, 1984–5*. Oxford: Clarendon Press.

Rowan, A. 1989. The Development of the Animal Protection Movement. *Journal of NIH Research* (November–December):1, 97–100.

Russell, N. 1986. *Like Engend'ring Like: Heredity and Animal Breeding in Early Modern England*. Cambridge: Cambridge University Press.

Slicer, D. 1991. Your Daughter or Your Dog? *Hypatia* 6 (special issue on ecological feminism):108–24.

Thomas, K. 1983. *Man and the Natural World*, Harmondsworth, England: Penguin.

Wieder, D. L. 1980. Behavioristic Operationalism and the Life World: Chimpanzees and Chimpanzee Researchers in Face-to-Face Interaction. *Sociological Inquiry* 50:75–103.

Wright, S. 1922. The Effects of Inbreeding and Crossbreeding on Guineapigs. *U.S. Dept of Agriculture Bulletin* No. 1090. Washington, D.C.

Zahava, I., ed. 1988. *Through Other Eyes: Animal Stories by Women*. Freedom, CA: The Crossing Press.

3
Carol J. Adams

Woman-Battering and Harm to Animals

A woman, a horse, and a hickory tree
The more you beat 'em the better they be

—folk proverb (cited in Straus 1977, 197)

Farmer John Wright lies dead. His wife has been arrested for suspicion of murder. At the secluded farmhouse where he died, the wives of the men investigating the crime begin to notice small signs that suggest a household in disorder: an odd quilt, an empty birdcage, a messy kitchen. These are unimportant concerns in their husbands' eyes, housewives' concerns, surely, but not those of men building a murder case. As the women survey the rooms, they discuss how Mrs. Wright had changed from a woman who enjoyed company and singing in a choir, to an isolated and dominated individual. They think of times when they ought to have visited, realizing how lonely she

55

must have been. The birdcage is an apt symbol, for she, too, once free, was imprisoned behind bars, albeit invisible ones.

Upon discovering a dead canary with a broken neck in the sewing box, they realize that what could be considered the accidental hanging of John Wright was instead deliberate. He had apparently murdered her sole companion. The evidence was literally in their hands, and they decide to hide it. Thus, Mrs. Wright is judged and freed by *A Jury of Her Peers* (Glaspell 1927).

Susan Glaspell prophetically identified the problem of harm to animals by men who control and abuse their wives or female partners. *A Jury of Her Peers* documented many women's lives, and anticipated circumstances such as this one:

> [A woman] who had been sexually and physically abused over a long period of time, shot her batterer at the point where he was attempting to steal her prized exotic pet bird. This act of psychological abuse toward the woman, through the abuse of her pet, went beyond the point of tolerability. (Dutton 1992, 27)

In fact, we now know that the murder of a pet often signals that the abuser's violence is becoming more life-threatening (see Browne 1987, 157).

Jean Baker Miller observed that until recently, the only understandings generally available to us were "mankind's," but now other perceptions are arising: "precisely those perceptions that men, because of their dominant position, could *not* perceive" (Miller 1976, 1). Susan Glaspell's short story *A Jury of Her Peers*, written eighty years ago, precisely portrays this insight. This essay plumbs the subject of Glaspell's short story as it is being experienced today by battered women and animals.[1] It extends Miller's insights into the working of dominance and subordination in our culture in terms of species *and* gender. My concern is both for what happens to the harmed animal and what is accomplished for the batterer vis-à-vis his control of his woman partner.[2] The killing of an animal as warning and to instill terror, or the sexual use of an animal and woman together result from and enact male dominance. This is precisely what woman-battering, and, I will argue, violence against animals, is all about.

Woman-Battering

Abusive men are the major source of injury to adult women in the United States.[3] According to United States Department of Justice's

Bureau of Justice Statistics, "women are six times more likely than men to be the victim of a violent crime committed by an intimate" (Harlow 1991, 1). According to the U.S. Bureau of Justice National Crime Survey, in the United States a woman is beaten in her home every 15 seconds (Harlow 1991). Testimony before the Senate Judiciary Committee indicates that as many as 4 million women are affected each year by woman-battering (see *Women and Violence* 1990). In the United States, a woman is more likely to be assaulted, injured, raped, or killed by her male partner than by any other assailant.

According to Anne Ganley (1989), battering is "assaultive behavior occurring in an intimate, sexual, theoretically peer, usually cohabitating relationship"; moreover, it is "a *pattern* of behavior, not isolated individual events. One form of battering builds on another and sets the stage for the next battering episode" (202). Battering is life-threatening behavior; a single attack can leave the victim dead or seriously injured.

When a man hits a woman, he has not lost control—he achieves and maintains control: *It is not so much what is done but what is accomplished.* Not only is he achieving and maintaining control, but he is reminding the woman of her subordinate status in the world:

> Battering may be done intentionally to inflict suffering. For example, the man may physically punish a victim for thinking/ behaving in a way that is contrary to the perpetrator's views. Or battering may be done simply to establish control in a conversation without intending harm. Regardless of the intent, the violence has the same impact on the victim and on the relationship. It establishes a system of coercive control. (Ganley 1989, 203)

Men who batter not only believe they have the right to use violence, but receive rewards for behaving in this manner—namely, obedience and loyalty. Battering guarantees that the man "wins" disputes, that the status quo in the relationship is maintained, and that the woman will not leave him (Stordeur and Stille 1989, 74). Battering erects an invisible cage: "Two key aspects of violence are threat and control. That is, the effects of battering are seen not only in the actual physical assaults, but in how fear of being hurt is used to manipulate and control a woman via threats" (Carlin n.d., 1).

In response to battering, the victim changes something about herself in an effort to accommodate the perpetrator. Frequently, this involves restricting her free will, ending relationships with friends or family to whom he has objected (which is usually all of her friends and family, since they all pose a threat to his control), or even quitting work. Often his behavior limits her access to a car or her ability to even leave the house. Meanwhile, she attempts to soothe and please the controlling man, complying with his demands, agreeing with his opinions, denouncing his enemies. She accepts blame when things are not her fault and squelches any anger for fear of igniting his. She makes excuses for him. All to no avail. "When a woman tries to keep a partner calm by pleasing him, he gains exactly what he wants. He exercises his power over her and gets his way on a daily basis. It is ironic that she thinks she is 'managing' best when in fact she is most under his control" (Jones and Schecter 1992, 36).

Battering is a component or kind of sexual violation, since it occurs against one's sexual partner. Catharine MacKinnon's insights on this matter are helpful:

> [Battering] is sexually done to women. Not only in where it is done—over half of the incidents are in the bedroom. Or the surrounding events—precipitating sexual jealousy.... If women as gender female are defined as sexual beings, and violence is eroticized, then men violating women has a sexual component. (MacKinnon 1987, 92)

Or as another feminist has put it: "violence *is* sex to those who practice it *as* sex" (Annie McCombs, quoted in MacKinnon 1987, 233, n. 23). Moreover, women are raped as a continuation of the beating, threatened with more violence if they fail to comply with their husband's sexual requests, forced to have sex with an animal, or forced to have sex to oblige the abuser's need to "make up" after a beating or the execution of an animal.

While MacKinnon's insight that battering is sexually done to women underscores that battering is an expression of male sexual dominance, one of the difficulties for a woman experiencing battering is identifying how it is that discrete aspects of her partner's behavior are abusive and represent his attempts at controlling her. Battering is a chronic situation marked by crisis events. But which moments, precisely, are a part of the chronic pattern?

Forms of Battering

Anne Ganley, a psychologist who has pioneered in victim-based counseling for batterers, has identified—for assessment purposes—

four forms of battering: (1) physical battering, (2) sexual battering, (3) psychological battering, and (4) the destruction of property and pets. She explains why she established these categories:

> Sexual battering overlaps with physical battering since both involve direct attacks on the victim's body. The destruction of property and pets overlaps with physical battering because both are physical acts against a person or object. However, the destruction of property and pets also overlaps with psychological battering since neither involves a direct attack on the victim's body. Too often sexual violence and the destruction of property/pets have been overlooked as part of the battering patterns. (Ganley 1985, 8)

Ganley perceptively discerns that in acts of destruction to property and pets, the batterer's goal is to affect the woman. It is not what is done but what is accomplished: "The offender's purpose in destroying the property/pets is the same as in his physically attacking his partner. He is simply attacking another object to accomplish his battering of her" (Ganley 1985, 15). But the destruction of property is qualitatively different from harm to animals or the execution of animals. Yes, for the batterer who threatens to injure or does injure animals, the animals' destruction may be like property destruction, that is, they are yet another object instrumentally used to represent the woman's fate. But, harming an animal inflicts physical damage, pain, and often annihilates someone—the animal. We cannot lose sight of *this* victim's perspective. What is so anguishing to the human victim about the injury of an animal is that it is a threat or actual destruction of a cherished relationship in which the animal has been seen as an individual. Thus it both inflicts psychological trauma on the woman and imposes a change in a valued relationship. Thus, I propose that this fourth form of battering be split into two separate categories: (4) destruction of property and (5) harm to animals.

The strength of these categories, as Ganley points out, is the identification as battering behavior of phenomena that are not ordinarily perceived as battering. This helps women recognize the interrelatedness of different kinds of behavior. As this essay argues, the establishment of a separate category for harm to animals is imperative for many reasons. When a batterer harms or executes an animal, he not only affects the woman, he also affects the animal. The results of such double control and such power over two living beings necessitate closer attention.

We do not know how many batterers harm animals, nor, I would submit, do we need to quantify this form of battering to establish its import. It should be sufficient that those who work in battered women's shelters often know of batterers who threaten, harm, or murder animals or force sex between an animal and the woman.

These workers have reported to me personally that cats are more likely to be stabbed or disemboweled, dogs to be shot, both may be hung, though a choke chain leash enables a batterer to act quickly against a dog; sometimes the pet simply disappears or dies mysteriously. Batterers have chopped off the heads or legs of cats, stepped on and thus killed a Chihuahua puppy. Cats have been found nailed to the front porch. An activist in the battered women's movement recounted how her grandfather, when angry with his wife, would go to the barn and relentlessly and systematically whip her favorite horse. Another activist who works at a battered women's shelter described at least six situations she was acquainted with, in the first half of 1993 alone, in which pets were victimized by battering: two women did not leave the men who battered them because of fear for the pet; two women left but returned because of concern over their pets; and two pets were killed. Sometimes batterers have turned their trained "attack" dogs upon their partners (one man was convicted of murder for ordering his pit bull to attack his girlfriend; she was bitten more than one hundred times). Other times batterers have beaten their partners *with* an animal. In one instance, a four-month-old Doberman-mix puppy was used to beat a woman; in another a man hit his wife with a frozen squirrel. *Time* magazine described a batterer, a violent man who was stalking his wife, who tried to flush a cat down the toilet (Time, 29 June 1994). My local paper described how one man slashed two pet cats to death and then threatened to turn the butcher knife on his wife and her dog.[4] In his Pulitzer prize–winning article "The Stalking of Kristin," George Lardner Jr. described the violent man—Michael Cartier—who eventually stalked and killed Lardner's daughter Kristin after she broke up with Cartier. In the wake of the first battering incident

> Cartier tried to make up with her. He gave her a kitten. "It was really cute—black with a little white triangle on its nose," Amber Lynch said. "It was teeny. It just wobbled around."

It didn't last long. Over Kristin's protests, Cartier put the kitten on top of a door jamb. It fell off, landing on its head. She had to have it destroyed. (Lardner 1992)

In order to illuminate what transpires when a man who batters harms an animal, I will provide details from two painful incidents that are representative of injury to animals by batterers. These accounts are unsettling; reading them can be upsetting. Yet, to recognize the meaning of the injury or murder of pets by batterers, we have to have an understanding of what transpires.

> Hal came back with the rifle. He pressed it against her temple and clicked the hammer, then began ramming it into her stomach, yelling, "I'll kill you, goddamn it! I'll kill you this time!" Finally, he laid the gun down and went outside. . . .
> When Hal left to get more beer, Karen fled, taking her small dog with her. Hal had nearly killed the dog several times when he was angry. She couldn't bear to leave it at home, knowing what would happen to it. (Browne 1987, 119)

She went to the police station and called a friend. The friend called Hal. Hal came to the police station and got her, and no one intervened.[5] He threatened her as he drove her home, she sheltered the dog.

> When they got to the house, Hal came around and jerked her door open. He yanked her out of the seat and onto the ground, then began kicking her in the ribs. Each blow knocked Karen farther across the driveway. . . . Finally, he stood over her, daring her to get up. Karen was afraid to move. The dog was still hiding in the truck; Hal carried it to the house and threw it against the concrete of the patio until he apparently thought he'd killed it. Then he made Karen go inside. (119–20)

Several days later, a friend helped Karen go to the emergency room of a local hospital. She had several broken ribs and her spleen had been damaged.

> She finally agreed to go to a local shelter and to receive outpatient care, but when they called to make arrangements they learned that the shelter wouldn't take dogs, Karen went home. The animal had survived, but it was badly hurt, and Karen felt responsible. She wanted to be there to take care of it; she knew Hal would kill it in retaliation if she left. (120)

Karen's inability to enter a shelter because they cannot take pets is confirmed by some battered women's shelter workers and volunteers, who told me that women were not leaving the abuser because they feared their pets would be killed.[6] Some who did leave would go back to the home within one to two days because of concern about the pet who had remained in the home. They would call to find out how the pet was and the husband would say, "I'm going to kill the animal."

In the other detailed incident we will consider, the batterer killed the animal. It was described in the *Los Angeles Times*, and later quoted by Diana Russell in her important book, *Rape in Marriage*:

> The dawn of Michael Lowe's madness came on a sunny July day as he watched his shaggy white sheepdog chase playfully after a pet chicken in the family's rural Ramona yard. "Come here!" shouted Lowe to the dog. The animal, bought for Lowe's wife as a puppy, pranced over and sat at her master's feet. "I told you not to chase the chickens," Lowe said to the dog. "I told you not to chase the chickens."
>
> Lowe went inside the house and returned with a .357 magnum revolver. Cecilia Lowe knew what was about to happen, having become uncomfortable at that look, that tone of voice. She fell to her knees, pleading with Lowe not to harm the animal. She grabbed her husband around the legs and begged while the couple's 20-month-old son stood by crying.
>
> Lowe casually pumped a shot into the dog. The sheepdog ran under the family's truck, cowering in pain as Lowe went back into the house and returned with a .30-.30 Winchester rifle. He called to the animal and made her sit in front of him as he fired five more shots, killing the family pet. Three months later he did the same to his wife. Then he killed himself. (Russell 1990, 296)

The *Times* implies that Lowe's actions were "madness"; however, they were consistent with the deliberate, calculated behavior of a man who wants to establish or maintain control. Cecilia Lowe's discomfort with his look and his tone of voice, also suggest a man who has used controlling behavior before, and who, with only a look or a specific tone of voice, can insure obedience.

Konrad Lorenz, in raising the issue of the morality of killing farm animals versus hunting nondomesticated animals, identifies the precise cruelty of a woman-batterer murdering a pet. While I do not agree with his confident assertion of the moral appropriateness of hunting, I do think he captures the cruel despotism that results through the institution of domestication:

> Morally it is much worse to wring the neck of a tame goose which approaches one confidently to take food from one's hand than it is, at the expense of some physical effort and a great deal of patience, to shoot a wild goose which is fully conscious of its danger and, moreover, has a good chance of eluding it. (Lorenz 1955, viii)

After being wounded by Lowe, the sheepdog still obediently came to him as he prepared to execute her. In this Lowe betrayed several relationships, not only with his wife and child, but also with the dog.

Psychological Battering in the Wake of Harm to Animals

Anne Ganley indicated that the execution of pets overlaps with psychological battering because it does not involve a direct attack on the primary victim's body. The psychological battering continues in the wake of harm to animals—especially the execution of a pet—by denying the woman the opportunity to express her reality, that is to mourn the loss of the pet. Part of the control that a batterer enacts is the doing of something that causes tremendous feelings and then not allowing the expression of those feelings. As Kathleen Carlin of Men Stopping Violence has observed, "It is a doubly powerful kind of sadistic control: 'I can hurt you so badly and then make it so that you cannot express it.' "[7] Wanting to have sex after executing an animal would be a further way of denying her reality.

Consider Cecilia Lowe's situation after the killing of her dog by her husband. The dog was hers.[8] We do not know whether Michael gave her to Cecilia or not, though this again would conform with the controlling behavior of batterers. (Recall Michael Cartier who gave Kristin Lardner a kitten.) To whom could she turn with her grief over the loss of her dog and the serious threat her husband's behavior posed?

After an attack upon a pet in which the pet dies or she takes the pet to a pound, the woman experiences many feelings. She has lost a beloved friend, and thus feels profound grief. As with marital rape, she needs someone with whom to share her earth-shattering experience. Unfortunately, as with marital rape, the person to whom one would most logically turn for support and consolation is instead the cause of the pain. And the environment he is creating is one that punishes any initiative, that enforces a constricted and flat emotional life: "Prolonged captivity undermines or destroys the ordinary sense of a relatively safe sphere of initiative, in which there is some tolerance for trial and error. To the chronically traumatized person, any action [including grieving] has potentially dire consequences" (Herman 1992, 91).

Mickie Gustafson's *Losing Your Dog* (1992) describes the range of feelings and reactions that occur upon the death of a pet:

> [A] dead animal is more than just a dead body. It represents happiness that has been lost and a bond that has been severed. Harmony is suddenly missing, and a wonderful source of happiness is no more. The resulting feeling of loneliness may feel overwhelming and almost unbearable. (14)
> –Those who experience great grief share an overwhelming sense of desertion and loneliness, as well as a yearning for the deceased, which may become almost unbearable at times.
> –Life appears unreal and meaningless to a grieving person, who may often become apathetic and deeply depressed. (21)

In these passages, Gustafson is describing the grief and emptiness in the wake of a pet's death from old age or from euthanasia. But the deaths that battered women mourn may be unexpected and sudden, or they may be expected—some women in fact may have been bracing themselves for such violence. In either case, the deaths occur within a context of violence and control. In addition to grieving, the woman may feel guilt, rage, hopelessness, for not being able to protect the animal from death at the hands of her partner:

> The kitten was sitting in the yard. Billy got his rifle, walked up to it, and shot it. Then he hunted down the other two cats and shot them. Kim was hysterical—following him around, tugging on him, jumping up and down and screaming. She begged him not to kill the cats, and after he had, she begged him not to leave them there. So he picked them up and threw them over the fence. After Billy went to sleep that night, Kim crept out, found the cats, and buried them. Then she lay down in the field and cried. She blamed herself for their deaths. She should never have brought them to live around Billy. It seemed like all that was left was for Billy to kill her. Her diary for that day reads, "I wish I were dead. I wish I had been shot, too." (Browne 1987, 154)

If a battered woman realizes the life-threatening nature of the batterer's behavior toward the animal while the animal still lives, she may decide to take the animal to the pound in order to protect him or her. This will be equally devastating in terms of her relationship with the pet. She will still need to mourn the ending of the relationship even if she can console herself that at least the animal continues to live. (Of course, given the pet overpopulation problem, the shelter may euthanize the animal.) Gustafson describes the specific feelings one experiences in response to forced separation: "Having to choose between keeping your dog and something else may lead to feelings of anger and disappointment at being forced to make such a choice" (Gustafson 1992, 106).

Gustafson identifies "exaggerated anger and irritation" (20) as characteristics of the grieving person after the death (or loss to the pound) of a dog. But anger is one of those emotions that battered women are not supposed to express, constantly monitoring their emotions so that they will be flat in relationship to the controlling man. This is both a survival strategy and a coping mechanism. Ann Jones and Susan Schecter describe how many women "push down their angry feelings for fear that expressing anger may trigger even greater anger in the controlling partner" (Jones and Schecter 1992, 44–45). In the case of an animal's murder, the anger may be all the more legitimate, while necessarily being all the more denied. Thus psychological control continues after the death of the animal.

One final step remains that many batterers take before the woman is truly "broken." As Judith Herman describes it: "the final step in the psychological control of the victim is not completed until she has been forced to violate her own moral principles and to betray her basic human attachments. Psychologically, this is the most destructive of all coercive techniques. . . . In domestic battery, the violation of principles often involves sexual humiliation. Many battered women describe being coerced into sexual practices that they find immoral or disgusting" (Herman 1992, 83). For some batterers, sexual coercion involves forcing sex between a woman and an animal. Thus, a batterer forces her to violate her basic attachments to others—human *and* nonhuman.

Forced Sex with Animals

A little-discussed form of battering involves the use of animals for humiliation and sexual exploitation by batterers and/or marital rapists. Batterers and marital rapists (and the two groups are neither mutually exclusive nor completely inclusive of each other) sometimes force sex between a woman and animal. For instance:

> –"He would tie me up and force me to have intercourse with our family dog. . . . He would get on top of me, holding the dog, and he would like hump the dog, while the dog had its penis inside me." (Walker 1979, 120)
> –One 25-year-old man raped his 16-year-old, menstruating, virgin girlfriend, by tying her spread eagled to the bed, and forcing his Doberman upon her. It took her eight years before she shared the story with anyone. (see McShane 1988, 73–75)
> –Linda "Lovelace" reports that she was forced—under threat of death by her batterer—to allow a dog to mount her in the production of a pornographic movie. "From then on if I didn't do something he wanted, he'd bring me a pet, a dog." ("Lovelace" 105–13, also 206)
> –In a California case in which a man was brought to trial for raping his third wife, his first wife "reported that her husband had purchased a large dog and trained it to have sex with her. Watching this occur enabled him to become sufficiently aroused to have intercourse with her." (Russell 1990, xii)

Pornography is often used when men force sex between a woman and an animal. It may be used as a desensitizing process. She is drawn into the process at first by him encouraging her to look at pornography with him—for instance, by watching videos together. This part she may like. But his goal is to raise her tolerance to the activities depicted so that she will duplicate them. Or, he consumes the pornography on his own and then wishes to reenact what he has seen.

> –He started taking me to sex shows where there were women and animals, esp. snakes. (*Pornography and Sexual Violence* 1988, 68, testimony by Ms. A)
> –This guy had seen a movie where a woman was being made love to [*sic*] by dogs. He suggested that some of his friends had a dog and we should have a party and set the dog loose on the women. He wanted me to put a muzzle on the dog and put some sort of stuff on my vagina so that the dog would lick there. (Russell 1984, 126)
> –One woman known to us related that her spouse always had a number of pornographic magazines around the house. The final

episode that resulted in ending the marriage, was his acting out a scene from one of the magazines. She was forcibly stripped, bound, and gagged. And with the help from her husband, she was raped by a German shepherd. (*Pornography and Sexual Violence* 1988, 104, testimony of Ms. Rice Vaugh)

Through pornography, dogs, snakes, and other animals help a man picture himself in the scene. They become stand-ins for the male phallus.[9] And this is true with watching forced sex between his female partner and an animal. Forced sex with animals is an indication of how abusive men extensively sexualize and objectify their relationships, including their relationships with other animals.

What does it mean in terms of the man's life-threatening behavior when he forces sex between a woman and an animal? I put this question to Kathleen Carlin of Men Stopping Violence. She replied:

They represent different types of danger—whatever it is that the man uses, if there is a stand-in for him, it increases the sense of omnipotence of the man watching. It feeds the sense of him that merges his omnipotence and his use of her as an object, whether it is an animal or a machine. In one sense that increases the danger because it heightens the level of acceptable abuse. It merges his sense of omnipotence and her objectifection. It intensifies her as an object. (conversation with author, autumn 1993)

From the abuser's point of view, he is sexually using an animal as an object, just as others may use baseball bats or pop bottles. The animal's status as object is what is important in this instance. But, then, so is the woman's. Objects used for sex in this way, including animals and the women victims, are denied individuality, uniqueness, specificity, particularity. It is not who they are that matters as much as what can be accomplished through the use of them. Forcing sex between his human female partner and a nonhuman animal reveals the way that a batterer objectifies both of them so that they have become interchangeable objects. They become to him no different—and no less expendable than a pop bottle. Ann Jones refers to instances such as these as pimping and categorizes forcible rape with an animal as torture (1994, 85, 93).[10] Surely, it is torture to the animal as well.

Forced sex with a pet animal may intensify the sense that a woman is betraying her basic attachments. Understandably, she will see this as immoral and disgusting. Coercive sex is always humiliating; coercive sex using an implement other than the man's body demonstrates how fully she, too, is an object without individuality, any particularity. When Linda Marchiano claimed her own name and her voice, she explained that forced sex with a dog made her feel "totally defeated. There were no greater humiliations left for me" ("Lovelace" 1980, 113).

Sexual coercion using an animal violates many women's moral, relationship principles. It is often the most unspeakable aspect of being a hostage to a violent man. For women political prisoners in Chile who had been raped by trained dogs,

> [t]his is evidently one of the most brutalizing and traumatic experiences suffered by women in prison. The survivors of this torment find it very difficult to report their exposure to this extreme sexual debasement. With sickening canniness, the torturers traumatize their victims into feeling shame for their own bodies. (Bunster-Bunalto 1993, 257)

Once safe, victims of sexual violence may move through a stage of remembrance and mourning in order to achieve healing. Through reconstruction of the story of the trauma, they transform "the traumatic memory, so that it can be integrated into the survivor's life story. . . . Because the truth is so difficult to face, survivors often vacillate in reconstructing their stories. Denial of reality makes them feel crazy, but acceptance of the full reality seems beyond what any human being can bear" (Herman 1992, 175, 181). Forced sex between an animal and a woman is so filled with shame and degradation that silence seems preferable to speaking. Because of the intensity of shame and silence in the wake of sexual attacks involving animals, healing from this victimization is rendered all the more difficult.

Forced sex with animals is an act that needs to be told but is so horrifying it almost guarantees the silence. During the Renaissance, bestiality was referred to in law books euphemistically as *"offensa cujus nominatio crimen est* [the offense the very naming of which is a crime]" (Serpell 1986, 126). The unspeakability of these instances of coerced sex indicate how destructive is the psychological control of the victim by the abuser. Forced sex with animals merges sexual experiences with torture, and as one activist commented "breaks all the circuits." While the human victim is denied her own voice because of shame and disgust, the other victim is seen as voiceless because animals do not communicate in human language. Both victims experience the unspeakable and are made unspeakable as well.

Animals and Batterers' Strategies for Control

Harming animals is in itself an act of violence against another living being. If the batterer executes the animal, he and everyone in his family perceive that matters of life and death are in his hands. Thus, he feels more powerful. Harming animals or using them sexually are also acts of instrumentalizing the animal to get to the woman.

The Chart of Coercion

After psychologist Alfred D. Biderman studied brainwashed American soldiers, his work was codified into a chart of coercion, which was published by Amnesty International. In her pathbreaking book, *Rape in Marriage*, Diana Russell demonstrated how Biderman's chart could also be used to understand the effects of torture on wives, as well as those who are seen ordinarily as "hostages." This chart of coercion is now used in battered women's shelters to help them identify the controlling tactics of their partner. Women can perceive numerous experiences that correspond with each general method of coercion.

In Table 1, I demonstrate how Biderman's chart can be used to reveal the variety of ways that animals are used coercively by batterers. Biderman's chart identifies the parallels between the experience of domestic captives, such as battered women, and political captives, and it depicts the way in which isolated cruel acts are actually interrelated. Table 1 establishes that anything that is coercive may and probably does include animals.

On the left side, Table 1 reproduces a modified chart of coercion (see Jones 1994, 90–91). On the right side are examples specific to woman-battering and harm to animals. Note that only one of these methods of harming an animal involves direct physical violence to the woman. Yet, all these methods generally occur in a situation in which a man has also used threats and bodily assaults against his partner. What these examples demonstrate is that harm to animals enacts a wide variety of coercive methods. Table 1 demonstrates the context of terror in which battered women live and through which animals are harmed.[11]

Table I

Biderman's Chart of Coercion and Examples of Harm to Animals
as a Form of Woman-Battering

Method of Coercion	Examples
Isolation	
–Deprives victim of all social support for the ability to resist. –Develops an intense concern with self. –Makes victim dependent upon interrogator.	Killing a pet animal reinforces isolation, often depriving the woman of her last significant relationship, increasing her dependence on her batterer.
Monopolization of Perception	
–Fixes attention upon immediate predicament; fosters introspection. –Eliminates stimuli competing with those controlled by captor.	Eliminates any competition from animals for attention by killing them; also eliminates the support a pet offers the victim.
–Frustrates all actions not consistent with compliance.	
Induced Debility and Exhaustion	
–Weakens mental and physical ability to resist.	Death or harm to animal induces physical reactions to grief (e. g., sleeplessness, headaches).
Threats	
–Cause her to live in terror.	Threatens to kill the pet; or kills the pet and says she is next.
Occasional Indulgences	
–Insure compliance. [Indulgences may be accompanied by a lessening or cessation of violent acts, but a context of terror remains. Because of underlying threats, the occasional indulgences provide a false sense of safety: she is never safe.]	Gives her an animal. [He gives her an animal not because he has really changed, but to maintain control over her.]
Demonstrating "Omnipotence"	
–Suggests futility of resistance.	Killing an animal in the presence of her and the children. [Separation assault: attacking her animal when she leaves him.]

Table I

Continued

Method of Coercion	Examples
Degradation	
–Makes cost of resistance appear more damaging to self-esteem than capitulation.	Raping her with an animal, sexually exploiting the animal as well.
–Reduces prisoner to "animal level" concerns.	Making her eat or drink from the animal's dishes.
Enforcing Trivial Demands	
–Develops a *forced* habit of compliance in the prisoner.	Refusing to allow her to feed an animal or let the animal in or out at a certain time.

Sources: Ann Jones, *Next Time She'll Be Dead* (Boston: Beacon Press, 1994), pp. 90–91, and Amnesty International, *Report on Torture* (1973), as adapted by the women's shelter of Northampton, Massachusetts. All examples and bracketed additions are by the author.

Control Strategies and Harm to Animals

When we examine the *reasons* a man may harm an animal as part of battering, we can perceive his deliberate attempts at controlling her. These are the strategies.

1. He harms an animal to *demonstrate his power.* Making someone watch the torture of another is ultimate mastery, saying through these actions "this is what I can do and there is nothing you can do to stop me." She may wish to protect the animal, but she realizes she is unable to. She may feel she let the pet down, or she may be hurt trying to protect the pet, and discover she cannot protect herself or the pet. Sometimes efforts to protect a pet may result in increased violence toward the woman (see, for instance, Dutton 1992, 27). In harming an animal, the man who batters simultaneously demonstrates his omnipotence and her complete loss of control.

2. He harms an animal to *teach submission.* Ann Jones describes the experience of one woman, whose husband decided to "teach submission" by forcing her to watch him "dig her grave, kill the family cat, and decapitate a pet horse" (Jones 1980, 298). Inconsistent and unpredictable outbursts of violence such as harming animals are meant to convince the victim "that resistance is futile, and that her life depends upon winning his indulgence through absolute com-

pliance"; the perpetrator's goal is to instill both fear of death and "gratitude for being allowed to live" (Herman 1992, 77).

3. He executes a pet to *isolate her from a network of support and relationship.* Her relationship with her pet may have been the last meaningful relationship she had been allowed to have. One way a man controls his partner is by severely limiting her social network, restricting her access to friends and families. In this way, he actively destroys her sense of self in relation to others (Herman 1992, 77). Murdering an animal severs a meaningful relationship. It also destroys the woman's sense of self, which was validated through that relationship. If this was the last remaining relationship she was allowed to have, in the loss of the pet she will see the loss of herself. Furthermore, the pet's presence may have helped her avoid adopting the batterer's point of view. It may also isolate her from friends who have pets, or make her feel dehumanized and hence alienated from other humans. She may be fearful around other people who have pets, feeling bad because she has lost her pet, and also feeling that, although she was not the perpetrator, the other animals may not be safe because her own animals are dead. Because she may feel uncomfortable watching other people with animals, or may fear for these animals, she will restrict her contact with other people who have pets.[12]

4. He hurts pets *because he is enraged when he sees self-determined action on the part of women and children.* He wishes to control their actions; their self-determined responses to others, including other animals, infuriate him. Allowed a self-indulgent rage by society, he expresses it with impunity.

5. He harms an animal to *perpetuate the context of terror,* so he may not need to do anything else. As Judith Herman observes, "It is not necessary to use violence often to keep the victim in a constant state of fear. The threat of death or serious harm is much more frequent than the actual resort to violence. Threats against others are often as effective as direct threats against the victim" (1992, 77). Furthermore, making someone watch torture is a particular form of terror:

> Torture or destruction of a loved pet may be an even more powerful abuse than personal abuse. One woman witnessed a succession of 12 kittens tortured and eventually killed by her batterer. (Dutton 1992, 27)

6. He harms a pet as a *preemptive strike against her leaving him, as a form of separation violence.* If harm to animals occurs during a

time that the woman is considering leaving the man who batters, *it works as a strong incentive to stay.* Often, just as a woman is getting ready to leave, a batterer may perform a careless act that endangers the animal(s). For instance, one man spilled bleach on the kitchen table and it "accidentally" poured into the cat's water dish. The message was quite clear: if she is not there, the animals are not safe. She is held hostage by threats to the pet.[13]

7. He *punishes and terrorizes her for leaving by stalking her and executing an animal.* She comes back to her current residence and finds the family pet dead—for instance, a dog shot and left on the doorstep, a cat hanging in the kitchen—she knows that he's been there, that she has been invaded, that there is nowhere where she can be safe.

8. He may *force her to be involved in the animals' abuse,* making her feel that she is a traitor to animals. She is in the position where she thinks animals should not trust her, because she is not going to protect them.

9. He harms animals to *confirm his power.* The act of harming or killing an animal may contain its own gratification.

Each of these reasons for harming a pet reveals motives of aggrandizing or regaining one's power. Yet, often harm to animals, rather than being perceived as deliberate acts of control, are seen, as in the case of Michael Lowe, as madness. The control inherent to the act is seen instead as loss of control. Thus harm to animals perpetuates his plan to make himself appear crazy, ruthless, cold, uncontrollable, invulnerable, and not responsible. That is what batterers want to do— they want people, especially their partners, to think of them as crazy, because it makes them more dangerous in their partner's eyes. When she sees him harm or execute an animal, she may think, "there must be something wrong with him, he must be mentally ill, emotionally ill, or he must have some serious unresolved conflict with his childhood, and how sad or shameful." She may also think, "this guy is really crazy and he scares the hell of me, he could do anything."[14] That is the purpose of psychological abuse: to baffle and confound her. This is his goal, as it successfully obfuscates his purposes.

Harm to Animals, Woman-Battering, and Feminist Theory

Harming an animal is a form of sexual mastery, the instantiation of dominance. It announces and reinforces the man's powerfulness, though it is cloaked in the deceptiveness of "madness." Several important reasons exist for recognizing harm to animals as a distinctive form of woman-battering.

1. Harm to animals exposes the deliberateness of battering.

The first reason to acknowledge harm to animals as a separate category of woman-battering is because *it exposes the deliberateness of battering, its control rather than loss of control.*

In talking with individuals who work with batterers, and especially those who run batterers' groups, I learned two seemingly incongruous facts: though each of them knew of instances in which a batterer had injured or killed an animal, disclosure of harm to animals rarely occurred in batterers' groups. Why was this phenomenon omitted when batterers acknowledged other forms of violence? Was it shame? Was it that there simply was not sufficient time in these groups to cover all atrocities, and a de facto triage effect excluded discussion of harm to animals?

I asked this question of Mike Jackson of the Domestic Violence Institute of Michigan. Jackson argued that it was a purposeful concealment for the men's own advantages. He found that men were more willing to talk about physical abuse than sexual abuse, and more willing to talk about sexual abuse than animal abuse. Jackson based his answer both on his subjective experience and on how many times these three items were discussed. Shame, he argued, was too simplistic a reason, an acceptance of the batterers' tactics. In fact, Jackson argued, batterers do not want people to know how purposeful, willful, and deliberate their actions are. Batterers can obfuscate why they batter when it is physical violence (claiming "I lost control and punched her"), and they can confuse the issue of sexual assault (asserting "she was teasing me and said she wanted it"), but loss of control in a relationship with an animal is harder to defend because the deliberateness of the violence is exposed in the description ("I 'lost' control and then cut the dog's head off and then nailed it to the porch"). Jackson contends that there is not much leeway for a man to say he tortured animals and it was out of his control. Talking about these specific acts of violence reveal their willfulness and purposefulness. Harm to animals is a conscious, deliberate, planned strategy. A facilitator in a batterers' group upon hearing of the torture and/or killing of an animal, would be able to pick that up and show precisely how purposeful the battering behavior is. It would become a point that refocuses on the agency of the batterer—that is, that he makes choices to be violent, and if he so chose, he could stop being violent.

Recall Michael Lowe's deliberateness: He calls to the animal, announces to the dog her infraction, walks into the house and returns with a revolver, ignores the pleas of his wife, the crying of his son, and shoots the dog. Lowe reenters the house, returns with a powerful firearm, calls to the animal, and then shoots her five more times.

Were Lowe to have reported that to a batterer's group, how could he possibly have claimed he lost control? Each step of the way, his deliberateness is evident.

Confirmation of Jackson's insight can be found in an all-male environment in which hostile expressions toward women are not merely condoned but encouraged. In such an environment where one's goal of humiliation and control can be openly acknowledged, harm to animals can be proudly described rather than silenced. And such bragging about these acts exposes how deliberate they actually are.

Consider the brutal male culture of the Citadel, the male military academy that endeavored to prevent the enrollment of Shannon Faulkner. Susan Faludi, in a *New Yorker* profile, evoking the violent, deliberately cruel environment of the Citadel, described how a common practice for Citadel students is bragging about humiliating ex-girlfriends. One cadet told how he had tacked a live hamster to a young woman's door. Another cadet "boasted widely that, as vengeance against an uncooperative young woman, he smashed the head of her cat against a window as she watched in horror." The cat story was his "calling card" (Faludi 1994, 72). Batterers, on the other hand, do not want to disclose their calling card—their deliberate decision to be violent.

2. Harm to animals and harm to children are closely related.[15]
Pet-keeping, according to Yi-Fu Tuan, is dominance combined with affection. So, too, is child-rearing. Proposing a fifth form of battering, harm to animals, of necessity indicates yet one more: harm to children. It is beyond the scope of this essay to argue this, but it may be helpful to highlight the connections between harming animals and harming children.

Harming animals is a way of controlling/threatening children or consolidating control of the children. Sometimes the children are warned that their pet will be harmed if they leave with their mother; one father threatened to disembowel the cat. His child was present when his father Michael Lowe killed the dog. When a batterer kills an animal, *the children, mother, and the batterer all see that there are few if any repercussions for killing a (nonhuman) member of the family.*

Forcing her to neglect or abuse the animal, or forcing her to force the children to abuse or neglect the animals, or forcing her to neglect her children exist within the same continuum of coercive control. "Shut that animal up" may be the command or "make that dog learn by making it stand outside in the cold." Whatever they then have to do to shut the animal up will be done. This dynamic is sadly similar to "shut that kid up" or "make that child learn by. . . ."

The batterer may influence the children to be abusive with the pets. Not only must the mother witness the children being coerced or willful in hurting animals, but she cannot intervene with them to stop the abuse, because if she stops them, she is going to "get it" or they are going to "get it." Again we see how closely intertwined are physical violence and psychological abuse.

Harm to animals, like harm to children, may be the act that convinces a woman of the necessity of separating from her partner. Just as injury to a child may convince women to leave, because their tolerance about what is acceptable toward the children has been violated, so the killing of pets often was the final sign that convinced a battered woman that her partner was capable of murder ("these incidents often seemed to the women a representation of their own death" [Browne 1987, 157]).

An estimated 90 percent of the children in families where there is battering are aware of the battering that occurs there. Yet a terrible denial pervades the household, as though the children do not know and thus are not harmed, and this occurs when an animal is killed as well. In the wake of an animal's death, the mother must model how to handle grief for her children, but recall the constricted environment in which she can express herself. Children need to vent their worries and be greeted with honesty in response to their feelings of despair. Instead they may find an atmosphere of silence, because it is not safe to express feelings in the presence of a controlling man. In addition, children may be concerned about themselves. According to Gustafson:

> The death of the dog will give rise to many questions in children, among them questions about their own death and how the parents would react to it. If the parents appear—in the eyes of the child—not to mourn a much loved animal, how would they

then mourn the child if the child were to die? (1992, 96, sexist language changed)

Harming animals forces denial upon women and children in many ways. She has to protect everybody—animal, children, herself. So, if a child approaches her and says "Mom, Sparky has a cut on his head," she may sit there and say, "No he doesn't." She does this because the batterer is also sitting there. She has to cut her feeling off for the animal. Strategically she learns denial as a survival mechanism. Purposefully denying that it matters to protect the cat, she must betray the cat. She has to demonstrate to the batterer that it does not matter, because she has learned that he hurts only the things she cares about, so she will pretend not to care about the animal. But to the children, not understanding this dynamic, they see their father hurt a dog or cat and think that their mother does not care. How do they interpret this?

Those 90 percent of children who are aware of battering behavior by their mother's partner may witness beatings, rapes, or injury to animals, thereby experiencing their mother's powerlessness. Even though they want to protect their mother or a pet, they usually are unable to do so and feel guilty about their inability to intervene. If they do attempt to protect their mother or the animal, they themselves may be injured. They may feel the mother's powerlessness as her fault and feel enraged with her, not the batterer.

The degree to which she or the children have an intense, respectful relationship with an animal is the extent to which he can harm her by harming the animal. And the degree to which she cares about her children is, similarly, the degree to which he can harm her by harming the children. He harms the animals or the children knowing he will harm her. As is the case with battering, it is his choice to be violent.

3. There are multiple forms of violence against women; harm to animals is consistently present.

Battering is one of several forms of male dominant behavior over women, along with rape, sexual harassment, and sexual abuse of children. Liz Kelly, for instance, in *Surviving Sexual Violence,* documents how "specific forms of sexual violence are connected to more common, everyday aspects of male behaviour. . . . The basic common character underlying the many different forms of violence is the *abuse, intimidation, coercion, intrusion, threat and force men use to* control women" (Kelly 1988, 75–76). So, too, injury to animals and the use of animals to sexually abuse a woman are methods of control. The threat or actual use of a pet to intimidate, coerce, control, or violate a woman is a form of sexual control or mastery over women by men and occurs in many instances of physically controlling behavior.

In 1993, in what became known as the "condom rape" trial (because the victim had requested that her assailant use a condom), the raped woman broke down only once when testifying: when recounting how the rapist had threatened to kill her dog, who was whimpering in the bedroom closet. The testimony of survivors of child sexual abuse reveal that threats and abuse of their pets were often used to establish control over them, while also ensuring their silence, by forcing them to decide between their own victimization or the pet's death. Sexual harassment often includes pornographic material involving explicit depictions of human-animal sexual activity or reference to this material. (See Adams 1994c for a more in-depth discussion.)

An abortion clinic staff member found her beheaded cat on her doorstep; later, when she arrived at the clinic, she was confronted with signs that read "What happened to your cat?" (Blanchard and Prewitt 1993, 259). Leaving a dead animal can be a warning, as two lesbians attempting to set up a retreat center for women in the South discovered in 1993 when they found a dog, dead, draped over their mailbox, with Kotex napkins taped to his/her body (Minkowski 1994, 73). One sex-specific form of torturing women political prisoners in Latin America was introducing mice into their vaginas. And, as noted, in Chile, female political prisoners were raped by trained dogs (see Bunster-Bunalto).

Harm to animals is a strategic expression of masculine power and can be found throughout male controls over women.[17]

4. There are multiple forms of violence against animals; harm to animals in woman-battering must be placed here as well.
Just as battering is one form of male dominance, so harm to animals through woman-battering is one form of animal abuse in which animals are objectified, ontologized as useable, and viewed instrumentally. Just as the status of women and children within the household is related to the cultural, economic, and ideological status of women in a patriarchal culture, so the status of animals in households is related to the cultural, economic, and ideological status of animals in a patriarchal, humanocentric culture: the violability of

what are generally regarded as high-status animals in the home, such as pets, is related to animals' low status in culture in general.

Battering exposes how contingent is the status of women and animals in patriarchal culture: one moment "pet" or "beloved," the next injured or dead. Battering eliminates the status that the culture had granted to specific animals, it levels "companion animals" to the violable status of most animals in our culture.

Feminist commitments to end violence err if they stop at the species barrier. A commitment to stop violence can succeed only when all forms of oppression are included within our analysis, and all forms of violence exposed and then challenged.

5. Harm to animals is violence in its own right and shows how violence is interconnected.

It was once thought that battering involved a series of discrete episodes: a slap here on this day, a hit there on that day. Such cataloging of separate events ignored the context of coercive control that the first slap initiated. It also often began its charting with "what did you do to provoke him?" The assumption was that A led to B, and that there were then C, D, etc. A linear analysis that maintained the separateness of each event was inadequate in establishing how battering behavior actually works. By identifying forms of battering, Anne Ganley aided the contextualization of battering; discrete actions, including how one speaks (batterers often linguistically objectify their partners), were interrelated. Similarly the chart of coercion provided a way of recognizing how a climate of terror is established by a violent man. (Indeed, it could be argued that when battered women's shelters attempt to impose linearity upon the chart of coercion—that is, this will happen first, then that—that they too are misreading a nonlinear phenomenon.) Neither of these tools could be linear in their analysis because battering is nonlinear, establishing an *environment* of control and fear. (Recall, it is not what is done but what is accomplished.)

Once theory is freed from a distorted and distorting dependence on linearity, then we are closer to understanding the dynamics of male control through battering against an individual woman and also its connection with other forms of (largely unchallenged) male control in our culture. The movement from a linear analysis to a recognition of interconnected forms of violence within the home (connections between physical and psychological battering in the home) and without (connections between battering and other forms of male violence) continues when we identify what happens to animals both within the home (harm to animals as a form of battering) and without (a male-dominant culture that with impunity eats, experiments upon, and wears animals).

In *The Sexual Politics of Meat*, I argued that violence against animals cannot be understood without a feminist analysis, because this violence is one aspect of patriarchal culture—arising within and receiving legitimation from the way male sexual identity is constituted as dominance. Gender is an unequal distribution of power; interconnected forms of violence result from and continue this inequality. In a patriarchy, animal victims, too, become feminized. A hierarchy in which men have power over women and humans have power over animals, is actually more appropriately understood as a hierarchy in which men have power over women, (feminized) men, *and* (feminized) animals.

Animals have been largely absent from battering theory, as much as women have been absent from conventional animal rights theory. But the way our culture countenances the construction of human male identity through control of others and the impunity with which women and animals are harmed reveals the errors of such linear approaches. Recognizing harm to animals as interconnected to controlling behavior by violent men is one aspect of recognizing the interrelatedness of all violence in a gender hierarchical world. The challenge now, as it has been for quite some time, is to stop it.

Notes

This essay is deeply indebted to conversations with activists in the movement to stop violence against women, especially Kathleen Carlin, David Garvin, Leigh Nachman Hofheimer, and Mike Jackson. Leigh, Mike, Josephine Donovan, Marie Fortune, and Susanne Kappeler provided close readings of an earlier version of this essay. I am extremely grateful for their attentiveness to this issue and my words. Thanks too for their support and conversations to Batya Bauman, Lisa Finlay, Gus Kaufman Jr., Leslie Mann, Ken Shapiro, John Stoltenberg, and DeLora Wisemoon.

1. This essay expands the preliminary work I have done on this subject (see Adams 1994c).

2. In this essay I use some terms that do not sit comfortably with me and other activists. For instance, I am uncomfortable with the term "battered woman," although it is one that the movement against violence against women has itself adopted. I agree with Sarah Hoagland (1988) that the term elides the agency of the batterer, while also ascribing an unchanging status

to his victim. However, because it is the commonly adopted term, and is used by the scholars and activists from whom I draw my examples, I use the term in this essay. I also use the conventional term "pet" to describe animals who are a part of a household. Those involved in the movement to free animals from human oppression prefer the term "companion animal." While I find this term helpful, the word "pet" is the word used most frequently within the battered women's movement. Thus, for consistency, I continue their usage. Furthermore, given the insights of Yi-Fu Tuan into the making of pets—dominance combined with affection (Tuan 1984, 2)—it may be deceptive for us to presume that there can be nonhierarchical relationships with domesticated animals at this point in history. Just how humans should relate to other animals in any intimate way, that is, the feminist implications of "pet" keeping and whether domestication of animals is consistent with a nonhierarchical feminist theory, is beyond the scope of this essay, but see in general Noske (1989), Tuan (1984), Serpell (1986), and Mason (1993). Finally, personally and philosophically, I find the use of the pronoun "it" disturbing when used to refer to nonhuman animals. However, again, for the purpose of continuity of the narrative, I do not intercede with [sic]s when "it" is used by other authors.

3. Much of the material in this section is taken from Adams 1994b, 11–21.

4. Reported in the *Dallas Times Herald*, 15 June 1991.

5. For a detailed analysis of the failings of law enforcement systems to protect battered women, see Jones (1994).

6. Battered women's shelters often cannot take pets because of Health Department regulations and the restrictions of their liability insurance. Feminists for Animal Rights is starting programs in various communities that offer shelter for the companion animals of battered women. For information on this program, see Adams 1994a or contact Feminists for Animal Rights, P.O. Box 8869, Tucson, Arizona 85738.

7. Conversation with author, October 1994.

8. Some would object to the notion of animals as property that this sentence countenances, but this was in fact the reality for the Lowes.

9. Insight of John Stoltenberg, conversation with author, May 1993.

10. "In fact, the batterer often is a pimp, forcing his wife to have sex with other men or with animals" (Jones 1994, 85).

11. In the past few years, some battered women's advocates have raised concerns about the use of Biderman's charts by shelters. They have focused their concern on several issues: (1) it cannot be seen as explaining woman-battering since it fails to contextualize the psychological effects from coercive controlling behavior within the social structure of male dominance; (2) shelters should not see the chart as a codification of every form of psychological battering, thus they should not assume that it is exhaustive in its identification of coercive controls; (3) it cannot be used as a tool to enable advocates to assess the life-threatening nature of the batterer's actions, nor does it indicate order and predictability. This chart does not mean that the batterer is going to act out in the order in which items are listed. Thus, it is

not a predictor of the safety of the woman. In other words, the chart functions best in offering an interpretive structure for a woman to understand the psychological battering she has experienced. When pressed into duty as a predictor of her safety or as a tool that explains *why* a man batters, it will lose its effectiveness. My purpose in reproducing it is to demonstrate just how fully insinuated within the coercive control of the batterer is his treatment of the animals in the household.

12. Insight of Mike Jackson, conversation with author, spring 1994.

13. Martha R. Mahoney proposes that the term "separation assault" be used to identify the struggle for control that occurs when a woman decides to separate or begins to prepare to separate. "Separation attacks," she argues, should be used to designate the "varied violent and coercive moves in the process of separation assault." Mahoney maintains, "*Separation assault* is the attack on the woman's body and volition in which her partner seeks to prevent her from leaving, retaliate for the separation, or force her to return. It aims at overbearing her will as to where and with whom she will live, and coercing her in order to enforce connection in a relationship. It is an attempt to gain, retain, or regain power in a relationship, or to punish the woman for ending the relationship" (Mahoney 1991, 65–66). This and the following example need to be seen as separation attacks, constitutive parts of separation assault.

14. Insight of Mike Jackson, conversation with author, spring 1994.

15. This section arose from conversations with Mike Jackson. I thank him for his close reading of a previous version, and his discussions with me about this issue. Jackson articulated clearly the need to identify parallels in the treatment of animals and children.

16. Using an animal to harm a woman is a way of exerting control; this explains why there are instances of lesbian attacks on their partner's pet. While human male violence is responsible for most of the damage to women and the other animals in cases of battering, a patriarchal, hierarchical culture will find expressions of this form of violence in some women's same-sex relationships. Where there is an acceptance of a patriarchal value hierarchy, some lesbians will wish to establish control (and be on top in terms of the hierarchy) through violence: "38% of the [abused lesbian] respondents who had pets reported that their partners had abused the animals" (Renzetti 1992, 21). These acts of battering are considered violent and coercive behavior (see Hart 1986, 188). The battered lesbian whose partner injures or destroys a pet faces a double burden: overcoming the invisibility or trivializing of lesbian battering and the invisibility or trivializing of abuse to animals.

References

Adams, Carol J. 1990. *The Sexual Politics of Meat: A Feminist-Vegetarian Critical Theory.* New York: Continuum.

———. 1994a. Sheltering the Companion Animals of Battered Women. In *Feminists for Animal Rights Newsletter* 8, nos. 1–2 (Spring-Summer):1, 8.

———. 1994b. *Woman-Battering.* Minneapolis, Minn.: Fortress Press.

——. 1994c. Bringing Peace Home: A Feminist Philosophical Perspective on the Abuse of Women, Children, and Pet Animals. In *Neither Man nor Beast: Feminism and the Defense of Animals*, 144–61. New York: Continuum.

Blanchard, Dallas, and Terry J. Prewitt. 1993. *Religious Violence and Abortion: The Gideon Project*. Gainesville: University Press of Florida.

Browne, Angela. 1987. *When Battered Women Kill*. New York: Free Press.

Bunster-Bunalto, Ximena. 1993. Surviving Beyond Fear: Women and Torture in Latin America. In *Feminist Frameworks*, 3d ed., ed. Alison M. Jaggar and Paula S. Rothenberg, 252–61. New York: McGraw Hill.

Carlin, Kathleen. n.d. Defusing Violence: Helping Men Who Batter. Available from Men Stopping Violence, 1020 DeKalb Avenue #25, Atlanta, GA 30307.

Dutton, Mary Ann. 1992. *Empowering and Healing the Battered Woman: A Model for Assessment and Intervention*. New York: Springer.

Faludi, Susan. 1994. The Naked Citadel. *The New Yorker*, 5 September.

Ganley, Anne L. 1985. *Court-mandated Counseling for Men Who Batter: A Three-Day Workshop for Mental Health Professionals*. Washington, D.C.: Center for Women Policy Studies. Originally published 1981.

——. 1989. Integrating Feminist and Social Learning Analyses of Aggression: Creating Multiple Models for Intervention with Men Who Batter. In *Treating Men Who Batter: Theory, Practice, and Programs*, ed. P. Lynn Caesar and L. Kevin Hamberger, 196–235. New York: Springer Publishing.

Glaspell, Susan. 1927. *A Jury of Her Peers*. London: Ernest Benn.

Gustafson, Mickie. 1992. *Losing Your Dog: Coping with Grief when a Pet Dies*. Trans. Kjersti Board. New York: Bergh Publishing.

Harlow, Caroline Wolf. 1991. Female Victims of Violent Crime. *Bureau of Justice Statistics* 5 (Jan).

Hart, Barbara. 1986. Lesbian Battering: An Examination. In *Naming the Violence: Speaking Out About Lesbian Battering*, ed. Kerry Lobel, 173–89. Seattle, Wash.: Seal Press.

Herman, Judith. 1992. *Trauma and Recovery*. New York: Basic Books.

Hoagland, Sarah Lucia. 1988. *Lesbian Ethics: Toward New Values*. Palo Alto, Calif.: Institute for Lesbian Studies.

Jones, Ann. 1980. *Women Who Kill*. New York: Holt, Rinehart and Winston.

——. 1994. *Next Time, She'll Be Dead: Battering and How to Stop It*. Boston: Beacon Press.

Jones, Ann, and Susan Schecter. 1992. *When Love Goes Wrong: What to Do When You Can't Do Anything Right. Strategies for Women with Controlling Partners*. New York: HarperCollins Publishers.

Kelly, Liz. 1988. *Surviving Sexual Violence*. Minneapolis: University of Minnesota Press.

Lardner, George, Jr. 1992. The Stalking of Kristin: The Law Made It Easy for My Daughter's Killer. *The Washington Post*, 22 November, 1992.

Lorenz, Konrad. 1955. *Man Meets Dog.* Trans. M. K. Wilson. Cambridge, Mass.: Riverside Press.

"Lovelace," Linda [Linda Marchiano], with Mike McGrady. 1980. *Ordeal.* New York: Berkley Books.

MacKinnon, Catharine. 1987. *Feminism Unmodified: Discourses on Life and Law.* Cambridge. Harvard University Press.

Mahoney, Martha R. 1991. Legal Images of Battered Women: Redefining the Issue of Separation. *Michigan Law Review* 90:1.

Mason, Jim. 1993. *An Unnatural Order: Uncovering the Roots of Our Domination of Nature and Each Other.* New York: Simon and Schuster.

McShane, Claudette. 1988. *Warning: Dating May Be Hazardous to Your Health!* Racine, Wisc.: Mother Courage Press.

Miller, Jean Baker. 1976. *Toward a New Psychology of Women.* Boston: Beacon Press.

Minkowski, Donna. 1994. Missouri Is Burning. *The Village Voice,* 8 February.

Noske, Barbara. 1989. *Humans and Other Animals: Beyond the Boundaries of Anthropology.* London: Pluto Press.

Pornography and Sexual Violence: Evidence of the Link. The Complete Transcript of Public Hearings on Ordinances to Add Pornography as Discrimination Against Women. Minneapolis City Council, Government Operations Committee. Dec. 12 and 13, 1987. 1988. Minneapolis, Minn.: Minneapolis City Council.

Renzetti, Claire M. 1992. *Violent Betrayal: Partner Abuse in Lesbian Relationships.* Newbury Park, Calif.: Sage.

Russell, Diana E. H. 1990. *Rape in Marriage,* rev. ed. Bloomington: Indiana University Press. Originally published 1982.

———. 1984. *Sexual Exploitation: Rape, Child Sexual Abuse, and Workplace Harassment.* Newbury Park, Calif.: Sage Publications.

Serpell, James. 1986. *In the Company of Animals: A Study of Human-Animal Relationships.* New York: Basil Blackwell.

Stordeur, Richard A., and Richard Stille. 1989. *Ending Men's Violence Against Their Partners: One Road to Peace.* Newbury Park, Calif.: Sage.

Straus, Murray. 1977. A Sociological Perspective on the Prevention and Treatment of Wifebeating. In *Battered Women: A Psychological Study of Domestic Violence,* ed. Maria Roy, 194–239. New York: Van Nostrand Reinhold Company.

Tuan, Yi-Fu. 1984. *Dominance and Affection: The Making of Pets.* New Haven: Yale University Press.

Walker, Lenore. 1979. *The Battered Woman.* New York: Harper and Row.

Women and Violence: Hearings Before the Senate Committee on the Judiciary. 1990. 101st Congress, 2d Session 117 (testimony of Angela Browne, Ph.D.).

4
Marti Kheel

License to Kill:
An Ecofeminist Critique
of Hunters' Discourse

Oh, never a brute in the forest and never a snake in the fen
Or ravening bird, starvation stirred, has hunted prey like men.
For hunger and fear and passion alone drives beasts to slay,
But wonderful man, the crown of the plan, tortures and kills for play.

—Ella Wheeler Wilcox, "Voice of the Voiceless"

We cannot have peace among men whose hearts
delight in killing any living creature. By every act that
glorifies or even tolerates such moronic delight in
killing we set back the progress of humanity.

—Rachel Carson, *Silent Spring*

Introduction

Most people conceive of the environmental movement as designed to curb or eliminate our society's destructive relation to the natural world. It may, therefore, seem puzzling to some that a growing number of environmental writers have endorsed an act of violence—namely, hunting. For an increasing number of writers, however, hunting is seen not only as morally acceptable, but as replete with moral and spiritual import. How did this phenomenon occur?

In the 1970s a number of environmental writers sought a different direction for environmental philosophy.[1] Having grown weary of the focus within environmental ethics on abstract principles and universal rules, they began to search for an ethic (more often called a "consciousness") that placed greater emphasis on the importance of experience. In distinct ways, the writings of deep ecologists, ecofeminists, and other radical ecologists all reflected this new orientation. For a number of writers, the valorization of experience was also accompanied by a turn to native cultures for practical inspiration for a new environmental consciousness. For some, hunting was viewed as an exemplary activity for grounding this new environmental consciousness.[2] Richard Nelson, a cultural anthropologist turned nature writer, who is frequently cited by environmental philosophers, illustrates this interest in the activity of hunting. In his words:

> Koyukon people follow a code of moral and ethical behavior that keeps a hunter in right relationship to animals. They teach that all nature is spiritual and aware, that it must be treated with respect, and that humans should approach the living world with restraint and humility. Now I struggle to learn if these same principles can apply in my own life and culture. Can we borrow from an ancient wisdom to structure a new relationship between ourselves and the environment? (The Gifts, 118–19)

Although the recent turn to hunting among environmental writers may appear anomalous, a review of the historical record reveals that the ties between hunting and the environmental movement have a long-standing history, beginning with the early conservation movement. It is my purpose here to identify and critique the mental and moral framework that underlies these ties.

I assess three major attempts to portray hunting as an activity that is not only morally admissible but morally praiseworthy as well. I focus on the attempt by some hunters and hunting proponents to ground the activity of hunting in ethical discourse—in particular, the discourse of the emerging field of environmental ethics—and on subsequent attempts by environmental thinkers to ground an environmental ethic in the ethical discourse of hunters. My intent is to delve beneath the explicit discourse of "hunting ethics" in order to uncover the subtextual ideology and philosophy upon which this discourse is based. In so doing, I hope to examine how the textual discourse on hunting ethics has functioned both to camouflage and to legitimate violence and biocide. In short, I attempt to lay to rest the ethic of the "good sportsman," as well as any notion that hunting may provide a sound conceptual "resource" for an environmental ethic, or any ethic at all.

I present a threefold typology of this discourse, based upon the narratives of three varieties of hunters and hunting proponents. I have named the categories the *happy hunter*, the *holist hunter*, and the *holy hunter*. This is not intended as a comprehensive analysis of all hunters; nor does it imply that no overlap exists within or among the categories. With this caveat in mind, the groupings may be summarized in the following way: the happy hunter claims to hunt for recreation and sheer pleasure, the holist hunter for the sake of the environment or the "biotic whole," and the holy hunter for the purpose of spiritual communion.

The hunters under analysis may also be distinguished from three other types of hunters who receive only passing mention in this paper. I have named these the *hired hunter*, the *hungry hunter*, and the *hostile hunter*. The hired hunter may be said to hunt for the sake of commercial profit, the hungry hunter for the sake of food, and the hostile hunter for the purpose of eradicating "villainous" animals. The latter three categories represent the attitudes of many white hunters prior to the emergence of the environmental movement. Although it could be argued that the hired, hungry, and hostile hunters did, in fact, operate by an implicit ethical code that sanctioned the killing of animals, this code was never developed as an explicit ethical or environmental discourse in books, journals, articles, etc., as has been the case with the happy, holist, and holy hunters.[3] Nor was it wed to an ideology of ethical restraint.

Although it could also be argued that Native Americans developed an ethical discourse on hunting through their myths and religious views concerning the hunt, they too appear to differ from the hunters in this study. Although generalizations about Native Americans can be made only at great risk, it appears that the primary motive for hunting among Native Americans was for the purpose of obtaining food, and they therefore constitute the prototypical example of the hungry hunter. Although the hunting narratives of the Native Americans bear some similarity to the narratives of the holy hunters, they differ from the holy hunters in that they do not appear to be endorsing the virtues of hunting as an activity in and of itself.[4] One does not hunt in order to attain a particular spiritual or religious state; rather, one hunts, first and foremost, for the purpose of procuring food.

My reasons for avoiding the simple distinction between those who hunt for survival and those who hunt for sport should become apparent in the course of this essay. As we shall see, only one of the categories of hunters in question (i.e., the happy hunter) admits to hunting in the name of sport. One of the common denominators among the three categories of hunters that I examine, however, is that all hunt out of desire, not out of need.

The third category of hunter, the holy hunter, receives the greatest attention in this essay, because I believe the spiritualization of violence engaged in by this category of hunter is particularly insidious. An additional reason for this emphasis is that the language and ideology that surround the "holy hunt" bear a disturbing resemblance to that of ecofeminist thought. I examine these apparent similarities and demonstrate that ecofeminist thinking not only differs from that of the holy hunter, but is diametrically opposed to it.

The latter part of the essay also examines the additional insights that an ecofeminist analysis can shed on the discourse of hunting ethics.[5] By all accounts, hunting always has been a predominantly male activity.[6] How have the ideologies and narratives that have surrounded and supported the activity of hunting helped to obscure the gender-specific nature of this activity? Can a subtextual analysis of hunters' discourse shed light both on the psychosexual roots of hunting and on the discourse that hunters have developed to justify the hunt?[7] In answering these questions, I hope to identify the violent underpinnings not only of hunting and hunting ethics, but of the environmental movement and the field of environmental ethics as well. In sum, I hope to facilitate the divorce of environmental discourse from its blood-stained marriage to the activity of hunting, thereby exposing the true function of this discourse—namely, the legitimization of violence and biocide; in other words, the license to kill.

All three varieties of hunters—happy, holist, and holy—believe that the activity of hunting has some redeeming benefit beyond individual satisfaction. Although each category of hunter has a different perception of the nature of this moral benefit, their narratives concerning the actual experience of hunting demonstrate certain common themes. Before turning to the ethical discourse of the three categories of hunters in question, it might, therefore, be helpful to examine these themes.

One of the recurring themes in the descriptions of hunting experiences in all three categories of hunters is the notion that hunting involves a momentary reversion to an earlier period of time before humans became removed from the natural world. Thus, the *New Hunter's Encyclopedia* states: "In this modern era hunting has largely become a social pastime—an opportunity to enjoy the companionship of kindred spirits and to commune with nature. Yes, and also to a certain extent, an opportunity to revert to the primitive" (quoted in Caras, 70). Similarly, D. H. Lawrence, who is cited with approval by deep ecologist George Sessions, bemoans the passing of the pagan era, when man hunted and lived in attunement with nature. In Lawrence's words, "It is better to be a hunter in the woods of Pan than it is to be a clerk in a city store. The hunter hungered, labored, suffered tortures of fatigue. But at least he lived in a ceaseless living relation to his surroundings" (227).

At other times, the reversion to a more primeval state is depicted as a return to an animal existence whereby one no longer feels in control. Thus, Ortega y Gassett, a biologist turned philosopher/historian, refers to hunting as a kind of "vacation from the human condition, achieved through an authentic 'immersion in nature'" (121). And Richard Nelson describes the moment at which he makes the decision to kill as one in which a different part of his mind is turned on. In his works, "it's a whole different way of thinking. It's incredibly elemental" (Exploring, 38).

For the hunters in question, the primeval, animal-like aspect of hunting is experienced as an instinctive urge which, like the sexual drive, cannot and should not be repressed.[8] Thus, Aldo Leopold, considered by many to be the "founding father" of the environmental movement, states, "The instinct that finds delight in the sight and pursuit of game is bred into the very fiber of the human race" (Goose Music, 227). Desire for hunting, according to Leopold, lies deeper than other outdoor sports. In his words, "its source is a matter of instinct as well as of competition" (Goose Music, 232). He elaborates, "A son of Robinson Crusoe, having never seen a racket, might get along nicely without one, but he would be pretty sure to hunt or fish whether or not he were taught to do so" (Goose Music, 232). In other words, for Leopold, a boy instinctively learns to shoot a gun and, moreover, instinctively wants to hunt and kill!

For many writers, the activity of hunting is not only essential for the attainment of full manhood, it is integral to the development of one's status as a full human being.[9] Thus, Paul Shepard states, "man is in part carnivore: the male of the species is genetically programmed to pursue, attack and kill for food. To the extent that men do not do so they are not fully human" (Tender Carnivore, 122–23). Similarly, Leopold claims:

> A man may not care for gold and still be human but the man who does not like to see, hunt, photograph or otherwise outwit birds and animals is hardly normal. He is supercivilized, and I for one do not know how to deal with him. (Goose Music, 227)

Sexual overtones, both subtle and explicit, can be found throughout many of the narratives of all three categories of hunters. Thus, Richard Nelson describes his encounter with a deer in these words:

> I am a hunter hovering near his prey and a watcher craving inhuman love, torn between the deepest impulses, hot and shallow-breathed and seething with unreconciled intent . . . I am consumed with a sense of her perfect elegance in the brilliant light. (The Gifts of Deer, in The Island Within, 274)

And, according to Lewis Mumford, hunting "opens up all one's senses, one's ears as well as one's eyes . . . [it] creates a silent communion between hunters, following their common purposes, akin to that which lovers enjoy" (95). And in the mind of Randall Eaton, the hunter "loves the animal he kills" (The Hunter as Alert Man, 110).

More explicitly, Leopold writes that he "tingled" at the recollection of the big gander that sailed honking into his decoys (Goose Music, 229); and Ortega y Gassett writes of the "exquisite" feel of the air that "glides over the skin and enters the lungs" (123). At other times, both write of hunting in more heated terms, using such words as "hunting fever" and the "drama" and "contagion" of the hunt. Indeed Ortega y Gassett goes so far as to assert the "unequaled orgiastic power" of blood, contending that wildlife photography is to hunting what Platonic love is to the real thing (92, 121).

The ethical discourse that I am examining here is predicated on the notion of restraining this aggressive, sexual energy and channeling it in appropriate ways.[10] Hunting itself is seen as an appropriate means of directing this erotic, aggressive drive, toward an acceptable target—namely, a nonhuman animal—rather than a human being. Thus, one hunter profiled in a booklet on *Values in Hunting* maintained, "Killing a deer is a relief; it takes out inhibitions, and it's good to take it out on animals" (quoted in Caras, 143). The environmental philosopher Holmes Rolston is more explicit in his assessment of hunting as a safety valve for sexual energy. He argues that "the sport hunt sublimates the drive for conquest, a drive without which humans could not have survived, without which we cannot be civilized" and goes on to conclude, "Perhaps the hunting drive, like the sexual urge, is dangerous to suppress and must be reckoned with" (91).

Although many hunters downplay the actual moment of the kill, most concede that it is an integral part of the hunt. Just as the male orgasm typically is seen as the denouement to the act of sex, so too, the death of the animal is seen as the narrative resolution of the hunt. Both the hunt and the sexual act are premised on the notion of the buildup of tension; the orgasm and the kill provide the sought-after relief. Significantly, in a frequently cited passage, Ortega y Gassett, claims that "one does not hunt in order to kill; one kills in order to have hunted" (96–97). Without the pursuit of orgasm, sex typically is thought to have no meaning or narrative structure;[11] without the intent to kill, the hunt, we are told, has none as well.[12]

A personal anecdote may help shed some light on the hunting-sex connection and thus on the rudiments of the ethic of self-restraint to which we shall subsequently turn. A number of years ago, I had the occasion to attend a hunter safety training course, a course that is required for every hunter to obtain a hunting license.[13] The instructor of the course, a Vietnam veteran, began by making several references to his "Bambi-loving wife" who, he joked, sometimes complained that he "loved his guns more than he loved her." It was the nature of the terminology used by the instructor, however, that was the most revealing. Bullets were called "balls," firing was called "discharge," and when a bullet hit an animal it was called "penetration." The power of a gun was referred to as its "penetration power." If a bullet was accidentally fired before the intended moment, it was labeled a "premature discharge." The law of "first blood" was also explained to us. According to an unwritten law, which is recognized by the Fish and Game department, whoever first "penetrates" an animal and draws the "first blood" has the "privilege" of "finishing the animal off," and claiming the body of the animal as his own. The law of "first blood" had a familiar ring.

The recurring theme throughout the course was self-control. In the words of the instructor, "Control is the name of the game. You lose control and you've been had." The importance of using the safety catch also was emphasized repeatedly. We were told that it was "easy to become excited" and to overlook the importance of this device. "Buck fever," according to the instructor, was a normal phenomenon that occurs "when your adrenalin starts pumping and you lose your common sense." The instructor proclaimed that it was, indeed, exciting to see an animal in the woods. "Even without a firearm," he conceded, it can be exciting. "It is for this reason that you must always use your safety catch. It is too easy to let your emotions carry you away," he cautioned. It is especially easy "when you are sitting alone in the woods, daydreaming about that ten-point buck that you would like to bag. But you must remember your safety catch," he cautioned over and over again. After numerous repetitions of this theme, it finally occurred to me where I had heard a similar refrain. The hunter-safety training class had all the trappings of a sex-education class. "Don't let your emotions carry you away . . . you must remember your condom" (or, rather, safety-catch). Substitute a few words, shuffle gender and species around, and the sentiment remains the same: the sexual urge must be exercised with control.

Having identified the major common ground in the experiences of all three categories of hunters, we are now in a position to examine the ethical code that is designed to reframe (or contain) these experiences. As we shall see, all three ethical codes are predicated on the need to harness an aggressive, sexual energy and to channel it in appropriate ways. In their distinctive fashion, all three ethical codes are thus premised on the notion of emotional and sexual restraint.

The Ethical Discourse of Hunters

Narrative I: The Happy Hunter

The first category of hunter, the happy hunter, freely admits to the pleasure he derives from the hunt. For the happy hunter, hunting is a form of recreation or sport; the animal killed is literally called "game." In the United States, the conception of hunting as a pleasurable, recreational activity emerged in the middle of the nineteenth century in response to increased urbanization and leisure time (Wilson, 24–25). This new "ethical" conception of hunting stood in stark contrast to an earlier attitude, which viewed hunting as a means of procuring meat and saw those who hunted for pleasure as worthy of scorn.

The stigma attached to the notion of deriving pleasure from violence has a long religious history.[14] The Puritans of New England viewed blood sports as frivolous activities on a par with gambling and other forms of "irresponsible pastimes."[15] Although the Puritans viewed the use of animals as "Man's" God-given right, the enjoyment of violence, like the enjoyment of sex, was seen as something to be shunned. The new ethical discourse was developed expressly to outline the parameters within which hunting for pleasure could be viewed as an *ethical*, even praiseworthy activity. It was from this marriage of hunting to ethical discourse that the environmental movement was born.

Despite disagreement over the extent of hunters' involvement, few historians deny that hunters played a significant role in the development of the early conservation movement. According to the historian John Reiger, hunters "spearheaded the early conservation movement" (54).[16] In Reiger's view, it was the hunters' response to the disappearance in region after region of "game" fishes, birds, and mammals, not concern for the forest, that generated the American conservation movement. Not surprisingly, the motive behind their effort was hardly altruistic. Hunters in the mid-nineteenth century had become increasingly distressed to find themselves in competition with commercial hunters and fishermen for the dwindling numbers of "game" animals. During the 1870s and 1880s, hunters responded to this situation by successfully lobbying local and state associations to pass laws to limit and regulate sport and market hunting. Significantly, the vast majority of the early environmentalists were avid hunters, anxious to ensure that enough wildlife remained to hunt. Environmental thinking was still in its early stages of development. Few appreciated the vital role played by predators in maintaining biological integrity and balance. In many cases, hunters were intent on eliminating as many predators as possible in an effort to enlarge the number of prey animals that they could kill.

The early conservationists, who were, by and large, from the upper

License to Kill

class, drew their inspiration from the British gentry and, in particular, the British tradition of fair play in field sports. In Europe, hunting had been a leisure activity of the upper class. For many hunters, the privilege of all Americans to hunt was an emblem of American democracy. Hunting was no longer seen as a utilitarian activity, whose sole purpose was to procure meat; nor was it seen as the savage (unrestrained) encounter with the "wild." Hunting was now seen as a democratic "sport," one which should be played according to a body of rules that purportedly gave the animals a "fair" chance.

The new ethic of the "good sportsman" quickly found expression in a spate of new journals, such as *American Sportsman* (1871), *Forest and Stream* (1873), *Field and Stream* (1874), as well as in sportsmen's clubs and associations. Together, these journals and associations helped hunters develop a common identity based on their allegiance to a well-defined code of conduct. According to Reiger, hunting had become more than a sport—it had become "something approaching a 'world view,' even a religion" (29).

The hunters in the early conservation movement were singularly unabashed about the enjoyment that they derived from the hunt. Thus Ernest Hemingway, who typifies this attitude, exulted after shooting live pigeons, "It's a good feeling, like hitting a fast ball" (quoted in Menninger, 53). Elsewhere, he boasted, "I think they (birds) were made to shoot and some of us were made to shoot them and if that is not so well, never say we did not tell you that we liked it" (Remembering Shooting, 152). A similar sentiment is expressed by a modern-day hunter in a 1967 booklet published by the University of Arizona's College of Business and Public Administration entitled *The Values of Hunting and Fishing in Arizona in 1965*: "I like the excitement of killing. You get a feeling of accomplishment when you kill something" (quoted in Caras, 142). Happy hunters saw hunting not only as a pleasurable activity, but also as a way of developing character, and, in particular, male character. Theodore Roosevelt, a prototypical happy hunter, felt that "the chase is among the best of all national pastimes; it cultivates that vigorous manliness for the lack of which in a nation, as in an individual, the possession of no other qualities can possibly atone" (vii).

In addition to the notion of the chase, the code of ethics of the good sportsman was also predicated upon the notion of emotional self-restraint. For the early conservation-minded sports hunters, the self-restraint that one exercised in the course of the hunt was the bedrock out of which good character was formed. Aldo Leopold's writings are premised upon this notion of restraint. For Leopold, hunting was not only an instinctive urge experienced by every normal man but was, moreover, a democratic right. Thus, the hunters who were decimating game animals were interfering with this "inalienable right." Leopold longed for the day when hunters would develop their ethical capacities to the point where they would be guided not by externally imposed limits but by their own ecological conscience. The land ethic, for which Leopold is so well known, was thus intimately tied to the practice of hunting and to the "good sportsman's" ethical code. One of the primary purposes of preserving the well-being of the land was to ensure that future hunters would have the opportunity to exercise their "hunting instinct." As Leopold states, "His instincts prompt him to compete for his place in the community but his ethics prompt him also to cooperate (*perhaps in order that there may be a place to compete for)*" (emphasis added; The Land Ethic, 239). In other words, the purpose of self-restraint is precisely to allow for the continuation of man's aggressive drive.

Narrative 2: The Holist Hunter

Aldo Leopold represents the consummate bridge between the first and second categories of hunters, the happy and the holist hunters. Although Leopold remained a happy hunter throughout his adult life, the land ethic that he developed in his later years also represents one of the earliest formulations of the holist philosophy that has come to characterize the second category of hunters discussed here. Unlike their predecessors in the early conservation movement, today's hunters are far less likely to make open pronouncements about the joys of hunting and killing animals. They are more apt to downplay the joy of "the kill," elaborating the many other benefits to be gained from the hunt—a sense of camaraderie with other hunters, the pleasure of being immersed in the natural world, and even the meat that is thereby procured. But an increasingly common explanation given by modern-day hunters is the argument that they render a service in "culling" the "excess" animals that would otherwise starve. The holist hunter claims to hunt not for the sake of pleasure, but rather for the well-being of the biotic community or "whole."

Leopold's land ethic is generally viewed as the first philosophical attempt to ground an environmental ethic upon an awareness of ecological principles. According to Leopold, "a thing is right when it tends to preserve the beauty, integrity, and stability of the biotic community. It is wrong when it tends otherwise" (The Land Ethic, 262). However, for Leopold, not only is the "beauty, integrity and stability of nature" not marred by the killing of animals; it is actually *enhanced* by it.[17] Although Leopold argued for the development of a "fellow feeling for all of life" based on an awareness of belonging to a common ecological community, his land ethic was never intended to extend to "fellow" individual animals.[18] Thus when Leopold admonishes us to "think like a mountain," since "only the mountain has lived long enough to listen objectively to the howl of the wolf," he is calling for a long-term, species-based, *objective ethic* (Thinking Like a Mountain, 137). It is this so-called objective, scientific aspect of his environmental philosophy that has come to prevail in forest and land use management.[19]

As the inheritor of this heritage, today's holist hunter comes fully armed not only with the best of today's modern machinery but also with an arsenal of "scientific facts." In an attempt to ground his conduct upon the science of ecology, the modern holist hunter claims to kill not in the name of recreation, but rather in the name of "objective science." Thus, the holist hunter seeks to convince the public that he is playing a vital, ecological role, comparable to other predators in the natural world. By killing the overpopulated animals, he argues, he is rescuing them from an even worse death. Hunters, according to this worldview, perform a charitable service for the natural world.

In reality, hunters bear little resemblance to other predators in the natural world. The vast majority of animals who hunt do so for reasons of survival; in contrast to humans, most predators would not survive without meat. In addition, unlike other predators who kill only the weak or sick, hunters typically select the biggest and healthiest animals for their prey, thereby promoting a kind of "evolution in reverse" (Teale, 161). In fact, it is hunters who are often responsible for the creation of overpopulation. This occurs through such activities as the killing of natural predators, sex-selective shooting, varying the length of hunting seasons, and habitat manipulation, and through the abnormally high reproductive rates that intensive hunting produces. In sum, hunters help create the ecological problems that they then claim to solve.[20]

The holist hunter has adopted not only the language of science but that of business management as well.[21] Leaving behind the realm of recreation and pleasure, the holist hunter has entered the business world. The express purpose of the holist hunt is to manage animal populations for the benefit of the natural world. Their "business partners" in this endeavor are the federal and state fish and wildlife agencies, which manage both the animals and the hunters themselves. But even some of the official "game management" publications reveal the true purpose of the "managerial kill." According to an article in the *Journal of Wildlife Management*, "The primary management plan has been the one directed at increasing the productivity of the whitetail deer through habitat manipulation and harvest regulation . . . to produce optimum sustained deer yields . . . and hunter satisfaction" (Mirarchi, Scanloni, and Kirkpatrick, 92). In a similar vein, Donald J. Hankla, former chief of management for all wildlife refuges, openly maintains that "wildlife refuges are managed in part to produce 'surplus game for hunters'" (brochure from The Committee to Abolish Sport Hunting). One state management plan also openly maintains that hunting "add[s] value to the quality of life for many citizens" (White-Tailed Deer, 3). Clearly, holist hunters are intent on "managing" animals so that sufficient numbers will remain for them to kill. Indeed, according to the writer Joy Williams, it is more accurate to say that the Fish and Game department plays the role of a "madam" for hunters, helping them to "procure sufficient numbers of animals to kill" (24).

In many ways, the holist hunter is the official face that happy hunters present to the public. It is the camouflage behind which a pedigreed happy hunter hides. Although the trade journals make little effort to obscure the pleasures that can be derived from the exploits of the hunt, most public pronouncements are likely to bear the mark of the holist hunt.

Holist philosophy has also found a home in the academic world, tracing its roots back to Aldo Leopold's thought. The major tenet of holist philosophy is the notion that the primary locus of value resides not in the individual parts of nature, but, rather, in the whole to which the individuals belong. Although the concept of the whole is conceived in various ways (i.e., as an "organism," a "community," or an "ecosystem"), all forms of holism maintain that the well-being of the whole must always take precedence over the individual parts. The early writings of Baird Callicott, a self-professed disciple of Aldo Leopold, represent the logical extension of this mode of thought. According to Callicott:

> To hunt and kill a white-tailed deer in certain districts may not only be ethically permissible, it might actually be a moral requirement . . . In every case the effect upon ecological systems

is the decisive factor in the determination of the ethical quality of action. (Animal Liberation: A Triangular Affair, 21)[22]

Most academic holists, like their holist hunting counterparts, downplay or decry the notion of hunting for pleasure. Thus, the environmental writer Martin Lewis claims that although hunting is often necessary "to cull fecund herbivores," he blasts the "happy hunting" Leopold, commenting that he "can only shudder on hearing an avowed environmentalist boast of the 'unspeakable delight' in the petty act of slaughtering another living being" (96).

Holist philosophers frequently contrast their philosophy with that of animal rights, arguing that the latter represents an anti-ecological stance.[23] Holists contend that the philosophy of animal liberation does not accord with the reality and necessity of killing in the natural world. Thus Paul Shepard comments that "the humanitarian's projection onto nature of illegal murder and the rights of civilized people to safety not only misses the point but is exactly contrary to fundamental ecological reality" (Animal Rights and Human Rites, 37). Similarly, Baird Callicott criticizes the humane movement for having a "world-denying or rather a life-loathing philosophy," arguing that "the natural world as actually constituted is one in which one being lives at the expense of others." Callicott goes on to argue that the neo-Benthamites (i.e., the "humane moralists" or animal liberationists) "have attempted to exempt themselves from the life/death reciprocities of natural processes and from ecological limitations . . . in the name of a prophylactic ethic of maximizing rewards (pleasure) and minimizing unwelcome information (pain)" (Animal Liberation: A Triangular Affair, 33). In a similar vein, Holmes Rolston charges animal rights proponents with a lack of biological and moral maturity. In his words:

> The ecological ethic which kills in place, is really more advanced, more harmonious with nature, than the animal rights ethic, which in utter disharmony with the way the world is made, kills no animals at all. Those who go out and kill for fun may have failed to grow up morally. Sometimes those who object to any killing in nature and in human encounter with nature have not grown up either biologically or morally. (91)

According to these philosophers, hunters are instruments of nature, carrying out her inexorable directives. The violence that they inflict merely reflects the violence of the natural world and is, therefore, beyond ethical reproach. Violence, including hunting, should not be shunned, but rather embraced.

Holist philosophy, with its grounding in science, has been a welcome arrival on the scene for happy hunters. Just as the public was beginning to look askance at the conjunction of pleasure and violence, holist philosophy came to the rescue, providing the happy hunter with the ideal shield from attack. Happily ensconced in the safe refuge of the holist camp, hunters could now successfully defend themselves against the charge of cruelty.[24] Armed with the claim that their mental state has been purified of the taint of pleasure, holist hunters contend that they are beyond rebuke. Although their official trade journals continue to enumerate the multiple pleasures to be found in the hunt, increasing numbers of holist hunters are now anxious to assume the camouflage of the holist hunt. The heyday of the happy hunter appears to be coming to a close.

Narrative 3: The Holy Hunter

Although happy hunters and holist hunters have had their share of literary and philosophical proponents, it is the third category of hunter, the holy hunter, that has received the greatest attention from the academic world. Often the writers who promote the notion of the holy hunt are hybrid writers, with academic backgrounds in multiple fields, such as anthropology, philosophy, and nature writing. Just as the happy hunter once sought legitimacy through the marriage of hunting to the language of ethical discourse, academic philosophers (both holist and holy) now seek to wed environmental ethics to the practice of hunting.

For the holy hunter, hunting is not a means of recreation; nor is it a form of charitable work. For the holy hunter, hunting is a religious or spiritual experience. Holy hunters are fond of contrasting their spiritual orientation with the crass and superficial mentality of the typical sportsman or happy hunter. Although all three categories of hunters emphasize the importance of a proper state of mind, for the holy hunter this assumes an overriding importance. For holy hunters, purportedly it is not the superficial pleasure derived from an act of conquest, nor the satisfaction of performing a "charitable" act. The only appropriate attitude for the holy hunter is the religious one of reverence and respect. Although the notion of emotional self-restraint is still emphasized, it is now seen as a by-product of a transformed worldview. Hunting is seen not so much as a game that requires adherence to rules of good conduct; it is more akin to a religious rite. Thus, one hunter quoted in the *Booklet of Values in Hunting* describes his feelings about hunting in these words: "It makes me feel almost religious, when I am sitting on a mountain waiting for a deer sometimes. I almost feel like praying." And according to James Swan, many hunters "feel that ultimately hunting is their religion" (35). In the words of Holmes Rolston, "hunting is not *sport*; it is a *sacrament* of the fundamental, mandatory seeking and taking possession of value that characterizes an ecosystem and from which no culture ever escapes" (91). Similarly, Paul Shepard insists that "Hunting is a holy occupation, framed in rules and courtesy, informed by the beauty of the physical being and the numinous presence of the spiritual life of animals" (Searching Out, 86).

One of the distinguishing features of the holy hunt is that the hunter not only claims to revert to a primeval, animal state; he also claims to identify with the animal that he kills. Thus, Randall Eaton states:

> What do I mean at the deepest level when I say I want to be a tiger? I really mean that I have affection for tigers and that I want to know the essential nature of the tiger. If the truth be known, I want to be a tiger, to walk in his skin, hear with his ears, flex my tiger body and feel as a tiger feels. (*Know Thy Animal*, 47)

And, in a similar vein, deep ecologist Gary Snyder believes that the hunter becomes "physically and psychically one with the animal." As he elaborates, "To hunt means to use your body and senses to the fullest; to strain your consciousness to feel what the deer are thinking today, this moment; to sit and let yourself go into the birds and wind while waiting by a game trail" (*Earth House Hold*, 120). And in Barry Lopez's opinion the "hunter wants to be a wolf" (*Of Wolves and Men*, 166).

The notion that through an identification with nature one can attain a sound ethical relation to the natural world has been popularized in recent years by deep ecologists. According to deep ecologists, the roots of our current ecological crisis can be traced to an overly narrow, atomistic sense of self. To remedy our problematic relation to nature, it is necessary to expand this narrowly defined sense of self first to family and friends, then to our species, and finally to all of life.[25] This process of identification is viewed as a matter of maturation according to which the expanded Self represents the most mature state of being. What is significant for our purposes, however, is the types of activities that some deep ecologists cite as helpful in promoting this expanded concept of Self. Thus, along with sunbathing, bicycling, skiing, and meditation, Bill Devall and George Sessions cite hunting as one of the activities that helps to promote a mature sense of Self (188).

What is curious about the notion of killing a being with whom one identifies is that deep ecologists and other environmental writers maintain that the purpose of identifying with nature is precisely so that one will wish to *avoid* harming those beings with whom one identifies. How then, do deep ecologists and other proponents of the holy hunt deal with this contradiction? It is at this point that the spiritual teachings of native cultures are imported into their narratives to bolster the notion of the holy hunt.

Deep ecologists and other environmental writers often contend that native cultures provide an exemplary model for ethical conduct toward the natural world (Devall and Sessions, Lopez, Nelson, Snyder, Shepard, and Swan). What is noteworthy about this contention is that these writers single out hunting as the activity with the greatest instructive value. Although native cultures engaged in myriad other practices (e.g., gathering, planting, cooking, weaving, singing, dancing), no other activity is seen to have the same moral relevance. Most of these environmental writers also ignore the vast cultural differences that existed among tribal people, referring to them as if they were a monolithic block.[26] But not all Native Americans hunted and not all showed "respect" for the animals they killed.[27]

Although it is not possible to generalize about all native cultures, it appears that the hunters within some (although by no means all) Native American tribal cultures experienced feelings of ambivalence and guilt about the killing of animals. One of the ways some native cultures seem to have dealt with their uneasy feelings is by developing a mythology or worldview according to which it was believed that the animal "gave" her or his life as a "gift."[28] Holy hunters have uprooted this notion of the "gift" from the context of native cultures and transplanted it into their own narratives of the hunt.[29] Thus, Richard Nelson repeatedly employs the teachings of the Koyukon elders to shed light on his own hunting experiences. He writes, "Koyukon elders maintain that animals will come to those who have shown them respect, and will allow themselves to be taken in what is only a temporary death" (The Gifts, 122). The animal's death is viewed not as a personal conquest, but rather as a "gift" to those who are worthy and who demonstrate the proper attitude. If a hunter fails to kill an animal, this failure may be attributed to some impropriety in the hunter's mental orientation. Given a proper attitude, it is argued, the animal willingly "gives" her or his life. Barry Lopez argues that a similar voluntary surrender of life occurs between nonhuman animals as well. Often this exchange between predator and prey is preceded by a locked gaze, whereby the prey animal conveys a willingness to give up her or his life. Lopez refers to this phenomenon as the "conversation of death" (94). According to Lopez, this constitutes a "ceremonial exchange, the flesh of the hunted in exchange for respect for its [sic] spirit. In this way, both animals, not the predator alone, choose for the encounter to end in death" (94).

After presenting this example of nonhuman hunting, Lopez goes on to refer to the hunting practices of Native Americans, whereby the death of the hunted animal is considered to be "mutually agreeable." In a similar vein, Gary Snyder refers to the "mutuality of death" in which animals help humans flourish by "giving" their lives in exchange for humans promoting their "fertility" (Earth House Hold, 120).[30] According to Snyder, the animal participates in this exchange on a willing basis out of "compassion" for the hunter. As he states, "Hunting magic is designed to bring the game to you—the creature who has heard your song, witnessed your sincerity, and out of compassion comes within your range" (Earth House Hold, 120). In Snyder's view, both "human nature and mother nature are on a path in which all things can come to fruition equally and together in harmony" (The Real Work, 73).

Holy hunters draw inspiration not only from tribal cultures, but from the science of ecology as well. Hunting and killing animals is seen as a means of actively inserting oneself into the food chain, thereby achieving a direct connection with the natural world. According to Shepard, hunting and killing "confirm the hunter's continuity in the complicated cycles of elements, in the sweep of evolution, and in the patterns of the flow of energy" (A Theory of, 509). Similarly, in explaining his urge to live not only on an island but from an island, Richard Nelson explains that, "In this way I can bring the island inside me, binding my soul and body more closely with this place." Nelson goes on to claim that "the experiences of hunting and fishing are the most powerful ones for reminding me of my dependence and connectedness with the Earth" (quoted in Leviton, The Island Within, 72).

Holy hunters contend that their intent is not to conquer nature, but rather to submit to the ecological reality of the natural world. According to Holmes Rolston,

> The hunter feels not "perfect evil" (Krutch), but "perfect identification" with the tragic drama of creation, the blood sacrifice on which sentient life is founded, which both *is* and *ought to be*. In ways that mere watchers of nature can never know, hunters know their ecology. The hunter's success is not conquest but submission to the ecology. It is an acceptance of the way the world is made. (92)

For holy hunters, the spiritual aspect of hunting derives from an understanding of the principles of ecology—in particular, the necessity and reality of death. The hunter is merely an agent of death, simply following (nature's) "orders," an innocent participant in a drama not of his own making. It is not only hunting that is seen as a spiritual, ecological, and reciprocal activity; the act of eating the dead animal is perceived this way as well. As David Barnhill points out, for Snyder the question "Where am I in the food chain?" is a religious question, "because ecological interdependence is the fundamental fact of the universe and the food chain is its basic physical structure" (Indra's Net, 25). Hunting and eating animals, according to Snyder, is a means of "communing" with nature and, therefore, is a cause for "celebration." In his words, "The evidence of anthropology is that countless men and women, through history and pre-history, have experienced a deep sense of communion and communication with nature and with specific non-human beings. Moreover, they often experienced this communication with a being they customarily ate" (*The Old Ways*, 13). Similarly, Paul Shepard cites with approval a statement made by Ortega y Gassett: "The greatest and most moral homage we can pay to certain animals on certain occasions is to kill them with certain means and rituals," claiming that he would add "and to eat them" (*Tender Carnivore*, 153). According to Shepard, "eating animals is a way to worship them" (Post-Historic Primitivism, 81).

As is the case with hunting itself, eating animals is often described in language that contains sexual undertones. According to Snyder, "intereating" is both a cause for "celebration" as well as a "giant act of love we live within" (Grace, 1). More explicitly, Shepard claims that the sexual energy that men have historically directed toward women is channeled into all aspects of the hunt. In his words,

The human hunter in the field is not merely a predator, because of hundreds of centuries of experience in treating the woman-prey with love, which he turns back into the hunt proper. The ecstatic consummation of this love is the killing itself. Formal consummation is eating . . . The prey must be eaten for ethical not nutritional value, in a kind of celebration. (*The Tender Carnivore*, 173)

Holy hunters have replaced the explicit notion of an inherently aggressive drive that must be contained through adherence to a code of good conduct with the blanket assertion that aggression does not exist. Holy hunters do not "kill" animals according to this world-view; rather, animals "give" their lives. Nor do the "holy hunters" perpetrate violence; instead, they are participants in an "equal exchange."[31] In effect, the holy hunter claims to restrain his aggression to the point of nonexistence—at least within his own mind. However, the notion that the animal chooses to end her or his life for the benefit of the hunter has no more validity than the idea that a woman who is raped "asked for it" or "willingly" gave herself to the rapist. In the end, despite the variation in language and conception, all three categories of hunters derive the morality of hunting first and foremost from their own mental and emotional state. Morality, thus, becomes a disembodied experience, with no tangible relation to the outside world.

The Hunt for Masculine Self-Identity

As we have seen, all three categories of hunters consider hunting to be an instinctive, sexually charged activity, which transports the hunter back to a primeval, animal-like state. The function of the hunters' ethical discourse is to set guidelines for how this aggressive, sexual energy might be discharged. Happy hunters do it in the name of recreation, holist hunters do it in the name of work, and holy hunters do it in the name of spirituality or religion. But despite these variations in language and emphasis, all three types of hunters include violence as an integral part of their ethical code, as long as it is restrained, renamed, or denied. What insights, then, can an ecofeminist analysis bring to bear on this phenomenon of violence and on the ethical discourse to which it is wed?

A growing number of feminist theorists have turned to psychological theory in an effort to explain the unconscious motivations behind the production of abstract philosophical ideas.[32] If we subject hunters' ethical discourse to the same psychological scrutiny, what light can be shed? One of the recurring themes found in the narratives of all three categories of hunters is the notion that hunting relieves men from a state of alienation from nature. Hunting is seen as a return to the "animal," a reversion to "the primitive," or as an immersion in the natural world. According to object relations theory this state of alienation is not, however, endemic to human nature; it is, rather, a particular feature of the psychology of men. Object relations theory claims that both boys and girls experience their first forms of relatedness as a kind of merging with the mother figure.[33] The child then develops a concept of self through a process of disengaging from this unified worldview. Unlike girls, boys have a two-stage process of disidentification. They must not only disengage from the mother figure, but in order to identify as male, they must deny all that is female within themselves, as well as their involvement with all of the female world.

According to Chodorow, since the girl child is not faced with the same need to differentiate her self-identity from that of the mother figure, "girls come to experience themselves as less differentiated than boys, as more continuous with and related to the external object world and as differently oriented to their inner object-world as well" (167). Girls, therefore, emerge from this period with a basis for "empathy" built into their primary definition of self in a way that boys do not. As Chodorow argues, "girls emerge with a stronger basis for experiencing another's needs or feelings as one's own (or of thinking that one is so experiencing another's needs and feelings)" (167).

Dorothy Dinnerstein extends this analysis to the masculine mode of interacting not only with women but with all of the natural world. For Dinnerstein, since a child's self-identity is originally viewed as indistinct from the surrounding world, self-identity for the boy child, in particular, later comes to be founded not only upon an opposition to women, but upon an opposition to nature as well. This process of developing an autonomous self then brings with it ambivalent feelings of rage and fear, and longing to return to the original coextensive self. The rage is, in reality, a rage against the "knowledge of fleshly transience" (246).

Simone de Beauvoir was the first to argue that women thus become for men the "other," the objects against which masculine self-identity is formed. According to de Beauvoir, women are relegated to this status as a result of what is perceived as their immersion in the natural world by virtue of such processes as pregnancy, menstruation, and childbirth. Authentic subjectivity is achieved to the extent that one raises oneself above biological necessity, and hence, above the animal world. Historically, men have transcended the world of contingency through exploits and projects, that is, through attempts to transform the natural world. For de Beauvoir, the prototypical activities of transcendence (hunting, fishing, and war) involve both risk and struggle. As she explains, "for it is not in giving life but in risking life that man is raised above the animal; that is why superiority has been accorded in humanity not to the sex that brings forth life but to that which kills" (72).

Paul Shepard also develops the theme of animals as the other. Shepard argues that animals, not women, are conceived as the other, and are necessary objects for the development of human identity. Shepard argues that children can come to understand who they are only by means of a negative identification with the nonhuman world, that is, by understanding what they are not. As Shepard states, "identity formation grows from the subjective separation of self from non-self, living from non-living" (*Nature and Madness*, 125). Although Shepard writes in gender-neutral terms, object relations theory suggests that the need he identifies is not found in all humans, but rather in men.

The transition of the boy child to adult masculine status is celebrated in initiation rites throughout the world. Many of these rites entail acts of violence toward both women and the natural world. Hunting and killing animals is a standard rite of passage out of the world of women and nature into the masculine realm.[34]

Having established a second and alienated nature, it appears that men then face a lifelong urge to return to the original state of oneness that they left behind. The return to an original undifferentiated state, however, is precisely what must be avoided, since such a return would constitute an annihilation of the masculine self. The conflict between these two drives may shed light on the hunter's urge to kill. The pursuit of the animal expresses the hunter's yearning to repossess his lost female and animal nature. The death of the animal ensures that this oneness with nature will not be attained. Violence becomes the only way in which the hunter can experience this sense of oneness while asserting his masculine status as an autonomous human being. By killing the animal, the hunter ritually enacts the death of his longing for a return to a primordial female/animal world, a world to which he cannot return.[35]

Echoes of this urge to return to a primordial oneness with nature can be found in the narratives of all three categories of hunters. The urge to connect with nature is—for the holy hunter, in particular—the major purpose of the hunt. The sense of merging with nature achieves its "ultimate consummation" for the holy hunters in the act of eating animals. According to Richard Nelson, "when we eat the deer its [sic] flesh is then our flesh. The deer changes form and becomes us, and we in turn become creatures made of death (The Gifts, 125).

Although holy hunters are more likely to call the ethic of the holy hunt "biocentric," it seems more accurate to describe this code of ethics as necrocentric. It is death, not life, that is seen to connect the hunter with other living beings. And it is death, not life, that elicits feelings of reverence and respect.

Although there are some women who hunt and some who have glorified it as well, the vast majority of hunters are still men. Whereas hunters have experienced their deepest feelings of connection to other forms of life through the infliction of death, many women have had similar feelings not through inflicting death, but rather through the act of giving birth (see O'Brien, Hartsock, Ruddick). Some holy hunters seem to be dimly aware of this birth analogy. Paul Shepard makes passing reference to it when he explains that it is not necessary or even possible for modern humans to become hunter-gatherers in their everyday lives. What is recommended is that "components" of the life-style of hunter-gatherers be incorporated into the modern "man's" life (Post-Historic, 79). One "component" that Shepard recommends is the experience of hunting, which he feels every man should have at least once in his life. In giving the rationale for his advice, Shepard explains:

> we cannot become hunter-gatherers as a whole economy, but we can recover the ontogenetic moment . . . the value of the hunt is not in repeated trips but a single leap forward into the heart-structure of the world, the "game" played to rules that reveal ourselves. What is important is to have hunted. It is like having babies; a little of it goes a long way. (Post-Historic, 86)

Thus, for Shepard, killing is seen as a transformational experience on a par with giving birth.

To understand how men can experience both a feeling of connection and a sense of being fully alive through the infliction of death, we might recall that it is through killing animals that male hunters are symbolically reborn.[36] In the process of killing the animal, the hunter (re)establishes his secondary identity, that is, his masculine self. It is, in reality, the mental construct of masculinity that is fed by violence and death.

One of the recurring themes in feminist and ecofeminist writing has been the notion of interconnection. According to Carol Gilligan, women's ethical conduct and thought derive more from a sense of interconnection with others, and the urge to maintain relationships, whereas men's derives more from the attempt to control aggression and conform to abstract principles and universal rules.[37] Many ecofeminists have seen in the notion of a sense of interconnection and caring for others the basis of a genuinely holistic ethic. What is of interest in the narratives of the holist and holy hunters is that although they emphasize, along with ecofeminists, the importance of a sense of interconnection, they seek to attain this state in a peculiar way, namely, through the infliction of death. According to Shepard:

> to be kindred . . . means . . . a sense of many connections and transformations—us into them, them into us, and them into each other from the beginning of time. To be kindred means to share consciously in the stream of life. (Searching Out, 87)

Needless to say, for many ecofeminists, killing and eating another living being is not the best means of "sharing consciously in the stream of life."

Ecofeminist philosopher Val Plumwood (1991, 1993) has criticized deep ecologists for advocating an expanded sense of identification that is too large and abstract to accommodate the more contextual ties of kinship connection as well as the relevant differences among living beings. Holy hunters represent a good example of the dangers that this form of identification entails. Although holy hunters claim to identify with the animal they kill, this identification is so abstract as to be meaningless. Although all three categories of hunters emphasize the keen sense of alertness and attention that characterizes the state of mind of the hunter, it is clear that the hunter is not alert enough to notice the true state of the animal he is about to kill. As Roger King has argued, "hunters are not truly alert to animals. They do not see the animal in their immediate context, but rather as abstracted from her or his relation to others" (83). If holy hunters were truly attending to nature, it would not be possible to rationalize the death of an animal as freely "given" out of "compassion" for the hunter. They would see in the hunted animal's eyes not "compassion" for the hunter, but rather terror and fright. They would see, in short, that nonhuman animals value their lives no less than do the holy hunters themselves.

Many feminists have emphasized the importance of the act of attention in helping to determine proper ethical conduct and thought.[38] According to Iris Murdoch:

> If we consider what the work of attention is like, how continuously it goes on and how imperceptibly it builds up values round about us, we shall not be surprised that at crucial moments of choice most of the business of choosing is already over. (37)

Morality, for Murdoch, is far from the rational control of an inherently aggressive will. When one directs a "patient, loving regard" upon a "person, a thing, a situation," according to Murdoch, the will is presented not as "unimpeded movement," but rather as "something very much more like obedience" (40).

According to Josephine Donovan, "women's relational culture of caring and attentive love" provides the basis for a feminist ethic for the treatment of animals (375). This caring, attentive love does not *command* us not to kill animals; rather, as Donovan argues, "We should not kill, eat, torture, and exploit animals because they do not want to be so treated, and we know that. If we listen, we can hear them" (375).

Although the holy hunters would claim that their act of attention is, in fact, an expression of an attentive, caring love, the meditative state that they describe is so diffuse as to be incapable of making crucial distinctions in the real world. The world of the holy hunters blurs over glaring differences. Theirs is a world in which death is equated with life, eating an animal is an "act of love," and taking an animal's life is a "gift." Thus Richard Nelson claims that "there is very little difference between moments when I only watch an animal and moments when I am hunting—they are part of the same thing, in the sense of a complete focus of mind" (Exploring the Near, 37). Similarly, Paul Shepard argues that he sees no difference between eating a vegetable and eating an animal. If these writers were truly attending to nature, however, they would discover that there is, indeed, an enormous difference between these activities. It is the difference of a sentient life.

This inability to attend to the actual experience of individual animals is characteristic of all three categories of hunters, as well as the environmental movement and environmental philosophy as a whole. All three categories of hunters employ ethical discourse as a means of shielding the hunter from the actual experience of the animal he kills, and as a means of renouncing personal responsibility.[39] The focus of the hunter is on his own interior mental state. As long as his mental attitude is said to conform to a particular ethical code, his violent behavior is thought to be legitimized. The emphasis on the instinctual (sexual) nature of hunting functions to further remove the hunters' conduct from ethical reproach, since hunting is seen as a natural and elementary drive.[40] The ethical discourse thus functions as a "decoy," focusing attention not on the state of the animal who is about to be killed, but rather on the hunter. What the holist and holy hunters see as a "reciprocal" activity is, in reality, a unidirectional morality in which the hunter formulates and follows his own moral directives. For all three hunters, the animal is reduced to an object, a symbol against which the hunter seeks to establish his masculine selfhood and moral worth.

Thus, despite the genuine variations in the conduct and discourse of the three categories of hunters, in the end, the differences among the three are less significant than the common ground that they share. All three partake of the quest to establish masculine identity in opposition to the natural world.

Conclusion

We live in a violent culture. If we are to change this state of affairs, we must begin to name the violence that exists as well as identify its psychological roots. It is necessary to recognize that the perpetrators of violence throughout the world are, by and large, men, and the victims of this violence are primarily women and the natural world. Language often obscures this reality. Crimes against women are classed as "homicides," and crimes against nature have no name at all. A first step in bringing the reality of gender-specific violence to the fore would, therefore, be to name these forms of violence. Violence against women should be named not homicide, but femicide, and violence against nature should have its own name, perhaps biocide. Both expressions of violence, however, must be recognized as products of a single frame of mind, namely, the masculinist mind which sees women and nature as objects to be manipulated, managed, and controlled in an attempt to establish masculine self-identity and worth. The happy, holist, and holy hunters are multiple expressions of the same theme, a trinitarian manifestation of the single "God": the masculine self.

Ecofeminism is still in the process of forging connections between feminism and the environmental movement. If ecofeminism is to rise to the challenge of its potential, it must begin to move beyond abstract statements concerning ethical conduct and thought. We have seen that it is not sufficient to rely on abstract language such as "holism," "biocentrism," or even "reverence" and "respect." We must begin to say what we mean by these words. When we speak of reverence and respect, we must ask "what precisely do we mean?" An emphasis on a spiritual sense of connection is, indeed, a praise-worthy goal. But a spiritual sense of connection must translate into genuine caring behavior for other living beings. Caring for other living beings cannot be conducted in the privacy of one's interior psychic state. It must take into account a genuine recognition of the response of the one we are caring for.[41] Saying a prayer before you kill an animal is no more acceptable than saying a prayer before a rape. It is our actions, more than our state of mind, that are crucial in the realm of ethical conduct. If these actions flow only from a men-tally constructed desire, they cannot take into account the needs of all parties in question. Moral actions must flow not only from the capacity to perceive our interconnection with others, but also from our ability to acknowledge—to morally attend to—the plight of other living beings as separate and distinct from our own needs and desires.

Environmental philosophy and the environmental movement as a whole have failed to incorporate a genuine concern for individual beings. Currently, no major environmental organization is willing to express opposition to hunting, and none takes a position on eating meat.[42] But until the environmental movement and environmental philosophy develop a concern for individual beings, they will be living in the shadow of their violent past. Hunters currently kill more than 200 million animals every year. They cripple, harass, and orphan millions more. An ecofeminist ethic must deplore this, along with all other expressions of violence. It must seek to sever the connections that historically have bound the environmental move-ment to a practice of violence. An ecofeminist ethic must help us to realize that, since we do not need to hunt or eat meat for survival, we should do neither. Rather, we should all engage in a genuine celebra-tion which recognizes that the best gift that we can offer to and receive from animals is their continued lives.

License to Kill

Notes

I would like to thank Carol Adams, Josephine Donovan, Clare Fischer, Greta Gaard, Dena Jones Jolma, Suzanne Kappeler, Ann Kheel, Martha Ellen Stortz, and especially Linda Vance for valuable criticisms and suggestions. Previous versions of this article were presented at the conference on Violence and Human Coexistence, Montreal, 13–17 July 1992; the Pacific meeting of the Society for Women in Philosophy, Sonoma State College, Rohnert Park, California, 9 November 1992; the Western Chapter Conference of the American Academy of Religion, California State University, Fullerton, 18–20 March 1993; the conference on Social Perspectives on Women and Ecology, sponsored by the Institute for Social Ecology, Plainfield, Vermont, 29 July–3 August 1994; and the Ninth Annual International Compassionate Living Festival, coordinated by the Culture and Animals Foundation, Raleigh, North Carolina, 30 September–2 October 1994.

1. I am employing the term "environmental philosophy" in a somewhat loose sense, so as to include a large body of nature writers who have engaged in philosophical speculation. Historically many nature writers have sought to generalize from their personal experiences in nature, so it is often difficult to distinguish their writings from more formalistic expressions of philosophy. Many of the writers I examine in this essay fall into this hybrid category, being both nature writer and philosopher.

2. Although ecofeminists are among those who have demonstrated an interest in native cultures, most do not appear to be endorsing hunting as an exemplary practice for our modern culture. In addition, most are not hunters themselves, as are many of the advocates of the "exemplary hunt." See, for example, Merchant; on a related theme, see Warren's use of an example of animal sacrifice from a native culture as an illustration of a purportedly sound environmental consciousness (1990).

3. It could be argued, for example, that the hostile and the hired hunters saw the eradication of predators as part of an ethical quest to "civilize" the land. This pioneer ethos valued "brute," unrestrained physical valor vis-à-vis the animal world. As Catherine Albanese writes of the legendary Davy Crockett, he "could outsavage any savage in hunt or fight. Indeed . . . he and his foes still acted like animals as they fought" (74). Coming before the era of "bag limits," Davy Crockett could also boast that he had killed 105 bears in the space of one year. The heroic ethic of these early pioneers, however, clearly differs from the ethic of the hunters in this study, both in its lack of the notion of self-restraint and in its lack of any connection to environmental thought.

4. This is not to say that factors comparable to the ones to be examined here were not also operative in native hunting practices. For example, it appears that the activity of hunting in native cultures also typically is tied to notions of masculine self-identity. Richard Nelson contends that multiple motivations seem to be operative in the hunting practices of the cultures he studied. In his words, "The Eskimo and Athabaskan Indians experience

great pleasure and something akin to adventure—if not adventure itself—as an integral element of hunting. While a prime motive is to provide food, it's extremely difficult to sort out and rank the motivations in something so emotionally bound as hunting" (quoted in Paul, 176). Interestingly, Nelson goes on to make an analogy with the sexual drive, which he claims is motivated both by the urge to reproduce as well as the desire for pleasure. Although it would be interesting to undertake a study of the ways in which native hunting practices conformed to or differed from the typology under investigation, this is not within the scope of the present study.

5. Portions of my analysis of hunting in this article are drawn from my "Ecofeminism and Deep Ecology." For other feminist critiques of hunting, see Abbot, Adams, Clifton, Collard, and Holliday.

6. According to a national survey published by the U.S. Department of Interior, in 1991 only 1 percent of females in the U.S. population of those sixteen years and older "enjoyed hunting." Of the 14.1 million people who hunted in 1991, 92 percent (13 million) were men and 8 percent (1.1 million) were women (36).

7. A related question that is raised but not developed here is whether all traditional (Western) ethical discourse is premised upon male psychosexual development.

8. The glorification of a return to the "primitive" first emerged as a common theme in the nineteenth century in the wake of Darwinian science. Men expressed a concern that they had become overly civilized and had lost contact with their "animal instincts" and "primitive needs." Citing the scientific evidence for humanity's animal nature, men increasingly spoke of their need to express their animal instincts and animal energy. Interestingly, according to Anthony Rotundo, the call for a "return to the primitive" was not directed at (or advocated by) women, whose only "primitive instinct" continued to be viewed as their maternal drive (see 227–32). At heart, the glorification of these animal instincts entailed a glorification of the male sexual drive. For further elaboration of the nineteenth-century glorification of the primitive, and its connection to male sexuality, see Anthony Rotundo.

9. Due to the careless use of the word "man," it is difficult to determine whether many of these writers intended to include women in the notion of "human being."

10. The characterization of hunting as an instinctive activity comparable to the sexual drive is found not only among hunters but among a wide variety of academic writers as well. See, for example, Washburn and Lancaster, Menninger, Ardrey, and Tiger and Fox. More recently, see the philosophers Holmes Rolston and Ann Causey.

11. Without speculating as to its basis in biology or socialization, one can acknowledge that emphasis on the importance of orgasm as the ultimate goal in sex is particularly characteristic of men. Evidence for this belief is cited in *The Hite Report on Male Sexuality*. Based on a survey of 7,000 men from throughout the United States, Hite found that "Most men who responded felt that male orgasm is the point of sex and intercourse" (468).

12. The idea is not that every hunt must end in the kill, nor every sexual act end in orgasm (see, for example, Randall Eaton, *Zen and the Art*, 48). Many hunters, in fact, appear to experience great exuberance on an occasion when they choose *not* to kill an animal. Nonetheless, the pursuit of the animal, like the pursuit of orgasm, always remains the original intent.

13. Lest there be any question as to why I was enrolled in a hunter safety training class, let me explain that in 1989 a lottery had been declared in California, the winners of which would be given the "privilege" of killing some of the remaining mountain lions. At the time, a number of animal liberation activists, including myself, entered the lottery in order to qualify for the privilege of *not* using our winning number to kill. To do this, it was necessary to obtain a hunting license, and in order to obtain a license, we were required to take a class in hunter safety training.

14. Although Christians for many centuries have supported wars and condoned the hunting and torture of animals, there has also been an ascetic tradition within Christianity that has maintained that these activities are inappropriate for holy men. It is interesting to note that countless stories proliferated throughout the middle ages of heroic saints who intercepted the arrows of hunters before they "penetrated" the animal's flesh. On a symbolic level, the saints appear to be engaging in a form of "coitus interruptus," shielding the animal from the arrows of death. According to Keith Thomas, "The medieval church had deemed [hunting] a carnal diversion, unsuitable for clergymen, and had (rather ineffectually) forbidden it to those in holy orders" (160). As with sexuality, the Church's prohibition was not intended to imply that hunting was at all times a moral evil. Just as sex was considered tolerable for those not in holy orders (as long as little or no pleasure was derived from the act), so too, hunting was considered acceptable for the laity, as long as it was undertaken for utilitarian purposes (i.e., procuring meat or killing "pests"). The intent was to prohibit all carnal sources of pleasure, whether they were derived from violence or from sex. (For a critique of the Church's denigration of both women and sexual pleasure, see Uta Ranke-Heinemann.)

15. According to historian Thomas Macaulay, the Puritans' concern was directed not at the pain inflicted upon the animal, but rather at the pleasure experienced by the participants in such violent sports (quoted in Thomas, p. 157). Keith Thomas suggests that part of the reason for the aversion to blood sports appears to have derived from the belief that by experiencing pleasure through the infliction of violence, one reduced oneself to the level of "beasts." The Puritans believed that the violence found in the natural world was a result of the Fall and was evidence of "Man's" sin, and thus should be viewed not as a source of enjoyment, but rather as something to mourn (Thomas, 157).

16. For an in-depth examination of the critical role of hunters in the origins of the conservation movement, see John F. Reiger. Despite the fact that Reiger is intent on demonstrating the positive contribution made by hunters, his book is a good chronicle of their central role.

17. It is noteworthy that the vast majority of chroniclers of Aldo Leopold's life gloss over his repeated allusions to the pleasures to be found in the hunt.

The discourse of the happy hunter has clearly become an embarrassment to many environmentalists who prefer the more dispassionate discourse of the holist hunter.

18. It is frequently maintained that Leopold had a conversion experience, which significantly altered his attitude toward hunting. Although Leopold did, in fact, undergo a "conversion" after shooting a wolf, which significantly influenced his environmental philosophy, he never renounced his love of hunting. Up until this event, he had been an unadulterated happy hunter intent on killing as many predators as possible so as to multiply the number of deer that hunters could kill. After shooting the wolf, however, and arriving in time to "watch a fierce green fire dying in her eyes," Leopold writes that he "sensed that neither the wolf nor the mountain agreed with such a view" (Thinking Like a Mountain, 138–39). Nonetheless, a careful reading of this passage demonstrates that Leopold did not believe any wrongdoing had been committed in killing the wolf. He had simply come to recognize the important ecological role played by predators and the need for hunters to demonstrate greater self control. Self-restraint is needed not to protect individual animals, but rather to ensure that only the right ones, in proper quantities, were killed.

19. Leopold's legacy of scientific management is, perhaps, not surprising in light of his dictum to "*think* like a mountain." Leopold does not ask us to *feel* what the inhabitants of the mountain might *feel*.

20. For book-length refutations of the typical arguments made by modern hunters, see Amory, Baker, Cartmill, Livingston, and Regenstein. See also the Defenders of Animal Rights pamphlet *The Case Against Hunting* and the Fund for Animal Rights Fact Sheets on Hunting.

21. For more on the confluence of the early conservation movement and the emerging field of scientific business management, see Hays.

22. Callicott has subsequently softened his earlier position in an attempt to achieve a reconciliation between animal liberation and environmental ethics (see "Animal Liberation and Environmental Ethics").

23. The environmental movement and environmental philosophy's condemnation of the animal liberation movement oscillates between neglect, dismissal, and vehement critique. For feminist critiques of the divisions between the philosophies of animal liberation and the environmental movement, see Marti Kheel, "The Liberation of Nature," and Josephine Donovan, "Animal Rights and Feminist Theory."

24. Cruelty typically is defined by reference to the state of mind of the perpetrator of a particular act. If I accidentally harm someone, it is not considered an act of cruelty. On the other hand, if I intentionally inflict harm and derive pleasure from this act, I am considered cruel. Since clearly many hunters derive great pleasure from hunting, they have faced a delicate predicament. To defend themselves against the charge of cruelty, they must either downplay or deny the pleasure that they derive from hunting, or they must convince the public that conventional conceptions of cruelty do not apply to nonhumans. Hunters typically have employed both strategies.

25. On the notion of "Self Realization" within deep ecology, see Devall and Sessions, Naess, and Fox.

26. "Indian" and "Native American" are culturally constructed categories. Prior to the European invasion, the indigenous population of North America did not see itself as a unified "race," but rather as separate peoples, often in hostile relation to one another. Recognition of this fact is increasing among Anglo historians; see, for example, Richard White (1–54). I am indebted to Linda Vance for the above citation.

27. Unfortunately, the question of whether Native Americans exhibited exemplary ethical conduct toward nonhuman animals is usually conflated with the question of whether they had a conservation ethic. According to Tom Regan, although Native Americans generally had a conservation ethic, at least prior to white contact, this conservation ethic was, in all probability, instrumental in nature and did not include a respect for the animals' "inherent worth." In Regan's opinion, their overall approach followed the precepts of a "shallow ecology," which sought to "conserve" nature for future (human) use (Environmental Ethics, 206–39). Baird Callicott also seeks to distinguish the instrumental notion of a "conservation ethic" from an "ecological consciousness," which accords a respect to all living beings. According to Callicott, the conservation ethic of Native Americans was primarily a *by-product* of an ecological consciousness which regarded all parts of the natural world as a single family or community (Traditional American Indian, 203–19). Other commentators, however, have argued that a number of Native American tribes killed animals indiscriminately, with little or no regard for the issue of "conservation" or for animal suffering. According to Calvin Martin, "the Indian was everywhere, except in the Rocky Mountain trade, the principal agent in the overkilling of furbearers" (2). And, according to Clifford Presnall, Indians engaged in "wasteful killing of buffalo, and to a lesser extent of antelope, deer, moose, and caribou, by driving them over precipices or into ponds" (458). One of the issues raised by both Regan and Callicott is the extent to which the hunting practices of Native Americans were governed by a "respect" for the inherent worth of animals, or rather by a sense of fear. The question centers around whether the "restraint" and propitiatory rites found in the hunting practices of Native Americans may have been due to fear of the "Animal Master" or the "Keeper of the Game," rather than to reverence for the animals themselves. In considering this question, it is worth noting that the prayers said by Native Americans were typically directed not to the slain animal, but rather to the Animal Master who controlled the hunt. For further challenges to the romantic contention that all tribal cultures treated animals with reverence and respect see Johnson and Earle, Hames, Carrier, Ornstein and Ehrlich, and Lewis. On Native Americans, in particular, see Dasmann, Moore, Rostlund, Martin, and Presnall.

28. For a speculative discussion of the origins of myth and religion as responses to feelings of guilt experienced by hunters, see Abbot.

29. The practice of invoking the myths and cultural practices of native cultures to give moral support to practices within our current culture is an increasingly common phenomenon. Thus, many people cite the example of

native cultures to defend their habit of meat-eating. The act of wrenching a narrative out of the context of one culture and grafting it onto another is not only disrespectful and self-serving, it is an act of violence in its own right. On the subject of "truncated narratives," see my "From Heroic to Holistic Ethics." For a discussion of appropriate criteria for evaluating the development and use of narrative, see Linda Vance, "Beyond Just-So Stories," in this volume.

30. It should be noted that Snyder's exchange is predicated on holist principles. The animal "gives" her or his *individual* life in exchange for the fertility of the *herd*.

31. Significantly, the celebration of killing and eating as an act of "love" is always at the animal's expense. A truly "equal exchange" would require "ecstatic celebration" wherein hunters are killed and eaten as well.

32. Jane Flax has referred to the feminist interest in the unconscious motivations and drives that underlie abstract theories and ideas as the "return of the repressed" (see "The Patriarchal Unconscious," 249).

33. My use of object relations theory is not intended to imply an unqualified acceptance of this theory. Object relations theory has been aptly criticized on a number of accounts, foremost among which are its presumption of cross-cultural validity; its focus on the heterosexual, nuclear family; its failure to identify the material and structural roots of male domination; its mono-causal analysis of women's subordinate status; and its simplistic (and problematic) "solution" for ending male domination by introducing male parenting into the nuclear family. While recognizing these cogent criticisms, I still believe that aspects of object relations theory can be useful for shedding light on the formation of masculine self-identity as it is conceived in opposition to not only the mother figure, but to all of the female (and natural) world. Object relations theory need not imply that this oppositional consciousness is learned exclusively in a heterosexual, nuclear family setting. Certainly, schools, the media, and other aspects of cultural conditioning exert an equally important influence. On object relations theory, see Nancy Chodorow, and Dorothy Dinnerstein. For feminist critiques of object relations theory, see Pauline Bart, "Review of Chodorow's *Reproduction of Mothering*," and Iris Young, "Is Male Gender Identity the Cause of Male Dominance?" in Trebilcot.

34. It is interesting to note that the subject of initiation has been one of the recurring themes of the men's movement. The lament has been the lack of appropriate male mentors in our culture who are capable of initiating men into masculine self-identity (see, for example, Sam Keen, and Robert Bly). In an excellent critique of the men's movement, Jill Johnston (1992) points out that what is crucial to the boy child, according to the men's movement, "is the boy's separation from his mother, who has to stay at home and take care of the boy, for the appearance of a male mentor to be significant or necessary. If the mother doesn't stay home, the boy will have no good emotional reason for being pried away. There would be no initiation story." Johnston goes on to conclude that "Male initiation *always* has to do with gender distinctions and the devaluation of women. If women were important, boys

wouldn't need to get away from them and mothers wouldn't need to cling to their boys" (29).

35. For a comparable analysis of the psychosexual roots of violence against women, see Hartsock.

36. The "birth-giving" properties of hunting find a parallel in the literature that describes hunting as a generative force not only in individual self-development, but in the development of culture as a whole. Thus, a number of authors have argued that hunting provided the evolutionary impetus for the development of a wide range of cultural practices, including technology, language, song, art, dance—in short, everything that is typically thought to define us as human beings. Hunting, according to this hypothesis, is seen not only to initiate men into masculine self-identity, but to initiate humans into the realm of culture as well (see, for example, Washburn and Lancaster, Laughlin, Dart, Ardrey, and Tiger and Fox). The "man the hunter" hypothesis has been countered by a number of feminist writers, who have pointed to the pivotal importance of gathering in the development of the human species (see, for example, Dahlberg). For a historical analysis of the popularity of the "man the hunter" hypothesis, see Cartmill.

37. Gilligan's work has inspired a large body of writing, which both supports and critiques the notion of an ethic of care. Critics argue that the proponents of an ethic of care lack a power analysis. Caring practices, they argue, are both a product of socialization and a strategy for survival under oppression. To endorse an ethic of care is thus to ask women to reinforce their own institutionalized oppression. In addition, a number of lesbian philosophers have pointed out that caring conduct is not universally appropriate. A woman in an abusive relationship, for example, would be better served by severing her connection with her abuser than by extending him more compassion and care (Hoagland, Lesbian Ethics and "Some Concerns About"; and Card, "Caring and Evil"). Despite these cogent criticisms of an ethic of care, I nonetheless believe that it is possible to speak of "appropriate care." The question then becomes, when is caring conduct appropriate, and what constitutes appropriate care—or what prevents the development of appropriate care. On the subject of an ethic of care, see Noddings, Manning, Tronto, and Ruddick. For a series of critical essays, see the anthologies by Card (Feminist Ethics), Kittay and Meyers, and Larrabee.

38. The connection between the act of attention and caring can be discerned in the use of the words "careless" and "careful." When we say that someone has acted "carelessly," we mean to say that they have failed to pay attention to a particular situation or thing; on the other hand, when we admonish someone to "be careful" we are, in effect, telling them to pay more attention to their surroundings. For other works on the topic of attention, see Weil, and Ruddick.

39. Carol Adams refers to a similar eliding of responsibility or agency in what she refers to as the "aggressive" and "relational hunts." Adams's "aggressive hunt" corresponds to what I have called the "happy hunt," whereas her "relational hunt" is analogous to my "holy hunt" (137–38).

40. For a philosophical development of the argument that hunting is an instinctual activity, which is therefore beyond ethical reproach, see Causey. Significantly, Causey avoids any speculation as to whether hunting is "instinctual" only to men. For a critique of Causey's argument, see Pluhar.

41. According to Tronto, an important aspect of caring entails the recipient's acknowledgment of the caring action. The problem in evaluating caring conduct toward animals, of course, is that we do not share the same language. Although we are often in positions where we have to use our imagination and empathy to infer what an animal's needs might be, I suspect that, at least for "wild" animals, the most caring thing that we can do most often is to leave them alone.

42. This is not to say that hunting and meat-eating are only matters of individual moral concern. Clearly, both activities have enormous repercussions for the environment as well (see, for example, Robbins, and Rifkin). The failure of the environmental movement to address the morality of these activities is all the more reprehensible in light of the far-reaching destructive impact of these activities. The mutual interest of the animal liberation and environmental movement in eliminating these activities could go a long way toward breaking down the divisions that currently plague these movements.

References

Abbot, Sally. 1990. The Origins of God in the Blood of the Lamb. In Diamond and Orenstein, 35–40.

Adams, Carol. 1991. Ecofeminism and the Eating of Animals. *Hypatia* 6, no. 1:125–45.

Albanese, Catherine L. 1990. *Nature Religion in America: From Algonkian Indians to the New Age.* Chicago: University of Chicago Press.

Amory, Cleveland. 1974. *Mankind? Our Incredible War on Wildlife.* New York: Harper and Row.

Ardrey, Robert. 1977. *The Hunting Hypothesis.* New York: Atheneum.

Baker, Ron. 1985. *The American Hunting Myth.* New York: Vintage.

Barnhill, David. 1990. Indra's Net as Food Chain. *The Ten Directions* 11, no. 1 (Spring/Summer):20–27.

Bart, Pauline. 1984. Review of Chodorow's *The Reproduction of Mothering.* In Trebilcot, 147–52.

Beauvoir, Simone de. 1974. *The Second Sex.* Trans. and ed. H. M. Parshley. New York: Vintage Books.

Bly, Robert. 1992. *Iron John: A Book about Men.* New York: Random House.

Callicott, J. Baird. 1989a. *In Defense of the Land Ethic: Essays in Environmental Philosophy.* Albany: SUNY Press.

———. 1989b. American Indian Land Wisdom? Sorting Out the Issues. In *In Defense of the Land Ethic*, 203–19.

——. 1989c. Animal Liberation and Environmental Ethics: Back Together Again. In *In Defense of the Land Ethic*, 49–59.

——. 1989d. Animal Liberation: A Triangular Affair. In *In Defense of the Land Ethic*, 15–38.

——. 1989e. Traditional American Indian and Western Attitudes Toward Nature: An Overview. In *In Defense of the Land Ethic*, 177–201.

Caras, Roger. 1970. *Death as a Way of Life.* Boston: Little, Brown.

Card, Claudia. 1990. Caring and Evil. *Hypatia* 5:101–8.

——, ed. 1991. *Feminist Ethics.* Lawrence, Kans.: University Press of Kansas.

Carrier, James. 1987. Marine Tenure and Conservation in Papua New Guinea: Problems in Interpretation. In McDay and Acheson, 142–70.

Carson, Rachel. 1962. *Silent Spring.* Greenwich, Conn.: Fawcett Publications.

Cartmill, Matt. 1993. *A View to Death in the Morning.* Cambridge: Harvard University Press.

Causey, Ann S. 1989. On the Morality of Sport Hunting. *Environmental Ethics* 11:327–43.

Chodorow, Nancy. 1978. *The Reproduction of Mothering.* Berkeley: University of California Press.

Clifton, Merritt. 1992. Killing the Female. *Agenda*, June, 26–29.

Collard, Andrée, with Joyce Contrucci. 1988. *Rape of the Wild: Man's Violence Against Animals and the Earth.* Bloomington: Indiana University Press.

Dahlberg, Frances, ed. 1981. *Woman the Gatherer.* New Haven: Yale University Press.

Dart, Raymond. 1953. The Predatory Transition From Ape to Man. *International Anthropological and Linguistic Review* 1, no. 4:201–17.

Dasmann, Raymond. 1988. Toward a Biosphere Consciousness. In *The Ends of the Earth: Perspectives on Modern Environmental History*, ed. D. Worster, 277–88. Cambridge: Cambridge University Press.

Defenders of Animal Rights. n.d. *The Case Against Hunting* [pamphlet]. Available from author, P.O. Box 4786, Baltimore, MD 21211.

Devall, Bill, and George Sessions. 1985. *Deep Ecology: Living As If Nature Mattered.* Salt Lake City: Peregrine Smith Books.

Diamond, Irene, and Gloria Orenstein, eds. 1990. *Reweaving the World: The Emergence of Ecofeminism.* San Francisco: Sierra Club Books.

Dinnerstein, Dorothy. 1967. *The Mermaid and the Minotaur: Sexual Arrangements and Human Malaise.* New York: Harper and Row.

Donovan, Josephine. 1990. Animal Rights and Feminist Theory. *Signs: Journal of Women in Culture and Society* 15, no. 21:350–75.

Eaton, Randall. 1985a. The Hunter as Alert Man: An Overview of the Origin of the Human/Animal Connection. In *The Human/Animal Connection,* ed. Randall L. Eaton, 2–19. Incline Village, Nev.: Carnivore Journal and Sierra Nevada College Press.

———. 1985b. Know Thy Animal, Know Thyself. In *The Human/Animal Connection*, 42–50.

———, ed. 1986. *Zen and the Art of Hunting: A Personal Search for Environmental Values*. Reno, Nev.: Carnivore Press.

Flax, Jane. 1983. The Patriarchal Unconscious. In *Discovering Reality: Feminist Perspectives on Epistemology, Methodology, and Philosophy of Science*, ed. Sandra Harding and Merrill B. Hintikka, 245–81. Boston: D. Reidel Publishing.

Fox, Warwick. 1990. *Toward a Transpersonal Ecology: Developing New Foundations for Environmentalism*. Boston: Shambhala Publications.

Fund for Animals. Hunting Fact Sheets. Available from the Fund for Animals, 850 Sligo Avenue, Suite 300, Silver Spring, Maryland 20910.

Gaard, Greta, ed. 1993. *Ecofeminism: Women, Animals, and Nature*. Philadelphia: Temple University Press.

Gilligan, Carol. 1993. *In a Different Voice: Psychological Theory and Women's Development*. 2d ed. Cambridge: Harvard University Press.

Hames, Raymond. 1987. Game Conservation or Efficient Hunting? In McDay and Acheson, 92–107.

Hartsock, Nancy C. M. 1985. *Money, Sex, and Power: Toward a Feminist Historical Materialism*. Boston: Northeastern University Press.

Hays, Samuel P. 1959. *Conservation and the Gospel of Efficiency: The Progressive Conservation Movement 1890–1920*. Cambridge: Harvard University Press.

Hemingway, Ernest. 1935. Remembering Shooting-Flying. *Esquire*, February.

Hite, Shere. 1981. *The Hite Report on Male Sexuality*. New York: Ballantine.

Hoagland, Sarah Lucia. 1988. *Lesbian Ethics: Toward New Value*. Palo Alto, Calif.: Institute of Lesbian Studies.

———. 1990. Some Concerns About Nel Nodding's *Caring*. *Hypatia* 5:109–14.

Holliday, Laurel. 1978. *The Violent Sex: Male Psychobiology and the Evolution of Consciousness*. Guerneville, Calif.: Bluestocking Books.

Johnson, Allen, and Timothy Earle. 1987. *The Evolution of Human Societies: From Foraging Group to Agrarian State*. Stanford, Calif.: Stanford University Press.

Johnston, Jill. 1992. Why Iron John Is No Gift to Women. *New York Times Book Review*, 23 February.

Jolma, Dena Jones, comp. 1992. *Hunting Quotations: Two Hundred Years of Writing on the Philosophy, Culture, and Experience*. McFarland & Company.

Keen, Sam. 1991. *Fire in the Belly: On Being a Man*. New York: Bantam.

Kheel, Marti. 1985. The Liberation of Nature: A Circular Affair. *Environmental Ethics* 7, no. 2:135–49.

——. 1991. Ecofeminism and Deep Ecology: Reflections on Identity and Difference. In Robb and Caseboalt, 141–64.

——. 1993. From Heroic to Holistic Ethics: The Ecofeminist Challenge. In Gaard, 243–71.

King, Roger J. 1991. Caring About Nature: Feminist Ethics and the Environment. *Hypatia* 6, no. 1:75–89.

Kittay, Eva Feder, and Diana Meyers, eds. 1987. *Women and Moral Theory.* Totowa, N.J.: Rowman and Littlefield.

Larrabee, Mary Jeanne. 1993. *An Ethic of Care: Feminist Interdisciplinary Perspectives.* New York: Routledge.

Laughlin, William S. 1986. Hunting: An Integrating Biobehavior System and Its Evolutionary Importance. In Lee and Devore, 304–20.

Lawrence, D. H. 1964. The Death of Pan. In *Phoenix: The Posthumous Papers of D. H. Lawrence 1936*, ed. Edward McDonald. New York: Viking Press.

Lee, Richard B., and Irven Devore, eds, with Jill Nash-Mitchell. 1986. *Man the Hunter.* New York: Aldine De Gruyter.

Leopold, Aldo. 1966a. *A Sand County Almanac: With Essays on Conservation from Round River.* Oxford: Oxford University Press.

——. 1966b. Goose Music. In *A Sand County*, 26–233.

——. 1966c. The Land Ethic. In *A Sand County*, 237–64.

——. 1966d. Thinking Like a Mountain. In *A Sand County*, 137–45.

Leviton, Richard. 1992. The Island Within. *Yoga Journal*, January/February, 52–70.

Lewis, Martin W. 1992. *Green Delusions: An Environmental Critique of Radical Environmentalism.* Durham, N.C.: Duke University Press.

Livingston, John A. 1981. *The Fallacy of Wildlife Conservation.* Toronto: McClelland & Stewart.

Lopez, Barry Holstun. *Of Wolves and Men.* New York: Charles Scribner's Sons.

Manning, Rita. 1992. *Speaking from the Heart: A Feminist Ethics.* Lanham, Md.: Rowman and Littlefield.

Martin, Calvin. 1978. *Keepers of the Game: Indian-Animal Relationships and the Fur Trade.* Berkeley: University of California Press.

McDay, B., and J. Acheson, eds. 1987. *The Question of the Commons: The Culture and Ecology of Communal Resources.* Tucson: University of Arizona Press.

Menninger, Karl A. 1951. Totemic Aspects of Contemporary Attitudes Toward Animals. In Wilbur and Muensterberger, 42–74.

Merchant, Carolyn. 1989. *Ecological Revolutions: Nature, Gender, and Science in New England.* Chapel Hill: University of North Carolina Press.

Mirarchi, Ralf E., Patrick Scanloni, and Roy L. Kirkpatrick. 1977. Annual Changes in Spermatozoan Production and Associated Organs of White-Tailed Deer. *Journal of Wildlife Management* 41, no. 1:92–99.

Moore, John. 1987. *The Cheyenne Nation.* Lincoln: University of Nebraska Press.

Mumford, Lewis. 1947. *Green Memories: The Story of Geddes Mumford.* New York: Harcourt Brace.

Murdoch, Iris. 1970. *The Sovereignty of Good.* London: Cox and Wyman.

Naess, Arne. 1989. *Ecology, Community, and Lifestyle.* Trans. and ed. David Rothenberg. Cambridge: Cambridge University Press.

Nelson, Richard K. 1987. The Gifts. In *On Nature, Landscape, and Natural History,* ed. Daniel Halpern, 117–31. San Francisco: North Point Press.

———. 1989. The Gifts of Deer. In *The Island Within,* 257–77. New York: Vintage Books.

———. 1991. Exploring the Near at Hand: An Interview with Richard Nelson. *Parabola* (Summer):35–43.

Noddings, Nel. 1984. *Caring: A Feminine Approach to Ethics and Moral Education.* Berkeley: University of California Press.

O'Brien, Mary. 1981. *The Politics of Reproduction.* London: Routledge & Kegan Paul.

Oelschlaeger, Max, ed. 1992. *The Wilderness Condition: Essays on Environment and Civilization.* San Francisco: Sierra Club Books.

Ornstein, Robert, and Paul Ehrlich. 1989. *New World, New Mind: Moving Toward Conscious Evolution.* New York: Simon and Schuster.

Ortega y Gassett, José. 1985. *Meditations on Hunting.* Trans. Howard B. Wescott, foreword by Paul Shepard. New York: Charles Scribner's Sons.

Paul, Sherman. 1992. *For Love of the World: Essays on Nature Writers by Sherman Paul.* Iowa City: University of Iowa Press.

Pluhar, Evelyn B. 1991. The Joy of Killing. *Between the Species* 7, no. 3:121–28.

Plumwood, Val. 1993. *Feminism and the Mastery of Nature.* New York: Routledge.

———. 1991. Nature, Self and Gender: Feminism, Environmental Philosophy and the Critique of Rationalism. *Hypatia* 6, no. 1:3–27.

Presnall, Clifford D. 1943. Wildlife Conservation as Affected by American Indian and Caucasian Concepts. *Journal of Mammalogy* 24, no. 4:458–64.

Ranke-Heinemann, Uta. 1991. *Eunuchs for the Kingdom of Heaven: Women, Sexuality, and the Catholic Church.* New York: Penguin Books.

Regan, Tom. 1982. Environmental Ethics and the Ambiguity of the Native American's Relationship with Nature. In *All That Dwell Therein: Essays on Animal Rights and Environmental Ethics,* 206–39. Berkeley: University of California Press.

Regenstein, Lewis. 1975. *The Politics of Extinction.* New York: Macmillan.

Reiger, John F. 1986. *American Sportsmen and the Origins of Conservation.* Rev. ed. Norman: University of Oklahoma Press.

Rifkin, Jeremy. 1992. *Beyond Beef: The Rise and Fall of the Cattle Culture.* New York: Penguin Books.

Robb, Carol, and Carl Caseboalt. 1991. *Covenant for a New Creation: Ethics, Religion and Public Policy.* Maryknoll, N.Y.: Orbis Books.

Robbins, John. 1987. *Diet for a New America.* Walpole, N.H.: Stillpoint Publishing.

Rolston, Holmes, III. 1988. *Environmental Ethics: Duties to and Values in the Natural World.* Philadelphia: Temple University Press.

Roosevelt, Theodore. 1893. *The Wilderness Hunter: An Account of Big Game of the United States and Its Chase with Horse, Hound and Rifle.* New York: G. P. Putnam's Sons.

Rostlund, E. 1960. The Geographic Range of the Historic Bison in the Southeast. *Annals of the Association of American Geographers* 50:395–407.

Rotundo, Anthony E. 1993. *American Manhood: Transformations in Masculinity from the Revolution to the Modern Era.* New York: Basic Books.

Ruddick, Sara. 1989. *Maternal Thinking: Toward a Politics of Peace.* New York: Ballantine.

Shepard, Paul. 1959. A Theory of the Value of Hunting. In *Proceedings of the North American Wildlife Conference* 24.

———. 1973. *The Tender Carnivore and the Sacred Game.* New York: Scribners.

———. 1974. Animal Rights and Human Rites. *North American Review* 259 (Winter):35–42.

———. 1967. *Nature and Madness: A Historic View of the Esthetics of Nature.* New York: Alfred A. Knopf.

———. 1978. *Thinking Animals: Animals and the Development of Human Intelligence.* New York: Viking Press.

———. 1991. Searching Out Kindred Spirits. *Parabola* (Summer):86–87.

———. 1992. A Post-Historic Primitivism. In Oelschlaeger, 40–89.

Snyder, Gary. 1969. *Earth House Hold: Technical Notes and Queries to Fellow Dharma Revolutionaries.* New York: New Directions.

———. 1977. *The Old Ways: Six Essays.* San Francisco: City Lights Books.

———. 1980. *The Real Work: Interviews and Talks 1964–1979.* New York: New Directions.

———. 1984. Grace. *CoEvolution Quarterly* 43 (Fall):1.

Swan, James A. 1995. *In Defense of Hunting.* San Francisco: Harper Collins.

Teale, Edwin Way. 1966. *Wandering Through Winter.* New York: Dodd, Mead.

Thomas, Keith. 1983. *Man and the Natural World: A History of the Modern Sensibility.* New York: Pantheon.

Tiger, Lionel, and Robin Fox. 1971. *The Imperial Animal.* New York: Henry Holt and Company.

Trebilcot, Joyce, ed. 1984. *Mothering: Essays in Feminist Theory.* Totowa, N.J.: Rowman and Allanheld.

Tronto, Joan C. 1993. *Moral Boundaries: A Political Argument for an Ethic of Care.* New York: Routledge.

U.S. Department of Interior, Fish and Wildlife Service and U.S. Department of Commerce, Bureau of the Census. 1993. *1991 National Survey of Fishing, Hunting, and Wildlife-Associated Recreation.* Washington, D.C.: U.S. Government Printing Office.

Warren, Karen. 1990. The Power and the Promise of Ecological Feminism. *Environmental Ethics* 12:125–46.

Washburn, Sherwood L., and C. S. Lancaster. 1986. The Evolution of Hunting. In Lee and Devore, 293–303.

Weil, Simone. 1951. Reflections on the Right Use of School Studies with a View to the Love of God. In *Waiting for God,* trans. E. Craufurd, 105–16. New York: Harper.

White, Richard. 1991. *It's Your Misfortune and None of My Own: A History of the American West.* Norman: University of Oklahoma Press.

White-Tailed Deer Species Management Plan. 1987. Missouri Department of Conservation.

Wilbur, George B., and Warner Muensterberger, eds. 1951. *Psychoanalysis and Culture.* New York: International University Press.

Wilcox, Ella Wheeler. 1917. The Voice of the Voiceless. In *The Collected Poems of Ella Wilcox,* 2:248–53. London: Gay & Hancock.

Williams, Joy. 1990. The Killing Game. *Esquire,* October.

Wilson, Alexander. 1992. *The Culture of Nature: North American Landscape from Disney to the Exxon Valdez.* Cambridge, Mass.: Blackwell Publisher.

Young, Iris. 1984. Is Male Gender Identity the Cause of Male Dominance? In Trebilcot, 129–46.

5

Maria Comninou

$\mathcal{S}$peech, Pornography, and Hunting

Introduction

The Constitution, says Catharine MacKinnon, "is a piece of paper with words written on it" (1987, 206). This piece of paper has become the ground over which battles of opposing interests are fought. Which group wins, in the short term at least, is likely to be determined by political appointees to the Supreme Court.

The failure to achieve consensus in problems that involve moral values and ethics is forcing all sides to rely on legislation, preferably at the federal, and failing that, at the state level. Issues that affect women profoundly, such as abortion or sexual harassment and pornography, for example, are moving from the public forum to the hands of the law and back. Their fate in terms of the law becomes a matter of interpreting the right to privacy in the case of abortion and the right to free speech in the case of sexual harassment and pornography. Depending on the case, the Constitution is either our ally and must be respected, or our foe and must be changed or reinterpreted. The disputes, expressed in the language of rights,[1] are really about drawing boundaries and deciding who is in and who is out.

While women and racial and sexual-orientation minorities are still fighting for a more secure position inside the circle of the privileged rightholders, another group is now pushing at the border. This group of "dumb," "subhuman brutes" can be represented only by advocates drawn from the ranks of its oppressors. It cannot give consent and has no ability to determine its own fate. In the hierarchy devised by Homo sapiens, nonhuman animals occupy the lowest rung, and they have lent their names to all kinds of metaphors for illtreatment.[2] On the contrary, no pejoratives that express direct contempt for the nonhuman animals[3] themselves come easily to mind, except for the straight-faced descriptions of modern technology: "animal models" and "biomachines."

Animals have still no legal "standing,"[4] and their advocates are often forced to protect them through subterfuge. Although we have no legislation protecting the rights of animals as such, we do have some anticruelty laws. However, some animals are even denied the "animal" label, which could activate a modicum of protection. Animal advocates have resorted to the courts to force the U.S. Department of Agriculture (USDA) to include mice, rats, and birds in the definition of "animals" covered by the standards of the Animal Welfare Act of 1970, but have not yet succeeded in overcoming the hurdle of acquiring legal standing.[5]

Even efforts directed toward passing legislation that will ban some of the most unnecessary practices in the treatment and commercial exploitation of animals—such as the Downed Animal Act, for instance—have not yet been successful (Hazard 1992). This act, the purpose of which was to provide humane and timely euthanasia for injured or sick livestock who can no longer stand or walk, was last introduced in the 103rd Congress and died there because there is some money to be made by marketing these spent creatures before disease claims them. A similar bill (Cal. S.B. 692) was signed into law in California in September 1994, but not before it was rendered toothless and ineffective by a few seemingly minor but key changes. The euthanasia provision, for instance, was replaced by the requirement to either take "immediate action to euthanize the animal or remove the animal from the premises" (Humane Farming Association 1994). Opposition efforts of a much wider scope, such as hunting harassment laws and sweeping legislation aiming at protecting ani-

Speech, Pornography, and Hunting

mal laboratory secrecy,[6] have been successful at the state and even federal level, in spite of the constitutionality issues they raise.

Religion is at the core of other constitutional disputes, and the signals on this front are mixed. Religious freedom has been upheld by higher courts in the case of some Christian Science parents who refused to seek mainstream medical treatment for their ailing children and relied instead on spiritual healing, even though the outcome was the death of the child (Goodrich 1992). On the other hand, the prohibition against the use of the narcotic plant peyote has not been lifted in connection with the religious rituals of American Indians. In the 1990 Smith case, the Supreme Court determined that the prohibition against peyote was neutral because it applies to everyone, and does not single out a particular group based on their religion.[7] The ruling has not pleased religious organizations, who saw in it an erosion of their free exercise of religion. Not surprisingly, when the issue of animal sacrifices in the name of religion surfaced, religious organizations ranging from Presbyterian to Jewish to Seventh-Day Adventist joined the American Civil Liberties Union (ACLU) in support of the freedom to practice religious rituals (Roman 1992a).

In this article I chronicle the unequal importance or protection that has been accorded to free speech in the seemingly unrelated cases of pornography and hunting. Comparing first the reactions to antipornography and hunter harassment laws, we find that we are dealing with situations in which those in power make and interpret the laws to suit their purposes. A comparison of sexual harassment and hunter harassment laws reveals further incongruities. If we want to take sides, it may appear superficially that we cannot side with women *and* animals without loss of consistency on the matter of free speech. Upon reflection, however, we find that we can trust our sympathies for both, because these inconsistencies dissolve if we recognize that pornography and sexual harassment are really about silencing women, just as hunter harassment laws are about silencing the animals' only advocates. Women and animals or their advocates may not always appear to sit on the same side of the argument, because the issues involved are being redefined before our very eyes, but no matter which side they seem to sit on, it is, so far, the losing side.

Pornography and Hunting

From the examples already mentioned, we may surmise that a narrow interpretation of the Constitution, one that allows a restriction on fundamental rights, is considered legitimate when the groups affected matter. Otherwise, the Constitution stands absolute. For instance, an avalanche of opinion and legal expertise, not the least from ACLU, will rush to defend free speech when the challenge comes from women seeking to pass antipornography legislation. But there is a deafening silence from the First Amendment defenders when the challenge comes from hunting groups. The defense of free speech in the latter case has fallen predominantly on the shoulders of animal rights activists. When a provision dealing with the "obstruction of a lawful hunt" was slipped into the anticrime bill H.R. 3355 under the guise of "recreational public safety," the ACLU belatedly woke up to the free speech problem.

Superficially, the failure of antipornography legislation and the quick success of hunter harassment laws,[8] are on opposite sides of the free-speech debate, and therefore simply point to inconsistency. But on a deeper level, both cases are about who "calls the shots." In this respect, the animal sacrifices case recently decided by the U.S. Supreme Court could have been enlightening. The city of Hialeah, Florida, passed ordinances banning animal sacrifices, but only in response to its open practice by followers of the Santeria religion.[9] Therefore, it was argued, the legislation was aiming to curtail the free exercise of a particular religion, and not to prevent animal cruelty or protect public health, as the city claimed. Because the ordinances failed to meet the criteria of "neutrality," specifically targeting religious slaughter while excluding other cases of animal slaughter, the Supreme Court ruled against Hialeah.[10] The decision was based on the Smith ruling that the use of banned drugs is not permissible even in the interests of religion and state separation.[11] Therefore, the question of whether animals may lose their lives in the interest of the free exercise of religion has not been answered, and must await a new case not hampered by the flaws in Hialeah.

The pornography issue has divided both the feminist block and the liberal block and has created some strange alliances.[12] Some feminists have opposed any legislation against pornography on the grounds that it is speech, and that any restriction of speech will disproportionately affect women. On the other side, some religious or right-wing conservatives have supported restrictions on pornography on the same grounds that they oppose obscenity: it offends community standards and debases family values. The feminists who oppose pornography, however, are not motivated by a puritanical morality. Instead, they see pornography as a political issue that affects the status of women in a male-dominated society.

University of Michigan law professor Catharine MacKinnon and feminist writer Andrea Dworkin together have drafted model anti-pornography legislation based on the premise that pornography violates women's civil rights, as evidenced by its detrimental effects on women as a class. Four injuries are recognized and made actionable: coercion in the production of pornography, forcing pornographic materials on others, direct assault caused by specific pornography, and trafficking in pornography (MacKinnon 1987, 179). Pornography is defined concretely, and excludes what is commonly known as erotica. A version of this legislation was passed in Indianapolis, but was later overturned as unconstitutional by the U.S. Supreme Court, which allowed a court of appeals decision to stand. In the words of MacKinnon, "this is a law that gives victims a civil action when they are coerced into pornography, when pornography is forced on them, when they are subordinated through the trafficking in pornography" (MacKinnon 1987, 210). A similar ordinance drafted for the city of Minneapolis was vetoed twice by the mayor. The antipornography legislation is an example of the uneasy coalitions formed on both sides.[13] According to Kaminer, "it was introduced in the Indianapolis City Council by an anti-ERA activist, passed with the support of the right, and signed into law by the Republican mayor" (Kaminer 1992). On the other hand, a group that includes Adrienne Rich and Betty Friedan formed the Feminist Anti-Censorship Task Force (FACT) in order to oppose such legislation.[14]

In his recent book, in a chapter entitled "The Gospel According to Catharine MacKinnon," free-speech absolutist Nat Hentoff criticizes the MacKinnon-Dworkin legal approach to pornography as censorship and cites opinions that express doubts about the link between pornography and violence against women (Hentoff 1992). Others have been less restrained in their opposition. A superb example of cooptation and identification with the male image of sex and pornography is presented by Camille Paglia in a breathless and florid attack directed toward the MacKinnon-Dworkin team, whom she dubs "the Mad Hatter and her dumpy dormouse" (Paglia 1992). "I am a pornographer," she declares in the opening line of her *Playboy* article, which alternates between imaginative insults ("Let's get rid of Infirmary Feminism, with its bedlam of bellyachers, anorexics, bulimics, depressives, rape victims and incest survivors") and a poetic exaltation of pornography ("Pornography is a pagan arena of beauty, vitality and brutality, of the archaic vigor of nature. It should break every rule, offend all morality. . . . Pornography lets the body live in pagan glory, the lush, disorderly fullness of the flesh"). Paglia's is a new, eloquent way of repeating the banality that women should enjoy degradation and violence if that is what turns on men, since sexuality is defined by men for both sexes.[15]

Whatever the merits of their arguments, the eloquence of pornography's supporters, such as Paglia, is equaled only by the prose of outdoors columnists in defending hunting. In a column of barely over 800 words, Gene Mueller manages to describe "the followers of America's newest religion, the animal-rights activists who hold the life of a rat dearer than that of a human" as "Bambi people" and "dandelion pickers" and ends his piece with a veiled threat: A startled hunter may shoot in reflex action and "what if birdshot scattered all over creation and found . . ." (Mueller 1992). His piece is meant to be humorous, of course, but its humor is the type that the people who are its targets don't seem to appreciate. On the contrary, Senator Burns, who introduced the hunter harassment section of the crime bill, portrayed hunt protesters as dangerous extremists from whom the hunters must be protected (Seelye 1994).

In a galloping legislative fervor, almost all states have already passed laws against activities that impede hunting. A few of these laws already have been or are being challenged for constitutionality, such as the 1985 version of the Hunter Harassment Act in Connecticut. The states are doing their utmost to avoid First Amendment challenges, including avoiding arrests or trying to drop the charges for those who violate the new laws (Bass 1992). A challenge to the amended 1990 Connecticut law, which still includes in its list of harassing activities "natural or artificial, aural, olfactory or physical stimuli to affect wildlife behavior in order to hinder legal hunting," has failed (see Bass 1992). The prosecutor of the case was quoted as saying that the right to privacy of the hunter "in the middle of the woods" trumps any First Amendment claims by the activists.[16] The concern for the protection of the hunter's privacy to shoot animals in the midst of public land, including our National Wildlife Refuges, forces those who sympathize with the hunted to risk arrest or stay out of public land during the endless sequence of special seasons for each "game animal," from duck to deer to pheasant to squirrel and rabbit, who may be hunted all year round. This overwhelming concern of states for the right to privacy does not seem to extend to women, whose privacy rights regarding reproductive choices have been eroded in recent years.

The constitutionality of hunter harassment laws not only had escaped the scrutiny of various First Amendment champions until their emergence in the crime bill in 1994, but had not even received the same serious discussion as other challenging legislation, such as the antipornography or sexual harassment laws. Even National Public Radio failed to mention the constitutionality issue in a segment describing an uneventful hunter harassment protest in Pennsylvania during the first day of the bear-hunting season in 1992.[17] The MacKinnon-Dworkin model managed to pass in Indianapolis, only to be overturned, as already mentioned. The only other place it received support in the U.S. was in Minneapolis, but it was vetoed twice by Mayor Donald Fraser (Hentoff 1992, 340). In contrast, hunter harassment laws met no such obstacles, as their swift passage attests.

Several explanations can be advanced for this discrepancy. One is put forward by MacKinnon herself to explain the failure of antipornography legislation: the harm caused by pornography to its victims is not considered as important as having pornography and pornographic materials available (MacKinnon 1989, 213). Hunter harassment, on the other hand, harms a lot of people who stand to gain by the promotion of hunting.

Another explanation is that the speech of certain citizens is more valuable than the speech of others. Thus, the failure of antipornography laws safeguards the free speech of men while silencing women; the passing of hunter harassment laws restricts the speech of animal rights activists, the majority of whom are women. In reality, of course, the speech of anybody venturing in the woods may be restricted, but only animal rights activists are targeted, because of their presumed intent to disrupt hunting. The Supreme Court of Connecticut conceded that free speech issues are involved, but nevertheless held that the hunter harassment statute was content-neutral, that is, it did not prohibit any particular message of the speech and could be regulated by the state.

A third, not unrelated, reason that pornography is considered to be speech, and is therefore constitutionally protected, while the speech of anti-hunting activists passes as conduct, and is therefore illegal,[18] is that both pornography and hunting are multibillion-dollar industries. This fact about pornography is well known, but the economic value of hunting may not be so obvious. Alan Farnham (1992) gives a breakdown of the $10 billion tag paid by hunters: the largest percentage of the money, 49 percent, goes for equipment, including guns, ammunition, and vehicles; 19 percent goes for food and lodging; 16 percent for transportation; 9 percent for access to land; and 4 percent for various government fees and permits. The beneficiaries of this largesse, including the government, are not going to deprive themselves in order to protect the speech of out-of-touch-with-reality Bambi lovers,[19] who are so characterized to prevent the public from identifying with them and sympathizing with their cause. Ironically, although the harm done by pornography is disputed or dismissed as indirect or irrelevant by free-speech liberals, pornography supporters, and the courts, there is no direct harm that can be attributed to the antihunt activists, except perhaps that of spoiling the fun of the kill for the hunters. On the contrary, the hunt protesters may be responsible for reducing the human carnage that is directly caused by hunters, by preventing their shooting as often (and as carelessly?) as they otherwise would. Although the total number of hunting accidents continues to decline, possibly due to mandatory safety courses for hunters in 47 states,[20] the number of human fatalities due to hunters (including self-inflicted fatalities) increased from 146 in 1990 to 160 in 1991 (Castaneda 1992). Obviously, the hunted animals, who are the real victims, are not counted as injuries or fatalities—to even suggest that they should be would seem absurd to those who engage in or promote hunting.

The issue of harm may be crucial.[21] In her writings and speeches MacKinnon often gives examples of other types of speech that are not protected because of the harm they may cause. Shouting "Fire!" with no reason in a crowded theater, giving an attack command to a specially trained guard dog, giving unlicensed medical advice, false commercial advertising, soliciting bribes, criminal conspiracies, threats, contracts that violate the law—none of these are currently protected as free speech, and nobody is complaining. Pornography, therefore, may be regulated under the same theory of harms that justifies the regulation of all these other forms of speech. The harms that can be attributed to pornography include harms during its production, harms to women in the form of increased sexual assaults and violence as a result of pornography, and harms from its use in sexual harassment (Sunstein 1993a). Similarly, objections that such regulation is not neutral because it restricts one viewpoint (presenting women as inferior) but not its opposite (presenting women as equal), can be answered by reference to the other examples of regulated speech. The fact that we fail to see the lack of neutrality, for instance, in banning the advertising of illegal drugs, while welcoming advertising *against* illegal drugs, is due to the widespread acceptance of such actions. Lack of neutrality becomes invisible when we deal with conventional or traditional views, but stands out when the views are nontraditional (Sunstein 1993a).

The issue of harm is also at the core of efforts to regulate hate or racist speech. It is true that some hastily drafted hate-speech codes in universities have been overturned by the courts or voluntarily withdrawn, and that the signals from Supreme Court cases are not encouraging.[22] However, there is increasing recognition of the damage that hate speech inflicts on its intended victims. New efforts are directed toward balancing First Amendment principles and victim's rights (see Matsuda 1989).

In the case of hunter harassment, the law is trying to protect the traditional activities of the special group of hunters, although in doing so it restricts the activities of a nontraditional group of zoophiles and even of hunting-neutral individuals who are uncomfortable remaining in parks while shooting goes on. The activities of hunt protesters who accost hunters and try to convince them to spare the animals do not cause a deprivation of something to which the hunters should be exclusively entitled. The protesters' exhortations that hunters respect the life of a deer or shoot with a camera instead of a gun cannot be characterized as "fighting words" or hate speech by any stretch.

Why should the animals in public lands be considered the property of hunters to kill and not of the hunt protesters to save? It is difficult to avoid here a comparison with the pro-life protesters who block entrance to abortion clinics. Their activities, as long as they are nonviolent, are still protected as speech, but the peaceful activities of hunt protesters are outlawed as conduct.[23] In contrast, the hunters may kill animals, who are independent subjects of life, as part of their right to privacy without interference from protesters; the privacy of women seeking the termination of pregnancy—or, to use the same language, the killing of a fetus that is not independently viable—is not always protected from the abortion protesters. The currently unfolding developments in Congress and in the courts have complicated the issue. Congress has enacted legislation to protect abortion clinics from violent protesters at the same time it has passed legislation to ensure the "safety" of hunters from those interfering with a "lawful hunt."[24] The ACLU supported the clinic protection bill but opposed the hunter harassment bill. The explanation for the difference in treatment may be that Congress, under the influence of the National Rifle Association lobby, lumped the animal advocates with violent demonstrators, while the ACLU, when it finally noticed the issue, was capable of distinguishing between violence against abortion clinics and the peaceful speech of hunt protesters.

Reexamining the differential treatment of free speech in the efforts to regulate pornography and hunter harassment in light of the previous observations, we may conclude that the discrepancy is best explained by recognizing that it is not a discrepancy at all. Antipornography laws restrict the speech of men only to the extent of giving some speech to women. From the perspective of women, who are the main victims of pornography, the antipornography laws are really laws for women's speech. The hunt protesters, who stand as surrogates for animals, are also asking for speech, speech that so far has been reserved for hunters. Their actions on behalf of animals are the nonviolent expressions of a viewpoint, and therefore speech.

Similarly, the actions of the hunters can also be interpreted as an extreme form of speech: if animals are mere objects and not persons, then killing them for sport is a form of speech in the same sense that flag burning is considered speech. The flag is a symbol that stands for a nation, a government in power, or a dominant ideology. Therefore, burning the flag can be seen as an expression of political belief protesting the status quo. Although no animals have legal standing, game animals are excluded from even the minimal protection afforded by anticruelty legislation. For hunters, game animals provide sport and a means of validation of their manhood or brotherhood with other hunters. Hunting and trapping are often part of the rites of passage into adulthood in rural communities. Hunting, therefore, can be a form of speech that expresses a masculine ideology of play, sufficiency, and dominance. It is an affirmation, not a protest, of the status quo. Since game animals have no legal rights or protection in hunting season, no harm is involved: hunting becomes speech. If this interpretation seems far-fetched, it is only because of its unfamiliarity and the fact that it has to be presented in a culture where animals do not really matter. Ironically, it is precisely the fact that animals do not count that allows us to consider hunting an expression of a viewpoint or speech in our society.

Seen in the light of speech for privileged versus marginalized groups, the contrasting histories of antipornography legislation and hunter harassment laws are in fact consistent. The two largely over-lapping groups, women and hunt protesters, are simply silenced under current law. The case for privacy is similar. Hunters can easily claim the right to privacy in order to fight off interference while they are shooting beings that do not belong to them in public areas, but women cannot receive the same protection in private abortion clinics without jumping various judicial and legislative hoops.

The hunted animals, who have been simply transformed into "game" to be "harvested" when ripe during the appropriate "season," furnish another example of the absent referent, which Carol Adams describes so aptly in connection with meat: "The animals have become absent referents, whose fate is transmuted into a metaphor for someone else's existence or fate . . . in this case the original meaning of animals' fates is absorbed into a human-centered hierarchy" (Adams 1990, 42). In fact, the metaphors of game and meat overlap in the case of hunted animals, as hunters increasingly try to justify their killing by consuming the object of their violence, or in some cases, try to receive absolution or the credit of beneficence by offering it to charitable organizations to be consumed by destitute or impoverished humans (DePass 1992). In this way, the poor become the unwitting accomplices in the demise of those who are even worse off than themselves. In a similar vein, money from the recognized symbol of pornography, *Playboy* magazine, has been contributed through the Playboy Foundation to feminist or women's causes (MacKinnon 1987, 134). We can pursue the analogy to the case of prostitution. The homeless[25] have so few options that their consumption of the hunters' bounty cannot be considered as approval of hunting, just as prostitution cannot be considered as a free choice even for the women who claim they engage in it out of choice (Giobbe 1990).

There is also a more straightforward connection between pornography and hunting. When not hunting, hunters can entertain themselves with other manly attractions provided for them in their hunting lodges: As Farnham (1992) reports, "you can get a striptease and a Bud for $1.50"; the stripper collects tips "off customers' noses. Not manually." It may indeed be entertainment or it may be psychological preparation, such as showing pornographic films to the Gulf War pilots on the eve of their "surgical strikes" against Iraq.[26] There is an even more gruesome permutation of this theme in the civil war in Bosnia. A captured Serb fighter revealed how he was trained in hand-to-hand combat using live pigs, whose throats he slit after immobilizing them. He was then asked to apply this practice on

Bosnian prisoners of war, and in the rape and murder of Bosnian girls. He claims he was following orders (Beeston 1992).

Sexual Harassment and Hunter Harassment

What does harassment mean? During the Anita Hill–Clarence Thomas Senate hearings and the accompanying report and surveys, we learned at least one thing about *sexual* harassment: most women said they knew what it was, but most men claimed they had no idea what women meant by it (Roman 1992b).

No such apparent confusion has surfaced in the case of hunter harassment, or at least the courts and the legislature failed to notice it. Let us examine the wording of one state's laws against sexual and hunter harassment. Michigan will serve the purpose, as its laws appear to be representative. As reported by Roman, most state laws consider sexual harassment as illegal sex discrimination. Sexual harassment of a woman is not something that happens to her because of what kind of woman she is, but simply because she is a woman. Nor is it a biological expression of all men, but even if it were, it would still be wrong. Arguments such as these are detailed by MacKinnon (1987) and show the steps the courts followed to arrive at the conclusion that sexual harassment is sex discrimination. Sexual harassment as sex discrimination is prohibited by Title VII of the Civil Rights Act (Furfaro and Josephson 1992), and the Equal Employment Opportunity Commission (EEOC) has codified the sexual harassment guidelines. EEOC's guidelines form the standard used by state laws such as Michigan's.

The Michigan law[27] specifies that "Discrimination because of sex includes sexual harassment which means unwelcome sexual advances, requests for sexual favors, and other verbal or physical conduct or communication of a sexual nature" and then proceeds to state the conditions that such conduct must satisfy. Such conduct generally takes one of two forms: the *quid pro quo* form, in which submission to or rejection of the conduct will influence the employment or education, housing, and other public services status or decision-making processes affecting the individual; or the *hostile environment* form, in which the climate created by the conduct interferes with the victim's functioning or psychological well-being (Furfaro and Josephson 1992). Under the hostile environment form, much conduct remains subject to interpretation and has invited the ire of free-speech defenders, especially since recent court decisions leave

Speech, Pornography, and Hunting

the determination of what constitutes a hostile environment to a "reasonable woman" standard. According to Plevan and Popper (1992, 25), "the court reasoned that the different perspectives of men and women regarding sexual behavior required the application of gender-based norms."

Although the overwhelming majority of the victims of sexual harassment have been women and the perpetrators men, a gender-based norm sanctified by law is not only unsettling to most men, who now begin to experience how it feels to be "the other," but it may on occasion boomerang on women and other minority-opinion groups in different contexts because of selective (discriminatory) enforcement. This has happened already in Canada. In the 1992 landmark Butler decision, Canada's Supreme Court took a pro-women stance on pornography by holding that restrictions on pornography that subordinates or degrades women do indeed infringe on freedom of expression, but that restrictions on such speech are justified because it causes harm to women.[28] However, the first publication to be targeted for prosecution under the new ruling was a lesbian magazine produced by women for women and which features pictures of bound, naked women (Varchaver 1992). Since lesbian pornography and victimization of women by other women is at most a minor social problem, we have here another example of how the law is applied selectively and more harshly to women[29]—though perhaps a more plausible view is that homosexual material had been targeted frequently under obscenity guidelines even before the Butler decision (Landsberg 1993).

The Michigan law on hunter harassment states:

(1) A person shall not obstruct or interfere in the lawful taking of animals by another person with the intent to prevent that lawful taking.

(2) A person violates this section when he or she intentionally or knowingly does any of the following:

   (a) Drives or disturbs animals for the purpose of disrupting a lawful taking.

   (b) Blocks, impedes or harasses another person who is engaged in the process of lawfully taking an animal.

   (c) Uses natural or artificial visual, aural, olfactory, gustatory, or physical stimulus [sic] to affect animal behavior in order to hinder or prevent the lawful taking of an animal.[30]

The law continues with the description of additional prohibited conduct. In comparing the sexual with the hunter harassment laws, there are some striking differences. Sexual harassment is defined, however inadequately according to some, as "unwelcome sexual advances." In the hunter harassment law, the word "harasses" appears in item (b) but is not specifically defined, unless it is meant as a synonym of "blocks" or "impedes." Another difference is that the harassed hunter must be engaging in a specific act, which is described, euphemistically only, as "the lawful taking of an animal." Does this sound like the killing of an animal? It is actually more reminiscent of the "lawful taking of his wife by a man," which is no longer lawful in Michigan since marital rape has been banned.[31]

In a sexual harassment case there are two parties involved, the harasser and the harassed, who is also the victim. In a hunter harassment case we have three parties, the hunter, the activist, and the animal. But who is the harasser, the harassed, or the victim? That depends on your moral or religious personal beliefs. In the eyes of the law or the hunters, there are only two parties, the animal being again the absent referent. In the eyes of the animal rights activists, and probably in the eyes of many who simply oppose sport hunting, the animal is the harassed victim and the hunter is the harasser. The following statement in the sports-section report of a fall 1992 hunt protest in Michigan definitely conveys a certain point of view on the issue: "[the head of the Department of Natural Resources enforcement unit] urged hunters who are victimized by protesters to keep cool and not react violently, because this kind of demonstration is designed to make hunters appear to be the aggressors" (Husar 1992). This must be one of the rare instances in which sportswriters assign negative connotation to aggressive behavior and pin it on those whom they normally dismiss as out-of-touch-with-nature Bambi lovers. Do the Michigan law and others like it, such as the 1990 Connecticut law that contains similar language, discriminate against the protesters' rights to free speech? As written, the law may be assumed to apply to anybody, including a nature devotee who decides to commune with the wood spirits by means of a ritualistic and leaf-rustling dance or by a mystical and loud incantation. Would these nature lovers be prosecuted to make the law pass the neutrality test, and thus declare public lands out of bounds to anyone who is not a hunter? Or will they not be prosecuted on the grounds that their intent was not to disrupt the hunt, but to commune with nature? If

Speech, Pornography, and Hunting

so, could the hunt protesters also argue that it is not their intent to impede the lawful taking of an animal, but simply to communicate an urgent message to a sister soul or even to protect the integrity of the maternal bond between the doe and her fawn?

One thing is certain: civil libertarians are slowly coming to the defense of the hunt protesters, and hunter harassment does not yet appear in the footnotes of books and articles that discuss the free-speech issues related to pornography and sexual harassment. Newspaper articles that touch on the issue in their sports or outdoors sections invariably make valiant efforts to demolish gender-related stereotypes by quoting women who hunt, although the number of women hunters is estimated to be "as high as 11% and growing" (Farnham 1992). It may be that outdoors writers subconsciously recognize the connection of hunting and hunter harassment with other feminist grievances and wish to defuse it. Traditional feminists have avoided any comparison with animal-related issues as inherently demeaning to women, but the recent ACLU involvement is bound to make the hunter harassment laws and free speech, if nothing else, at least a respectable subject of debate.

What can we conclude from the comparison of sexual and hunter harassment laws? The striking difference in acceptability is illuminated if we realize that the true harassers in both cases are predominantly members of the male sex. The hunt protesters are not there to harass anyone, but to protect or warn animals that do not belong to hunters. The hunters are there to engage in the ultimate harassment: killing. By subtracting the animals from the discussion of the hunt, the law succeeds in converting the harasser into harassed. As in the pornography case, what superficially appears as an inconsistency is at a deeper level consistent. The true harasser is in a position of dominance and must be protected, either by converting his conduct to speech, as in pornography and sexual harassment, or by transforming his speech into conduct to be protected on the grounds of privacy, as in hunting. The speech of victims and surrogate victims is either nonexistent, as in pornography and sexual harassment, or is converted into conduct so that it can be suppressed, as in hunting harassment.

Rape and Hunting

When ethical arguments against entrenched behavior fail, scientists and hunters, who are predominantly male, use "nature" and the example of other animals to exonerate the less attractive propensities of the human male, or to justify their own behavior. And whereas their usual argument in favor of experimenting on animals or killing them and eating them is that humans are superior because of their unmatched rationality and intelligence, when it comes to rape and hunting, other animals and nature itself often serve as their models and excuses. In the case of rape, Anne Fausto-Sterling (1985) exposes the attempts by prominent sociobiologists to mold their observations of reproductive behavior in mallard ducks and insects and fish to fit the definition of rape. By casting rape as an adaptive strategy dictated by evolution, these scientists redefine a human crime as a genetically programmed behavior that enhances the biological fitness of the male. The conclusion is that rape is inevitable and we should not waste our efforts to prevent it unless we can change the nature of men.

Similarly, hunters proclaim their right to kill on one level by claiming that "animals are here for our consumption" and on the other by asserting that hunting simply confirms "their animal status" in the chain of being: "By killing, he [the hunter] willingly couples himself into the chain of life and death binding all other predators and prey. And thus bound, he experiences nature in a way far more intimate than whale watching: He watches it, and then eats it" (Farnham 1992). Marti Kheel has analyzed the writings of deep ecologists Randall Eaton, José Ortega y Gasset, and Aldo Leopold on the subject of hunting and found that for them hunting is not "a necessary means of subsistence but rather a *desire* that fulfills a deep psychological need" to identify with the animal (Kheel 1990). This is an impossible task, since the animal is killed, but for ordinary hunters eating the dead flesh is obviously sufficient for identification purposes. It is not clear how women hunters will interpret their kill-mediated connection with nature, but Farnham's article provides some hints. After informing us that Jane Fonda also hunts, he describes a long list of the hottest paraphernalia and other products or services one can buy: muzzleloaders, scents and lures, calls (instruments), prey acquisition systems such as infrared binoculars and Bionic Ears, how-to videos, special classes, corporate leases, etc. (Farnham 1992). Such abundance of consumer goods may appeal to the adherents of the "shop 'til you drop" credo of both sexes and recruit some women (and men) from their current "hunting for bargains" to a "shopping for the hunt."

It is not great news that protection of speech is applied selectively. On one hand, it is difficult to impose regulations on speech when pornographers make money and women are the victims, but on the other, free speech issues are almost invisible when hunters and the hunting industry stand to benefit and only the speech of animal rights activists is silenced. Similarly, sexual harassment laws are criticized often and at length as unclear or infringing on free speech, but hunter harassment laws have largely escaped such scrutiny. When viewed in this light, neither the application of the laws nor the stance of women (who comprise the majority of animal advocates) relative to issues of free speech are inconsistent. The legal system still protects the free speech of the dominant class at the expense of the free speech of the subordinate or minority groups. To this end, it may resort to various contortions, such as portraying the hunters as the victims of harassment and converting the expressions of opinion of the hunt protesters into conduct. Similarly, women are consistent when they support antipornography laws and oppose hunter harassment laws. In both cases they argue for their right not to be silenced in speaking out against exploiters who objectify women or animals in very similar manner.[32]

Concerning women, there seems to be a change in the air that may or may not be short-lived. The historic Butler ruling in Canada may pave the way for new antipornography legislation; there is a greater awareness of sexual harassment issues after some recent high-profile cases and an apparent change of heart at the ACLU;[33] and new anti-stalking laws will finally offer some urgently needed protection to women often pursued to death by ex-husbands and boyfriends (Holstrom 1992). However, it is already expected that the constitutionality of these laws will be challenged. Unfortunately, animal advocates have recently lost on appeal some legal battles they had won in lower courts.[34]

At the same time we see the phenomenon of successful women adopting the standards of men with a vengeance. Will women's march to power ascendancy, won against all odds, mean that they too will choose to flaunt their preferences for red meat, animal skin, sport hunting, and even bullfighting?[35] As women are swelling the ranks of biomedical science, many have adopted the practice of animal experimentation.[36] Will animal exploitation become the ultimate symbol of equality with the white male? Or will the rising number of women attorneys change the way the law treats both women and animals?

Notes

I would like to acknowledge Carol Adams for her encouragement and insistence that I write this article. I would also like to thank the anonymous reviewers for helpful suggestions and Josephine Donovan, Susanne Kappeler, and Katherine Malin for their close readings of my article.

1. The language of rights has been criticized by feminists as being patriarchal, but it is embedded in the legal system and stamped on our consciousness. As different ways of thinking also become officially accepted, the word "rights" may change its connotation. In this article it is used as a convenient shorthand to convey a broader set of ideas—including care, consideration, liberation, and legal standing.

2. Such as "bitch," "swine," "rat," "cow," "mole," "shark," and, of course, "beast," "brute," "animal," and "meat." See the Dunayer article in this volume.

3. I use the word "animals" as a shorthand for "nonhuman animals," as in everyday speech.

4. Lack of standing means roughly that the law does not recognize animals as entities that have interests in themselves. Animals have no personhood, although corporations currently do. Recent cases brought by animal rights activists have attempted to establish the standing of animal protection/rights organizations to sue on behalf of animals, but, after some initial success at the lower court level, these efforts have failed. See notes 5 and 32.

5. The case against USDA, *Animal Legal Defense Fund v. Madigan*, 781 F. Supp. 797 (D.D.C. 1992), was brought by the Animal Legal Defense Fund (ALDF), the Humane Society of United States (HSUS), and two other individuals in federal court. USDA lost at the lower court level, but the decision was overturned on appeal, in *Animal Defense Fund v. Mike Espy*, 23 F.3d 496 (D.C. Cir. 1994). The court did not recognize that the organizations or the individuals, one of whom was a researcher, had standing to sue because they could not show they were directly harmed. Note that the species excluded from the rudimentary protection of the Animal Welfare Act comprise the vast majority (85 percent) of laboratory animals.

6. See, for example, the Utah Code Ann. Sec. 76-10-2002 (Michie 1990).

7. *Employment Div., Dept. of Human Resources of Oregon v. Smith*, 494 U.S. 872 (1990). See also "Hialeah's Affront to Religious Freedom," *The Chicago Tribune*, editorial, 8 November 1992.

8. According to Heidi Prescott of the Fund for Animals, by 1993, 48 states had already passed hunter harassment laws. Connecticut's law, which had been overturned on constitutional grounds, has been redrafted and upheld in *State v. Ball*, 226 Conn. 265 (1993). The constitutionality of the Montana

law was upheld by that state's supreme court, *State v. Lilburn*, 875 P.2d 1036 (Mont. 1994), but the Idaho Supreme Court struck down Idaho's hunter harassment law, *State v. Casey*, 876 P.2d 138 (Idaho 1994). See Motavalli (1994). The Recreational Hunting Safety and Preservation Act of 1994, Pub. L. No. 103-322, which was inserted in the "crime bill," provides a penalty up to $5,000 for anyone who "intentionally [engages] in any physical conduct that significantly hinders a lawful hunt." When physical contact involves violence or threat of violence, the penalty is $10,000.

9. "Church and State: Necessary Sacrifice?" *The Economist*, 14 November 1992, World Politics and Current Affairs section.

10. *Church of the Lukumi Babalu Aye, Inc., et al. v. City of Hialeah* 61 U.S.L.W. 4587 (U.S. 1993). See also "Excerpts from Supreme Court Opinions on the Ritual Sacrifice of Animals," *The New York Times*, 11 June 1993, Section 1.

11. Although the Hialeah decision was unanimous, three justices expressed disagreement with the Smith ruling (see note 7). In a concurring opinion, Justice Blackmun, joined by Justice O'Connor, wrote: "This case does not present, and therefore I decline to reach, the question whether the Free Exercise Clause would require a religious exemption from a law that sincerely pursued the goal of protecting animals from cruel treatment."

12. For an analysis of the tensions between feminism and liberalism when sex is involved, see Leidholdt and Raymond (1990).

13. The Hialeah case is another example of mixed alliances: The ACLU and various Christian and Jewish organizations sided with the Santeria Church of Lukumi Babalu Aye in support of animal sacrifices as religious expression. Predictably, many animal welfare and animal rights organizations sided with the City of Hialeah. The latter, as the Supreme Court noted, not only deems the killing of animals for hunting, fishing, and food as necessary, but did not even consider the use of live rabbits for training greyhounds as animal cruelty.

14. For a critique of the opposition to antipornography legislation, see MacKinnon (1990).

15. This point is made often in MacKinnon's writings.

16. See Bass (1992) and note 8 for an update on the Connecticut law.

17. National Public Radio, *Morning Edition*, 3 December 1992.

18. Flag burning also involves action, but is still protected as speech. I credit Josephine Donovan for this observation, which is considered at the end of this section.

19. Animal rights activists are habitually derided as "Bambi lovers" or "bunny huggers" when the object is to protect the practice of animal killing for sport or food. The epithets are meant to imply that the activists are overly emotional and wrongly anthropomorphize animals. On the other hand, when the issue is animal experimentation, the epithet of choice is "terrorists." The term "terrorist" was given official sanction by the then Secretary of Health and Human Services Louis Sullivan, who used it on the

eve of the historic March for the Animals at Washington, D.C., in June 1990. This characterization prompted a prominent animal rights leader to quip, "We used to be little old ladies in tennis shoes, now we have become terrorists!"

20. This is the official explanation given to justify these courses. Animal advocates charge that the courses are used to recruit children into hunting and trapping activities.

21. The discussion in this paragraph has been influenced by and closely follows the arguments presented by University of Chicago Professor Cass Sunstein in a seminar on Pornography and the First Amendment given 14 April 1993 at the University of Michigan. For a detailed exposition, see Sunstein (1993b).

22. For a detailed history and analysis of the University of Wisconsin's code in light of recent court decisions, see Siegel (1993).

23. The case against the hunt protesters who peacefully followed hunters in the woods of the Pinckney State Recreation Area, Michigan, in October 1992 was dismissed on a technicality. Judge Bronson of the 14th District Court did find that the hungers were interfered with and harassed, but ruled that they were not engaging in lawful hunt at the time because they were illegally present in the woods before the posted park hours of 8:00 a.m. to 10:00 p.m. The prosecution argued that the hunters were exempt from the posted restrictions, but the assistant park manager, called by the defense, testified that there was no such written exemption, and that the park rules were selectively enforced for nonhunters only.

24. I do not mean to compare hunting and abortion here, but only to compare how women and hunters fare under law when faced with protests of their activities. There were two possible interpretations of the Supreme Court decision in *Bray v. Alexandria Women's Health Clinic*, 113 S. Ct. 753 (U.S. 1992): one was that a federal civil rights law could not be used to protect abortion clinics against protesters who illegally blocked access (Shatz 1993); the other was that the federal civil rights laws *could* be used in this way, provided the standard of proof was held high (Pines 1993). The scene changed drastically in 1994, when two physicians performing abortions were murdered by abortion foes: the Supreme Court held that the federal Racketeer-Influenced and Corrupt Organizations (RICO) Act could be used against antiabortion or pro-life groups that conspire to close down abortion clinics, *National Organization for Women v. Scheidler* 114 S. Ct. 798 (1994); and Congress passed broad legislation to protect abortion clinics, Freedom of Access to Clinic Entrances Act, 18 U.S.C.S. Sec. 248 (1994).

25. A homeless person "living in the shelter system" of Ann Arbor, as he described it, told me at the annual vegan food sampling of Washtenaw Citizens for Animal Rights (March 1993) that several persons who were vegetarians for religious reasons found there was not much they could eat there.

26. "US Censored News of Pilots' Pre-raid Porno Movies," *The Reuter Library Report*, 26 January 1991.

27. Elliott-Larsen Civil Rights Act, Article 1, Mich. Comp. Laws Ann. Sec. 37.2103 (West 1985).

28. "Canada's High Court Upholds Anti-pornography Law," *The Atlanta Journal and Constitution*, 28 February 1992, Foreign News section.

29. Lois Forer has documented, from her experience as a judge, that women, children, and the elderly are not treated equally in the courts. See Forer (1991).

30. Mich. Comp. Laws Ann. Sec. 300.262a (West Supp. 1992).

31. Mich. Comp. Laws Ann. Sec. 750.520L (West 1991).

32. For parallels in the objectification of women and animals, see Adams (1990).

33. The ACLU changed its position regarding the definition of sexual harassment. It no longer requires that the harassing behavior be directed toward a particular individual (Gailey 1993).

34. In *Animal Legal Defense Fund v. Secretary of Agriculture*, 813 F. Supp. 882 (D.D.C. 1993), the Animal Legal Defense Fund won its case against the USDA in the matter of the USDA's failure to enforce requirements of exercise for dogs and environment enrichment for primates. A year later, this decision was overturned, *Animal Legal Defense Fund, Inc. v. Espy*, 29 F.3d 720 (D.C. Cir. 1994). See "ALDF Forces USDA to Protect Animals in Labs," *The Animals' Advocate*, Spring 1993; and "Appeals Court Reverses Key Decisions," *The Animals' Advocate*, Fall 1994.

35. Spain has now its first woman bullfighter (Hayley 1993).

36. Observation based on my ongoing monitoring of animal research at the University of Michigan from documents obtained through the Freedom of Information Act.

References

Adams, Carol J. 1990. *The Sexual Politics of Meat.* New York: Continuum.

Bass, Carole. 1992. Protesters Dodge Acquittal to Challenge Harassment Law. *The Connecticut Law Tribune*, 12 October.

Beeston, Richard. 1992. Serb learnt rape and murder, *The Times* (UK), 14 December.

Castaneda, Carol. 1992. Carelessness, Hunters Equal a Deadly Season. *USA Today*, 2 December, News section.

DePass, Darlene. 1992. Maryland Hunters Feed Venison to Poor. *The Washington Times*, 16 December, Part B.

Farnham, Alan. 1992. A Bang That's Worth Ten Billion Bucks. *Fortune*, 9 March.

Fausto-Sterling, Anne. 1985. *Myths of Gender.* New York: Basic Books.

Forer, Lois. 1991. *Unequal Protection.* New York: Norton.

Furfaro, John, and Maury Josephson. 1992. Sexual Harassment. *New York Law Journal*, 4 September, Labor Relations section.

Gailey, Philip. 1993. ACLU Weakens Its Commitment to Free Speech. *St. Petersburg Times*, 11 April, Perspective section.

Goodrich, Lawrence. 1992. Florida Court Overturns Spiritual-Healing Case. *The Christian Science Monitor*, 6 July.

Giobbe, Evelina. 1990. Confronting the Liberal Lies about Prostitution. In Leidholdt and Raymond, 67–81.

Hazard, Holly. 1992. Downed Animals: Historic Bill in the Making. *The Animals' Advocate*, Winter, 2–3.

Hayley, Julia. 1993. Spain's Only Woman Bullfighter. *Reuters*, 18 February.

Hentoff, Nat. 1992. *Free Speech for Me But Not for Thee*. New York: Harper Collins.

Holmstrom, David. 1992. Efforts to Protect Women from "Stalkers" Gain Momentum at State, Federal Levels. *Christian Science Monitor*, 22 December.

Humane Farming Association. 1994. October 1994 mailing of the Humane Farming Action Fund, legislative branch of the Humane Farming Association.

Husar, John. 1992. Protesters Try, Hunters Keep Cool. *Chicago Tribune*, 8 October, Sports section.

Kaminer, Wendy. 1992. Feminists Against the First Amendment. *Atlantic Monthly*, November.

Kheel, Marti. 1990. Ecofeminism and Deep Ecology: Reflections on Identity and Difference. In *Reweaving the World*, ed. Irene Diamond and Gloria Feman Orenstein. San Francisco: Sierra Club Books.

Landsberg, Michele. 1993. Supreme Court Porn Ruling Is Ignored. *The Toronto Star*, 14 December, D1.

Leidholdt, Dorchen, and Janice Raymond, eds. 1990. *The Sexual Liberals and the Attack on Feminism*. New York: Pergamon.

MacKinnon, Catherine. 1987. *Feminism Unmodified*. Cambridge: Harvard University Press.

———. 1989. *Toward a Feminist Theory of the State*. Cambridge: Harvard University Press.

———. 1990. Liberalism and the Death of Feminism. In Leidholdt and Raymond, 3–13.

Matsuda, Mari. 1989. Public Response to Racist Speech: Considering the Victim's Story. *Michigan Law Journal* 87(8):2320–81.

Motavalli, Jim. 1994. Hunters' Free Speech. *E*, October, In Brief.

Mueller, Gene. 1992. Rightists Wrong to Disrupt Hunts. *The Washington Times*, 23 December, Part D.

Paglia, Camille. 1992. The Return of Carrie Nation: Feminists Catharine MacKinnon and Andrea Dworkin. *Playboy*, October.

Pines, Deborah. 1993. Leeway Is Seen in Rulings on Abortion Protests. *New York Law Journal*, 22 April.

Plevan, Bettina, and Seth Popper. 1992. An Expert Can Gauge Perceptions: Harassment. *The National Law Journal*, 9 November.

Roman, Nancy. 1992a. Ritual Sacrifice Poses Hazards, High Court Told. *The Washington Times*, 5 November, Part A.

——. 1992b. Harassment Headlines Help Muddy Definition of Crime. *The Washington Post*, 13 December, Part A.

Seelye, Katharine Q. 1994. Protecting the Targets of Protests: A Debate Now Shifts to Hunting. *The New York Times*, 11 June, Section 1.

Shatz, Steven F. 1993. Misconstruction of Reconstruction; Supreme Court Gives Operation Rescue a Green Light. *Legal Times*, 5 April, Points of View section.

Siegel, Barry. 1993. Fighting Words. *Los Angeles Times*, 28 March, Magazine section.

Sunstein, Cass R. 1993a. Pornography and the First Amendment. Seminar given at the University of Michigan Law School, 14 April 1993.

——. 1993b. *The Partial Constitution.* Cambridge: Harvard University Press.

US Censored News of Pilots' Pre-raid Porno Movies. *The Reuter Library Report*, 26 January 1991.

Varchaver, Nicholas. 1992. Protecting Women from Themselves. *The American Lawyer*, September 1992.

6
Gary L. Francione

Abortion and Animal Rights: Are They Comparable Issues?

Abortion is a terribly complicated legal and social issue, and so is the issue of animal rights. Indeed, these topics have accounted for a great deal of recent writing in the fields of moral philosophy and applied ethics, social theory, and feminist studies. Although some feminists who support the right to terminate pregnancy have voiced strong support for animal rights, many others have refused to commit themselves or, worse yet, have indicated hostility to animal rights because they believe that recognition of animal rights will be one step down the road toward recognition of fetal rights.

Similarly, although some animal rights advocates are staunch supporters of a woman's right to choose to terminate her pregnancy, many animal rights advocates either are reluctant to express a view on abortion ("my issue is animal rights") or, worse yet, are opposed to freedom of choice on the ground that if animal life should be protected, then the argument for fetal protection is even stronger.

The present stand-off between advocates of animal rights and supporters of the right to choose can be traced to the fact that opponents of choice claim that the arguments advanced by animal advocates apply equally to fetuses, and that failing to apply such arguments is simply irrational on the part of animal advocates. For example, Peter Singer argues that nonhumans, like humans, are sentient and, by virtue of that sentience alone, are entitled to have their interests treated equally in the utilitarian balancing process (Singer 1991). Anti-choice advocates claim that if sentience, in and of itself, is sufficient to establish moral consideration for nonhumans, then fetuses (at least some of whom are sentient) are entitled to similar moral consideration. Indeed, opponents of choice view the failure to apply animal protection views to fetuses as demonstrative of misanthropy on the part of animal rights advocates.

In this essay, I want to examine the two primary theories that have been articulated in the literature to advance the cause of animal protection. It is my view that although both theories are properly applied to issues involving nonhuman animals, they cannot automatically be applied to the abortion context without recognizing that there are very significant differences between these two moral situations. When a vivisector seeks to exploit a nonhuman in a biomedical experiment, the situation is much more analogous to one of child abuse, not abortion. The state can regulate vivisection—and child abuse—in a way that does not fundamentally intrude on the basic privacy rights of vivisectors or parents. The state cannot, however, regulate abortion in the absence of a patriarchal intrusion of the law into a woman's body, and we generally do not tolerate that sort of bodily intrusion anywhere else in the law.[1]

That is, even if we grant that the fetus is sentient (at least at some phases of its existence), or that a fetus is a rightholder in the sense that philosopher Tom Regan (1983) intends, we are still confronted by the question as to who is the appropriate moral agent to resolve any conflict between the primary rightholder (the woman) and the subservient rightholder (the fetus).[2] The only choices are to let the primary rightholder decide, or to relegate the responsibility to a legal system dominated by actors and ideologies that are inherently sexist. In the abortion context, there are no other choices, as there are when the state attempts to regulate animal abuse or the abuse of minor children.

In this essay, I examine briefly the *consequentialist* and *deontological* views advanced by animal advocates[3] and argue that neither framework really can address the moral issue of abortion, because abortion presents a unique moral issue. That is, there is a fundamental difference between the abortion issue and the other moral contexts in which we generally seek to employ these frameworks. This difference does not mean that our discourse about the morality of abortion ends; it means only that our reliance on moral theories of animal protection do not commit us to reject abortion on the same grounds.

I should state at the outset that I anticipate that many feminists will object to my focus on the welfarist or rights structure as being itself patriarchal, both as a matter of history and theory. For example, many feminist theorists reject animal rights because a right is a male-created concept that reflects the hierarchical thinking so typical of the male mind (Glendon 1991). Although I embrace such alternatives as the ethics of care as expressions of the highest form of moral thought, I am concerned that we not reject traditional moral thought on the matter for two reasons.

First, it is my view that the source of a moral concept tells us little, if anything, about the sexist or nonsexist status of that concept. Virtually every intellectual concept used in our culture was formulated originally by white men, who held (and to a very considerable degree still hold) exclusive control over education and publication. That origin, however, does not mean that every concept is itself patriarchal in some way apart from its admittedly patriarchal origin. The concept of rights can be used in a patriarchal way to oppress; but then, so can any other moral concept that seeks political expression, including the ethic of care.

Second, and more important, however, is my view that in a diverse and highly populous political system, there must be some mechanism that can be used to resolve the inevitable conflicts that will arise among individuals, irrespective of whether the society in question is matriarchal or patriarchal. Many feminists argue that the ethics of care should replace what they view as the patriarchal notion of rights; that is, that a collective notion of concern, not based on competition and conflict, is preferable to rights theory. In many ways, this argument is somewhat similar (albeit different in material respects) to Marx's critique of rights. Marx believed that the concept of rights was bourgeois because it reinforced the notion of people as individuals in a society that should (and, if historical materialism is true, will) regard itself collectively.

One day, if we ever achieve a society without sexism, racism, homophobia, and economic injustice, perhaps the whole concept of the individual will, like Marx's state, "wither away" and be an unnecessary component of moral theory. For the foreseeable future, however, individual conflicts are likely to arise in any society, and there must be some set of principles that may be used to evaluate claims and to resolve conflicts. Even in a matriarchal society that employs an ethic of care, there will still be notions of individuality that delimit intrusions on one's body by men or women. The concept of the individual is here to stay; it may find itself conceptually melted into a more communitarian society in which many *individualistic* values are traded away for the sake of the whole, but there will still be some individual left—however meager—whose individuality will in some sense be defined by laws that limit personal intrusion.

In short, something like rights is necessary, and cannot be rejected out of hand. Even if we did achieve a society even more utopian than those being proposed by our few remaining idealists, it is highly improbable that we will eradicate conflict entirely. And when conflict does arise, we will need some mechanism to resolve it. This mechanism may be based on collective consequences without consideration of the individual, or it may be based on individual concerns. If the latter is chosen, it seems that something very much like rights will be needed.

Sentience, Animal Welfare, and Animal Rights

In 1976, Australian philosopher Peter Singer produced *Animal Liberation*, a work that has been credited widely with renewing interest in the topic of animal rights. Although the importance of Singer's work may not be underestimated, it should also not be forgotten that this book had nothing to do with animal rights. That is, Singer presented a consequential moral position; specifically, he presented a utilitarian version of consequentialism that had been espoused by Bentham in the nineteenth century, except that Bentham viewed pleasure as the intrinsic value to be maximized while Singer regards preference-satisfaction as the primary value to be maximized. Bentham argued that it was irrational not to include nonhuman animals in using the utilitarian calculus to determine the morality of various actions. According to Bentham, the question is not whether animals can reason or talk, but whether they can suffer (Bentham 1789, chap. 17, sec. 1).

Neither Bentham nor Singer argued that animals (or humans) were entitled to moral rights as a matter of consequential theory; rather, both philosophers maintained that because nonhumans were, like humans, sentient, both types of beings should have their interests considered in determining what was the best moral outcome (greatest aggregate pleasure or preference-satisfaction) for the largest number. Humans and nonhumans alike were to be counted as "beings" for purposes of the recognition and respect of these interests. The approach posited by Bentham/Singer is quite consistent with the philosophical doctrine of animal welfare—that is, that humans may justifiably exploit animals as long as human or animal suffering is considered as part of the utilitarian calculus.[4]

Those who accept the Bentham/Singer position on the moral significance of sentience often argue that if it is irrational not to include the interests of nonhumans in the utilitarian calculus, it is similarly irrational to exclude human fetuses. There are at least two responses to this argument. It is not clear whether and to what degree human fetuses are sentient. Although there is little doubt that second- and third-trimester fetuses exhibit signs of sentience, the overwhelming number of nontherapeutic abortions are performed during the first trimester, and there is substantial evidence that there is little, if any, sentience during this period. If human fetuses in the first trimester experience little (if any) pain, then there is no sentience about which to be concerned and which must be weighed in the utilitarian calculus. In any event, it would be difficult to compare the sentience of a first-trimester fetus with that of a human being or a dog.

Moreover, the sentience argument neglects an important aspect of modern animal protection theory: rights advocates do not regard sentience as playing the same theoretical role. For example, philosopher Tom Regan uses sentience only as a starting point in his theory. Regan claims that a being must have a psychological status sufficiently complex so that we may say that the being has preferences, fears, hopes, mood changes, etc. Regan calls such an individual the "subject-of-a-life" and claims that such attributes constitute a sufficient but not necessary condition for a being to be said to have moral rights. If we rely on the rights response, however, we may be able to avoid some of the difficulties raised by exclusive reliance on the sentience argument. That is, it is at least arguable that even if some fetuses are sentient, at least some of those lack in salient respects the very characteristics that rights theorists see as sufficient for status as a subject-of-a-life or as a rightholder. Under a rights view, a fetus arguably cannot be analogized to a primate that is to be used in experimentation or to a cow that is to be consumed by human beings, because the fetus does not possess the qualities normally associated with personhood.[5] Of course, the rights theorist can argue (as Regan does) that fetuses may have moral rights even if they are not subjects-of-a-life because that criterion is only a sufficient and not a necessary one for having rights.

It should be noted that neither Regan nor Singer uses his respective theory to condemn abortion. Singer openly endorses choice and, when justified by the consequences, even infanticide (Singer and Kuhse 1985). Regan argues that the subject-of-a-life criterion is inexact and that in the case of newborn infants and fetuses of mature gestation, we should probably err in favor of granting rights. But that would only mean that there was a conflict of rights between the mother and fetus. Moreover, Regan makes it clear that fetuses in early term do not have moral rights.

The Problems of the Prevailing Theories and the Politics of Abortion

Whether one chooses a consequentialist approach such as Singer's, or a deontological approach, such as Regan's, it must be understood that these theoretical frameworks have been developed largely in contexts in which there are conflicts between separate entities. In particular, these viewpoints address what we should do when we are confronted with a conflict between, for example, a chimpanzee who is to be used in experimentation and the vivisector who seeks to use the chimpanzee. Alternatively, these moral frameworks may help us to determine whether and when the state may intervene to protect a child from an abusive parent.

As such, both Singer's and Regan's approaches may help us to find our way out of the moral thicket when we are confronted with a conflict between two separate and independent entities. Abortion, however, presents us with a completely unique moral issue that is replicated nowhere else in nature. That is, in the abortion context, the conflict is between a woman and a being who resides in her body. Vivisection should not be viewed as analogous to abortion; it should be viewed as similar to infanticide or murder. In my view, this feature of abortion makes it very different from the normal moral conflicts that we may try to resolve by recourse to moral theories concerning our treatment of animals.

A critic may respond that this seemingly peculiar feature of abortion is morally irrelevant to the ultimate determination of the abortion issue. That is, if the fetus is sentient (in Singer's view) or is the subject-of-a-life (in Regan's view), then its sentience or inherent value should matter as much as the sentience or inherent value of any other being ought to matter. But this criticism fails to understand the politics of abortion, the morality of privacy, and the mechanisms that are required to vindicate fetal life.

Even before *Roe v. Wade* (1973), American law recognized—correctly in my view—that there were areas of privacy that were simply off limits to governmental control. For example, basic principles of criminal liability have generally rejected imposing culpability on human thought. The privacy principle in this situation arguably derives from a combination of the First Amendment protection of people's right to think (and say) what they choose, as well as from a general revulsion to punishing people for what goes on in their heads alone. Similarly, in *Griswold v. Connecticut* (1965), the Supreme Court held that marital privacy was violated by a state law that forbade the use of contraceptives. In *Stanley v. Georgia* (1969), the Court, relying on the right to receive information and to be free of governmental intrusions into one's privacy, forbade criminalizing the possession of obscene material for private use.

The underlying theory present in all of these decisions is the notion that it is sometimes impossible to enforce certain laws without committing heinous (and morally unacceptable) intrusions into the realm of personal privacy. If the state is going to criminalize possession of obscene materials for private use, or the use of contraceptives, these laws can be enforced only by having the constable stand in the bedroom—an intrusion that I would hope most of us would see as completely inconsistent with the existence of a free society.

That is precisely why the Court decided *Roe* in the way that it did; in order to enforce abortion laws (especially in the first trimester of pregnancy), the state would have to intrude in a way that is arguably as repulsive as the intrusion in *Griswold* or *Stanley* would be; the state would have to "invade" and manipulate the body of the woman in order to vindicate any interest it had in the protection of fetal life. In *Roe*, the Court drew the line at various trimesters and held that at certain points relative to the line the state's interest in protecting fetal life could justify a violation of the woman's privacy (at least in certain circumstances).[6]

The same invasions of personal privacy are not involved, however, when the state seeks to protect the well-being of a minor. That is, if a parent is abusing a minor, the state can come in and remove the

Abortion and Animal Rights

child from the hazardous situation without literally entering the parent's body or otherwise mandating the odious manipulation of the woman's body in order to protect the well-being of the child. Similarly, if the state seeks to protect nonhuman animals, it can do so without crossing the privacy line that is crossed in the abortion context.[7]

Those who seek to argue that issues of animal exploitation are no different from abortion not only neglect the clearly empirically different nature of the issues involved; they also fail to understand how moral decisions are played out in the context of other moral principles that are often ignored. To put it another way: questions about abortion are not decided in a philosophical vacuum, and careful consideration of the consequences of political oppression of the disenfranchised is morally necessary in order to resolve these conflicts.

This is not to deny that there are important political dimensions that accompany our attempts to apply philosophical theories to "balance" animal interests against human interests. The philosophical "balancing" apparatus may be theoretically correct, but the process can almost never work fairly because of the political status of nonhumans. Animals are regarded as the property of humans and incapable of having rights because they are property; similarly, humans have rights—and most notably, they have the right to own and use private property. In human/animal conflicts, the human is usually seeking to exercise property rights over the animal. In any "balancing" situation, the animal will almost always be the loser. So the philosophy looks great, but the results are less than desirable. Nevertheless, should the state choose to do so, it could protect at least some animal interests over at least some human interests simply by removing animals from abusive situations. Such action would arguably violate the human's property interest in the animal, but the regulatory action would not require that the state invade the privacy of the human in the way it does when it prohibits or restricts abortion.

The application of utilitarian or deontological theories cannot ignore the reality that when a conflict is presented between a woman and a fetus, there are, as a practical matter, only two ways in which the issue may be resolved. One of the two parties involved in the conflict may make the decision, and since it is difficult for fetuses to make decisions, the woman is the only other available decision maker. Alternatively, we may have the state make the decision through laws that prohibit (or permit) abortions. Many opponents of abortion appear to think that this second resolution is acceptable:

that the state, through the political process, should be able to make the decision as to whether the woman can terminate the pregnancy.

If the decision-making power is relegated to the state, the state will probably enforce that power by literally entering the body of the woman and dictating what she can and cannot do with her body and her reproductive processes. The state can act only by invading that woman's privacy in a most basic way, and the state must proceed in this manner given the patriarchal nature of our legal system. This is very different from the state removing a minor child from an abusive situation where, although family disruption may result, the level of state intrusion is qualitatively different and the insidious effects of patriarchy are at least ostensibly less apparent.

Moreover, the current political climate surrounding abortion demonstrates more than ever that even when we accord reproductive rights to women, those rights, which are interpreted within the strictures of a patriarchal legal system, are precarious at best. It must be remembered, for example, that irrespective of the progressive nature of *Roe*, the Supreme Court was careful to articulate that the right to terminate pregnancy belonged to a woman *and her doctor*. Similarly, the abortion litigation of the recent decade has continually encroached on the right to choose through the adoption of the "undue burden" test. That is, the Court has generally upheld state prohibitions on the right to choose as long as those restrictions do not impose "undue burdens" on the freedom to choose. The problem is that this standard has been used to justify everything from parental and spousal notification to waiting periods. We have absolutely no reason to believe that women will ever enjoy privacy over their reproductive systems if the legitimacy of abortion is left to the political or legal systems.

Conclusion

Contrary to what the Reagan/Bush administrations would have had us believe, virtually all progressives—women and men alike—recognize that abortion raises serious moral issues. It was not my intention in this essay to argue that abortion should be treated as a non-issue. Rather, I have argued that a commitment to animal rights does not necessarily lead to a rejection of freedom to choose abortion, because animal exploitation and abortion present different moral dilemmas. In the former, there is a conflict between two discrete individuals: a human being and an animal that the human seeks to exploit. I argue that the state can protect the animal's interest without invading the privacy of the human in a manner that we would see as repulsive or as inimical to our basic liberties.

I also argue that abortion presents a unique moral dilemma, in that even if we accept that fetuses have rights, the conflict is between the primary rightholder—the woman—and the subservient rightholder, who resides in her body. In these circumstances, someone must resolve the conflict, and if that task is relegated to the state, the task of fetal protection can be accomplished only through the state's literal entry into the body of the primary rightholder.

Notes

I am deeply indebted to suggestions that I received from my colleague and partner, Professor Anna Charlton, codirector of the Rutgers Animal Rights Law Clinic. This essay is dedicated to Carol Adams, who got the ball rolling.

1. I am aware that some feminists do not accept privacy as a legitimate ground for reproductive freedom. See, e.g., MacKinnon (1989, 184–94). Although I think MacKinnon's arguments are interesting, I do not agree that the right to privacy necessarily means that no social change is required, nor do I accept her argument that a right of privacy means that "women are guaranteed by the public no more than what they can get in private—what they can extract through their intimate associations with men" (1989, 191). I do agree, however, that at present, our legal concept of privacy is impoverished for many of the reasons that MacKinnon states. It is at least conceivable to have a legal system that recognizes certain privacy rights and certain other rights that guarantee the exercise of those privacy rights. That is, the right of privacy could protect the right to terminate pregnancy at the same time that the legal system recognized that if privacy rights are to be meaningful, then public resources should be used to ensure that all women could meaningfully exercise those rights.

2. My distinction between the woman as primary rightholder and the fetus as subservient rightholder finds historic support throughout legal doctrine. For example, abortions have almost always been permitted when the life of the mother is at stake.

3. Consequentialism is the doctrine that says that the moral quality of actions is dependent in some way on the consequences of particular actions or actions of a general type. For example, one version of consequentialism is utilitarianism, which, although formulated in various ways, holds that the morally right act is that which maximizes happiness (or pleasure, liberty, wealth, etc.) for the greatest number. Act utilitarianism states that the principle of utility is to be applied directly to individual acts. Rule utilitarianism states that the principle of utility is to be applied to acts of a type. That is, an act utilitarian might be inclined to tell a lie if the consequences of tell-

ing the truth in that particular situation were disastrous. A rule utilitarian might argue that lying as a general matter will destabilize society and have even worse consequences than telling the truth in the particular situation; so a lie would not be required, or justified, under rule utilitarianism.

Deontological thinking formulates criteria for the moral quality of acts on considerations other than consequences. For example, many rights theorists argue that people (or animals) have rights because of their inherent value as individuals and not because of consequential considerations.

4. The fact that utilitarian theory may be used to justify animal exploitation is demonstrated by the work of R. G. Frey (1983).

5. Regan does argue, however, that being the subject-of-a-life is a sufficient but not necessary condition of possessing inherent value, and he argues that fetuses are entitled to moral consideration (1983, 319–20).

6. Of course, this is not to say that *Roe* was an ideal decision; indeed, there are many grounds upon which to criticize *Roe*. In my judgment, the most serious problem with the decision is that it dealt more with the right of physicians to perform abortions rather than the right of women to get them. Moreover, the Court provided protection to the decision made by the woman and her doctor.

7. I recognize that certain religions recognize the right to inflict serious corporeal punishment on children, and resent any state interference aimed at preventing abuse to the children. Putting aside the rather unusual views held by this relatively small group of persons, the state interference involved is still not as intrusive as state-mandated manipulation of the body.

References

Bentham, J. 1789. *The Principles of Morals and Legislation*. London: Methuen.

Dworkin, Ronald M. 1993. *Life's Dominion*. New York: Knopf.

Frey, R. G. 1983. *Rights, Killing & Suffering*. Oxford: Clarendon Press.

Glendon, Mary Ann. 1991. *Rights Talk*. New York: Macmillan.

MacKinnon, Catharine A. 1989. *Toward a Feminist Theory of the State*. Cambridge: Harvard University Press.

Regan, Tom. 1983. *The Case for Animal Rights*. Berkeley: University of California.

Singer, Peter. 1991. *Animal Liberation*. 2d ed. New York: New York Review of Books. Originally published in 1976.

Singer, Peter, and Helga Kuhse. 1985. *Should the Baby Live?* New York: Oxford University Press.

Tribe, Laurence. 1990. *Abortion: The Clash of Absolutes*. New York: W. W. Norton.

Wenz, Peter S. 1992. *Abortion Rights as Religious Freedom*. Philadelphia: Temple University Press.

Part 2

Alternative Stories

7

Linda Vance

Beyond Just-So Stories:
Narrative, Animals, and Ethics

Introduction

A naturalist does not toss stones into a pond to make the frogs "do something." Even if it's only a vernal pond, only a silted puddle lined with rotting oak leaves and pine needles. Even though it's little more than a depression where runoff hesitates before soaking in or moving on. But I'm restless, impatient as the runoff, eager to be on my way, and my hand twitches greedily. I'm hungering to pick up a stone, turn it casually over in my fingers, and almost accidentally lob it into the deepest part of the pond.

I was drawn here by the absurd croaking. Rounding a corner of the road that meanders through the woodland park behind my home, I was greeted by a cacophonous chorus of grunts, groans, cackles, squawks, and caws. Could it be ducks, I wondered, as I approached the sound, a flock of ducks stopping on the way to a yet more northern pond? Or geese, perhaps? Or could I have stumbled onto a grand assembly of the Raven People? When I found the source, this tentative pond, I realized it was frogs, newly active in the warming spring day, not yet confident in their vocal abilities. And as soon as I came close, of course, the sound stopped. The rounded brown heads I had only just noticed bobbed quickly below the surface; on the far edge of the pond, I saw slim bronze bodies slip easily down the smooth muddy bank from the forest. Straining to peer beneath the surface, I could see them swim for the cover of the last slab of surface ice hovering precariously near the inlet. And then nothing: no sound, no movement.

So now I'm standing here alone beside the pond, on the margin of a thicket of raspberry canes, a thorny discouragement of my other desire, which is to lie down and watch the frogs at their face level. They are holding absolutely silent. I stand a while longer, scanning the leaves on the far bank for some errant croaker, imagining that if I can at least classify its species, I will be content. But there are no fugitive frogs, and my gaze wanders, climbing the pine tree up to the sky beyond. Faded muslin spring clouds drift across the chambray blue sky, now obscuring the sun, now revealing it. When the sun appears, it sparks the fernheads to brilliance, illuminates the mosses on the rocks and tree trunks, brings green to the world like a sneeze, sudden and unfamiliar. New Englanders in the springtime are connoisseurs of green, but language fails us: we can merely blink or wince at the apparition, saying "Green," "Oh, look, green," breathlessly, over and over, like an invocation, or an exhalation of hope, of trust in the air to come.

At the far end of the pond, a narrow channel draws the water slowly downward, and from somewhere along its lengths, just out of my range of vision, I hear a loud, grating croak. Have I missed the show? Have the frogs moved stealthily away from me, slinking across the muddied bottom one by one, as fluid as the water surrounding them? Is this my reward for restraint? But no. The first one may have been a scout, foolishly sounding an all clear, or maybe she simply goaded the others to bravery, but in any case a half dozen voices now rise to meet hers, then a dozen, then a score more, all absolutely out of time and out of harmony, like members of an orchestra who are inexplicably tuning their instruments each to a different key.

They'll get their chorus right soon enough, I suppose, and I, passing by, will cease to hear them, their well-practiced songs fading to the commonplace of background noise. Then one day the sound will have gone, will have shrunk and disappeared like the ephemeral pond that brought it to life. Perhaps I will note these facts, that the croaking has stopped, that the pond has shriveled, that a tiny ecosystem has vanished, that this small corner of the woods, the park, is less diverse than it was. Perhaps I will wonder about the frogs themselves, will worry whether they've found a new habitat. Or perhaps I will simply dismiss all thoughts of frogs from my mind. After all, it's a Hobbesian life for frogs in spring ponds: nasty, brutish, and short, just enough time to learn your song before you cease to sing it.

Let us assume that this is the whole story: Frogs are born, live, reproduce, and die. Humans enter the natural world, observe it, and move on, taking whatever moral lessons we find. So what is the lesson of the frog pond? That life is ephemeral, of course, although this is not a moral favored by people all too aware of mortality. I could stretch the story of the frogs out for a better one. Oh, the pond will dry up in a few weeks, I could tell you, but the runoff canals will remain wet through the summer, will be home to aquatic plants and black fly larvae, will be a watering spot for the deer and raccoons. That's a more popular moral: to everything there is a season. Or I could call on process models of ecosystems, describing to you the flow of energy that is the matrix of all life, the field in which a frog, or a human watcher, is only a momentary apparition. Everything flows, I'll tell you, and you will nod.

The problem with moral tales, of course, is that they require us to depart from the particular, and to chase after the general, universalizable truth. The frogs are effectively gone, then, long before the pond dries up; they disappear as soon as I impose a narrative on them. But the point of most human narrative, of course, is to illuminate the *human* experience, so it should come as no surprise that narratives about animals and nature tend to be human centered, or to exist for human edification.

If this human centeredness were only a curious feature of nature writing, an increasingly popular genre but a minor one nonetheless, it might not be cause for concern. But unfortunately, story-making is not so limited. One of the major contributions of postmodernism thus far has been to challenge us to recognize that all human knowledge is essentially narrative, just story in the making. We do not so much discover the natural world as we construct it; this is true whether we are nature writers or ecologists, environmental lawyers or ethicists, historians or geographers. We impose our cultural and descriptive narratives on the world like templates, text creating text.[1]

So if it is a feature of all these story-making activities that nature's particularity, and especially animals' particularity, is obscured, then there is cause for concern among all of us who care for animals as individual entities and not abstractions. In this essay I touch lightly on narratives from ecology and history, but my main focus, given my own cultural and disciplinary leanings, is on the narratives imposed on animals by ethics. In the next section, "Ethics Constructs the Animal," I hope to make evident that even the best-intentioned ethical narratives have "silenced" animals just as surely as similar ones have silenced women. This is a story in itself, and a discouraging one at that. But the following section, "Ethical Narratives," will, I hope, gather energy toward a "happy ending," exploring the potential of distinctly feminist ethical narratives for bringing voice to animals and the natural world. After all, until recently, women have been denied the chance to be the artisans who created the templates. But times have changed. So sharpen your carving tools. Put on your aprons. Clear a space. There will be work to do.

Ethics Constructs the Animal

Historian William Cronon, looking specifically at U.S. environmental history, has observed that there are three cherished narratives that students of the past impose on nature. In one version of American history, the narrative is an upbeat one of linear progress, the taming of wild nature and the triumph of humans. In a second version, the story line is similar but unfolds in a more dialectical manner: progress is periodically interrupted or set back when Nature rises on her haunches and challenges the human usurpers. Nonetheless, humans meet the challenge and become more heroic in so doing. The third story is a sad tale of declension: nature was fine until human populations began to alter it; now human acts have brought us, and the natural world, to the brink of destruction. In fact, in this version, it is precisely the first narrative, the tale of progress, that lured humans into a downward slide in the first place. What all these versions of history have in common is that they order facts and events along a temporal line with a fixed starting and ending point, which, not incidentally, are opposite from each other. In the first and second versions, things start off bad and get good; in the third version, they start good and get bad. This is a critical feature of narrative,

Cronon reminds us, whether of history or anything else. Stories, at least in American Anglo culture, have a telos or direction, with one event leading to another. To "work," a narrative needs to show change from its beginning point to its end point.

It isn't hard to guess which version of the past is most popular in the historical profession these days, since it's the same one that seems to hold sway on our collective American consciousness: human hubris has led us to make a mess of the planet, and we need to act fast to correct it. This is also, of course, the starting point for most environmental philosophers and ethicists, because the expectations of narrative structure govern our meaning-making efforts, too. We know how we want our stories to end: whatever our particular ethical persuasion, we all believe it will lead to "better" interactions between humans and the nonhuman world. By definition, then, our current interactions must be judged as potentially or demonstrably harmful. We are fallen humanity, with only a few visionaries to point the way to salvation.

Most ethical theories about animals reflect one of three ideological positions, each corresponding to one of these narratives: (1) humans have a right to exploit animals, and therefore either minimal or no obligations toward them; (2) humans have a right to exploit animals, but only to the extent that such exploitation will provide the greatest (human) benefit in the long run; and (3) humans have no right to exploit animals or to dominate nature, since we are merely a component part of nature, and to ignore that fact will lead us to our doom.

The first position has prevailed in Western culture for centuries, and in some ways hardly needs restating.[2] In contemporary times, it reflects the "progress" narrative: we have been put on earth for a purpose—that is, to subdue nature—and we are moving steadily toward achieving that end. Nature, in this story, is hostile and unyielding: it deserves to be tamed.

The second position is the anthropocentric utilitarian imperative toward nature; as a maxim, it might be characterized as "Dominate Wisely!" This stance is rapidly gaining most-favored-position status in environmental policymaking. Briefly characterized, it is the "dialectic" narrative, the "progress" story with some struggle, mistakes, failure, and redoubled effort thrown in to make the journey more intriguing. Here nature is a "worthy antagonist of civilization," requiring us to scope out the probable consequences of our actions, and to always watch out for trouble stirring at our flank.

The nondominance position is conceptually and practically the most far-reaching, and takes many forms. Sometimes characterized as *ecocentric* or *biocentric* (as, for example, with deep ecology and the land ethic) or *zoocentric* (as with animal liberation), or simply antianthropocentric (as with ecofeminism), nondominance positions are supported by a declensionist narrative, which moves nonhuman nature into a "noble victim" role.

These are the grand themes, the "big stories." Ethics also spins out lesser narratives, stories that operate within, and are influenced by, these larger spheres. Let me pursue this theme for awhile, examining how the three ideological positions and their supporting narratives shape the smaller stories we tell about humans and animals, and thus construct our interactions.

Small Tales 1: Progress

In dominationist fantasies, animals are good or bad, depending on whether they function usefully as instruments to human ends and/or property. Like women in masculinist fantasies, animals are seen as having no individuality, no significant life-plan, no preferences, and, ultimately, no real concerns. It is true, of course, that both our legal and ethical systems contain certain norms that govern the treatment of animals, but even haphazard scrutiny reveals the core assumption that animals are mere objects. For example, traditional Western ethical positions about animals are reflected in laws that categorize animals by the circumstances under which they may be killed: either they may never be killed, or they may be killed at specific times, or they may be killed when they behave in a specific way, or they may be killed at random. Songbirds, for instance, may never be killed; so-called game animals may be killed during prescribed seasons; predators like wolves, bears, mountain lions, and coyotes may be killed either during a designated season or when they "deserve it," that is, when they have become a threat to crops or livestock; and animals that are the property of humans (livestock, household pets, and lab animals) or which are a nuisance (rodents), or are simply abundant and "inconsequential" (frogs, mice, insects) may be killed at any time.[3] In the process of setting these limits on the killing of animals, laws (and by implication traditionalist ethics) construct a number of story lines about them: besides "good animals" and "bad animals," there can be too few, too many, or "just enough" animals; animals that count because they are beautiful or useful; and animals that *don't* count because they are useful. But the central story line behind all these is that animals are the individual or public property of humans, and their fate is ours to decide. We are on the road to progress; they had best stay out of it if they can't be of use.

Small Tales 2: Dialectics

Most contemporary environmental ethicists operate in opposition to the belief that nature is ours to exploit as we will; that belief is, in fact, the point of departure for most ethics, the "bad" situation that will be transformed into a "good" one if we will merely subscribe to the "right" ethical approach. In mainstream ethical circles, and in most environmental policymaking, the "right" approach is some variant on anthropocentric utilitarianism, wherein the alternatives to be chosen are those that will provide the greatest pleasure for the greatest number of humans. To the extent that this differs from a straight dominance approach, it does so because it recognizes some autonomy in nature: by the simple fact that nature is not endlessly bountiful and productive, it resists human domination, and must therefore be approached with some respect. Still, this is not so much because nature's essential otherness is recognized; instead, it is because failure to do so will imperil existing and future generations of humans.

Anthropocentric utilitarianism can justify both exploitative and protectionist practices in regards to animals. Some utilitarians, like Theodore Vitali, take the position that if meat consumption, or hunting, or vivisection, or extermination of predators will yield the greatest pleasure for the greatest number of humans, then their effects on animals are irrelevant. But it is also possible to argue *for* animal protection from a human-centered perspective. For example, one can oppose meat eating on the basis of its ill effects on human health, or on the human environment, or, for that matter, upon human spirit. We can say that hunting is wrong because it is a form of violence, which should be checked, rather than encouraged, if we hope for a truly peaceful society. We can make similar arguments about vivisection: that it does not in fact yield cures to human diseases; that the moral harm done to humans by treating fellow creatures callously outweighs the good; that the money involved would be better spent on prevention, etc. The problem with such arguments, however, is that they are merely factual and thus open to challenge on factual grounds, with moral issues taking a back seat.[4]

169
Beyond Just-So Stories

Anthropocentric utilitarianism shares a number of fantasies about animals with strict dominance. Once again, animals are characterized as "good animals" (those that increase human pleasure) vs. "bad animals" (those that increase human pain); there is an idea that there can be too few, too many, or just enough animals to serve human ends now and in the future; some animals are held to count for more than other animals in the satisfaction of human desires; and some animals are held not to count at all. Indeed, the only real difference between dominance theories and anthropocentric utilitarian theories is that the latter acknowledge the world does not consist of ever-expanding resources.

In anthropocentric narratives, then, humans are fallible. Greedy, or lacking foresight, or merely succumbing to temptation, we can make mistakes. Animals, therefore, are *more* than objects that can be used and discarded at will. They have symbolic significance as well, as markers in the human game of progress. Sometimes we make the wrong move with them and lose our turn, as is the case when human folly or error leads to a species' extinction; sometimes we land on a square that allows us to advance a number of places, as is the case when genetic engineering yields a "new and improved" lab rat. But in either case, animals are merely stepping stones on our way to our goals, and while our forward march may not always go smoothly (because of our mistakes, often pointed out to us by those animals), in the end, we will succeed.

Small Tales 3: Declension

Theorists who reject dominance and anthropocentrism may style themselves and their positions as biocentric, ecocentric, zoocentric, or simply antianthropocentric, but all have a common starting point: they see no reason why moral considerability should begin and end with humans. Instead, it should extend to animals, to ecosystems, even to biochemical processes, not merely as an addendum to humanism, but as an alternative.[5] The arguments are many and varied, but underlying them all is a sobering "truth": traditional attitudes of dominance have led us to the wholesale slaughter of billions of animals, and have led the world to the brink of ecological disaster. There is no time for half measures; if we do not completely reverse our ways, we are doomed.

In these ethics, animals (or ecosystems or processes, depending on one's choice of theories) receive at least prima facie equal consideration with humans in any decision-making situation. However, the actual outcome of a given situation or dilemma will depend, in part, on whether the ethical position is one that can be broadly characterized as *individualist* or as *holistic*. Individualist ethics, as the term implies, focus on the duties and responsibilities we have toward individuals—for example, individual animals—while holistic ethics emphasize duties and responsibilities toward all of nature. Either approach might seem to promise "improved" story lines vis-à-vis animals, but perhaps surprisingly, this is often not the case. Let me briefly explore three popular theories to expose some of the complexity of nonanthropocentrism, and to illuminate another set of curious tales about animals.

Animal liberation.

Although theorists such as Carol Adams, Marti Kheel, and Andrée Collard have attempted to base animal liberation philosophies on ecofeminist principles,[6] the animal liberation mainstream still insistently treats humans as paradigmatic beings. From the time of Aristotle, there has been an ethical imperative to treat like beings and situations alike; animals therefore have equal moral considerability with humans to the extent that they are considered to be *like* humans—that is, to feel pain and pleasure as humans do, to have wants and desires, to be able to act intentionally and so on. Thus Peter Singer, a utilitarian, draws the line between humans and animals at the point at which animals cease to experience pain in the ways humans do; in practical terms, this means excluding invertebrates from moral consideration (171–74). Tom Regan, a rights theorist, distinguishes between mammals and nonmammals, and even within that category would withhold full rights from young nonhuman mammals, because they lack the intellectual sophistication to be (in his words) "subjects-of-a-life" (367). Under these theories, if I wanted to drain the frog pond because I consider it a breeding ground for mosquitos and blackflies (a source of displeasure for humans), I would be within my rights to do so. As a sentient adult mammal, my interests would override those of the insects and frogs in the pond. In fact, the insects would be morally negligible to both Singer and Regan, and Regan would only reluctantly give "the benefit of the doubt" to frogs, not letting them die "unnecessarily" (367).

There is an even gloomier side to these animal liberation theories: because they grow out of classic ethical theories, they cannot help but share those theories' worldviews. Ethics has been a field of inquiry concerned with checking humans' bad impulses, that is, with imposing restraints on our self-interest. The picture of human nature painted by most traditional ethical theories is a somber one: we are cruel, competitive, and self-serving. We agree to ethical restraints only because others promise to do the same, a sort of moral protection racket.

What does all of this say about the world? First, it imagines a state of nature in which both humans and animals are opposed to each other, a competitive free-for-all in which the meanest survive. There is no room in this narrative for kindness, affection, delight, wonder, respect, generosity, or love. And, in fact, these ethical theories operate only when there is a conflict: neither rights theories nor utility theories have any application whatsoever until two or more beings—characteristically a human and an animal—come into conflict with each other.[7] Second, nothing happened prior to the ethical conflict; it has no context. The social, ecological, historic, economic, and political factors that made the conflict possible are rendered invisible; as Marti Kheel observes, we are simply "given truncated stories and then asked what we think the ending should be" (From Heroic to Holistic Ethics, 249). Third, the narrative of animal liberation theories imagines winners and losers. Since everyone, human and animal alike, is in struggle, and since, in the absence of conflict, there would be no story for these theories to tell, when they do tell a story, someone wins and someone loses. Someone has a "better" right than someone else, whose wants are thus thwarted. Someone's desired action will increase the good of the whole, usually at someone else's expense. Fourth, animal rights theories are premised on abstract individualism, the notion that rights-bearing entities are interchangeable, with no room for positionality, particularity, historicity, or in fact anything that makes a real individual in the world. And finally, there is little reason for optimism. These theories pay little heed to the actual power imbalances that exist between animals and humans; their worldviews are rooted in mythic beliefs that people (and animals) have fallen from grace. Some versions of the fall from grace are religious, others secular, but all follow an essentially similar, declensionist line: once there was a time when humans lived in harmony with all nature; a turning point came (the serpent and the apple, or encounters with other, unknown humans, or agriculture); life has been harsh ever since, and without some near-magical redemption, it will continue its downslide. Thus, even though we should have no quarrel with animal liberation theories to the extent that they produce desirable results (opposition to meat-eating, fur, vivisection, etc.), we should be aware, and somewhat wary, of the whole-world story they tell.

The land ethic.

Another popular theory that tells a story about animals is "the land ethic," a characteristically holistic approach that encourages humans to stop imagining ourselves as superior beings morally entitled to dominate nature, and instead to see ourselves as simple citizens of a biotic community, no more or less privileged than a frog, a tree, or a river. The important unit of moral consideration is "the land," the entire community of beings and processes. Aldo Leopold, whose work has formed the basis of much subsequent holistic theorizing, believed that all action could be judged according to a single moral principle: "A thing is good when it tends to preserve the integrity, stability and beauty of the biotic community. It is wrong when it tends otherwise" (224). Generally stated, then, the land ethic takes no notice of individuals except insofar as their presence or absence affects the community.

Although it avoids the crude "good animal/bad animal" fantasy of anthropocentric positions, the land ethic continues to distinguish between classes of animals. For domestic animals, the outcome of the story is predetermined: they will be meat. For wild animals, a degree of chance is possible: although, as land ethic proponent Baird Callicott observes, "the most fundamental fact of life in the biotic community is eating . . . and being eaten" (57), wild animals may exercise their own cunning, luck, and strength to effectively co-author their life stories.

Most significantly, however, the land ethic does not allow for the consideration of particularly situated individuals: everything exists as a specimen, a representative of a type, and is judged as such. An individual life has no value—unless, of course, that individual is among the last of its kind. And while conflicts between individuals may arise, they are irrelevant unless their resolution will affect "the land."

Deep ecology.

The ethical position of deep ecology, another holistic approach, is based on the principle of self-realization articulated by Norwegian philosopher Arne Naess. Where Western humans go wrong, Naess claims, is in imagining the human self in individualist terms. Instead

Beyond Just-So Stories

self should be seen as Self, a continuous identity shared by all natural beings, processes, and forces. We are not merely a part of the land, or of a particular ecosystem, but a part of all things: we are, in fact, all things. Just as my arm has no identity apart from the rest of my body, the individual self has no existence apart from the larger Self. When we recognize and accept that ontological position, we also realize that we as humans are personally diminished by anything that diminishes diversity and complexity in the world, or that hinders a part of it from realizing its full potential. We are all intimately and irrevocably connected; the bell that tolls for the frog tolls for me.

Deep ecology barely acknowledges the existence of animals as animals, or, indeed, of any creature as an embodied individual. As ecofeminist Val Plumwood (1991, 1993) has argued, it is a philosophy of mind, an abstraction that renders our daily existence inconsequential. In this respect, it makes possible stories about animals that are just as discouraging as those spun out by any other ethical theory. Like the land ethic, deep ecology takes notice of particular specimens of animal, that is, those that are rare or endangered, but only because their disappearance would make the world less diverse and complex, and thus diminish the Self. One could, of course, extend the idea of self-realization to animals, and attempt to argue that hunting an animal, or killing it for food, prevents it from realizing its full potential, but deep ecology seems unconcerned with such matters. In fact, Naess supports so-called "wildlife management" (*Ecology, Community, and Lifestyle*) while Americans Bill Devall and George Sessions go so far as to suggest that hunting can help develop a "sense of place and intuitive understanding of the connections between humans and nonhumans, with a respect for the principle of biocentric equality" (188). And in this country, at least, deep ecologists are notoriously contemptuous of domestic animals, condemning them as human artifacts having negative impact on diversity. In short, from a deep ecology perspective, both humans and their animal creations are quintessentially bad animals, embodied forms to be scorned and rejected in pursuit of union with abstract "nature."

Ethical Narratives

I have, of course, been telling a story of my own, and the expectations of narratives should now bring me to the end, since I have already given you a beginning and a middle. And, typically, the end of my story should be an upbeat one: having demonstrated some of the shortcomings of other theories—"bad theories," if you insist—I should now offer you a good one, the theory that will solve our problems and allow us to claim victory. Sorry. At the risk of seeming disingenuous, I will tell you instead that I am an ecofeminist, and that in the feminist tradition, we eschew the creation of "grand theories," metanarratives to govern all actors in all situations at all times.

Shall we just tell stories then, simply chronicle the events of our lives, and leave the meaning-making to others? I think not, in part because I doubt it would be possible for us to do so. The point I have been attempting to make up until now is that we make meaning as much by accident as by design. Just as theorizing is a form of story-telling, so too is storytelling a form of theorizing. Our theories reflect our beliefs—our stories—about how the world works; our stories about how the world works lead us, consciously or not, to the creation of theory, as we repeat and revise them.

In the introduction, I told you a story, a first-person narrative of an encounter with nature. "Let us assume," I said, "that this is the whole story: frogs are born, reproduce, and die. Humans enter the natural world, observe it, and move on, taking whatever moral lessons we find." There was more to this narrative, of course, although this was indeed the core I chose to emphasize to illustrate my subsequent points.[8] The narrative itself included a brief mention of my "role"—a naturalist—and the expectations this imposes on me. It told you that I restrained my impulse to startle the frogs because of that role expectation, and that I expected a reward, namely a performance by the frogs; it also mentioned that I restrained another impulse (to stretch out and watch the frogs) because of my self-interest (not being scratched by raspberry canes). And it told you that ultimately I will forget the frogs, that they will cease to have consequence for me, because frogs, in my life, do not matter. Embedded in this seemingly innocuous account of a few moments on a spring day, then, was a fairly complex and textured description of an ethical approach to the natural world.

If neither grand theories nor innocent narratives are possible, what is left? What we can strive for, I think, are what feminist legal critics Fineman and Thomasden call "theories of the middle ground" (xi–xii). Such theories would mediate between the "stories"—that is, the material facts and circumstances of human/animal coexistence—and the grand realizations that environmental ethics have humanist biases and that relationships between humans and animals have been driven by power inequalities. Once we recognize that narratives and the social circumstances they reflect don't come out of thin air, we can start to develop a theory that *will* illuminate their origins, and that will help restore some balance between humans and animals.

My contribution to this effort is a beginning theory about the kind of narratives we might construct to take into account the realities of animals' lives. Your contribution—well, it's implied, but I'll leave the execution up to you. But before I begin, I want to discuss some of the attempts that have been made recently to blend environmental ethics with narrative.

Storytelling is by definition an act done in community. When I tell you, or my students, or my friends the story of the frog pond, or stories like it, I am engaging in a form of ethical discourse, modeling, as it were, my beliefs about human/nature relationships. My stories shape others' stories; their stories shape mine. Imagine, then, the power of *conscious* narrative, of myths and tales intentionally constructed and repeated that would inform and instruct us in "proper" attitudes toward nature. This is not so different from the type of storytelling that has emerged from feminism over the past twenty years. We have told each other our stories, have discerned the patterns that emerge from them, have chosen the patterns that seem best suited to a liberated future, and have repeated those again and again, with appropriate modifications and variations, until a relatively clear "feminist ethos" of caring, relationship, compassion, and attentiveness has been called into existence.[9]

It is no wonder, then, that ecofeminists would advocate a similar approach to the creation of a new environmental ethos. For Karen Warren, first-person narratives can "give voice to a felt sensitivity often lacking in traditional ethical discourse, namely, a sensitivity to conceiving of oneself as fundamentally 'in relationship with' others"; they can express "a variety of ethical attitudes and behaviors often overlooked or underplayed in mainstream Western ethics"; and they can suggest "*what counts* as an appropriate solution to an ethical situation" (135–36). These consciously chosen narratives, Jim Cheney suggests, rightfully extend out to include "not just the human community but also the land, one's community in a larger sense." What we want, he says,

> . . . is language that grows out of experience and articulates it, language intermediate between self, culture, and world, their *intersection*, carrying knowledge of both, knowledge charged

with valuation and instruction. This is language in which, in Paul Shepard's words, "the clues to the meaning of life [are] embodied in natural things, where everyday life [is] inextricable from spiritual significance and encounter." (Nature and the Theorizing of Difference, 9)

Both Warren and Cheney (and Shepard as well) find examples of such narratives in Native American myth and ritual. But look, for a moment, at the examples they choose. Warren recounts a Sioux child's introduction to hunting, wherein the boy learned to

... shoot your four-legged brother in his hind area, slowing it down but not killing it. ... look into his eyes. The eyes are where all the suffering is. Then, take your knife and cut the four-legged under his chin, here ... and as you do, ask your brother, the four-legged, for forgiveness ... Offer also a prayer of thanks to your four-legged kin for offering his body to you just now ... And promise the four-legged that you will put yourself back into the earth when you die, to become nourishment ... (145–46)

Cheney, for his part, cites Tom Jay's discussion of the role played by salmon among Indians of the Pacific Northwest:

... salmon were not merely food. To them, salmon were people who lived in houses far away under the sea. ... When the salmon people travelled, they donned their salmon disguises and these they left behind perhaps in the way we leave flowers or food when visiting friends. To the Indians, the salmon were a resource in the deep sense, great generous beings whose gifts gave life. ... The Indians understood that salmon's gift involved them in an ethical system that resounded in every corner of their locale. The aboriginal landscape was a democracy of spirits where everyone listened, careful not to offend the *resource* they were a working part of. (Jay, 112)

Both these stories are cited by the authors with approval; Warren, in fact, comments:

As I reflect upon that story, I am struck by the power of the environmental ethic that grows out of and takes seriously narrative, context and such values and relational attitudes as care, loving perception, and appropriate reciprocity, and doing what is appropriate in a given situation—however that notion of appropriateness eventually gets filled out. (146)

Warren would argue, I am sure, that this tale has nary a hint of anthropocentric utilitarianism in it; after all, the child is being instructed to feel the otherness of the deer, to experience its pain, and to recognize his own mortality, and his connection to the earth. But the point remains: killing the animal is all right, because it serves human ends. The only issue is whether the killing is done "the right way," namely, the way that will bring future deer, will sustain a connection with nature, and will teach the hunter appropriate humility. Cheney's chosen narrative is the same: the salmon are mythologized so that they may be killed and eaten with impunity.

Both Cheney and Warren take a holistic approach to ethics, and so it is perhaps predictable that they would fail to see how these narratives obliterate the lived experience of particular animals. And it is true that such narratives may have been appropriate in a particular culture at a particular time where food alternatives were scarce. But it is equally true that they are not appropriate in Western culture *now*, nor are they appropriate as models of a narrative form in which the natural world has a right of coauthorship. In contemporary America, the deer and the hunter are not cohabitants of a balanced ecosystem: they are carefully manipulated components of a closely monitored management unit.[10] The "animal master" has been replaced by state and federal fish and wildlife agencies. The hunter is not one of a number of natural predators: he is the *only* predator, his position secured by the intentional elimination of his competitors. And most significantly, the deer is not necessary food for the hunter; a healthy vegetarian diet based on simple, regionally appropriate agriculture is within reach of virtually everyone in the lower forty-eight states.

I think we must learn to be discriminating about narrative, at least the narrative that we put forward as what Cheney calls "ethical vernacular" (Postmodern Environmental Ethics, 134). It is always true that narrative may offer insights into the psychology of the storyteller, or the worldview of the culture from which she speaks, and in that sense all narrative has value. But insights alone do not make it *good* narrative. Good narrative—that is, narrative that can form the basis of an ethic that recognizes both individual and general others—requires more. If we are to propose the creation of intentional narratives, myths to live by, we must also establish criteria by which to judge them.

The kind of narratives we want, I think, should satisfy four criteria: (1) they should be ecologically appropriate to a given time and place; (2) they should be ethically appropriate in that time and place;

(3) they should give voice to those whose stories are being told; and (4) they should make us care. I'll expand on each of these criteria separately.

A good narrative should be ecologically appropriate to a given time and place.

While there is some danger in assuming that ecology is an exact mirror of the world—it is, after all, a human enterprise, and as such subject to the sorts of unconscious meaning-making I have been describing in this article—it does, I think, provide us with a parameter for our narratives. Cronon's remarks about environmental history are equally appropriate here:

> . . . the biological and geological processes of the earth set fundamental limits to what constitutes a plausible narrative . . . Insofar as we can know them, to exclude or obscure these natural "facts" would be another kind of false silence, another kind of lying. (1372–73)

It is absurd, I think, for white Americans to advance narratives that feature animals willingly presenting themselves to be killed, or as humans traveling in a fish "disguise," which they leave behind as a sort of bread-and-butter note. However much descriptions of the world are open to interpretation, it seems fairly indisputable that wild animals shy away from humans, and that when forced into confrontation, attempt to preserve their lives through flight, artifice, or counterattack.

Similarly, it is inappropriate to craft narratives that present the world as an unlimited storehouse of resources awaiting human use, or which posit human ingenuity as the single driving force behind change, or which, for that matter, extol the virtues of human manipulation of the natural world. The tale of human progress, whether strictly linear or dialectically unfolding, has outlived its usefulness, if indeed it ever had any. And while declensionist narratives may seem too overwhelming, too fatalistic, or too much a manipulative stage setting for salvation fantasies, it does us no good to avoid the unpleasant truth: there are ecological limits. So let's tell the stories of dammed and polluted rivers, disappeared ecosystems and species, plains and prairies and tundra ravaged by inappropriate agriculture and grazing, forests leveled for exports, the unnecessary slaughter of millions of animals.

But at the same time, let's also tell the stories about how we *could* live in harmony with the rest of nature. Our narratives could remind us of the integrity and complexity of the natural world, and the need to embrace limits with joy and humility. They could be models of ecologically responsible and respectful interactions, both among animals and between humans and animals. They could inspire us to see beauty and feel delight in natural forces.

None of these stories require that we ignore "the facts," or turn away from elements of the natural world that seem harsh or cruel, like predation, or starvation, or natural disaster, or competition. Our narratives about nature, about animals, about ourselves—all must ultimately be judged by their credibility; we must therefore tell stories that are as accurate as we can make them.

A good narrative should be ethically appropriate
to a given time and place.

In the past twenty years, environmentalists and ethicists have invested considerable energy in establishing ecology as a normative discipline, not just a descriptive one. A healthy ecosystem, they tell us, is not only a model of how the natural world is, but also of how it ought to be: interdependent, sustainable, and diverse, a web of beings-in-relationship that emerges as a whole far greater than the sum of its parts, and which cannot be reduced to its parts without destroying its integrity. How do we move from what *is* in nature to what *ought* to be, or from ecologically appropriate narratives to ethically appropriate ones? The first move, I would suggest, is the easier of the two, despite the number of pages it has consumed in journals devoted to philosophy and ethics.[11] Like Holmes Rolston, I think we can say that facts and values in the natural world are discovered simultaneously; our values affect what we perceive as facts, and vice versa. This is especially true when we consider the words used to describe natural ecosystems, as Don Marietta points out:

> Such words as *stability, diversity, unity, balance, integrity, order,* and *health* can be employed in strictly scientific, value-neutral ecological research papers, but they also show up in expressions of appreciation for the environment and in normative discourse. (201)

Thus moral obligation is contextual, a matter of *is-with-ought* rather than *is-implies-ought.*

When we speak of ethically appropriate *narratives,* however, we need to add another dimension. It is entirely possible for a narrative to be ecologically accurate, and to suggest or model behavior that accords with the ecological facts, while nonetheless presenting an ethically inappropriate rationale for the behavior. Suppose, for example, that I perceive the frog pond as a delicately balanced microcosmic universe, however temporary it may be. Having learned from ecology (and culture) that balanced and complex ecosystems are functionally good, I conclude that tossing a stone or a bag of garbage into it would be wrong. Asked my reason, I reply that disturbing an ecosystem is a wrongful act because it violates God's design, or because it might ultimately threaten human well-being. Indeed, most contemporary utilitarian ethicists (and deep ecologists) advance the notion that the natural world is an interrelated whole of which humans are a part, and that anything that threatens our environment threatens us. Therefore, it is in our interests not to harm the environment. In a similar vein, I might advance the importance of self-restraint. In my opening narrative, you may recall, I "restrained" myself from picking up a stone and tossing it into the pond, but I expected the frogs to entertain me as a "reward." My action was good, but my stated reason for it was questionable at best.

How, then, do we judge the ethical appropriateness of a narrative? Here I think we can have recourse to principles of ecofeminism. While there is certainly no one formulation of ecofeminist ethics, a number of guidelines—what Karen Warren calls "boundary conditions"[12]—can be suggested. Besides being ecologically appropriate, good ecofeminist narratives should reject the notion that any part of the world, human or animal, exists for the use and pleasure of any other part; in particular, any kind of instrumental characterization of animals implies an endorsement of human power-over. Ecofeminist narratives should emphasize lived experience and context, and the ways in which perception of the world is socially negotiated. When possible, they should remind us of the intersection of oppressions. But instead of presenting humans as compulsive destroyers who can control our bad impulses only with great effort, they should emphasize the pleasure we take in relationships and in identification with nature and animals, and the importance of caring, attention, kindness, playfulness, trust, empathy, and connection. They should demonstrate that ethical behavior toward the nonhuman world is a kind of joyfulness, an embracing of possibility, a self-respecting and respectful humility.

Theorizing about the natural world and human relationships to it all too often focuses on goals, whether they be the execution of a divine design or the reestablishment of some mythical arcadian harmony. If we behave in such and such a way, we are told, things will work out fine; this is the message of the progress narrative, and, insofar as it calls upon us to change our ways, the declensionist one as well. But what if we ground ourselves in the present, asking not so much what we hope to achieve in the future, but who we want to be right now? Ethics should not be about a Herculean labor, wherein right action will lead to a desired end. We are already in relationships with each other and with the natural world, even though these relationships may not always be mutually beneficial. We should be asking, I think, not what we will *get* from being more attentive, more loving, more joyful, more empathic, and more trusting, but simply how to do it. Ethically appropriate ecofeminist narratives would begin to show us the way, and to remind us that a vision can illuminate the present as well as the future.

> *A good narrative should give voice to those*
> *whose stories are being told.*

In the mythic narratives of the hunt such as those suggested by Warren and Cheney, the animal's story is never really told. Instead, human desires are centralized, while the animal becomes a universalizable animal "Other." And, like the classic female/mother "Other" of masculinist discourse, the universalizable animal is offering itself up as food/sacrifice. In the same way, the narrative freezes a particular moment in time—the moment of the animal's death—thus denying the rich, textured, purposeful, and unique life that the animal led prior to the encounter with the hunter.

The story of "the one that got away," as a hunting tale, is of course just another version of the story of the kill, since it focuses only on the events of the hunter/animal encounter. But what if the story continued: Where did the animal go when s/he got away? Where had s/he come from to begin with? What, after all, is an animal's life?

When I speak of an animal's life, I mean to do so in both factual and mythic ways, because I think our narratives should be informed by both observation and imagination. There are abundant observations of animals in the wild, the best of which record animal's life histories without manipulating them; from these we can learn a great deal about animal thought, feeling, needs, desires, joys.[13] But we can also rely on direct knowledge. In our lived experience, animals communicate with us in many ways: through companion relationships, in which most of us engage at some point in our lives; through scolding, swooping, hissing, circling, or bursting from cover as we walk through the woods or across the desert; by their absence, in the places that humans have rendered uninhabitable for them; by the scat, chewed twigs, faint trails, empty burrows, and nest holes they leave behind; by their cleverness, in pursuing their own lives all around ours, as is the case with raccoons, ravens, starlings, coyotes, rabbits, and the like; by their confined presence and passivity in fields, on rangelands, and in feedlots; and by their fate, when we see their remains in the supermarket meat section. Even intermittent attentiveness to our surroundings brings knowledge about the animals who share the place with us.

An animal's life history can be told in factual ways, and it can be told in mythic ways as well. I am somewhat hesitant to propose this, because mythologizing has so often been used to objectify animals, but that objectification, I think, is more a function of the worldview of the mythmakers than of mythology itself. In dreams, in fantasies, in visions, animals often speak to us—and who is to say that this is not a form of communication? As long as a myth does not contravene observed fact—as do the hunting myths—or exist simply to prove the mythmaker's theory, it can be a way of translating animal consciousness into a form humans can apprehend, and thus admit animals into our dialogue.

Giving voice to something that does not speak is a challenge we should not take lightly. Indeed, as María Lugones and Elizabeth Spelman have pointed out in "Have We Got a Theory for You!," many white feminists have displayed a remarkable lack of talent for giving voice even to those "others" who do speak. Of course, we need not think that communication is only verbal; for both humans and animals, instinct, emotion, and action can be a form of speech. But the test, I think, for determining whether the voice we give to animals is accurate will lie in the behavior it calls forth from humans.[14] If an animal's "voice" dictates action that serves human ends but compromises the animal, we had best try listening more carefully.

A good narrative should make us care.[15]

Marti Kheel writes that "we cannot even begin to talk about the issue of ethics unless we admit that we care (or feel something)" (The Liberation of Nature, 144). Therefore, even if a narrative satisfies all the other conditions I have laid out, if it fails to make us care, we cannot judge it to be a good narrative. But what do we mean by "care"?

For these purposes I think that caring is best defined as a state of consciousness and a form of behavior, each inextricably linked to the other.[16] Sara Ruddick's work on maternal thinking is useful in this regard. For Ruddick, mothers learn to care, to think "maternally," by doing it; it is a practice that grows out of the requirements of the work. In the case of mothers, the work requires above all that the child be nurtured, protected, and trained. These in turn require attention both to the individual and its environment, that is, an awareness of and sensitivity to the child's needs *and* to the community (or context) in which the child is to grow up.

Awareness of and sensitivity to the needs of the individual requires what Ruddick calls "attentive love,"[17] the habit of asking "What are you going through?" and *waiting for the answer.* Like empathy, it requires us to experience the other's feelings as though they were our own, but without projecting our own feelings onto that other. And it requires us to celebrate as well as suffer:

> . . . it is equally important and sometimes as difficult to really look at her excitements, ambitions, and triumphs, to see her quirky, delighted, determined independent being and let it be. Attention lets difference emerge without searching for comforting commonalities, dwells upon the *other,* and lets otherness be. (121–22)

Nonetheless, attentive love requires more than simply asking, waiting, and hearing: it has to imply a commitment to action, and in particular, to the action that will help preserve the other and let her flourish.

Applying concepts of maternal thinking to narrative suggests that good narratives will model attentiveness to individuals as well as to the context in which they live, and will inspire us to appropriately preservative actions. By "appropriately preservative" I mean to indicate actions that promote the evolution of an individual animal's life history in ways that are consonant with its community/context. Attentive love directed toward a child, for example, would require us to save it from a (human or animal) predator; predators are not (or should not be) a part of a human child's life story, in the context that healthy human lives are lived. But attentive love toward a deer, or a bighorn lamb, or a ruffed grouse does not require us to devise schemes to frighten off every wolf, eagle, and fox; predation *is* a part of the life story of at least some wild animals. Therefore a narrative that had humans intervening to protect an animal from a natural predator could be judged as modeling a misguided form of caring, one that was ignorant of context.

For the purposes of narrative, decisions about what constitutes an individual's context can be guided by common sense and by the other requirements of good narrative. For instance, to care about an individual chicken in context means more than caring that it is being humanely treated while it awaits death; the context, in this case, must be extended beyond the immediate material circumstances of its existence to the larger ecological and ethical circumstances. In other words, narratives about chickens should make us care enough to put an end to meat-eating.

Crafting narratives that will give voice to animals and make humans care about them in appropriate ways is no easy task. We want to avoid anthropomorphizing animals even though that has proven itself an effective tactic for mobilizing public sympathy toward them.[18] We need to be faithful to their stories, not our own. The goal is not to make us care about animals because they are like us, but to care about them because they are themselves.

Epilogue: Can This Narrative Be Saved?

It is usually the prerogative of a theorist to sketch out the parameters of a theory and then leave the work of applying it to others, as I have tried to do with you. And who knows: perhaps you are whittling away already, making template after template, or perhaps you've finished and are out searching for a text. But I have a text of my own to revise, one I produced initially in a self-interested effort to demonstrate that not all narratives are created equal. Could that story be retold in line with my own criteria? I am compelled to try, if only to illustrate that what I have said need not drive us to the creation of grand narratives, narratives for all time, any more than we should strive for grand theories. Sometimes we can just have fun with the simple stories.

Why do the wood frogs sing so absurdly in the spring, out of tune and out of sync? In the summer, when they hop around on the forest leaves, so light- and shadow-mottled you can barely see them, they're silent. But in the spring every one of them sings, and each has a different song. Why?

One morning as I walked through the woodland park behind my house, I heard them singing, and so I decided to ask. I made a place for myself at the edge of a vernal pond, pushing the raspberry canes aside and stretching out on the bank. This was apparently a suspect move, because the frogs became very, very quiet. But so, curiously enough, did everything else. Even I was quiet. I watched the surface of the pond, and I watched the leaf litter in the woods, and I looked upward at the pallid blue sky, and I peered down into the muddy chocolate water, where mosquito larvae and salamander eggs lay in clusters. I imagined myself a deer, bent low to drink from the stream-fed trickle that the pond would soon become. I imagined myself a raccoon, sensitizing my fingers by dipping my paws in the water, a raccoon's idea of an *aperitif*. I imagined myself me, the scent of newly thawed earth in my nostrils—but then, of course, I remembered I *was* me.

"Cuhr-roawk," said a frog, and another answered "Curh-romph." My heart gave a little lurch, and just then I saw an amazing thing: a leaf had popped out on the raspberry cane nearest my cheek, and a mushroom had sprung up under the maple across the pond. Then a shiny brown frog drifted to the surface, as casually as you please, just as though she were a stick that had broken free of some underwater anchor. I lay still, belly down and legs splayed out; she did the same, but she was floating, and the movement of the water eased her toward me. We looked back and forth at each other, the sun warming our backs. Then another frog croaked, "Cree-ukha," startling us both, and this time I saw a salamander egg begin to hatch. Can this be, I thought? The frog in front of me gave a little "ahh-ruk," and I swore I heard a rush of sap in the tree. "Would you do that again?" I asked her, as politely as I could, and sure enough, she gave forth another little "ahh-ruk," and this time I was quite certain I heard the sap rise higher. And then another frog went "ahhroo-roak," and a trout lily burst into bloom.

And so it went: cuhr-roawk, and there was another raspberry leaf! Cuhr-romph, and out came a mushroom. Cree-ukha, and a sala-mander egg hatched. Ahh-ruk, and the sap rose. Ahhroo-roak, and the forest was bursting with trout lilies.

The shiny brown frog drifted downstream a bit, basking in the sun, looking, perhaps, for a tree that needed her. Nice work if you can get it, I thought, better even than making theory. But like theory, it must get tiring. And with that, I lay my cheek on the sweet damp earth and slid into a nap.

Notes

It would be impossible to identify all the conversations and exchanges that contributed to this essay. Still, I know that my thinking in this area has been challenged and sharpened by a number of my students—most notably Neysha Stuart, Karen Villemaire, and Linda Clark—and by my friends and colleagues Judy Anhorn and Gail Wheeler. Marti Kheel has heard every idea and example in this article in some form or another, and has been an inexhaustible source of ideas and examples of her own. She deserves much credit, then, for anything that seems insightful, wise, or provocative; the pedestrian thinking, however, is entirely my own.

1. I owe the notion of narrative and template, with text creating text, to Judy Anhorn.

2. There are a number of excellent works on the history of environmental consciousness and attitudes toward nature. In particular, I recommend Carolyn Merchant, *The Death of Nature* (New York: Harper & Row, 1978); Roderick Nash, *The Rights of Nature: A History of Environmental Ethics* (Madison: University of Wisconsin Press, 1989); Keith Thomas, *Man and the Natural World: A History of Modern Sensibility* (New York: Pantheon, 1983); and Max Oelschlaeger, *Contemporary Wilderness Philosophy: From Resourcism to Deep Ecology* (New Haven: Yale University Press, 1991). Former Secretary of the Interior Manuel Lujan summed up the traditional position when he stated his own worldview: "I believe that man is at the top of the pecking order. I think that God gave us dominion over these creatures" (Ted Gup, "The Stealth Secretary," *Time*, 25 May 1992, 58).

3. Although it seems paradoxical that animals may be killed at the whim of their "owners" but not treated cruelly, the explanation is simple: acts of brutality, or even exposure to those acts, have long been considered demoralizing to *humans*. See the discussion of the American Society for the Prevention of Cruelty to Animals (ASPCA) and its founder Henry Bergh in Gerald Carson, *Men, Beasts, and Gods: A History of Cruelty and Kindness to Animals* (New York: Scribner's, 1972), 95–106, esp. 105.

4. In a letter responding to an excerpt from Jeremy Rifkin's book *Beyond Beef*, which had appeared in the *Utne Reader*, the editor of a meat industry journal took exception to a half dozen facts ranging from the weight of the world's cattle to the percentage of methane gas attributable to them. Rifkin responded by elaborating on the initial information to "prove" that beef consumption is indeed harmful to humans. At the conclusion of his response, he stated the Beyond Beef Campaign's goal: to reduce U.S. beef consumption by at least 50 percent "to improve our health, preserve the environment, alleviate world hunger, and *decrease animal suffering*" (emphasis added; *Utne Reader*, May/June 1992, 8–9). This was the only time in the whole exchange that the concern of any nonhuman being was raised. For those of us who believe that animal suffering is the central issue, the relegation of animals' concerns to fourth place is at best disingenuous and at worst a reflection of the low regard in which they are held.

5. The extension of moral considerability to animals and ecosystems is discussed below. For a discussion of ethical obligations toward biochemical processes, see generally Charles Birch and John Cobb, *The Liberation of Life* (Athens, Ga.: Environmental Ethics Books, 1990).

6. For further elaboration on ecofeminist principles, see note 12 and the accompanying text.

7. Feminist theory has been critical of rights and utility theories generally, largely because such theories are premised on an abstract individualism, do not take into account the context in which human lives are lived, and are indifferent to such values as compassion, trust, and generosity. For a more detailed analysis, see Moira Gatens, *Feminist Philosophy: Perspectives on Difference and Equality* (Bloomington: Indiana University Press, 1991), esp. 122–35; Martha Minow, *Making All the Difference: Inclusion, Exclusion and American Law* (Ithaca: Cornell University Press, 1990), esp. 146–74; and Elizabeth M. Schneider, "The Dialectic of Rights and Politics: Perspectives from the Women's Movement," *New York University Law Review* 61 (1987):589–652. For a feminist critique of animal rights theories, see Josephine Donovan, "Animal Rights and Feminist Theory," *Signs: Journal of Women in Culture and Society* 15, no. 2 (1990):350–75.

8. I confess that this narrative was calculated; while the setting and "events" were real, my responses were invented to advance my argument, namely that narratives do not necessarily model good ethics.

9. For a more detailed treatment of women's stories and autobiographies, see the essays in Bella Brodzki and Celeste Schenck, eds., *Life/Lines: Theorizing Women's Autobiography* (Ithaca: Cornell University Press, 1988).

10. David Ehrenfeld compares current models of game management to the linear systems approach used to manage large industrial systems like nuclear power plants, and suggests that a better, more ecologically astute model would be the complex systems approach used in air traffic control. See "The Management of Diversity: A Conservation Paradox," in *Ecology, Economics, Ethics: The Broken Circle*, ed. F. Herbert Bormann and Stephen R. Kellert, (New Haven: Yale University Press, 1991).

11. Some of this debate is reviewed in Don E. Marietta Jr., "The Interrelationship of Ecological Science and Environmental Ethics"; and in Callicott, *In Defense of the Land Ethic*, 117–27.

12. See Warren, "The Power and the Promise," 139. Warren's boundary conditions are similar to the ones set out here: an ecofeminist ethic should generally (1) oppose domination; (2) be contextualist; (3) recognize diversity; (4) honor theory-in-process; (5) include the perspectives of oppressed persons; (6) deny the validity of "objectivity"; (7) emphasize such values as care, love, friendship, and trust; and (8) reject ahistoric abstract individualism. See also my article "Ecofeminism and the Politics of Reality"; for additional readings on ecofeminism, consult Carol Adams, ed., *Ecofeminism and the Sacred*, and the works discussed in my bibliographic essay "Remapping the Terrain: Books on Ecofeminism."

13. In *Primate Visions: Gender, Race, and Nature in the World of Modern*

Science (New York: Routledge, 1989), Donna Haraway discusses both the racism and sexism of much recent primatology, and the ways in which it could be done so as to advance the agendas of animals and humans other than the researchers. Barbara Noske's *Humans and Other Animals* (London: Pluto, 1989) is an intriguing anthropological examination of animals, respecting and recognizing their "otherness" while examining language, culture, toolmaking, and the like. See also Daisie Radner and Michael Radner, *Animal Consciousness* (Buffalo, N.Y.: Prometheus Books, 1989).

14. Patrick Murphy makes a similar point in "Ground, Pivot, Motion: Ecofeminist Theory, Dialogics, and Literary Practice," *Hypatia* 6 (1991), 152–53.

15. Cronon (1992, 1374) claims this is the central difference between historical narrative and mere chronicles of events; I go further in calling it a compelling test of the value of a narrative.

16. There have been a number of books and articles devoted to the notion of caring as a distinctly feminist ethic. Two useful anthologies are Eva Feder Kittay and Diana T. Meyers, eds., *Women and Moral Theory* (Totowa, N.J.: Rowman and Littlefield, 1987) and Eve Browning Cole and Susan Coultrap-McQuin, eds., *Explorations in Feminist Ethics: Theory and Practice* (Bloomington: Indiana University Press, 1992). Joan Tronto's *Moral Boundaries* (New York: Routledge, 1993) offers an excellent summary of work on caring, and posits a number of guidelines for an ethic of care. For a detailed ethic of care that manages to exclude animals from its purview, see Nel Noddings, *Caring: A Feminine Approach to Ethics and Moral Education* (Berkeley: University of California Press, 1984); see also her exchange with Josephine Donovan in *Signs: Journal of Women in Culture and Society* 16, no. 2 (Winter 1991):418–25. Rita Manning's *Speaking From The Heart: A Feminist Perspective on Ethics* (Lanham, Md.: Rowman & Littlefield, 1992) develops an ethic of care that does include animals, but it is nonetheless incompatible with a strong animal liberation perspective.

17. Ruddick's work on attentive love draws on the writings of Simone Weil, especially as developed by Iris Murdoch. See Simone Weil, *The Simone Weil Reader,* ed. George A. Panichas (Mt. Kisko, N.Y.: Moyer Bell, 1977) and Iris Murdoch, *The Sovereignty of the Good* (New York: Schocken, 1971).

18. Lisa Mighetto's *Wild Animals and American Environmental Ethics* (Tucson: University of Arizona Press, 1991) examines some self-conscious attempts by preservationists to make wild animals, especially wolves and bears, seem more like humans; see especially her chapters "Science and Sentiment" and "Working Out the Beast."

References

Adams, Carol J. 1990. *The Sexual Politics of Meat: A Feminist-Vegetarian Critical Theory.* New York: Continuum.

——, ed. 1993. *Ecofeminism and the Sacred.* New York: Continuum.

——. 1994. *Neither Man Nor Beast.* New York: Continuum.

Callicott, J. Baird. 1989. *In Defense of the Land Ethic: Essays in Environmental Philosophy.* Albany: State University of New York Press.

Cheney, Jim. 1989. Postmodern Environmental Ethics: Ethics as Bioregional Narrative. *Environmental Ethics* 11:117–34.

———. 1990. Nature and the Theorizing of Difference. *Contemporary Philosophy* 13, no. 1:1–14.

Collard, Andrée, with Joyce Contrucci. 1988. *Rape of the Wild: Man's Violence Against Animals and the Earth.* Bloomington: Indiana University Press.

Cronon, William. 1992. A Place For Stories: Nature, History and Narrative. *Journal of American History* (March):1347–76.

Devall, Bill, and George Sessions. 1985. *Deep Ecology: Living as if Nature Mattered.* Salt Lake City: Peregrine Smith.

Fineman, Martha Albertson, and Nancy Sweet Thomasden. 1990. *At the Boundaries of Law: Feminism and Legal Theory.* New York: Routledge.

Jay, Tom. 1986. The Salmon of the Heart. In *Working the Woods, Working the Sea,* ed. Finn Wilcox and Jeremiah Gorsline, 101–17. Port Townsend, Wash.: Empty Bowl.

Kheel, Marti. 1985. The Liberation of Nature: A Circular Affair. *Environmental Ethics* 7:135–49.

———. 1993. From Heroic to Holistic Ethics: The Ecofeminist Challenge. In *Ecofeminism: Women, Animals, and Nature,* ed. Greta Gaard, 243–71. Philadelphia: Temple University Press.

Leopold, Aldo. 1949. *A Sand County Almanac.* New York: Oxford University Press.

Lugones, María C., and Elizabeth V. Spelman. 1986. Have We Got a Theory for You! Feminist Theory, Cultural Imperialism, and the Demand for "The Woman's Voice." In *Women and Values: Readings in Recent Feminist Philosophy,* ed. Marilyn Pearsall, 19–31. Belmont, Calif.: Wadsworth.

Marietta, Don E., Jr. 1979. The Interrelationship of Ecological Science and Environmental Ethics. *Environmental Ethics* 1:195–207.

Naess, Arne. 1973. The Shallow and the Deep, Long-Range Ecology Movements. *Inquiry* 16:95–100.

———. 1989. *Ecology, Community, and Lifestyle,* trans. David Rothenberg. Cambridge: Cambridge University Press.

Plumwood, Val. 1991. Nature, Self and Gender: Feminism, Environmental Philosophy and the Critique of Rationalism. *Hypatia* 6:3–28.

———. 1993. *Feminism and the Mastery of Nature.* New York: Routledge.

Regan, Tom. 1983. *The Case for Animal Rights.* Berkeley: University of California Press.

Rolston, Holmes, III. 1975. Is There an Ecological Ethic? *Ethics* 85:93–109.

Ruddick, Sara. 1989. *Maternal Thinking: Towards a Politics of Peace.* New York: Ballantine.

Singer, Peter. 1991. *Animal Liberation.* New York: Avon.

Tronto, Joan. 1993. *Moral Boundaries.* New York: Routledge.

Vance, Linda. 1993. Ecofeminism and the Politics of Reality. In *Ecofeminism: Women, Animals, and Nature,* ed. Greta Gaard, 118–45. Philadelphia: Temple University Press.

——. 1993. Remapping the Terrain: Books on Ecofeminism. *Choice* (June):1585–93.

Warren, Karen. 1990. The Power and the Promise of Ecological Feminism. *Environmental Ethics* 12 (Summer):125–46.

8
Karen Davis

_T_hinking Like a Chicken: Farm Animals and the Feminine Connection

Prologue

In the mid-1980s I became interested in how the philosophy of deep ecology harmonized with the philosophy of animal rights. This happened during the time when my interest in animal rights was becoming increasingly centered on the plight of farm animals. Years earlier, an essay by Tolstoy that included an excruciating account of his visit to a slaughterhouse had opened my eyes to what it meant to eat meat.[1] After that, except for occasional fish, I stopped eating meat and drifted away from eggs. However, I continued to consume dairy products until a description of the life and mammary diseases of dairy cows ended my consumption of those products.

I was well into my thirties and had been a semivegetarian for nearly a decade before I realized that a cow had to be kept pregnant in order to give milk or thought about the strangeness of continuing to nurse after infancy or of sharing a cow's udders with her offspring, let alone shoving her offspring out of the way so that I could have all of her milk for myself. My growing preoccupation with the plight of farm animals did not particularly arise from the clear perception I now have of the exploitation of the reproductive system of the female farm animal, epitomized by the dairy cow and the laying hen. However, two important things happened, one through reading and the other through personal experience, to clarify my thoughts and, ultimately, my career.

My reading led me to two contemporary essays in which chickens are represented as a type of animal least likely to possess or deserve rights. One was by Carl Sagan. In "The Abstractions of Beasts," Sagan argues against the view that, in the words of John Locke, "Beasts abstract not." He shows that chimpanzees, at least, have demonstrated the ability to think abstractly through a variety of behaviors, including maltreating a chicken. A researcher watched two chimpanzees cooperating to lure a chicken with food while hiding a piece of wire. Like Charlie Brown to the football, the chicken reportedly kept returning, revealing that "chickens have a very low capacity for avoidance learning," whereas the chimpanzees showed "a fine combination of behavior sometimes thought to be uniquely human: cooperation, planning a future course of action, deception and cruelty" (Sagan 1977, 108). Sagan poses the question whether nonhuman species of animals with demonstrated consciousness and mental ingenuity should not be recognized as having rights. At the top of the list are chimpanzees. At the bottom somewhere are chickens.

The second essay derived from the field of environmental ethics. In "Animal Liberation: A Triangular Affair," J. Baird Callicott draws upon "The Land Ethic" of A Sand County Almanac by Aldo Leopold to argue that domesticated and wild animals have differing moral statuses and that, similarly, individual animals and species of animals have differing moral statuses. Wild animals and species of animals have characteristics entitling them to a moral considerateness that is intrinsically inapplicable to the characteristics of domesticated and individual animals. The smallest unit of ethical considerability is the biotic community of which the individual "nonhuman natural entity" is a component of value only insofar as it contributes, in Leopold's words, to the "integrity, beauty, and stability of the biotic community" (Callicott 1980, 324–25).

Regarding domesticated versus wild animals, the relevant distinctions for Leopold are between things that are "unnatural, tame, and confined" and things that are "natural, wild, and free." Domesti-

cated animals, farm animals in particular, "have been bred to docility, tractability, stupidity, and dependency." They are "creations of
man," making "the complaint of some animal liberationists that the
'natural behavior' of chickens and bobby calves is cruelly frustrated
on factory farms" about as meaningful as "to speak of the natural
behavior of tables and chairs. . . . Leopold to all appearances never
considered the treatment of brood hens on a factory farm or steers in
a feed lot to be a pressing moral issue" (Callicott 1980, 314, 330).[2]

In the midst of these reflections I moved to a place where for the
first two years the owner continued her practice of raising a flock of
about a hundred chickens each summer for slaughter. That is how I
became acquainted with Viva, the chicken hen, the first chicken I
ever really knew. In the essay that I later wrote about her, I have
described how one day in August, I was surprised to discover the
chicken house, which I had gotten into the habit of visiting, deserted.

Then I saw her. She was stumbling around over by the feed
cylinder on the far side where the low shelf piled with junk
makes everything dark. A shaft of sunlight had caught her, but
by the time I was able to get inside she had scrunched herself
deep in the far corner underneath the shelf against the wall. She
shrank as I reached in to gather her up and lift her out of there. I
held her in my lap stroking her feathers and looked at her. She
was small and looked as if she had never been in the sun. Her
feathers and legs and beak were brownstained with dirt and
feces and dust. Her eyes were as lusterless as the rest of her, and
her feet and legs were deformed. I let her go and she hobbled
back to the corner where she must have spent the summer,
coming out only to eat and drink. She had managed to escape
being trampled to death in this overcrowded confinement shed,
unlike the chicken I had found some weeks earlier stretched out
and pounded into the dirt. (Davis 1990, 34)

I took Viva into our house, where she lived with my husband and
me until she died a few months later in November. She was severely
crippled but resourceful, and determined to get around. To steady
herself, she would spread her wings out so that the feather ends
touched the ground, and standing thus she would totter from side to
side in a painstaking adjustment before going ahead, a procedure that
had to be repeated every other step or so. Just one unsuccessful foray
off the rug onto the hardwood floor caused her to avoid bare floors
thereafter. Viva was not only strong-willed and alert; she was expres-

sive and responsive. One of the most touching things about her was her voice. She would always talk to me with her frail "peep" which never got any louder and seemed to come from somewhere in the center of her body which pulsed her tail at precisely the same time. Also, rarely, she gave a little trill. Often after one of her ordeals, in which her legs would get caught in her wings, causing her terrible confusion and distress, I would sit talking to her, stroking her beautiful back and her feet that were so soft between the toes and on the bottoms, and she would carry on the dialogue with me, her tail feathers twitching in a kind of unison with each of her utterances.

This kind of nature and experience did not seem to have a niche in environmental ethics, including the radical branch of deep ecology, making environmentalism seem in a certain sense to be little more than an offshoot of the prevailing scientific worldview with its hard logical categories and contempt for the weak and vulnerable. Concerning farm animals, even the animal community tended to stand clear and, as ecofeminist animal advocate Harriet Schleifer pointed out, to hedge on the issue of "food" animals and vegetarianism, making the public feel "that the use of animals for food is in some way acceptable, since even the animal welfare people say so" (Schleifer 1985, 70).

During this time a letter appeared in *The Animals' Agenda* from a woman requesting that more coverage be given to farm animals, coverage similar to that accorded to whales. The editor's note that followed explained that "the plight of whales remains a high priority with both animal advocates and environmentalists." Whales, wrote the editor, are "intelligent, amazing, and benevolent creatures" whose increasing fund of world sympathy, built up by the agitation on their behalf, had yet to protect them. "Given that, if we can't protect the whales, what chance do we have of protecting the chickens of the world?" (Dahl 1987, 47). It seemed, however, fair to ask what chance there could ever be of protecting the chickens of the world if their only defenders viewed their plight as less than a "high priority."

This dilemma, crystallized for me by my recent encounters with Sagan, Callicott, and Viva, led me to compose an essay, "Farm Animals and the Feminine Connection," on the triangular affair between feminism, farm animals, and deep ecology. I argue that although nonhuman animals are oppressed by basic strategies and attitudes that are similar to those operating in the oppression of women, it is also true that men have traditionally admired and even sought to

Thinking Like a Chicken

emulate certain kinds of animals, even as they set out to subjugate and destroy them, whereas they have not traditionally admired or sought to emulate women. Animals summoning forth images of things that are "natural, wild, and free" accord with the "masculine" spirit of adventure and conquest idolized by our culture. Animals summoning forth images of things that are "unnatural, tame, and confined" represent a way of life that Western culture looks down upon. The contrast can be vividly seen in our literature. Whereas in Herman Melville's *Moby Dick* the hunters of the great white whale conceive of their prey as an awesome, godlike being, in William Golding's *Lord of the Flies* the little boys view the nursing sow, whom they violently rape with a spear, as an object of disgust.[3] The analogy between women and nonhuman animals overlooks perhaps a more specifically crucial comparison between women and farm animals.

Not only men but women and animal protectionists exhibit a culturally conditioned indifference toward, and prejudice against, creatures whose lives appear too slavishly, too boringly, too stupidly female, too "cowlike." Moreover, we regard conscious logical reasoning as the only valid sort of "mind." Evidence that chimpanzees possess such a mind is a primary reason why many are now insisting that they should be granted "human rights." Human rights for chimpanzees? Yes. Human rights for chickens? Meaningless.

This brings in the question of deep ecology. The philosophy of deep ecology, with its emphasis on the ecosphere as a whole, including both sentient and nonsentient beings, presents a salutary challenge to the reductionist logic and homocentric morality of Western culture. As the branch of environmentalism that emphasizes the spiritual component of nature and of our relationship to the natural world, deep ecology offers deliverance from the Western exfoliative global enterprise based on mechanistic models and unbridled greed of acquisition and inquiry masquerading as progress.

However, like its parent stock of environmentalism, deep ecology is infested by a macho mystique, whereby "things natural, wild, and free" continue to be celebrated and phallicized as corresponding to the "human" order of experience and idealized existence. Activities such as hunting, fishing, and meat-eating are extolled on recreational and spiritual grounds as part of the challenge posed by Leopold to "think like a mountain." Homage is paid to the "hunter-gatherer" lifestyle, with virtually all of the tribute going to the hunter and none to the gatherer. Armed with the new ethic, men essentially give to themselves a new lease to run with the predators, not the prey, and to identify with the "wild" and not the "tame." Western culture's smug identification with the "knower" at the expense of the "known" stays intact, albeit mysticized in a headdress claimed to derive from the Mythic Past.

Thus it is not surprising that many proponents of deep ecology cannot find an ethical niche for farm animals or for the qualities of mercy and compassion and the desirability of treating others as we wish to be treated. I discussed these issues in a further essay, "Mixing Without Pain," and there things stood until my participation in the 1992 Summit for the Animals meeting recalled them to my attention so vividly that I wrote a reply, "Clucking Like a Mountain," the kernel of the present essay, this time from the viewpoint of a battery-caged "laying" hen.

In the meantime, a year and a half before the Summit for the Animals meeting, in October 1990, I had founded United Poultry Concerns, a nonprofit organization that addresses the treatment of domestic fowl in food production, science, education, entertainment, and human companionship situations and promotes the respectful and compassionate treatment of domestic fowl as fellow creatures rather than a food source or other commodity. United Poultry Concerns grew out of the above experiences, and from my volunteer internship at Farm Sanctuary (an enterprise based on the rescue of factory farm animals) where I extended my acquaintance with chickens and got to know turkeys, ducks, and geese.

Back home I discovered that another lame hen had been left behind following the owner's removal of the flock to the slaughterhouse. Tulip was my beloved friend for a year until she died of a heart attack, to which chickens bred for rapid growth and excessive muscle tissue ("meat") are susceptible. Since then, chickens have become the center of my personal and professional life. I had an enclosure built onto our kitchen for rescued chickens who have the run of our three-acre yard. Amid the darkness of my knowledge of the horrible experiences inscribed within billions of chickens by our species, they are the peace and the light.

The Summit meeting had as its featured speaker environmentalist-historian Roderick Frazier Nash, who presented the attractive holistic concept of environmentalism along with the, to me, unattractive outlook in which species and biosystems prevail over the individuals composing them—except in the case of the human species, for which environmentalism in general seems to provide an

Thinking Like a Chicken

exemption. Concerning hunting, the familiar justifications were given, including the inquiry how and why the sacrifice of one or two deer should matter as long as the herd or species is preserved from decimation or extinction. Humans are predators by nature. In Nash's "dream of Island Civilization" essay, the ecotopian future is one in which "Humans could take their place along with the other predators . . . in an expanded ecological brotherhood" of all beings (Nash 1991/92, 2). Ideally, an intensely urban culture would flourish on the basis of a hunter-gatherer society complete with predator initiation rites. The exciting hunter part is vividly evoked; the boring gatherer part is left for the reader to infer.

As usual, farm animals are relegated to the wasteland of foregone conclusions in which they are considered to be not only ecologically out of tune but too denatured and void of autonomy for human morality to apply to them. The recognition that human beings are specifically and deliberately responsible for whatever aberrances farm animals may embody, that their discordances reflect our, not their, primary disruption of natural rhythms, and that we owe them more rather than less for having stripped them of their birthright and earthrights has not entered into the environmentalist discussions that I've encountered to date. The situation of these animals, within themselves and on the planet, does not appear to exact contrition or reparations from the perpetrators of their plight, while the victims are per se denied "rights," of which the most elemental must surely be the right of a being to be perceived before being conceptually trashed.

In an article following "Triangular Affair," Callicott assigns farm animals a fixed, degraded niche in the conceptual universe. "Barnyard animals, over hundreds of generations, have been genetically engineered (by the old-fashioned method of selective breeding) to play certain roles in the mixed community [human communities including domesticated animals]. To condemn the morality of these roles . . . is to condemn the very being of these creatures" (Callicott 1988a, 167). I think to myself, listening to the trumpet blasts and iron oratory of environmentalism, how could the soft voice of Viva ever hope to be heard here? In this world, the small tones of life are drowned out by the regal harmonies of the mountain and their ersatz echoes in the groves of academe. A snottish article in *Buzzworm: The Environmental Journal* (Knox 1991) on animal rights versus environmentalism clinched matters.

This is how I came to write "Clucking Like a Mountain" (contained within this essay), in which I examine the ethical foundations of environmentalism from the imaginary viewpoint of a factory-farm battery hen via a human interpreter. Leopold's plea for humans to think ecoholistically—"like a mountain"—has been taken by some environmentalists as a mandate to exclude from substantive and ethical consideration the individuated existences that help constitute the mountain, particularly those classified in Leopold's terms as "unnatural, tame, and confined" in contrast to those regarded as "natural, wild, and free." The ontological result is a holism devoid of contents, resembling an empty shell. The ethical result is moral abandonment of beings whose sufferings and other experiences are inconsequential compared to the "big realm." I raise questions concerning our moral obligations to genetically altered and weaker creatures, especially those debilitated by our activities, pointing out, moreover, that domesticated chickens have been shown to retain their ancestral repertoire of behaviors, which undermines the prima facie assumption that they have been rendered docile and servile through breeding for specific traits.

Clucking Like a Mountain

"Why do you keep putting off writing about me?"
It is the voice of a chicken that asks this.

—Alice Walker (1988, 170)

In answering the call of ecologists to think like a mountain, I have to know whether this would conflict with my effort to think like a chicken. For I have chosen with the American writer Alice Walker to be a microphone held up to the mouths of chickens to enable them to step forward and expound their lives. I am glad that I have been able to see and identify with a chicken, though I grieve that my ability to communicate what I have seen and have identified with may be limited by profound but obscure obstacles which it is nevertheless my task to try to traverse. To think like a mountain implies a splendid obligation and tragic awareness. Environmentalist Aldo Leopold coined this image in 1949 to contrast the abiding interests of the ecosphere with the ephemeral ones of humans, arguing that unless we can identify with the ecosphere and "think like a mountain," our species and perhaps even our planet are doomed.[4]

Individuals inspired by Leopold and others have poignantly expressed on occasion the yearning of many humans to break out of our isolation as persons and as a species and to recover, through the story that connects us with all beings, our larger identity in the heartbeat of the living universe (see Seed et al. 1988, 57). I prize these thoughts but have been saddened that Aldo Leopold may not have intended that chickens, too, should give voice in the Council of All Beings along with California Condor, Rainforest, Wombat, Wildflower, and the rest of the biotic host convened in empathic rituals designed to reconstitute the experience in humans of a larger ecological Self. In the Council of All Beings, says a workshop guideline, "the beings are invited to tell how life has changed for them under the present conditions that humans have created in the world" (Seed et al. 1988, 111).

Megaphone please.

> I am a battery hen. I live in a cage so small I cannot stretch my wings. I am forced to stand night and day on a sloping wire mesh floor that painfully cuts into my feet. The cage walls tear my feathers, forming blood blisters that never heal. The air is so full of ammonia that my lungs hurt and my eyes burn and I think I am going blind. As soon as I was born, a man grabbed me and sheared off part of my beak with a hot iron, and my little brothers were thrown into trash bags as useless alive.
>
> My mind is alert and my body is sensitive and I should have been richly feathered. In nature or even a farmyard I would have had sociable, cleansing dust baths with my flock mates, a need so strong that I perform "vacuum" dust bathing on the wire floor of my cage. Free, I would have ranged my ancestral jungles and fields with my mates, devouring plants, earthworms, and insects from sunrise to dusk. I would have exercised my body and expressed my nature, and I would have given, and received, pleasure as a whole being. I am only a year old, but I am already a "spent hen." Humans, I wish I were dead, and soon I will be dead. Look for pieces of my wounded flesh wherever chicken pies and soups are sold.

According to Callicott, the treatment of hens on a factory farm has not been morally important in the development of environmental ethics. Ecologically, this hen, like other domesticated "farm" animals, is not on a moral par with the authentic and autonomous creatures of the world but with all of the intrusive human technologies, from dune buggies to hybrid corn, doing their dirty work of contributing to the despoliation of the biotic community into which they had been inserted. Moreover, it is about as absurd to complain that the natural behavior of a chicken on a factory farm is frustrated as it would be to talk about the "natural behavior" of a piece of furniture. Black slaves were "metaphysically autonomous." Wild animals are metaphysically autonomous. Even caged wild animals retain metaphysical autonomy as "captive, not indentured, beings." But cows, pigs, sheep, and chickens? Veal calves and domesticated turkeys? Callicott asserts, "They have been bred to docility, tractability, stupidity, and dependency. It is literally meaningless to suggest that they be liberated" (Callicott 1980, 330).[5]

This *lasciate ogni speranza, voi ch'entrate*[6] focused my concern about the fate of domesticated animals in environmental ethics. This burgeoning branch of philosophy seems in large part to cloak the old macho mystique of unrestricted power, conquest, and disdain for the defenseless, idolized by our culture, in pseudoscientific, pseudopoetical distinctions between beings who are "natural, wild, and free" and things that are "unnatural, tame, and confined" (Leopold 1966, xix). Pity—look down on but do not sympathize or identify with—all the dodos and dunces in the history of the world too dumb to succeed in the cosmic power plays wherein the metaphysical autonomy of just one species is ensured.

This attitude contains errors of fact and logic and draws attention to certain unfavorable elements in our cultural and even species psychology. In *Where the Wasteland Ends* historian Theodore Roszak says, "The experience of being a cosmic absurdity, a creature obtruded into the universe without purpose, continuity, or kinship, is the psychic price we pay for scientific 'enlightenment' and technological prowess" (1973, 154). The fact is, we are not the only ones paying this price, nor is a psychic price the only one paid, as 16 billion chickens worldwide can tell us now. A Nietzschean analysis might suggest that the "rational" relegation of domesticated animals to the moral wasteland in environmental ethics is yet another instance in our species' history of the "irrational" heaping onto other creatures, to be punished and banished in our stead, of things that we fear and hate in ourselves, such as the capacity for enslavement and the destructibility of our personality, identity, and will by conquerors more powerful than ourselves. We project our existential anxiety and inanity onto our victims: "I am not the creature obtruded into the universe without purpose, continuity or kinship but this genetically altered cow, this egg-laying machine of a dumb-ass chicken. I created them, which gives me the right to despise and abuse them. They let me 'create' them, which gives me the right to despise and abuse them." The next step is to assert that these animals wanted, even chose, to resign their metaphysical autonomy to the will of humans on the darkling plain of evolution.

Environmentalism challenges us to think about how we view and treat the weaker and more pacific beings in our midst, be they nonhuman or otherwise. It invites us to explore how we want, on principle, to regard these beings. Are we content to maintain that a genetically altered creature, or a docile and perhaps even stupid one, deserves to be morally disdained or abandoned? Do we believe that a weaker creature is less entitled to justice and compassion than more vigorous types? Do we suppose that creatures whose lives we humans have wrecked do not have paramount moral claims on us?

Environmentalism has a tendency to blame such victims. There are implications that ecological sophistication comports with turning away from them sniffily, like a bored husband, or Dr. Frankenstein, to things more "interesting" and grand, like a mountain or, more aptly, to "thinking" like one.

Adherents of environmentalism have rapped animal rights advocates on the knuckles for caring about "little things," like individuals and beings with feelings. By contrast, environmentalists operate in the big realm:

> They at least attempt to listen to the entire fugue of rocks and trees, amoebas and heavy metals, dodos and rivers and styrofoam. Animal rights, by contrast, is a one-note samba. Where environmentalists worry about salt marshes and all the plants and creatures therein, animal rights activists worry about the suffering of individual animals. Where environmentalists worry about the evolution of island endemics, animal rights activists worry about the suffering of individual animals. Where environmentalists worry about species extinctions, animal rights activists worry about the suffering of individual animals. (Knox 1991, 31–32)

A question for environmentalism concerns the nature of the big realm it claims to represent and worry about.[7] If, ecologically regarded, the concrete manifestations of existence are inconsequential, what substance does this realm possess? What are its contents and where do they reside exactly? Can the ecosphere be thus hollowed out without being converted to a shell? An ecologist once said in an interview that the individual life is a mere "blip on a grid" compared to the life process.[8] Yet, it may be that there is no "life process" apart from the individual forms it assumes, whereby we infer it. The "process" is an inference, an abstraction, and while there is nothing wrong with generalizing and speculating on the basis of experience, to reify the unknown at the expense of the known shows a perversity of will. How is it possible, as the environmentalist asserts, to worry about "all the plants and creatures" of a system while managing to avoid caring about each and every one? Why would anyone *want* not to care?

I know of no composer or lover of music who disparages the individual notes of a composition the way some environmentalists scorn the individual animals of this world. Maybe this is because the musically educated person perceives in each note the universe of song that note in turn helps to create. The poet William Blake said that we must learn to see the universe in a grain of sand. We must learn with equal justice and perception to hear the music of the spheres in the cluck of a chicken, starting with the hen who, historian Page Smith says, "is rich in comfortable sounds, chirps and chirrs, and, when she is a young pullet, a kind of sweet singing that is full of contentment when she is clustered together with her sisters and brothers in an undifferentiated huddle of peace and well-being waiting for darkness to envelop them" (Smith and Daniel 1975, 334). If I think like a mountain, will I be able to hear this hen singing?

To accept the environmentalist argument that the suffering of individual animals is inconsequential compared to the ozone layer, we must be willing to admit that the sufferings of minority groups, raped women, battered wives, abused children, people sitting on death row, and our loved ones are small potatoes beneath the hole in the sky. To worry about any of them is, in effect, to miniaturize the big picture to portraits of battered puppy dogs.[9] Or does environmentalism shift to the more convenient ground, when it comes to humans and oneself, where all species are equal but one species is more equal than others and membership has its privileges? An environmentalist writes: "We care about bears and buttercups for themselves, but also for us humans. That's the selfish, Cartesian bottom line: I think, therefore I deserve a hospitable environment" (Knox 1991, 37). The reasoning may or may not be sound; the sensibility makes my hackles rise.

This sensibility has placed many environmentalists at a distance from so-called "farm" animals and allowed them to patronize the nature of these animals without checking the facts. Environmentalism has two major moral arguments against agricultural animals.

One is that agricultural animals disrupt the natural environment. Environmentalists and animal rights advocates agree that large-scale, intensive animal agriculture is ecologically inefficient and unseemly, and ethically obscene. The United States poultry industry pollutes fields and streams with 14 billion pounds of manure and 28 billion gallons of waste water each year. According to a report, "Thousands of poultry farms and processing factories churn out millions of birds everyday—along with carcasses and chemicals that contaminate the land and poison the water with toxic wastes" (Giardina and Bates 1991, 8). This is detestable, but it is not the chickens' fault. It is ours.

Environmentalism's second major moral complaint against domesticated, farm animals is that they lack the behavioral repertoire and élan vital of wild animals, including their own ancestors. As a result, farm animals are disentitled to equal moral consideration with wild animals. If this is true, the blame is not on them; it is on us. Morally, we owe them more, not less, for bungling their birthright. But how diminished is the nature of these animals genetically? Two researchers who have been studying the behavior of "laying" hens for years state:

> A good place to begin thinking about what a hen needs for a decent life would be in the jungles of Southeast Asia where, with persistence, one can track the red jungle fowl ancestors of the domestic chicken. These wary birds live in small groups of between four and six, and are highly active during the day— walking, running, flying, pecking and scratching for food, and preening. At night they roost together in the trees. Domestic chickens released on the islands off Queensland, Australia, and the west coast of Scotland showed remarkably similar patterns of behaviour. David Wood-Gush and Ian Duncan, of the Agricultural and Food Research Council's Edinburgh Station, observed that the Scottish birds formed small, discrete social groups which spent much of their day foraging either separately or together, then returning at dusk to roost. The hens concealed their nests and raised and defended their broods. In short, there is no evidence that genetic selection for egg laying has eliminated the birds' potential to perform a wide variety of behaviour. (Nicol and Dawkins 1990, 46)

This snookers the industry claim, which has been brought by environmentalists, that "laying" hens have been "bred" for the battery cage and are genetically accommodated to a sterile, docile, and slavish existence that would drive humans and wild animals mad. How many environmentalists are aware that, in addition to the routine debeaking and sometimes even claw removal of these birds (to help "adaptation" along), efforts have been made to fit them with contact lenses to "calm" their "uneconomical" frenzy by destroying their vision (Davis 1992)?[10] Dr. Nedim Buyukmihci, a veterinary ophthalmologist at the University of California, Davis, says of even these birds that upon release from the cage and removal of the lenses, following a period of adjustment, those hens in his care "would do *all* the things hens normally would do if allowed: scratch for food, dustbathe, spend time with one another or apart from one another, make attempts at flight, stretch their wings and legs simultaneously, preen, and the like. Preening, of course, was severely curtailed due to the mutilation of their beaks" (Buyukmihci 1992).

Contrary to the unexamined assumption that "laying" hens are our metaphysical slaves, Dr. Page Smith, the cultural historian of the chicken, correctly observes: "Chickens are, on the whole, very sturdy creatures or they could not have survived the experiments that have been performed on them in the last fifty or seventy-five years in the name of scientific chicken raising" (Smith and Daniel 1975, 331).[11]

Paradoxically, like most of us, chickens are sturdy and vulnerable and, in situations that insult their nature, pitiable. Their experience of being alive in the flesh—be it one of pain, joy, or learned helplessness—is as much a part of the biosphere as the composite experience of a mountain. It feels good to think like a mountain and experience the Romantic Stone Age sensations of a predator (not prey) and a hunter (who in ecology has taken equal trouble to ramify the gratifications of being a gatherer?). It does not feel good to think like a battery hen and view oneself and one's species through her eyes, not as an autochthonous Hero in Chains but as a bewilderingly cruel creature who punishes her and has no mercy.

Epilogue

I submitted "Clucking Like a Mountain" to *Environmental Ethics*, "an interdisciplinary journal dedicated to the philosophical aspects of environmental problems," because it seemed to provide the best opportunity to meet the environmentalist community on its own conceptual grounds. The editor turned it down.[12] Of the two referees, one favored and the other opposed publication. The one in favor did not "share the author's views," but considered it a "highly worthwhile essay . . . a provocative piece, challenging the views that generally dominate the pages of *Environmental Ethics.*"

The second reader, seemingly a poultry researcher, insisted that the arguments ignored "much factual information," for instance, that "it is in the interest of those individuals that raise hens in battery cages that the welfare of those hens is not so ignored that egg production is impaired" and that "the industry has made considerable strides in determining the proper mesh size for battery cages to avoid leg entrapment." The two major problems of hens in battery cages, as in all intensive animal agriculture, are (1) that when things go wrong they go wrong in a big way and (2) waste disposal. I had failed to mention the major benefit of "increased productivity through a savings in time and labor." Moreover, I had implied that hens could care about the death of other chickens and ignored the disadvantages of free-range production, making the imaginary viewpoint of a factory-farm battery hen via a human interpreter read like "lopsided anthropomorphism."

In rejecting the manuscript, the editor said it ignored much material that readers of the journal are familiar with, including Callicott's " 'Triangular Affair,' which discusses chickens in some detail," and Birch and Cobb's *The Liberation of Life,* "which specifically contrasts the lives of chickens with chimpanzees" (Hargrove 1992). The editor has a policy of not publishing papers on animal welfare ethics unless they pertain specifically to environmental ethics. The point of a revised paper would have to continue to be that domestic chickens should be a concern of environmental ethicists from an environmental perspective, supporting Callicott's argument in "Back Together Again" (1988a) that we need a single ethic.

I believe that we need a single ethic in which we are a voice not only for life but for lives—for all of the soft and innocent lives who are at our mercy. I share Callicott's Darwinian view that we and other animals have a common biosociality rooted in evolutionary kinship and, in the case of domesticated animals, direct interactions that often include mutual affection. However, I do not share his position in "Back Together Again" that "barnyard" and other domesticated animals have an a priori ontological status whereby their very being is synonymous with the diminished roles humans have assigned to them as food sources, plow pullers, and pets. Nor do I believe that there is a kind of evolved, unspoken social contract between "man and beast" in the so-called mixed community of humans and domestic animals (Callicott 1988a, 167), in which the "beasts" just happen to be our slaves and inferiors whom we treat exactly as we please, as in our manipulation of their reproductive systems for market efficiency and other purely human ends rather than species fitness or their individual and social happiness. The will of the domesticated animal is no different from that of a human slave in being at the mercy of an "owner" backed by a legal system that defines the slave as property.

The contract idea ignores these and other facts, such as the innumerable diseases of domestication which, pertinently, have created a flourishing animal research, pharmaceutical, and veterinary industry. It romanticizes and exonerates our relationship to domesticated animals and teasingly suggests that species that in other environmentalist contexts are rigorously denied moral agency and autonomy, in some sort of lopsided scapegoatism, just happen to have them here.[13] Domesticated animals were themselves once wild and free. "Egg-type" chickens released into wild habitats they personally have never known revive their suppressed behavioral repertoire. Whether farm and other domesticated animals could survive under feral conditions, it is inappropriate to refer to an "unspoken social contract" between themselves and their human "masters."

The editor of *Environmental Ethics* cites Birch and Cobb's contrast between the life of a chicken and the life of a chimpanzee. In *Matters of Life and Death,* John Cobb, a professor of Christian theology, raises contemporary issues including whether humans have the right to destroy the environment and exterminate or cause extreme suffering to other species. In a section on animal rights, he distinguishes between the life of chickens, veal calves, tuna, and sharks and the life of humans, nonhuman primates, and marine mammals, arguing that while God's perspective comprises both groups, "the right to life applies much more to gorillas and dolphins than to chickens and sharks" (Cobb 1992, 36). Understandably, chickens and sharks regard their lives as most important. However, "judgment" regards their death to preclude further experiences of much less distinctive value than does the death of a primate or sea mammal, and their contribution to the divine life to be much less significant. In Cobb's view, the potential experiences of veal calves, chickens, and others consigned to their class are "not remarkably distinctive"; these animals' fear of death is "not an important factor in their lives," and their death "does not cause major distress to others" (Cobb 1992, 40).

In short, the editor's letter, with its suggested reading, acts out my own analysis. It seeks to shout down the voice of the individual animal and author and to delegitimize me as a speaker who knows chickens in deference to the "experts" with whom the world order and divine mind just happen to agree that animals humans like to eat (such as chickens, veal calves, and tuna) and animals who like to eat humans (such as sharks) have less valuable personal and interpersonal experiences and a lesser part in the universe. How do the experts know? They decided.

I have been impressed by the realization that a few men have virtually "decided" what experiences count and even exist in the world. The language of Western science—the reigning construct of male hegemony—precludes the ability to express the experiential realities it talks about. Virtually all the actual experiences of this world, expressed through the manifest and mysterious characteristics of all the different beings, are unrepresented in the stainless steel edicts of experts. Where is the voice of the voiceless in the scientific literature, including the literature of environmental ethics? Where do the "memory of suffering and the truths of subjugated knowledge" fit into the domineering construct of our era (Adams and Procter-Smith 1993, 302)?

Carol J. Adams and Marjorie Procter-Smith ironically observe that "the voice of the voiceless offers a truth that the voice of the expert can never offer" (1993, 302). This voice requires a different language from the language of experts, a verbal and lyrical equivalent of the subjective and intersubjective experiences linking humans to one another and, through an epistemology rooted in our evolutionary history, to other animals and the earth. Significantly, the poultry science referee of my "Clucking" essay chides me with "too much first person singular" and snorts that "sixteen billion chickens cannot tell me the psychic price of scientific enlightenment."

If women feel bludgeoned by this oppressive mentality, how must the animals be affected by it? Let us consider not only the pain that we impose on them, but the moral ecology within which we inflict it—the belittling, sniggering atmosphere of pompous hatred and contempt that we emanate in which countless billions of beings are forced to live. This moral ecology is as distinctive a human contribution to the range of experiences in the world as anything else that our species has conferred.[14]

I have a photograph of a poultry researcher posing for the media in an experimental battery hen unit with a scientifically blinded and defeated hen in his arms and a smile on his face (Greene 1992, A-6). I have a letter from a poultry experimenter who writes: "I think you will agree that the human species is the only one that has any compassion for its prey. . . . I perceive in your literature the proposal that chickens be treated as pets. The child who is holding a Plymouth barred rock hen should stay near a supply of clean clothes. I have been involved with many thousands of chickens and turkeys and I don't think they are good pets, although it is evident that almost any vertebrate may be trained to come for food" (Jukes 1992).

This is the voice of the expert so insensitized that the image of a little girl tenderly holding a hen in her arms produces only thoughts of the hen's defecation—a reminder that his involvement with thousands of chickens and turkeys is such that they evacuate when he touches them. In being barred from entering the environmentalist dialogue by way of "Clucking Like a Mountain," I cannot help wondering how far the delegitimization process acts as a form of intellectual protection against the mute importunities and soft dialogues of all the Vivas in the world. There is no comfort in seeing the eyes of a hen staring out of the cage built especially for her. The supposition that she has no expression, nothing to express, is, however, a great comfort.

Notes

1. This extended essay on "food" animal slaughter and vegetarianism was written in 1892 as a preface to the Russian edition of Howard Williams's *Ethics of Diet* (1883). Williams's book is a biographical history of philosophic vegetarianism from antiquity through the early nineteenth century.

2. See Callicott (1980, 315): Toward the "urgent concern of animal liberationists for the suffering of domestic animals . . . Leopold manifests an attitude which can only be described as indifference."

3. In *Lord of the Flies* (Golding 1954), see chapter 8, "Gift for the Darkness."

4. Says Leopold (1966, 137): "Only the mountain has lived long enough to listen objectively to the howl of a wolf."

5. See also Callicott, "Farm Animal Feminism" (1988b). Cf. Ursula K. Le Guin, "She Unnames Them" (1985, 27): "Cattle, sheep, swine, asses, mules, and goats, along with chickens, geese, and turkeys, all agreed enthusiastically to give their names back to the people to whom—as they put it—they belonged."

6. "Abandon all hope, you who enter here," the inscription on the entrance to hell in Dante's *Inferno* 3.9. See also Davis, "Farm Animals and the Feminine Connection" (1988b); "Mixing Without Pain" (1989); and "Farm Animal Feminism" (1988a).

7. For a valuable consideration of this issue, see Michael Allen Fox, "Environmental Ethics and the Ideology of Meat Eating" (1993). He says, for instance, concerning the environmentalist dismissal of dietary ethics and the suffering of individual animals, that it is "ethically myopic and no more than self-serving; it is an example of the kind of compartmentalized thinking that humans have practiced far too long and from which environmental ethicists had promised to deliver us. It is a kind of thinking that must be abandoned if human and other forms of life are to coexist and flourish on this planet" (122).

8. In Pacelle, "The Foreman of Radical Environmentalism" (1987), David Foreman of Earth First! is quoted as saying: "I see individual lives as momentary energy blips on a grid" (8).

9. In "The Rights Stuff," Knox (1991, 37) concludes that "Those who would fight the earth's battles can't help but make common cause with animal rights activists where their interests coincide—but carefully, lest the ever-elusive big picture doesn't get miniaturized into portraits of battered puppy dogs."

10. See Karen Davis, "Red Contact Lenses for Chickens: A Benighted Concept" (1992). Available from United Poultry Concerns, Inc., P.O. Box 59367, Potomac, MD 20859.

11. The 1994 report *Laying Hens* by the Swiss Society for the Protection of Animals upholds this claim, noting, "Neither thousands of years of domestication nor the recent extreme selective breeding for productivity have fundamentally altered the behaviour of chickens. The frequently expressed view that the brooding instinct has been bred out of present-day hybrid birds has been proved wrong. Hens repeatedly become broody even under intensive production conditions" (11). My personal experience with domesticated chickens over the past ten years supports these observations.

12. Except for some sentence tightening, "Clucking Like a Mountain"—this essay within the essay—is represented here exactly as it was submitted to the editor of *Environmental Ethics*.

13. See, e.g., Mary Anne Warren, "The Rights of the Nonhuman World" (1992).

14. On the concept of the moral ecology of pain and suffering, see Karen Davis, "What's Wrong with Pain Anyway?" (1989).

References

Adams, Carol J., and Marjorie Procter-Smith. 1993. Taking Life or "Taking on Life"?: Table Talk and Animals. In *Ecofeminism and the Sacred*, ed. Carol J. Adams. New York: Continuum.

Birch, Charles, and John B. Cobb Jr. 1981. *The Liberation of Life: From the Cell to the Community*. Cambridge: Cambridge University Press.

Buyukmihci, Nedim C. 1992. Letter to the author, 9 March.

Callicott, J. Baird. 1980. Animal Liberation: A Triangular Affair. *Environmental Ethics* 2:311–38.

——. 1988a. Animal Liberation and Environmental Ethics: Back Together Again. *Between the Species: A Journal of Ethics* 4:163–69. Reprinted in *The Animal Rights/Environmental Ethics Debate: The Environmental Perspective*, ed. Eugene C. Hargrove. Albany: State University of New York Press, 1992, 249–61.

——. 1988b. Farm Animal Feminism. [letter to editor]. *The Animals' Agenda* (June):3–4.

Cobb, John B., Jr. 1992. *Matters of Life and Death.* Louisville, Ky.: Westminster/John Knox Press.

Dahl, Ruth [Mrs. Richard A.]. 1987. Thinks We Show Favoritism to Whales [letter to editor]. *The Animals' Agenda* (June):47.

Davis, Karen. 1988a. Farm Animal Feminism [letter]. *The Animals' Agenda* (June):4.

——. 1988b. Farm Animals and the Feminine Connection. *The Animals' Agenda* (January/February):38–39.

——. 1989. What's Wrong with Pain Anyway? *The Animals' Agenda* (February):50–51.

——. 1989. Mixing Without Pain. *Between the Species: A Journal of Ethics* 5:33–37.

——. 1990. Viva, The Chicken Hen (June–November 1985). *Between the Species: A Journal of Ethics* 6:33–35.

——. 1992. Red Contact Lenses for Chickens: A Benighted Concept. Potomac, Md.: United Poultry Concerns, Inc.

Fox, Michael Allen. 1993. Environmental Ethics and the Ideology of Meat Eating. *Between the Species: A Journal of Ethics* 9:121–32.

Giardina, Denise, and Eric Bates. 1991. Fowling the Nest. *Southern Exposure* 19(2):8–12.

Golding, William. 1954. *Lord of the Flies.* N.p.: Wideview/Perigree Books.

Greene, Jan. 1992. Cal Poly Chicken Study Ruffles Feathers: Animal Rights Groups Blast Contact Lens Study. *Telegram-Tribune* (San Luis Obispo, Calif.) 13 March, A-1, A-6.

Hargrove, Eugene C. 1992. Letter to author, 18 October.

Jukes, Thomas H. 1992. Letter to author, 4 September.

Knox, Margaret L. 1991. The Rights Stuff. *Buzzworm: The Environmental Journal* 3(3):31–37.

Le Guin, Ursula. 1985. She Unnames Them. *The New Yorker*, 21 January, 27.

Leopold, Aldo. 1966. *A Sand County Almanac.* New York: Ballantine Books. Originally published 1949.

Nash, Roderick Frazier. 1991/92. Island Civilization: A Vision for Planet Earth in the Year 2992. *Wild Earth* (Winter):2–4.

Nicol, Christine, and Marian Stamp Dawkins. 1990. Homes Fit for Hens. *New Scientist* (March 17):46–51.

Pacelle, Wayne. 1987. The Foreman of Radical Environmentalism: A Discussion with David Foreman of Earth First! *The Animals' Agenda* (December):6–9, 52–53.

Roszak, Theodore. 1973. *Where the Wasteland Ends: Politics and Transcendence in Postindustrial Society.* New York: Anchor Books.

Sagan, Carl. 1977. *The Dragons of Eden: Speculation on the Evolution of Human Intelligence.* New York: Random House.

Schleifer, Harriet. 1985. Images of Life and Death: Food Animal Production and the Vegetarian Option. In *In Defense of Animals,* ed. Peter Singer, 63–73. New York: Basil Blackwell.

Seed, John, et al. 1988. *Thinking Like a Mountain: Towards a Council of All Beings.* Philadelphia, Pa.: New Society Publishers.

Smith, Page, and Charles Daniel. 1975. *The Chicken Book: Being an Inquiry into the Rise and Fall, Use and Abuse, Triumph and Tragedy of Gallus Domesticus.* Boston: Little, Brown.

Swiss Society for the Protection of Animals STS. 1994. *Laying Hens: 12 Years of Experience with New Husbandry Systems in Switzerland.* Bern: Kummerly & Frey AG.

Walker, Alice. 1988. Why Did the Balinese Chicken Cross the Road? *Living by the Word: Selected Writings 1973–1987.* New York: Harcourt Brace Jovanovich.

Warren, Mary Anne. 1992. The Rights of the Nonhuman World. *The Animal Rights/Environmentalist Ethics Debate: The Environmental Perspective,* ed. Eugene C. Hargrove, 185–210. Albany: State University of New York Press.

9
Diane Antonio

Of Wolves
and Women

Developing an ethic of care and respect toward nonhuman animals is a challenge to the feminist moral imagination. It will necessitate an examination of our relationship not only to the similarities underlying all animal life, but also the development of new ways of relating to the differences. Such an examination touches on the sources of racism and classism, for ecofeminism generally contends that moral failures of perception and imagination between human and nonhuman realms of nature are symptomatic of similar failures between men and women, races, and social classes.[1]

In contemporary theorizing about the human-animal relation, both those who build theories of natural and/or legal animal rights and those who draw oppositions between *women and nature* and *men and culture* may be criticized for being self-referencing or anthropocentric in relation to the natural world. In certain versions of the former theory, rights are extended to animals because of their likeness to humans, insofar as they are experiencing subjects of their own lives or independent individuals (Rigterink 1992). Animal species are not necessarily or primarily regarded as lifeways possessing intrinsic value, and nonhuman animal rights claims become competitive with human rights claims. In some accounts of the latter theory, those who focus upon a certain equivalence between nature and women, also emphasize similarity, neglecting a relation to difference. In fact, there are serious differences to be addressed if we are to be true to our goal of a robust and more equitable relationship with nonhuman animals. And while we should not fall into glorifying nature in the abstract, as though it were something dancing "out there" on the other point of a dualism, or try to stamp out all fellow feeling for the qualities and interests of our own human species, neither may we facilely dismiss nonhuman animal qualities and values as being ontologically inferior to our own.[2]

Ecological philosophers like Deane Curtin provide a promising alternative by calling for a caring relationship to nonhuman life (1991, 60–75). But as others have pointed out, the idea of care is just a starting point for approaching nature on its own terms; it is not there a priori as a concept ready for use. To be consistent with general ecofeminist theory, it has to be forged out of the stuff of our own experience with an individual animal or out of a concrete situation in nature, such as imminent species extinction. (In my case, an interest in wolves began, not with an encounter with an individual wolf, although I have observed a wolf pack in captivity, but as a result of my acquaintance with an admirably wolf-like canine, an American pit bull terrier.)

In this essay, I suggest a way of shaping an ecofeminism or ethical theory of "care respect" (to use Robin S. Dillon's term; 1992, 73) that includes a deeper relationship of women to difference.

The Ethic of Care Respect

Women who seek to develop "respect" for the wolf may do so through rational analysis of the natural history of the wolf. To reach a respectful understanding of what wolves value, we must first educate ourselves about wolf behavior and imagine lived experience from the wolf's point of view. Second, we can attend to the wolf's needs for survival and a life without physical or emotional pain. Third, we can acknowledge wolves' inherent value as living creatures. At the same time as we attend to the wolf's need for us to live with better economy and equity on the earth, we would be recognizing our own moral need to give respect to nonhuman animals. In this way, we may help transform the phenomenal world according to our moral valuations in communication with wolves' observable valuations of activities, relationships, and events in their environment. As a practical matter, this transformation would be wrought first, according to a human valuation of the good—such as, for example, the continuity of sacred life or preservation of beauty on earth. Such public witnessing of our own valuations, based on women's self-respect as self-defined moral agents, is an exercise of political power. Then, by recognizing not only the similar but the differing values of the wolf—for example, acknowledging the wolf's service of balancing the ecosystem through predation—the ecofeminist would properly empower the animal as part of the earth community.[3]

So far "respect" has been defined as attentiveness to both the mutual interests of and the differences between human and nonhuman animals. But this is only half the picture of "care respect." What then constitutes "care" of the wolf?

"Care" is the desire to preserve the existence and to promote the good of wolves. It is a way for us to express respect for them and, in order to be complete, should result in our active moral response to their needs. As discussed above, respectful knowledge of what at first appears to be the other (wolves) results initially from recognizing the "similarity or affinity of the subject with the object of affection" (Aristotle, *Ethics*, bk. 6, sec. i). This respectful understanding arising first from similarity will in turn engender the desire to care for the nonhuman animal.

In loving a friend, one chooses to love one's own good, the "good" being the friend and the friend's virtues. Women align with wolves in the area of our desire *of* and their instincts *for* the good represented by their survival. Our desire for their continued existence directs our moral will to act respectfully on their behalf, even though the care can never be fully reciprocated in kind. Consider in this context the model of a mother with children, who does not seek equal benefit for the benefits she bestows but who rejoices nonetheless over her children's continued healthy existence. This paradigm can be broadly applied to the relationship of care between humans and wolves.

However, although ecofeminists might seek to conserve the wolf purely because of its intrinsic value as a life form and should not expect full reciprocity in kind, there *are* three forms of wolf reciprocation for human care. First, wolves do provide women, as children provide mothers, with the opportunity to satisfy our needs to "act or forbear acting out of benevolent concern" (Dillon 1992, 71) for living creatures, in order to become self-defined moral beings.

A second example of incidental but beneficial wolf response to our care is that the lifeway of wolves offers a socially empowering image of females as leaders, equal to or, in the case of young alpha females, exceeding that of alpha males in the survival skills required by the pack. Women's appreciation of these similarities in virtue between wolves and women—the female wolf's "spirit," which resembles human courage; or the "prudence" in survival ability, which in human terms is the political virtue par excellence—also offers an opportunity for creating a sense of our community with wolves. Physiological similarities, such as the fact that we share parts of our brain with the reptiles and other mammals, and emotional congruence—the fact that wolves display feelings of sadness, rage, disappointment, loss, joy, affection, embarrassment—further link us through our bodily natures, and make it that much easier to take into account the good of all animals, human and otherwise.

Finally, male/female human relations are greatly illuminated by considering how Western males relate to difference vis-à-vis *Canis lupus*. In her book *Pure Lust* (1984, 282–84), feminist philosopher Mary Daly explores the analogy between male violence toward women and the torture of animals (wild cows). If it is true that one builds relationship, initially, through identification of mutual interest, it would be fruitful to pursue a causal relation between men's cultural and philosophical concepts about women as incarnations of evil and the violent treatment of wolves, which has pushed them even to the brink of extinction. Western woman—in the guise of the irrational, the unlimited, the bestial, the inferior "other" end of the good/evil duality—had unleashed all the evils of Pandora's box upon the Classical world, preyed upon the sensuality of dreaming Jewish men, and caused males to be flung out of Paradise. Not incidentally, the European witch burnings of the Middle Ages coincided with Church-sponsored programs against the wolf, the archetype of the ravening beast in literature and folklore. And while "human" werewolf burnings ended in the eighteenth century, nonhuman wolves are targeted for torment to this day. The "other"—which is often typified by Western woman and which becomes, in this case, exemplified by a particularly hated nonhuman animal—is still perceived by some men as being irredeemably "evil."

Many ecofeminists rightly agree that our emotional attachments to individual animals and species are moral realities that need to be illuminated by feminist discourse. This discourse may help us expand the boundaries of the moral domain to include what has been seen to be, for both men and women, ontologically "other"—that is, nonhuman nature. In articulating a relation of care respect, then, we must move beyond the limiting concept of similarity, once it has been examined in the context of male mythmaking, and press for a more complete apprehension of the wolf in its concrete particularity of differences. In Josephine Donovan's words, we need to create a human ethic "in consideration and consultation and communication with other species" (1991, 424).

Despite similarities, or areas of mutual valuation, in so many ways, wolves are not like us, will never reason like us, and for all we know, would gain no advantage in "feeling" as we do about moral issues. For instance, from time to time, wolves bring down prey far in excess of food needs, destroy sick pups, and, contrary to popular opinion, have killed humans in North America, notably Inuit and other Native American hunters, who share territory and prey (Lopez 1978, 27, 51, 54, 69). That is not to say that human beings do not slaughter in excess of survival needs but that in the areas in which wolf behavior comes into conflict with our collective mores, we must enlarge our concept of moral virtue.

In her essay "Care and Respect," Dillon properly defines the virtue of "care" as a cherishing respect that manifests the "object's special worth." In this sense, an act of care not only reveals the presence of virtue in the one who cares and protects but reciprocally indicates virtue in those who are cared for and protected, helped to "pursue their ends," and assisted in satisfying their "wants and needs" (73).

The notion of an active "virtue" of care when applied to the behavior of a nonhuman animal is a problematic one, to be sure. Because of the rationalist bias of much traditional Western ethical philosophy (such as Platonist or Kantian theory), which requires, among other things, the voluntary intellectual cultivation of good judgment so that one may make sound moral choices, nonhuman animals may seem to be excluded from the realm of moral agency. Appearing to be devoid of choice of activity, or motivated by instincts alone, they often have been thought to be "virtuous" only in the pleasure or utility found in them by human beings.

However, as documented by Rick Bass in his book *The Ninemile Wolves* (1992), there may be enough behavioral variation in nonhuman animal individuals to allow for some choice, at least in degree, in the performance of their instinctual behaviors. For example, the so-called "Good Mom" (36, 103), a she-wolf living in the Ninemile Valley of Montana with her six cubs, shared a meadow with a herd of cows and chose not to teach her cubs to kill them. (Bass believes that wolves must be taught to prey on cattle.) This act of forbearance, not shared by all wolves who come upon grazing cattle, was virtuous in two senses. First, it was a caring act of protection of her cubs, who would have been persecuted had they become cattle killers. Second, the "Good Mom's" peaceful coexistence with cattle was virtuous in human economic terms, that is, she "respected" the ranchers' turf and did not "steal" from them. (I am not suggesting, however, that the "Good Mom" was cherishing the cattle, and thus revealing the presence of virtue in them!) Another example of differential caring behavior among wolves would be an individual wolf's choice or refusal to use force to seize food from pups (Bass 1992, 29).

Barry Holstun Lopez (1978) also argues for differing "personalities" and, therefore, variation in virtuous behavior, among wolves (33). Some babysitting adults, he says, are more playful and therefore more effective in teaching cubs how to hunt. He also discusses the great range of "feelings," "facial expressions," and "moods" displayed by wolves (44).

In addition to the idea of the virtue of caring being exhibited by individual nonhuman animals, there is already fertile ground in feminist thought for the development of a theory of "communal virtue" in regard to nonhuman creatures. Marilyn Friedman, in "Feminism and Modern Friendship: Dislocating the Community" (1992), has provided a useful paradigm for such a discourse. Her notion of a "communitarian self" or moral agent "constituted and defined by its communal attachments" (88) fits nicely with the notion of the strong social bonds of a wolf pack, for example. Wolves also share with humans the three types of communities outlined by Friedman: the "found" community into which one is born, the voluntary community of mating and companionship, and the nonvoluntary community of place in which the young and the old must dwell in order to survive (92–95). For the purposes of this essay, and taken in the context of a human cultural or nonhuman animal social structure—if not within an absolute value system, religious or otherwise—communal virtue may be provisionally defined as an attitude or quality or set of attitudes or qualities of character that are mutually beneficial to the individual and his or her social community. These positive qualities are generally manifested, in the case of nonhuman animals, in physical gesture, vocalization, and social behavior. It is interesting to note that wolves themselves recognize virtue in this sense, deferring to evinced individual leadership qualities, and allowing each wolf to contribute according to talent and inclination.

Yet, an obstacle to the wolf's claim to American women's special interest and protection is the "Disney Dilemma," in that the bloody details of the wolf's worthy ecological service of preserving nature's balance (i.e., by thinning out overpopulated deer or caribou herds) may conflict with our cultural bias for the relative aesthetic value of the nonpredator species that wolves feed on. The recent popular Disney film *Beauty and the Beast* depicted a snarling wolf pack that endangered both Beauty and Beast. To enlarge our concept of moral agency in this context becomes the work of the imagination.

So first of all, in attempting to create an imaginative new relationship to difference, we can initiate a celebration or *hymein* of the mystery of difference whenever we are tempted to punish or repress it. Second, we can take a cue from the Seneca native culture and find a basis for trust in the notion that a wolf may be trusted always to behave like a wolf.

On a collective level, feminist acts of imagination like these have the potential for causing sweeping moral change. As Aldo Leopold observed, "No important change in ethics was ever accomplished without an internal change in our intellectual emphasis, loyalties, affections and convictions" (1966, 246). Let us look now at the wolf of the Western imagination—through the eyes of religion, philosophy, gender issues, and anthropology—and try to see how we can change it.

Whose Wolf Is This Anyway?

Religion

In his sympathetic and intelligent treatment of the lupine, *Of Wolves and Men*, Lopez reminds us that from an historiocultural point of view, at least, humans "create" wolves. Leaving aside for the moment the obvious question of *techne*—that is, who is doing the creating—it is intriguing to recognize that the root of the Greek word for wolf, *lukos*, is so close to the word "light," *leukos*, that it has often been mistaken in translation (Lopez 1978, 209). The Latin homology *lupus/lucis* further elucidates the linguistic linkage of twilight-prowling wolves with the fallen lightbearer (*lucem ferre*) or Lucifer (Lopez 1978, 210). Lucifer was, of course, the prince of angels who—like the Judaic Lilith, the first woman—rebelled against the Father, and thereby "turned into" a devil, the quintessence of darkness in a Judeo-Christian tradition that suppressed the Mother Goddess in all her many forms (Koltuv 1987, 6–7).

So much of our atavistic memory of wolves seems to be dominated by this essentially religious concept of the devouring demon, augmented in legend by a Grimm romanticism of evil. Again and again, throughout Western history, Europeans played out mass Manichean dramas of the beast against the light. In the fifteenth century there were great organized drives against wolves. At the height of the "burning times"—the sixteenth through eighteenth centuries—hundreds of thousands, perhaps millions of women were condemned by the Inquisition for being lupine shape-shifters. For generations of our ancestors, the werewolf, not to mention the she-wolf, became the personification of pure evil. (In North America, Navajos also have werewolves, but, in contrast, they are usually male.)

To be fair, it must be noted that wolves have not only been hounded to extinction throughout most of Europe (there are none left in the British Isles), but their populations have also been substantially reduced in India as well as in the Near and Middle East. Still, the West has had a particularly fatal attraction to the wolf.

In contemporary America, there is increasing concern for the survival of the wolf. But there are also the pernicious images of the lone wolf, the Big Bad Wolf, a wolf in sheep's clothing, wolfing it down, Saturday night wolf. This is typical and troubling linguistic abuse of a species that usually mates for life, can pursue temporary solitude while maintaining a highly cooperative social group, typically shuns or even patiently tolerates humans, feeds its old, and collectively cares for its playful young in a way roughly analogous to an extended human family.

According to *National Geographic*, wolves of the high arctic are known to be intelligent, resourceful, and not easily fooled by humans. They are patient hunters, trekking long distances over harsh terrain to find food for the pack, food that even the alpha pair leaders will feed first to the pups. It may take up to three hours to bring down their musk oxen prey, which are much larger than wolves and can only be approached by the collective pack. The wolves husband their energy for the good of the group.

At this point, alerted by the bad fit of observed reality to idea, a time-honored test of scientific theory, we North American women might well ask of culture: whose wolf is this anyway?

Philosophy

In addition to the foregoing brief examination of the religious basis for negative attitudes toward the wolf, it may be useful here to make a similar historical survey of pertinent philosophical concepts, especially those concurrent with the early European settlement of this country.

We may recall that in "On the Generation of Animals," Aristotle negatively defined the female role in reproduction in terms of the female's inability to transmit the active life principle or spirit to her offspring; in his view, she offered only dumb, inferior matter. We may further recall that this pseudoscientific theory of reproduction was later taken up by the English biologist William Harvey. In 1651, after doing anatomical studies on the doe's reproductive system, Harvey published his finding that Aristotle was, basically, right (Anderson and Zinsser 1988, 96)!

In seventeenth-century France, meanwhile, René Descartes was denying a soul to animals altogether, describing them as cunning automata, upon which vivisection could be practiced with impunity. Compatible with such ethical arguments upholding human superiority over the creatures, the English empiricist John Locke told his fellow men that it was their God-given duty to "subdue" the wilds of the North American continent (1952, 21), as did New England theologian Cotton Mather. Given this proprietary view of nature and, dating back to the Greeks, the oft-made identification of women with the "inferior" natural functions, it is hard to escape the conclusion arrived at by Ursula Le Guin in her essay "Woman/Wilderness": that for many American men, the chaotic wilds, psychologically speaking, include women (1989).

Gender Issues

It is important to note here that in modern Minnesota, for example, the aerial hunters who waged wolf "genocide" from the safety of hovering helicopters were mostly, if not all, males of our species. Although this wholesale wolf killing was banned in 1972, male outrages against this particular animal continue. Lopez, who relates the "unrestrained savagery" of the perpetrators of U.S. bounty programs—den dynamiting, poisoning, wolfing for sport, and other national pogroms against the wolf, such as the Canadian wolf war in the 1950s—believes that hunting is "ingrained" in men and that ranchers were simply defending their Lockean property rights. He says he cannot blame them (1978, 198). Nonetheless, he suggests, it is true that when it comes to wolves many men do not seem to know their own place in the natural scheme of things. They hunt too much, they hate too much, they hurt too much. They will not share, and they do not act sensibly within the larger natural economy. Whatever reasons are given for it, Lopez says, all wolf killing is "rooted in the belief that the wolf is 'wrong' in the scheme of things, like cancer and has to be rooted out" (165).[4]

While I would agree that many men have underestimated the value of the role of wolves and overestimated their own (human) importance within the ecosystem, as well as the strength of some of their more dubious claims (e.g., the right to hunt soon-to-be-endangered species), I would also suggest that the problem goes much deeper and that it is gender based. Lopez relates two anecdotes that support my thesis. The first concerns a favorite ruse among cowhands, who would stake out a female dog in heat to attract a wolf. Then, while the two canines were joined in a copulative tie, and unable to break apart, the men would club the wolf to death (196). Significantly, if we look back to linguistic roots again, we find that the Latin word for "whore," *lupa*, is a homophone for "wolf." The sexual imagery embedded in the Western imagination is inescapable.

Literature and folklore also provide supportive examples of the link between the wolf and female, which is to say, sinful sexuality. Dante called his damned seducers "wolves," and in the medieval villages of the Caucasus, it was believed that adulteresses were punished by becoming *werewolves* for seven years.

One more account will serve to illustrate poignantly the connection between male sexual violence against women and wolf killing. In the 1970s, three "fun-seeking" Texas men on horseback lassoed a female red wolf, dragged her around the prairie until her teeth broke out, stretched her between their horses with ropes, and for a finale, beat her to death with a pair of fence pliers. To complete the humiliation of the scapegoat, which strongly suggests innumerable newspaper accounts of the prolonged torments of some rape victims, the wolf was taken to a few bars in a pickup, then flung into a roadside ditch to rot (Lopez 1978, 152).

I am not trying to suggest here that men's cruelty or ascription of only instrumental value to animals is exclusive to wolves (or that women are exempt from these attitudes, but that is another matter). That other species are similarly targeted can be seen in examples of bear baiting, cockfighting, and whaling, in which the sperm whale was hunted to extinction by the New England trade and others. Nonetheless, it could be argued that pursuit of the wounding or death of individuals of these species (some wild) was primarily motivated by an economic interest, such as gambling stakes or sperm oil, rather than by irrational hatred. It is probably also true that sadistic pleasure in the animals' pain was present in some members of the pit audience or whaling crew, thus giving an economic enterprise a secondary "entertainment" value. With the exception of the brutalities of the wolf bounty system, wolf torture often has no primary economic value.

Perhaps a better model of an irrationally persecuted species, this time domestic, would be the cat, which is again a creature traditionally associated with female witches. Even in recent years there have been TV news reports of cat mutilations. Still, with *Canis lupus*, from the Middle Ages to our own era, the impulse or impulses of men that result in either fatal economic interest or in random persecution of these other animals has repeatedly exploded into fullblown Church- or State-sponsored war against wolves.

Even as I was revising this essay, I came across a disturbing but somehow not surprising announcement in the *New York Times* of 19 November 1992. The government of Alaska had given permission for up to 80 percent of the state's endangered grey wolf populations to be destroyed by aerial tracking and shooting. The reason given was that the 7,000 grey wolves were acting like wolves and devouring some of the million strong caribou and moose herds, thereby depriving hunters of the pleasure of killing the deer themselves, at a convenient location close to home. Quite apart from the moral question of valorizing hunters' pleasure over conservation of what is an endangered species all over the country and around the world, the Alaskan wolf-control policy was irrational. Without wolf predation, ungulate populations would decline even more drastically through famine and disease, not only in numbers but in quality and evolutionary diversity. Due to the international efforts of conservationists who threatened a tourism boycott, former Alaska governor Walter J. Hickel postponed the massacre, pending an ecological conference. In the spring of 1993, the *Los Angeles Times* announced that the Alaska government had decided to allow the destruction of 150 wild wolves beginning in the fall. It would take place in a 200-square-mile region southwest of Fairbanks and would not include aerial hunting. The presumption was that with most tourists locked into their plans for the summer, the wolf kill could proceed without delay. With this sort of ecological betrayal, not only of Alaska but of the whole continent, the future of the Alaskan wolf was tenuous. What is already an endangered species elsewhere in this country would soon be hunted down in their last American stronghold. In 1994, under this "game management" plan, approximately a hundred Alaskan wolves were slaughtered. As we go to press, the wolf kill has been canceled, granting the wolf a reprieve. But the game management forces in the Alaskan state legislature are strong: the wolves are still gravely at risk.

Why this genocidal attitude toward wolves? Why yet another irrational campaign against them? Could it be that, more markedly than other animals, man's wolf is, metaphorically speaking, a woman?

Anthropology

There is some anthropological evidence that Western man's wolf is a woman. In the East, birthplace of the major Western religions, one symbol of the Great Mother goddess was, indeed, a she-wolf (Walker 1988, 393). Wolves, in popular imagination, bay at the moon. It has been well documented by Merlin Stone and others that the moon was another symbol of the goddess, from Arabia to Zimbabwe. The Chinese depict the raven as a wise grandmother or crone, another guise of the goddess (Hecate to the Greeks and Romans), and in the wild, wolves and ravens are companions who play tag and find prey together.

The Sioux named the December moon "The Moon When the Wolves Run Together." For European-American women, there is the tradition of the historical wolf clans. The Celts had them, the Romans too. Women would go out into the forest dressed in wolfskins, sing, dance, and ritualize the wild side or celebrate the mystery of difference. They knew then how to combine the domesticated dog necessary to a smooth-running society and the freedom-seeking wolf, their existential sister, within their own hides. Best of all, it appears they were not afraid to relate to their own bloodthirstiness, power, and sensuality—antinomies to their prescribed cultural roles—and did not need to project these qualities onto nature "out there."

The Native American tribes, of course, have not forgotten what the loss of the wolf would mean in the depths of the American psyche. However, the Native American relation to nonhuman animals, while respectful and spiritually rich, is still largely representative of the male hunter-prey paradigm. The question of real moral responsibility for violence against animals, and a relationship of care respect for difference needs further exploration by feminists.

Interestingly, in the lore of tribes with special interest in the wolf, such as the Sioux, women are associated with wolves through marriage or caring relationships (Lopez 1978, 121). There are stories of female shamans who are either named after or are aided by wolves. There may be an empirical basis for this association of wolves with feminine power—an alpha female usually outlasts five alpha males as leader of the pack, is the swifter hunter when she is young, and is often relied upon for her experience in the hunt.

My Ántonia: One Woman's Wolf

In contrast to male derogation of wolves in fiction and folklore, American novelist Willa Cather creates a powerful if subtle emotional alliance between *Canis lupus* and the eponymous Ántonia of *My Ántonia*.[5] In chapter 9, narrator Jim Burden repeats Ántonia's story of the Russian immigrants Pavel and Peter, who were once the groomsmen of an ill-starred Ukrainian wedding party sledding home through the snow:

> The wolves were bad that winter, and everyone knew it, yet when they heard the first wolf cry, the drivers were not much alarmed. They had too much good food and drink inside them ... The wolves ran like streaks of shadow; they looked no bigger than dogs, but there were hundreds of them. (Cather 1988, 38)

The horses and riders of five of the wedding sledges are devoured by the wolves. Pavel, co-driver of the sixth and lead sledge, flings the bride and the groom who defends her to the wolves in order to lighten the sledge and gain time for the two men to escape.

Although the two survive, they become social and spiritual pariahs—Pavel's own mother "won't look at them"—and misfortune follows them even to America.

Cather, interestingly, never focuses on the gruesome predation of the wolves. She couches the macabre scene in mild, even poetic terms: for example, "they saw behind them a whirling black group on the snow" (39). In this passage, the evocation of a painterly chiaroscuro creates a dreamy aura. This kind of softening aesthetic treatment together with the far from graphic description of the carnage serves to distance the reader from the full human horror of the episode. One might almost say Cather approaches the killing itself from an amoral or wolven perspective.

However, in assessing the events leading up to the killing, the author definitively enters the realm of ethical judgment. Cather places the full weight of moral responsibility first upon the drunken drivers, who are grievously remiss in their duties to their passengers, and then upon Pavel. The heaviest burden of blame falls upon Pavel because, in contrast to the wolves, predators who simply act like predators, this character eschews his common humanity with the bride and groom, and behaves like an amoral animal bent on survival.

In other words, wolves may be trusted to act like wolves, whereas humans may not be trusted always to act like rational, ethical humans, especially toward women. This story obliquely suggests that the bride was in the grip of a society that devalued her and, in the crunch, preyed upon her for its own survival. The townspeople may have been shocked at Pavel's cold-bloodedness, but how many of their families had betrayed their daughters into dreary or abusive marriages for economic or social advantage or repressed women's wild, natural creativity in order to preserve the status quo?

There is a dual lesson for animal ethicists in this story. In developing a deeper ethical relationship to difference, it is incumbent upon us to take into consideration the survival needs and behaviors of wolves before we condemn or punish them for their rapacity. And we must recall our own rapacity, usually less pure in its motivation, and far less forgivable in the face of our supposed ethical development as a species.

There is one more clue to Cather's sympathies with the wolf/beast/instinctual life in her surprising ending to the chapter. One might imagine that the girl Ántonia and her friend, Jimmy, might be terrified by this tale of death in the snow. It is quite the contrary. They cherish it and repeat it with a secret, even sensual, thrill:

For Ántonia and me, the story of the wedding party was never at an end. We did not tell Pavel's secret to anyone, but guarded it jealously—as if the wolves of the Ukraine had gathered that night long ago, and the wedding party been sacrificed, to give us a painful and peculiar pleasure. At night, before I went to sleep, I often found myself in a sledge drawn by three horses, dashing through a country that looked something like Nebraska and something like Virginia. (41)

Ántonia, the young girl, had obviously been sufficiently impressed by the story to preserve it in her memory and pass it on to Jim. Yet again, one might suppose a little girl to be traumatized by this nightmarish yarn, and to try to repress it. Why does Ántonia take such voluptuous pleasure in the story of the Russian wolves?

In framing an answer to this question, it is not proper just to assume an essentialism or equivalence between nature and little girls. Rather, I would argue for a child's—in contrast to an adult's—purer or more immediate response to the demands of instinct because she has not yet been "socialized" or acculturated out of it. The animal nature represented by the wolves may symbolize to Ántonia her existential freedom to be, to create, to range the wilderness, outside of the restrictions of a patriarchal, turn-of-the-century society oppressive to female Others.

The analogy becomes even more resonant when one considers that the female wolf leaders are equal in power, status, and opportunity to alpha males. A Jungian like Clarissa Pinkola Estés (*Women Who Run with the Wolves*, 1992) might also want to point to a "wild wolf woman" archetype or center of psychological energy (which itself may be cultural in genesis) in the girl-child's psyche that cries out for expression. But one need not subscribe to Jungian notions to discern in this scene the secret need for a young girl to connect with her sensory life. Notice that Ántonia fails to identify with the victim bride. Rather, in her imagination, she "sacrifices" the powerless maiden again and again, to the "wolves"—that is, her own creaturely nature—the nature of that which is playfully free to be herself, sexually, artistically, emotionally, and to validate the sensory life as a trustworthy mode of cognition. Unfortunately, as contemporary feminist observers like Carol Gilligan (1982) have pointed out, it is this instinctual nature that typically gets deracinated and withers away in girls after puberty. Ántonia's secret pleasure in wolves reminds women of the danger of relying too heavily upon the kindness of human society. It is better, she seems to be saying, to recognize and feed one's inner wolves, than to have them loom up behind you in the dark, frightening the horses and the men who might just throw you to the pack.

Reinventing the Wolf

In light of the foregoing examination of women's religious, philosophical, anthropological, and gender identification with wolves, I would like to propose that ecofeminists find our own images of the wolf, based on its fierce maternity (one may nourish ideas and projects other than or in addition to child bearing); strength in solitude; sensitivity to small but important changes in the environment, emotional or physical; intelligence, sensuality, playfulness, resilience, and powerful hunting instincts (one may hunt for truth or value in life, as well in physical nourishment); and, as Ántonia understood, enjoyment of freedom and sensory richness.

Konrad Lorenz even saw the rudiments of a political ethic in the social organization of wolves, based on cooperation rather than domination, something akin to Riane Eisler's feminist "win-win" model (Eisler 1987).

In any case, there is no need to idealize the she-wolf; just accept her, imaginatively, as one of our planet's own, the way Romulus's and Remus's wolf mother accepted them, trans-species. Of course, this is easier to do with wolves when they behave like us. When they do not, we might try stretching our moral space to let in the differences. This goes beyond the bare minimum of according humanlike rights to nonhuman members of our planetary community.

In "The Will to Believe," William James offered a radical empiricist epistemology in which human minds are seen as centers of creative activity. Our will (faculty of attentiveness) to know makes things more knowable (see Myers 1986, 202–3). Perhaps if we are attentive to the wolf in all its nonhuman differences, we may enlarge the field of what we know in the phenomenal world.

And, finally, a deep concern: If American women do not attend to wolves and their fading spirit, if we do not will them continued existence, admire and long for both their familiar and feral qualities, as did the Nations and the ancestors, if we do not take collective moral action to save them, then the wolves will surely leave us. Since the extinction process, worldwide, has already begun, it is time for us to ask ourselves, "Why wolves?"

Notes

1. Coined by Françoise D'Eaubonne in 1974 as a call to arms for a feminist ecological revolution, *ecofeminism* is an umbrella term covering a variety of feminist theoretical positions in the field of environmental ethics. While some ecofeminists are concerned about the interconnected domination and abuse of women and nonhuman animals in Western rationalist culture and elsewhere, others think discussions about animals, including the eating of animals, are irrelevant to ecofeminist discourse.

2. For more on *speciesism*—according a higher ontological value to the human species than to others—see the Nel Noddings and Josephine Donovan exchange in *Signs* 16, no. 2 (Winter 1991): 418–25. The debate over the definition of speciesism and its acceptability in any form in the discourse of ecofeminism is a complex and ongoing controversy, which has crucial implications for the issues of sexism and racism. It is also beyond the scope of this essay. However, both ethicists who accept the propriety of basing human moral prescriptives upon species differences and those who seek attentiveness to species difference without making hierarchical evaluations share a common interest in developing a stronger theory of human relationship to difference. This is especially so in regard to the questions of which animals we eat and the conditions of their captivity and slaughter.

3. Robert Sessions (1991) makes a good case for the compatibility of a deep ecology that generally does not acknowledge the androcratic sources of Naturism and an ecofeminism that does. To this end, Sessions suggests a slight shift in perspective among the deep ecologists, who seek a quasi-mystical oneness with nature and look to traditions like Taoism or thinkers like Spinoza for theoretical support. Rather than focusing solely on ideal unity, Sessions says, humans should try for a sense of community with the animal nations. Although there is unquestionable value in transpersonal unitive experience, I think for many women a sense of "community" with wolves is, in fact, a more immediately realizable goal.

4. In nineteenth-century America the argot used for wolf killing was identical with the jargon of "Indian killing": "loafer," "renegade," the phrase "the only good Indian/wolf is a dead Indian/wolf." In my view, this is another piece of linguistic evidence of the psychological linkage forged by men between the despised Other and the wolf.

5. Another work of fiction that depicts an interesting woman-wolf connection is Elizabeth Marshall Thomas's *Reindeer Moon* (Boston: Houghton Mifflin, 1987).

References

Anderson, Bonnie S., and Judith P. Zinsser. 1988. *A History of Their Own: Women in Europe from Pre-History to the Present.* Vol. 2. New York: Harper & Row.

Bass, Rick. 1992. *The Ninemile Wolves*. Livingston, Montana: Clark City Press.

Cather, Willa. 1988. *My Ántonia*. Boston: Houghton Mifflin. Originally published 1918.

Cole, Eve Browning, and Susan Coultrap-McQuin, eds. 1992. *Explorations in Feminist Ethics: Theory and Practice*. Bloomington: Indiana University Press.

Curtin, Deane. 1991. Toward an Ecological Ethic of Care. *Hypatia* 6, no. 1 (Spring):71.

Daly, Mary. 1984. *Pure Lust: Elemental Feminist Philosophy*. Boston: Beacon Press.

Dillon, Robin S. Care and Respect. In Cole and Coultrap-McQuin, 73–78.

Donovan, Josephine. 1991. Reply to Noddings. *Signs* 16, no. 2 (Winter):423–26.

Eisler, Riane. 1987. *The Chalice and the Blade*. New York: Harper & Row.

Estés, Clarissa Pinkola. 1992. *Women Who Run with the Wolves: Myths and Stories of the Wild Woman Archetype*. New York: Ballantine.

Friedman, Marilyn. 1992. Feminism and Modern Friendship: Dislocating the Community. In Cole and Coultrap-McQuin, 89–97.

Gilligan, Carol. 1982. *In a Different Voice*. Cambridge: Harvard University Press.

Koltuv, Barbara Black. 1986. *The Book of Lilith*. York Beach, Me.: Nicolas-Hays.

Le Guin, Ursula K. 1989. Woman/Wilderness. In *Dancing at the Edge of the World*, 161–64. New York: Grove Press.

Leopold, Aldo. 1966. *A Sand County Almanac: With Essays on Conservation from Round River*. New York: Ballantine.

Locke, John. 1952. Of Property. Chap. 5 in *The Second Treatise of Government*, ed. Thomas P. Peardon. Indianapolis: Bobbs-Merrill.

Lopez, Barry Holstun. 1978. *Of Wolves and Men*. New York: Scribner's.

Myers, Gerald E. 1986. *William James: His Life and Thought*. New Haven: Yale University Press.

Noddings, Nel, and Josephine Donovan. 1991. Comment and reply. *Signs* 16, no. 2 (Winter):418–25.

Rigterink, Roger J. 1992. The Surgeon Moralist Has Determined That Claims of Rights Can be Detrimental to Everyone's Interests. In Cole and Coultrap-McQuin, 40.

Sessions, Robert. 1991. Deep Ecology vs. Ecofeminism: Healthy Differences or Incompatible Philosophies? *Hypatia* 6, no. 1 (Spring):90–108.

Walker, Barbara G. 1988. *The Woman's Dictionary of Symbols and Sacred Objects*. New York: Harper Collins.

10
Marian Scholtmeijer

$\mathcal{T}$he Power of Otherness: Animals in Women's Fiction

Contextualizing the Problem

In her introduction to *Buffalo Gals and Other Animal Presences*, Ursula Le Guin raises the issue of talking animals in literature and conceives of the alienation of the Other in the following superb analogy:

> In literature as in "real life," women, children, and animals are the obscure matter upon which Civilization erects itself, phal-lologically. That they are Other is . . . the foundation of language, the Father Tongue. If Man vs. Nature is the name of the game, no wonder the team players kick out all these non-men who won't learn the rules and run around the cricket pitch squeaking and barking and chattering! (10)

Le Guin's image is lighthearted: phallological civilization is a game, and the indifference of "these non-men" to the rules of the game leads merely to their being barred from the field. There are benefits to such lightheartedness. It mocks reified attitudes toward the Other, renders those attitudes absurd, and prepares the way for dismissal.

Change the arena, however, and deadlier implications emerge. Change the arena, for example, to the site of the bullfight or rodeo, to the slaughterhouse, to the dissecting table, to the zoo—or to any place where humans use the otherness of animals as the rationale for cruelty and exploitation, and the issues become much more resistant to ridicule. The injustices suffered by women—the suppression, silencing, and violence—are arguably an extension of the more easily identified abuse of animals. The otherness of women from an androcentric perspective finds a correlate in the more radical otherness of the animal from an anthropocentric perspective. On both scores—the magnitude of abuse and the extent of alienation—the analogue of animal otherness is an idea that can serve to free women from the equivocation that might lead them to collude with their abusers. If the object of feminism is to defeat androcentric culture, then animals offer an ideational model for ontological defiance. Despite abuses up and down the scale, animals have not come over to the side of their oppressors.

There is a further consideration here as well. In terms of practice and politics, anthropocentric culture *is* androcentric culture. Many of the most pointed cruelties toward animals are authorized by asinine notions of virility, as in hunting, the bullfight, or the rodeo. In sociohistorical terms, one might note that attention to open cruelty toward animals can reveal hidden violence toward women. Coral Lansbury's brilliant work *The Old Brown Dog: Women, Workers, and Vivisection in Edwardian England* demonstrates the point. In Lansbury's analysis, Edwardian women saw and felt the cold arrogance of the sciences and the medical profession, the ideology and practice of which originated with men. Subconsciously or consciously, they caught the analogy between the image of the dog strapped down for vivisection and images of the bondage of women in pornography. The victimized animal gave a point of focus for rage against men and the social forces victimizing women, forces which, being generalized and nebulous, seemed to elude direct anger. Lansbury's analysis can be extended to the culturally ingrained ideology of the conquest of nature, which can now be seen as androcentric politics masquerading as anthropocentrism. Anthropocentrism is not a given; it is not "natural." Anthropocentrism springs from the same ideology of dominance that elevates the interests of men over the interests of women and sustains those who possess power in practice in the position that allows them to determine that power means oppression.

Though conceiving of women as "other," then, might seem to represent a capitulation to male-determined dualism, it is the first and most important stage in alienation from a culture which, considering its treatment of nonhuman animals, founds itself upon cruelty and contempt. Who would not wish to detach herself (or himself) from a culture that rests upon violence toward all those beings designated "other"? The political thrust of my argument here comes not from denial of the status of other for women and animals, but from denial that "otherness" presupposes weakness. Indeed, as has already been suggested above and as women's acknowledgement of animals in fiction confirms, the radical otherness of nonhuman animals provides a double source of power: recognition of the degree to which women are victimized by androcentric culture, and realization of solidarity in defiance of cultural authority. In their work on animals, moreover, women writers perform that most anti-androcentric of acts: thinking themselves into the being of the wholly "other," the animal. It turns out that this act is not an act of self-sacrifice but of empowerment.

Establishing the legitimacy of outcast experiences is precisely the political cultural work that needs to be carried out in real life for the sake of all beings disenfranchised by sanctioned value systems. In narrative, writers can actualize the power to discount dominant ideology, just as dominant ideologies have effectively discounted much that is genuine in human and animal life. In this essay, I examine some of the ways in which women writers of fiction defy standard conceptions of nonhuman animals and animal/human relations.[1] I am seeking to demonstrate, ultimately, that women employ the creative freedom of narrative to liberate otherness from the norms of dominant ideology. Women writers use fiction to concretize, affirm, and empower the state of being "other," which dominant ideology objectifies as a site of weakness, but which finds living expression in nonhuman animals.[2]

Because nonhuman animals *are* radically "other," there are certain risks in yoking feminism and animal rights. The identification of women with nature and the inferior social status entailed by that identification has been reviewed and contested in ecofeminist literature.[3] The posited identification of women with animals represents a more substantial threat to women than identification with nature. Nature in the abstract is grand and important; animals, particularized, seem lesser beings than ourselves. In the abstract, nature is a powerful system that competes with culture, whereas nonhuman animals seem inherently to have lost the battle with the human species. The suggestion that the otherness of nonhuman animals can inform the otherness of women, therefore, appears to be counterproductive, to pull women down into a condition of defeat along with the animals. It is, however, only from an anthropocentric perspective that animals are defeated. The otherness of the animal remains free and clear, despite human assaults. The responsibility for seeing and honoring otherness resides with the source of the trouble: resides, that is, with culture.

With fiction, we are in the domain of culture. Fiction can expose and then dismantle the unexamined belief systems that authorize violence against free beings. One of the preconditions for acknowledging the rights of animals is freeing them from the cultural constructions human beings have imposed upon them. With animals, this does not mean replacing one cultural construction with another that just happens to work in their favor; it means coping with the animal's autonomy from culture in general. Admittedly, this is a difficult task. One has to use the resources of culture to argue that culture is not all-in-all, is not the omnipotent arbiter of change. Yet if we note that the whole idea of cultural supremacy is a formal extension of the hierarchy of dominance that elevates humans above animals and men above women, it becomes obvious that the liberation of animal otherness from cultural constructions delivers a blow to the whole structure. The radical alienation of animals from culture can be projected in literature, and that alienation is not just ideationally but politically advantageous to feminism. Indeed, the very difficulties and convolutions necessary to honor the animal's defiance of culture within a cultural medium are by themselves valuable to feminism: the infrastructural persistence with which culture denies animal autonomy suggests the magnitude of the problem facing women.

The three divisions in the following analysis of the import of animals in women's fiction[4] proceed from the core idea that otherness is powerful. Given this assertion, beginning with the subject of victims,[5] or perhaps simply raising the issue of victimization in any form, has certain risks. Since the focus of the discussion is otherness, one of those risks is the perception that social and cultural outsiders are quintessential victims and that we cannot escape the mechanisms of conquest established by the in-group. The fact that it is not obvious to culture that animals *are* victims, however, enables women writers to wrest the victimization of both animals and women from the structures of thought that mandate victimization. Women can subvert the assumptions on which victimization is founded through allegiance with animals. The second part of my analysis follows logically from this idea. Identity is the key term here. In this section, we find animal identity confronting and embarrassing cultural presuppositions about the state of the individual as a subject. Finally, in the third section, I focus on three works of fantasy that envision communities of animals and humans. These fantasies show the way toward opting out of dominant culture and joining up with the animals, who already occupy worlds apart from ours. "Otherness" is an overarching concern in these stories; it becomes the occasion for imagining a new social system, one that does not frame itself upon victors and victims.

Victims

Humankind's root cultural relationship with animals is that of aggressor to victim. In narrative, as in life, it is difficult to escape the paradigm of victimization when it comes to animals. In narrative, animal victims make for dramatic action; often writers coopt animal tragedies to enhance the impression of pain in the world or simply to round out a plot. Indulgence in the narrative efficacy of killing an animal reinforces the conception of animals as congenital victims who call for the abuse they receive. Too often, the logic of the narrative affirms that the victimization of animals is only natural. Women writers subvert the traditional narrative use of animal victims in several ways. One way is ensuring that animals are not alone in their pain. By means of a posited kinship between victimized women and victimized animals, women writers both reclaim the fact of women's suffering and challenge the isolation of human from animal that permits aggression against animals in the first place. A second way of undermining the idea that animals are foreordained victims is to allow the animal to escape. The freed animal inherently questions abuse founded upon anthropocentrism. Finally, and with great difficulty, women writers invent the terms whereby power relations are reversed and animals can assault the species that assaults them.

Loneliness is probably one of the most terrible features of suffering. Each animal victim is acutely alone. Nothing signals the status of animals as outcasts more thoroughly than the systematic singling out of individual animals for death coupled with the denial of individuality that society practices for the very purpose of victimizing animals. In other words, cultural abrogation of the individuality of animals leaves the animal victim more chillingly isolated than if their aloneness were at least acknowledged. Thus, the narrative act of conjoining human and animal victims is a step toward affirming the importance of animal suffering. At the same time, the psychic unity of woman and animal victim underscores the pointed rejection of women from the social nexus. In the first two stories, the woman protagonist's fondness for animals signals more than ideological opposition to the forces in society that injure and kill animals: it indicates estrangement so complete that only concurrence with the animal's pain can tell of the entirety of the woman's isolation. Mary Webb and Doris Lessing use the link between women and animal victims to analyze the extent of socially authorized aggression against otherness.

In the novel *Gone to Earth* (1917), Mary Webb creates a female character who does not and cannot belong in the given, social world. Hazel is an outsider, a different kind of being from the others around her. She possesses the innocence and vitality of the wild. Within her personality, two strains, deemed incompatible by Western culture,[6] coalesce: she is sexually alive *and* she loves animals. By means of contradictory options in male lovers, Webb points to society's incapacity to accept a woman like Hazel. Hazel has the choice of a minister who can be brought to love animals but cannot satisfy her sexually and a squire who satisfies her sexually but loves to kill animals. Hazel's outrage at acts of cruelty toward animals elevates her morally above conventional society: she is supercivilized. Hazel's lack of restraint in sexual expression, however, aligns her with the natural world: she is a more "natural" being than those who are civilized and sexually repressed. Thus Webb works with the persistent and peculiar belief in Western culture that sexually passionate, "natural" people must have a lust to kill animals, while those who are "civilized" and care about animals must suffer from libidinal deficiencies. That such a convention is foolish does not mean that it has any less power to shape personality or that it presages any less terrible a fate for an outsider like Hazel. The logic of Hazel's very existence is antithetical to the logic of the normal world. Furthermore, Webb creates a convincing character in Hazel.

Hazel seems right in herself, not artificially thrust by the author into her position as an outcast.

Narratively speaking, however, Hazel has to die. In her very nature, she is too much of a contradiction to the social norm—perverse as that social norm is—to survive the novel. In addition to being a living affront to society, she moves within an atmosphere of animal suffering. She is deeply attuned to animal pain, and given the extent and persistence of animal pain, it is little wonder that her story has a tragic end. Hazel dies trying to save her totem animal, a young female fox, from the wealthy and religious folk who have banded together to hunt foxes.

Foxy is the emblem of the wild spirit in Hazel that belongs nowhere in human society. Yet Webb has not converted Foxy into a mystical being. Foxy's otherness, and hence Hazel's, is firmly grounded in physical particularity. As is consistent with the tragic vision of the novel, Foxy is most vividly a real fox when she is under assault by human beings. Her totemic value, then, consists not only in representing Hazel's otherness, but also in focusing social and cultural cruelty toward the Other. As Hazel runs from the hunters with Foxy in her arms, the burning image of her fox's impending death enters her mind; she hears the cry the animal would utter as hunters and hounds tear the fox's body to pieces. Hazel's life is completely integrated with Foxy's: "She knew that she could not go on living with that cry in her ears" (286). Chased to the edge of a stone quarry, she leaps over and carries her fox with her into death. Both creatures have "gone to earth," as the ironic last line in the novel tells us. The earth alone is home to these two beings whom the world persecutes.

Human society is no home to animals; and human society exiles something essential in women as well. Doris Lessing brings together an old homeless woman and an animal outcast in "An Old Woman and Her Cat" (in *The Temptation of Jack Orkney*, 1974). Tibby, a battered old tomcat, is Hetty's totem animal. Tibby and Hetty manifest the same determination to survive outside of social institutions. The first part of the story finds Hetty living in a tiny, dirty London flat; she collects junk; she frightens people. Addressing Tibby, Hetty speaks with affection the sentiments that society tacitly and callously applies to herself: " 'You nasty old beast, filthy old cat, nobody wants you, do they Tibby' " (24). Hetty seizes hold of social hostility toward herself and converts it into fondness for another individual who is like her. An outsider, she is not weak, then, but strong: so strong that she can translate rejection into love. She escapes the fate of being effectively "put to sleep" in a "Home" for the elderly—they will not let her keep her cat—but Tibby is less fortunate. Hetty freezes to death in a ruined building: she dies free. An animal, Tibby takes the brunt of social aversion to the frightening "others" who roam city streets. He is dirty and decrepit; no one would want him for a pet, despite his willingness to give affection. The city pound kills him. Reflexively, the cold rationality that determines Tibby's end puts into focus social antipathy to Hetty and women like her. Like Mary Webb's Hazel, Hetty has no place in the world; the home for her heart is her companion animal. The measure of Hazel and Hetty's status as outcasts *is* their love for animals. In turn, the measure of society's contempt for this definitive quality in Hazel and Hetty is its cold-blooded treatment of their animals.

If it is fairly easy to link female outcasts and animal victims, it is harder to drive a narrative toward the liberation of the animal scheduled for death. From the perspective of the system that imprisons and kills animals, the act of releasing them appears absurd. On this score, the fate of the farm animal is unequivocal: since the farm animal's whole purpose in life is determined by her death, the idea of liberty cannot enter into conceptions of her being. Where would she go, what would she do, what would she *be,* if not delimited by human-kind and its plans for her? Liberating an animal whose only significance resides in her incarceration and death subverts cultural meaning in the most radical way imaginable. When Alice Munro and Janet E. Aalfs envision the incredible—the escape of farm animals—they simultaneously defy notions of domesticity that oppress women.

Alice Munro explores the correspondence between women and animals in a world defined by men in her first-person narrative "Boys and Girls" (in *Dance of the Happy Shades,* 1968). The setting is a fox farm. Freedom is a property that men, not women, possess, and men express their freedom in the slaughter of animals. Cultural images of adventurous men, explorers and heroes, surround the girl whose story this is. One sign that she is becoming a "girl" in the conventional sense is the reversal of her role in her own fantasies; no longer the heroine who rescues others in her daydreams, she becomes the victim, the one who needs rescuing. Ironically, the girl's one attempt at heroism disbars her permanently from the man's world. Acting on impulse, and no doubt on identification, the girl opens a gate wide for a mare fleeing from the men who mean to shoot her. The girl's impulse is fruitless. Her father and the hired man recapture the horse Flora and kill her: it was her destiny all along. The only real-life opportunity the girl gets to act as a savior marks her as an irrational female. The masculine world converts what should be an act of triumphant rebellion into a shameful capitulation to girlish weakness: "I was on Flora's side," the narrator says, "and that made me no use to anybody, not even to her." Only fools, weaklings, and girls oppose the butchering of animals—at least according to men and farmers. In this story, the two points of view are one and the same, and both the girl and the horse are victims of the combination. Nonetheless, in order to demonstrate the full-scale oppression of masculinist culture, Munro has yoked the idea of female opposition with the idea of the literal liberation of an animal.

Where horses bear the symbolic implication of freedom, chickens are radically excluded from any such idea, culturally speaking. Chickens are archetypal victims, fated for the dinner table or life as an egg-producing machine, and determined by us to be quintessentially witless. To rationalize the liberation of chickens in a narrative, a writer has to heave off a terrific burden of cultural attribution.

Janet E. Aalfs achieves a permanent escape for a chicken in "A Chicken's Tale in Three Voices" (in Corrigan and Hoppe, *And a Deer's Ear*, 1990) because she breaks the boundaries of "reality" and has the chicken speak. In the story, Aalfs interweaves a chicken's fate with that of a girl whose resistance to the whole idea of marriage with a man manifests itself in chicken-like behavior. The girl, who has fled her family cackling and flapping her arms, reappears in the part of the story told by the chicken. The chicken's dream at the end of the story finds the girl in the embrace of a female lover, happy, complete, and ready once again to call the chicken by name. The bond between the girl and her lover reminds the chicken of the chicken's sisters, who have been killed to feed the girl's family. In effect, the chicken transforms the girl into an honorary chicken. What else would freedom and self-possession mean if a chicken told the tale of the world? The chicken-like behavior that in the first part of the story was a stigma and mark of victimization becomes a victorious assertion of otherness. By reversing human and animal roles in this manner, Aalfs asserts the power of otherness despite imparting a human voice to an animal. The chicken's view of life holds sway at the end of the story.

Women are, of course, acutely aware of power relations and of the extraordinary effort required to turn those relations around. Although tales of menacing animals are a staple in popular literature, stories that allow animals final victory are rare. A return to peace usually means the death of the animal, or its submission one way or another. In "Attack at Dawn" (in Corrigan and Hoppe, *With a Fly's Eye*, 1989), Cris Mazza arranges for a truce between an angry rooster and a frightened woman, without forcing either one into the position of victim.[7] The woman has shared the warmth of her bed with this rooster when he was a chick. As an adult penned in a coop, he attacks her whenever she comes near him. Her fear causes her to do the masculine thing at the peak of their conflict: she smacks the rooster on the "red earlobe" (the detail is particularly painful) with a wooden dowel. No victor emerges from this conflict. Panic alone motivates the woman's violence, and she deeply regrets having hurt Clarence. Clarence lives to attack again; he does not yield. The woman changes weapons; in the future she will use a broom, bristle end forward, simply to keep Clarence at a distance. Mazza conveys the emotion of the conflict with singular intensity. She does not fudge either the fear on the woman's part or the aggression on the rooster's to produce the conventional outcomes of conquest or friendship. The distance remains between these two beings; the woman finds a way to work with the rooster's otherness instead of fighting it.

On a larger scale in the reversal of power relations, one can cite Daphne du Maurier's "The Birds" (in *Echoes of the Macabre*, 1952), which presents a vision much more apocalyptic than that of Alfred Hitchcock's movie version of her story. Du Maurier gives final victory to the birds, who wreck humankind's technology and evidently annihilate most of the human population. She sides with the birds even to the extent of denying both humans and readers that most human of needs: explanation.[8] Knowledge of the reason for the bird's revolt would perhaps make their victory tolerable, but du Maurier does not make this concession to reason. The vision alone is satisfying. We have made war upon the animals for so long that successful retribution from them is pleasing to imagine. At the same time, the destruction of human society and the denial of explanation imitates the animal's perspective under the assaults of humankind. Du Maurier puts humankind in the role of the victimized animal: helpless, disorganized, and completely confused. Granted, the whole of humankind, men and women alike, falls before the power of the birds. Yet there is singular pleasure in the uprising and absolute victory of those who have been conceived of as thoroughly conquered even in their very being.

Women know what it is like to be victimized, to have one's difference used as a rationale for suppression and violence. Instead of reproducing the conventions of conquest, and using those conventions to compose the narrative of the animal, the women writers discussed here expose and subvert the assumptions underlying victimization. While most admit that there is little hope of toppling hierarchies of dominance, they give their allegiance to the animal victim. These writers reclaim the totality of women's status as victim by kinship with the more obviously victimized animal, grant freedom to the animal, however temporary, and sometimes dramatize that truly inconceivable phenomenon: the literal indomitability of animal otherness.

Identity

We have seen identification with animals in stories women write about animal victims. The issue of identity qua identity arises in women's narratives, likely because women recognize the cultural devices that deny animals a sustaining sense of individuality. The idea of otherness takes the foreground in analysis of women's stories that address the rift between animal and human identity. In the stories I discuss for their work upon identity, women writers examine the distance that Cris Mazza acknowledges in "Attack at Dawn." These stories provide a corrective to anthropomorphism. Anthropomorphism may appear unavoidable in literary uses of animals, yet the writers discussed in this section politicize projections of human qualities onto animals at least as far as questioning those projections.

Harmless as such projections might seem, even children's literature can come in for criticism over anthropomorphism. As early as 1974 (early, that is, in the history of our rethinking of ideas about animals) Deirdre Dwen Pitts spoke of the talking animal as a "pathetic mechanism" in children's stories and demanded that children's literature respect "the dignity of [the animal's] ordered world" ("Discerning the Animal of a Thousand Faces"). Pitts is well ahead of her time, and ours, in insisting that literature honor the otherness of animals. Clarice Lispector and Nadine Gordimer, among others, locate the animal's identity in the dignified silence the animal preserves.

Nevertheless, this section does cover some talking animals: a wolf in Ursula Le Guin's "A Wife's Story" (in Le Guin, *Buffalo Gals*, 1988), buzzards in Zora Neale Hurston's *Their Eyes Were Watching God* (1937), and a cat in Stephanie T. Hoppe's "What the Cat Brought In" (in Corrigan and Hoppe, *With a Fly's Eye*, 1989). In many works of literature, the insertion of words into an animal's mouth entails a kind of violence. The talking animal too often represents a violation of the otherness similar to that evident in the performing animal: it reflects human aggression toward the animal's natural being. In Hurston's, Le Guin's, and Hoppe's stories, however, animal speech is used to communicate, rather than erase, animal otherness. Animals "speak" in quite a different sense in the stories in which identity is a central issue.

Finally, I discuss Alice Walker's unique contribution to literature on women and animals, *The Temple of My Familiar* (1989). Walker's novel occupies the boundary between identity and community, the third dimension of power and otherness to be analyzed in this essay. One of the most extraordinary features of this novel is Walker's successful evocation of a kind of utopianism, not of society, but of individual identity. The human image she achieves in her novel is the lovelier for its association with animals. We turn first, though, to the conceptual abyss separating human from animal identity.

Often in Clarice Lispector's stories, human beings stare at animals across a space that divides them. In the "Chronicles" section of *The Foreign Legion* (1964), Lispector says that she regards animals "as closest to God, matter which did not invent itself, something still warm from its own birth" (148). Some of her short stories locate animals in a godlike position, not by projecting sacredness on them, but by casting them in the role of silent, distant witnesses to human confusion. Her nonfiction theme upon horses, "The Dry Point of Horses" (*Soulstorm*, 1974), explains that the distant gaze of the animal in fact divides the human being from herself. Noting that she has "a horse within [her]," she also reverses this identification when she recalls stroking a horse's mane: "Through his aggressive, rugged mane, I felt as if something of me were seeing us from far away" (108).

Aware, then, that animals possess the pure identity that gazes at us when we gaze at them, Lispector brings animals into moments of self-realization for her characters. Massaud Moises (1971) describes these encounters as episodes of "ontological transference" ("Clarice Lispector: Fiction and Comic Vision," 275), though it must be added that Lispector is clever enough to avoid simply passing qualities from human to animal or vice versa. Instead, human and animal qualities seem to meet in her stories, leaving the individual beings more wholly "other" than they were before the encounter. The human characters become "other" to themselves, an experience that Lispector sometimes indicates with the idea of death-in-life or simply fainting away.

One of Lispector's most complicated invocations of the power of animal otherness occurs in "The Buffalo" (in *Family Ties*, 1985). In this story, she works with the projection of qualities of love and hostility onto animals. A woman wanders through a zoological garden, asking the caged animals to " 'teach [her] only to hate' " (123). She needs to find among the animals confirmation of her hatred for a lover who has rejected her. What she sees in all the animals, or what she projects onto them, however, is love, nothing but love—at least until she arrives at the compound that holds the buffalo. The buffalo is the first animal she sees after she has, without knowing it, reclaimed her rage. Just the sight of the buffalo brings her peace, but the punctuating experience is the animal's indifference. The buffalo turns his back to her—a natural act, hardly surprising in zoo animals—but the woman calls out to him, trying to provoke a response. As these two beings stare into each other's eyes, the woman sees what she takes to be hatred. Woman and buffalo are "caught in mutual assassination" (131), and the woman faints. Since there is no literal death in the story, the metaphoric assassination instead addresses the fragmentation of identity that comes from the buffalo's total denial of the importance of the woman's existence. Lispector elicits a "fatal" otherness in the buffalo; "hatred" is only the name that the woman gives to yet another disconfirmation of her identity. For the woman in the story, such an assault upon her identity can hardly be taken as a boon, especially when it results in fainting, essentially a loss of self. Yet there is something reprehensible in the need to force other beings to reflect one's desires, and the story becomes a statement to readers about finding strength in one's own identity.

Likewise, Nadine Gordimer gives clear and crisp expression to the phenomenon of animal assault upon identity in "The Soft Voice of the Serpent" (in *The Soft Voice of the Serpent*, 1952). The story is similar to Katherine Mansfield's "The Fly";[9] both writers use insects to throw human readings of life off balance, and perhaps even to negate those readings entirely. Insects, of course, are vastly removed from human existence and yet they maintain an identity (hence the value of Kafka's having turned a man into one in "The Metamorphosis"). An interesting connection between Gordimer's story and Lispector's "The Buffalo" (and, in fact, Mansfield's "The Fly" as well) is that the central character is struggling both to think and not think about the key conflict in his or her life. The man in Gordimer's story has had a leg amputated. He spends his days in a wheelchair, reading and suppressing full awareness of his loss: he "never let the realization quite reach him; he let himself realize it physically, but he never let it get at him" (2). Society, of course, prescribes such stoicism.

The central event in the story does not seem momentous. One day, a large locust attracts the man's attention. He studies the locust; almost a third of this very short story is taken up with his microscopic observations of the locust's physical features. The locust, it turns out, has also lost a leg. The man begins to use the locust to come to terms with his own injury; his wife pities the creature, while he jokes about providing it with a tiny wheelchair. Just at the point when he identifies with the locust completely, laughing and speaking of " 'the two of us,' " the locust gets up and flies away. Both man and wife "had forgotten that locusts can fly." Locusts have a talent and a mobility that humans have not. One imagines that the man and the woman must feel a kind of amazed pain at finding themselves disadvantaged by a seemingly insignificant creature. The animal's negation of identification is as harsh in this story as it is in Lispector's. As in "The Buffalo," too, the animal's silent rebuff casts the person back upon his or her own devices, more fully conscious than before the encounter of personal existential aloneness.

Assaults upon characters give way to assaults upon readers in the next three stories. They twist the facile conventions of anthropomorphism around to perplex and provoke readers to thought. The true otherness of animals has power to determine the course of the narrative and undermine the very conventions with which the narrative works.

A narrative rebuff to the reader occurs in Ursula Le Guin's "The Wife's Story." Le Guin practices a deception upon the reader. She leads her readers to believe that they are listening to a woman tell the tale of her love for a man and of the fear that grows as the man begins to behave oddly, frightening the children and coming home with strange odors hanging about him. Clearly, the reader is meant to think that this is a werewolf story, in which the husband's metamorphosis into a beast fully explains the woman's fears. Le Guin retrieves the true horror of the conventional werewolf story in the scene, witnessed by the wife, of the husband's metamorphosis:

The hair began to come away all over his body. It was like his hair fried away in the sunlight and was gone. He was white all over, then, like a worm's skin. And he turned his face. It was changing while I looked. It got flatter and flatter, the mouth flat and wide, and the teeth grinning flat and dull, and the nose just a knob of flesh with nostril holes, and the ears gone, and the eyes gone blue—blue, with white rims around the blue—staring at me out of that flat, soft, white face. (70)

Next—horror of horrors—the husband rears up on his two legs! What we are witnessing is the metamorphosis of a wolf into a man; and what the reader experiences along with the wolf-wife is the ugliness of the human shape from the animal's perspective. How much lovelier are the long ears and muzzle, the array of sharp teeth, the deep brown eyes, compared to human features. "The Wife's Story" forcibly divides the reader from attachment to the human image. We are "other," and not in any complimentary fashion. By investing in the animal the power to define the natural state of being, Le Guin undermines human identity. The effect is simultaneously disturbing and liberating.

Zora Neale Hurston produces a similar effect when she lends a voice to animals in *Their Eyes Were Watching God*. On the subject of the politics of voice in this novel, it is difficult to expand the territory of Carol Adams's analysis. Adams uses the episode in which Janie persuades her second husband, Joe Starks, to purchase and free an abused mule to illustrate the idea of "muted voices" (*The Sexual Politics of Meat*, 1990). Her commentary hinges on the fact that freeing a mule from servitude " 'ain't no everyday thought' "—to use Janie's words (*Their Eyes*, 70). Adams points out that Janie "is empowered to speak on behalf of another being" and that this "empowerment may arise from recognizing the fused oppression of women and mules—silenced and overworked" (77). It is not only their joint status as silenced victims that Janie acts on, but also their resistance to being treated as such: the old, wasted mule fights back when some townspeople torment him; he "jerked up his head, laid back his ears and rushed to the attack. . . . [H]e had more spirit left than body" (68). Adams observes that, although Janie has the revolutionary thought of saving the mule, her husband receives the glory (77). This analysis goes to the heart of the politics involved in Janie's association with the mule.

Both the honesty of the vision and the complexity of the political issues involved in the African-American experience, however, lead Hurston into apparent contradictions. For one thing, she appears to approve of the fact that Janie's third husband, the one she loves passionately, slaps her around "a bit" out of jealousy, then pampers her afterwards (176). She also admires Janie's ability to "shoot a hawk out of a pine tree and not tear him up. Shoot his head off" (158). One cannot condone either of these acts of violence, but it is possible to use an aspect of identity to explain them. Prescriptive values are under attack in this novel. Hurston subjects any norm that binds free people to challenge on behalf of vitality. Censure of the conventions that slapping a woman is a sign of love, and that a woman who is able to shoot animals is a powerful woman, might be obliged to yield to the novel's defiance of repression in any form.

Hurston employs a curious animal metaphor, for example, to convey the foreignness of the changes Joe Starks introduces as he seizes the position of mayor in the unincorporated town of Eatonville. Joe uses gilt spittoons, ignoring the traditional tomato can favored by Eatonville men. Of Joe and his innovation, Hurston writes:

> It was bad enough for white people, but when one of your own color could be so different it put you on a wonder. It was like seeing your sister turn into a 'gator. A familiar strangeness. You keep seeing your sister in the 'gator and the 'gator in your sister, and you'd rather not. (59)

Hurston's metaphor appeals primarily to experience, not judgment. One could denounce Joe's gilt spittoons as an ostentation coming from the white world, but Hurston is more fascinated that condemnatory. Although one might "rather not" see one's sister turn into a 'gator, the image is not horrifying in context. Nor is it playful. The violation of rigid categories speaks to the general emancipatory character of Hurston's novel. Hurston treats the crossing of boundaries between human and animal as a literal possibility. Like the liberation of the mule, Hurston's fusion of animal and human identity in this metaphor "ain't no everyday thought."

Nor are the developments surrounding the mule's death. The mule dies a natural death. That is to say, no human being kills him. Once again, however, Hurston crosses identity boundaries: the mule "fought [Death] like a natural man" and he dies "on his rawbony back with all four feet in the air" (72). He dies like a man and like an animal. The mule has become such a favorite in the community that all of the townsfolk, with the exception of Janie, gather in the woods for a Rabelaisian funeral. Joe delivers a mock eulogy, and another man speaks of "mule-heaven" and "mule-angels" (74). Are they mocking the mule? A sentimentalist might say so. If appeals must be made to heaven and to angels, there is no reason to suppose that animals are excluded from such divine offices. Hurston, however, locates the terms of the mockery on the other side of the equation: the participants in the ceremony, she writes, "mocked everything human" (73). The mule's death provides the community with a legitimate occasion for throwing off the restraints of everyday identity. As further confirmation of the importance of animals, Hurston goes beyond the human "funeral" to an animal funeral for the mule, conducted by buzzards. She parts company with the realistic mode and speaks in the voice of the folk—that is, the voice that delivers the folktales in which one finds talking animals. The buzzards circle the mule's carcass and engage in a question-and-answer session. " 'Who killed this man?' " the lead buzzard asks. " 'Bare, bare fat,' " replies the chorus (75). The mule who has died like a man is both a man and a meal to the buzzards. Theirs is the earthy perspective. Hurston uses animal identity to challenge ideological norms, including the literary norm of realism. We are free to pick and choose among the acts of defiance practiced by Hurston's characters, but there is no doubt that animals are a significant source of disturbance to strictures upon identity in *Their Eyes Were Watching God.* Metaphorically and literally, Hurston's animals are politicized in so far as they assault cultural convention.

Hurston shifts to the speaking animal of the folktale as the culminating literary development out of an African-American community's mockery of that most sober of cultural conventions, the funeral. Le Guin's alienation from humankind licenses the attribution of speech to an animal which, in a different context, would be a violation of the animal's otherness. Lispector's story and Gordimer's predicate the identity upon the animal's actual and metaphoric silence: animals do not "speak" to us literally; nor will they respond to the meanings we impose upon them. Their silence is articulate. It is also, as Stephanie T. Hoppe realizes, world-sustaining. Her self-reflexive story "What the Cat Brought In" (in *With a Fly's Eye*) builds consciously upon the idea of animal speech by treating the power of the writer's cat to speak in coherent human language as a kind of thought experiment. Naturally, in this story, the cat's power to speak proves unsettling to the writer—as it would should our own cats begin addressing us in actual human words. Hoppe understands, furthermore, the vastness of the disruption that would be caused by the talking animal. When silent, the writer's cat had held the world in place; now that she speaks, the world begins to dissolve. The writer realizes that she has to write the very story that she is writing in order to keep the world from disappearing into a fog. "What the Cat Brought In" closes with words to the reader indicating that we will all have to write and talk without stopping, now that the animal speaks. Is this not what we do already: write and talk the animal into silence and the world into a construction that suits our sense of order?

"What the Cat Brought In" corners us in the paradox that we must do obsessively what we think we do out of freedom and power: employ language to uphold the world-identity that we take to be reality. As with many women's stories, Hoppe's passes power over to the animal as an animal. The silence we think of as a defect in the animal is in fact the force that graciously permits us to maintain our beliefs about the nature of the world. Hoppe plays with our habit of founding animal and human identities upon language or the "lack" of language. Since the story is self-reflexive, it violates the distance between narrative and reader at the same time as it violates the presumed distance between animal and human. Its finest achievement is to politicize the abstraction of language. Something similar occurs in Ursula Le Guin's "She Unnames Them," discussed in the next section.

The deconstruction of human identity by means of the animal is clearly a theme in the works discussed to this point. The reconstruction of human identity by means of the animal is a rare event, but one that Alice Walker accomplishes in *The Temple of My Familiar*. The characters in her novel work upon their own identities, strive to become complete people at peace with themselves and capable of loving well. Perhaps most pleasing to any woman reader is that Walker shows male characters learning how to love women as women want to be loved—and does so credibly. Animals come into the story in association with women. The animals do not speak:

> "The animals can remember [says the character Miss Lissie]; for, like sight, memory is renewed at every birth. But our language they will never speak; not from lack of intelligence, but from the different construction of their speaking apparatus. In the world of man, someone must speak for them, and that is why, in a nutshell, . . . goddesses and witches exist." (199)

The very existence of the most powerful cultural identities women can assume depends upon nonhuman animals. Indeed, since Walker's character puts the question of animal speech in the context of "the world of man," women are cast as others whose power comes from speaking for animals.

Despite the mention of goddesses and witches, and despite the emphasis on memories of past lives, *The Temple of My Familiar* remains firmly grounded in accessible contemporary experience. In a way, although their presence is most potent in Miss Lissie's paintings and stories of her past lives, the animals humanize the characters. The mother of one of the characters recalls an episode involving a dog, her own mother, and the woman from whom her mother learned how to live, Mama Shug. The period is just after World War II, the place the American South. The speaker remembers the " 'casual, vicious, unfeeling' " cruelty to animals practiced by the people around her. Her mother is particularly cruel to a dog named Creighton, going out of her way to insult, blame, beat, and kick the dog. The dog responds by cringing and fawning upon her, trying to lick her hands when she is most cruel. Miss Shug takes Creighton away for a summer and effectively restores his identity to him. When he returns he is " 'no longer a slave; he [is] a dog' " (312); and good dog that he is, he bites the speaker's mother when she tries to beat him again. In turn, the speaker's mother changes: " 'She began to feel for *everything*: ant, bat, the hoppy toad flattened on the road' " (312). Proud, free beings neither give nor accept abuse. Empathy for animals is a prerequisite for humanness.

What human beings consume, what we put into ourselves, is also a theme in this novel. Diet is a key element in the creation of identity. Here and there throughout the novel, characters recommend fresh foods to other characters: fruits, whole grains, and green leafy vegetables. In context, the advice takes on greater significance than the standard prescriptions of books on health food and vegetarianism. Body and psyche are allied in the matter of diet. Indeed, Walker goes as far as to integrate diet and feminist politics (as Carol Adams has done in her sphere). Among several excursions into the history of cultural origins is the story told by an old South American woman to her daughter about the earliest of times in her tribe when women created men; when men and women lived apart and men worshipped women; when the woman, who "was entirely used to herself," would cover her body in brightly coloured muds and decorations made of feathers, shells, and flowers; and when women "lived quite well on foods other than meat" (48–50). Similarly, and reaching even further back in time, Miss Lissie relates a dream memory of living as a pygmy among nonhuman primates: her people hunt animals, but she prefers hunting for plants to eat as her primate "cousins" do. Among her people, men and women live in separate communities, but she prefers to live with her mate in imitation of her animal cousins who "seemed nearly unable to comprehend separateness." Our nearest animal relatives are held up as examples of good conduct. A later part of this dream memory finds "fathers and uncles," larger versions of the pygmies, killing the animal cousins with spears and eating them (84–86). In these stories about origins, Walker attributes the loss of an attachment to animals and the practice of killing and eating them to male aggression. She grounds modern confusion over human and personal identity upon the literally essential issues of diet, gender, and original history.

The whole matter of gender and human/animal relations is securely attached to identity in Miss Lissie's final revelations. To the character Suwelo, she has said that throughout her past lives she has always been a black woman (53). A tape that she leaves for him to listen to after she has died reveals that she was once a white boy and once a lion. As a white boy, she seems to have been a genetic mutation, a source of discomfort to the women who protect him from his disfigurement by darkening him with juices mixed with nut fat. The girl who is his first lover reveals his deformity to him. The sight of his penis rubbed clean of dye fills him with shame. The girl's expressions of natural grief only cause him anger, and in his rage he kills her familiar, a strange little serpent with wings (361–62). The compression in this story is remarkable. Here, in effect, we have the source and long history of the white male's crimes and misery summed up in one revelation. The fact that the speaker is a proud black woman who cherishes animals emphasizes the depth of shame associated with the identity she once possessed.

As a lion, Miss Lissie lives through the radical change in relations between men and women, and the consequent change in human relations with animals. The crucial turning point comes with the merging of the men's camp with the women's. Women lose "their wildness, that quality of homey ease on the earth that they shared with the animals" and men assert "themselves, alone, as the familiars of women" (367). The lions and other animals back away from the strife resulting from this merging of camps. Of course, "not even the most cynical animal" could have predicted the aggression men would practice upon animals to preserve their status as the familiars of women. The whole human race loses their knowledge of animals. The shock in this story of a past life comes from the denaturalization of male relations with women. What could be more natural, one undoubtedly thinks, than that the boon companion of a woman should be a man? What could be less natural than a woman choosing an animal for company over a man? Men and women are a pair; they compose each other's identities. Nonhuman animals do not figure in the creation of human identity at all. Obviously, Walker defies these deep-seated "givens." She subverts current relations by composing a contrary history of origins, a history, that is, of otherness.

Adroitly combining gender and animal identity, Walker ends her novel with an animal image: a painting of a lion done by Miss Lissie shortly before her death. The lion *is* Miss Lissie, Lissie with "dare-to-be-everything lion eyes." "Dare to be everything" is right, for the woman's love of finery is incorporated into the painting: on her/his (for he is a "great maned lion") left back paw, the lion wears a "very gay, elegant, and shiny red high-heeled slipper." The animal has absorbed the woman; the lion is not a tag-along familiar but the very essence of the woman's identity. The inner lion, the inner animal, in Miss Lissie, and in all women, surfaces, to explain and render powerful that correspondence between women and animals when they exist in separateness. The "temple" of my familiar is myself. The slipper is the token of female constructedness, recognition of difference, acknowledgement of accord.

Although this section begins with the animal's assault upon human identity, it ends (as did the section on victimization) with the overwhelming power of the animal to remake the world. The animal's refusal to assist in personal conflicts is clear enough: animal defiance of humanization bears decided relevance to feminism and the powerful effects of preserving self-identity-in-otherness against the tyranny of culture. Animal identity cannot be shaped and re-shaped at the whim of culture or personal need. As Hurston's, Le Guin's, and Hoppe's stories reveal, animal otherness can take hold of the narrative process and bend it out of shape. Walker goes farther, inventing new stories to counteract the old ones. She rescues the human image from the misery produced by male and human dominance over matters of identity. Indeed, Walker reverses the order of analysis to achieve her end; instead of projecting her novel toward an allegiance of feminist and animalist politics, she works from the premise that the two politics are one and derives a new image of humankind from that allegiance. As we find in the next section, men are simply obliged to lag behind or come up to standard in the kind of feminist/animalist utopia that Walker locates in the individual in *The Temple of My Familiar.*

Community

Communion is a constant in human relations with animals. For all that the human species practices unrelenting assault upon animals, the individual animal remains a reliable source of solace in the face of unhappiness. When no one else in the world understands us, when we are hurt and lose our way, we turn to animals for comfort and reconfirmation. Harriet E. Wilson describes this experience in *Our Nig; or Sketches from the Life of a Free Black* (1859). In Wilson's novel, the mulatto girl Frado makes a confidant of her dog Fido: she "told him her griefs as if he were human; and he sat so still and listened so attentively, she really believed he knew her sorrows" (41–42). Frado is utterly different from the white people who have power over her, and her difference draws contempt and physical abuse from some of these people. There is a certain utility in her appeal to Fido, for "the only time she forgot her hardships . . . was in his company" (42). Despite the simplicity and familiarity of this experience, considerable existential complexity stands behind the communion Frado shares with her dog. Frado herself is "other," at least as far as the power system is concerned. She does not identify with Fido in his more obvious otherness, but gains in his company the freedom of her own otherness. The simple comfort obtained from the kind of communion Wilson describes has broad implications: those humans who are outcast from established power structures find strength and freedom in the absolute otherness of the animal. By means of the liberation of otherness in the abstract (i.e., as a principle), communion with animals can be translated into community.

In view of the radical, ontological separation of humans and animals in contemporary life, the mere thought of a community of animals and humans demands full-scale revisioning of the ways of the world. Arbitrary anthropomorphism subsumes animals and fails to recognize their real-life autonomy from culture. It reenacts the dominance that allows us to victimize them; their own beings are a matter of indifference to us. At the same time as ethical philosophers strive to extend the human community to include animals,[10] women are employing fiction to envision world communities not predicated on the assimilation of animals.

In Judy Grahn's *Mundane's World* (1988), Carol Emshwiller's *Carmen Dog* (1990), and Ursula Le Guin's "She Unnames Them" (in *Buffalo Gals*, 1988), the establishment of communities that honor the animal does not entail the humanization of animals but the infusion of the world with otherness. I hesitate to say "with animality" here, because the phrase presupposes specific qualities predefined by humans. Grahn, Emshwiller, and Le Guin create strange worlds that defy human normalcy. The pertinence to feminism of the whole-world revision for the sake of the other is obvious. The worlds these writers imagine, however, are givens; that is to say, the stories do not strain to make concessions to the bothersome animal but are simply informed by irregularity. One real-world place to seek for community in defiance is, of course, among women. Within these stories, women are the founders of the social state that achieves accord with animals.

Men are barely in evidence in the clan system Grahn imagines for the human community in *Mundane's World*. Women sustain a loose communal life by means of clan divisions in labor and ritual; daily life is purposeful yet informal. The resolution to the plot in *Mundane's World* is the discovery of a "human-designed magnetic disturbance" (184) within the grid that holds human and animal communities in harmony. Plans to build a temple at a certain site disrupt natural fields of force and cause a death. An adolescent girl solves the mystery as she dreams herself flying over the site in the shape of an owl. The overarching "grid" system is open and organic, not rigid and controlling. The macrocosmic consciousness Grahn engages in order to invent a world-myth of this sort relies, however, upon an intense appreciation of the microcosmic subjectivity of animals and plants.

Grahn employs a "camera-eye" technique to draw the reader into the mazy world of animals. It is fitting to the point of the argument that I am making here that beetles, ants, and a fly are significant among those subjects Grahn chooses for the exercise of this technique. She gets down among the roots of an oak tree, for example, to explore the activities beetles and ants perform simultaneously as human activities go on up above (36, and passim). In the middle of the story, the perceptions of a newborn fly suddenly become important and temporarily steer the course of the narrative (88–94). The fly is not a player in the human narrative, just a subject whose own story, Grahn indicates, merits the author's and the reader's attention. The

Animals in Women's Fiction

openness of Grahn's story itself subverts the literary systems that exploit animals. The imagined coexistence of human and animal realms in *Mundane's World* is achieved out of Grahn's willingness to shift between those realms anarchically, in violation of conventional narrative logic.

Envisioning a human/animal community does appear to entail a kind of happy anarchy. Where Grahn imagines coexistence in difference, Emshwiller imagines a fusion of human and animal, with the animal providing the corrective to the oppressive orderliness of human-dominated, but specifically, male-dominated society. Women, in *Carmen Dog*, are metamorphosing into animals, while female animals are at the same time metamorphosing into women. Culture is a central element in Emshwiller's novel, since Pooch, the dog-becoming-woman whose story this is, has aspirations to sing at the opera. Early in the novel, Emshwiller uses the anarchy of the metamorphoses to increase the traditional excitement of attendance at the opera. The scene is Lincoln Center; the animal element in the women creates the thrill that should always exist on such occasions but seldom does, as human operagoers strive to remain discreet and sophisticated:

> What a wonderful diversity exists among the women! What feathers, scales and furs! What sounds! Laughs and shrieks that reach the highest C. Seeing them, one might wish also for banana women, apple women, pine-tree women, but one can't have everything and this suffices to all but the greediest seekers after life. (11)

Emshwiller's playfulness with costume (very much akin to Walker's) and with sounds reinforces the idea that the introduction of the animal into such a scene represents an elevation in the life-quotient.[11] The height of culture, the opera, is revivified by the presence of animals.

In *Carmen Dog*, the leader of the rebel group of women-animals is a lumpy, elderly woman who is changing into the abominable snow-woman: "savage, silvery white and abominable, but abominable in all the best ways" (82). The motto she establishes for them, and which she delivers in cryptic, growling speech, is " 'not win, or lose all.' " Fortunately, there is little need for the women-animals to fight for supremacy. The masculine opposition to the changing shape of existence is stupid rather than vicious; the men seek to preserve order through scientific institutions, which prove wholly ineffectual. The metamorphoses are global, inexorable, and systemic. The women-animals are not obliged to "win." The whole system finally succumbs to the joyous freedom of the carnival. Emshwiller simply overwhelms the systems of dominance that victimize women and animals. She enshrines a holiday atmosphere. In her vision, animal vitality infuses culture and in effect "rehumanizes" it—much along the same lines as Walker's achievement with identity.

With Le Guin's "She Unnames Them," we are closer to home. As is the case with Grahn and Emshwiller's communities, aggression has no place in Le Guin's vision, despite the fact that her story hinges upon the overthrow of language as the agent of reality. Le Guin capitalizes upon the too-familiar experience of masculine deafness to women's voices. The animals and the woman in "She Unnames Them" achieve a victimless insurrection. An unnamed woman and all the animals decide to give back to "the donor" their names and classifications. The woman, it turns out, is Eve, but she gives her name back to Adam before it is ever written into the story. Far from being angered by Eve's quiet mutiny, Adam is too preoccupied to listen to what she is saying. The now truly unnamed woman simply leaves him to his little enterprises and withdraws with all the rest of the unnamed beings. Male indifference to the passive opposition of women and animals is a cultural truth; Le Guin renders Adam's assumptions about what is true and worthy in life simply absurd. The first woman—at least of Judeo-Christian myth—stands for all women. That she is able to renounce her identity and join the community of animals holds promise for all women, even if that means leaving men behind. Le Guin takes the ingrained cultural negation of the animal, most firmly authorized in language and naming, and turns it to her own account. She uses that negation as the means of withdrawal from culture itself. She reverses the hierarchical arrangement that sees us stooping to liberate animals. In "She Unnames Them," animal indifference to language shows a woman the way out of the stories culture tells about women and animals. What kind of community the woman and the animals will establish remains a mystery, but the step over the edge into unobstructed communion suggests possibilities both blissful and frightening.

Mundane's World, Carmen Dog, and "She Unnames Them" are fantasies. By definition, fantasy has little authority among modes of thought. Yet if only within its protected realm of literature, fantasy can shake the realities of dominant culture. Indeed, one might entertain the paradox—particularly with respect to the defiance of power structures—that fantasy's very lack of authority challenges authoritarian culture. There is truth in Rosemary Jackson's comment in *Fantasy: The Literature of Subversion:*

> [F]antastic literature points to or suggests the basis upon which cultural order rests, for it opens up, for a brief moment, on to illegality, on to that which lies outside the law, that which is outside dominant value systems. The fantastic traces the unsaid and the unseen of culture: that which has been silenced, made invisible, covered over and made absent. (4)

Jackson's comment puts into focus the human-assumed silence and lawlessness of animals and the efforts of women writers to assert other, entire value systems against anthropocentrism. Grahn, Emshwiller, and Le Guin inform us that the obstacles to community with animals are in us and not in them. Ironically, "others" vastly outnumber the beings who have claimed control over reality. If animals will not rise up and destroy us, as du Maurier envisions them doing, then the least we can do is recognize that the realities we take to be all-consuming are in fact fatally abbreviated. Perhaps it is only in the abstract that "otherness" has the power to subvert dominant culture's confidence. *Mundane's World, Carmen Dog,* and "She Unnames Them" substantiate otherness out of the realization that real, experiencing "others" possess this property. Seeking community with animals, these stories create whole worlds in defiance of obdurate conceptions of reality.

Conclusion

Having begun with Le Guin's playful image of a host of "others" rushing about the cricket pitch and bringing the game to a halt, this essay ends appropriately with the touch of sadness implicit in fantasy. Where animals are concerned, victimization is systemic, too deeply ingrained in human institutions for optimism over the immediate effects of reconceptualization. Perhaps, however, there is reason for some slight hope, not in the creation of new conceptualization of animals, but in the changes to institutionalized ways of thinking that literary works are able to exemplify. Women's stories do not arbitrarily assert different images of animals against conventional ones. They root through fundamental aspects of human and animal relations; they activate those critical and imaginative faculties that tend to remain inert with respect to animals.

Many of the writers discussed here consciously employ feminist analyses of dominance to invoke animal resistance. At the same time, they use appreciation of animal resistance to advance the politics of feminism beyond the realm in which some minor tinkering does the work of correction. Wholesale disruption of orthodox ideas of normalcy has to occur before culture and society can understand the fullness of the "other's" being. Excluded, women are in a good position to comprehend otherness and to use otherness to subvert the self-designated "realities" of authorized culture. Indeed, warning marks belong on "reality" and not on otherness. Otherness in the abstract bridges feminist and animal causes. Literature gives material reality to otherness, and women's narratives empower otherness by locating it securely in bodies, identities, and worlds. It is not the "otherness" embraced by reason that challenges dominant culture, but all of the "others" who live alongside the culture that denies them.

Notes

I wish to express my gratitude to the reviewers who offered comments on the draft version of this essay; to Josephine Donovan, Susanne Kappeler, and Carol Adams for both general and specific criticisms; and to Michael Bresalier for assistance with the initial research.

1. The isolation of women's stories is itself a political act. In her article "Animals in Folklore: A Cross-Cultural Study of Their Relation to the Status of Women" (1986), Mary A. Johnson cites C. R. Farrar's observation that in the late nineteenth century, when collectors of folktales had a choice between a man's version of a story and a woman's, the man's version was given preference (Johnson 1986, 180). The existence of three anthologies of women's writings about animals, two of which are cited here (the third is *Through Other Eyes: Animal Stories by Women*, edited by Irene Zahava), also provides a rationale for seeking special qualities in women's stories about animals. In a similar fashion, an anthology of men's stories about animals might be put together, and gender tendencies sought therein. In "Animal Rights and Feminist Theory" (1990), Josephine Donovan uses a footnote to sketch out some of the distinctive features of women's fiction containing animals (371–72). All of these diverse pieces of evidence suggest the importance of bringing together the widely dispersed writing of women in order to construct an alternative view of human/animal relations.

2. In the current postmodern climate, I feel the need to defend the use of fiction as a means of tapping a condition—otherness—which, I insist, is real and has political import precisely because it is real. Postmodern theory tends to treat the idea of fiction as an analogue for the constructedness, and hence artificiality, of beliefs about life which we take to be true; see, for ex-

ample, Donna Haraway's references to narrative in *Primate Visions* (New York: Routledge, 1989) and Jim Cheney's "Postmodern Environmental Ethics: Ethics as Bioregional Narrative," *Environmental Ethics* 11 (1989). Taken as a concept, "fiction" is certainly useful for loosening the stranglehold of ideational constructs such as anthropocentrism. In general, however, fiction qua fiction is subversive. Encounters with "otherness" are the virtual raison d'être of all literature. Literature has the capacity to embrace the unknown minus the need to "know" it. The uncertainty that is built into the production of literary works informs and empowers the representation of the "other." The representation of the "other," furthermore, becomes particularly dynamic, and gains special political force, in stories written by "others" whose words have been discounted by dominant culture. Fiction does compel us to confront realities, regardless of the quite powerful "fictions" on which dominant culture relies.

3. Simone de Beauvoir's *The Second Sex* is seminal among these works. Her observations on the inferior status presupposed by the association of women and nature have been challenged by ecofeminists. Among others who outline, question, and revise the import of connections between women and nature are the following: Sherry B. Ortner, "Is Female to Male as Nature Is to Culture?" in *Women, Culture, and Society,* ed. Michelle Zimbalist Rosaldo and Louise Lamphere (Stanford, Calif.: Stanford University Press, 1974); Susan Griffin, *Woman and Nature: The Roaring Inside Her* (New York: Harper & Row, 1978); Carolyn Merchant, *The Death of Nature: Women, Ecology, and The Scientific Revolution* (San Francisco: HarperSanFrancisco, 1990; originally published 1980); Karen J. Warren, "The Power and Promise of Ecological Feminism," *Environmental Ethics* 12 (Summer 1990); and Val Plumwood, "Nature, Self, and Gender: Feminism, Environmental Philosophy, and the Critique of Rationalism," *Hypatia* 6 (Spring 1991).

I should also observe that women are foremost, in several fields, among those who are examining and challenging our relations with nonhuman animals. Among historical analyses, Coral Lansbury's *The Old Brown Dog: Women, Workers, and Vivisection in Edwardian England* (Madison: University of Wisconsin Press, 1985) is a major study, as is Harriet Ritvo's *The Animal Estate: The English and Other Creatures in the Victorian Age* (Cambridge: Harvard University Press, 1987). Barbara Noske employs sociological methods to critique human uses of animals in *Humans and Other Animals: Beyond the Boundaries of Anthropology* (London: Pluto Press, 1989). In the field of cultural anthropology, Donna Haraway's *Primate Visions: Gender, Race, and Nature in the World of Modern Science* (New York: Routledge, 1989) is an extraordinarily detailed, groundbreaking study. In literary criticism, Margot Norris's *Beasts of the Modern Imagination* (Baltimore: Johns Hopkins, 1985) adapts postmodern theory to suggest that artists and thinkers can "write with their animality speaking" (1). In ethics, one cannot ignore the contributions of Mary Midgley (e.g., *Animals and Why They Matter* [Penguin, 1983]) nor of a slim and courageous volume, *The Dreaded Comparison: Human and Animal Slavery* (London: Heretic Books, 1988) by Marjorie Spiegel, which does draw the "dreaded comparison" between the treatment of human slaves and the treatment of animals in bold and striking images and text. Carol Adams's *The Sexual Politics of Meat: A Feminist-Vegetarian Critical Theory* (New York: Continuum, 1990) and "Ecofeminism and the Eating of Animals," *Hypatia* 6 (Spring 1991) show how we can opt out of one form of institutionalized aggression against animals. Marti Kheel has pointed to the interrelationship of feminism and animal rights in "Animal Liberation is a Feminist Issue," *The New Catalyst* 10 (Winter 1987/88) and "Ecofeminism and Deep Ecology: Reflections on Identity and Difference," in *Reweaving the World: The Emergence of Ecofeminism*, ed. Irene Diamond and Gloria Feman Orenstein (San Francisco: Sierra Club Books, 1990).

4. My primary research into stories about animals has been performed without regard to the gender of the author. The tripartite structure of this essay emerges out of the isolation of women's stories about animals from an ungendered survey of the field. In fiction, men and women alike engage in reconceptualization of animals and, in the process, do well by animals. Of course, the reverse is also true: one finds men and women alike simply reproducing pernicious conventions in thought about animals. My effort to this point has been to establish the theoretical principles on which we as readers and critics can separate good work on animals from that which degrades animals and runs contrary to the cause of animal rights.

Looking over the field again, with a feminist politic in mind, I find that many women writers are doing interesting and distinctive work on animals, many more, indeed, than could be included here. With this essay, I have tried to organize that work into a feminist scale of values, a scale of values that, in its own way, covers the history of modern feminist thought as it has moved from recognition of oppression (victimization), to the assertion of holistic selfhood (identity), and on toward the larger vision of new societies (community). Stories have been chosen to illustrate key principles in each of these matters of concern. As with my other work, I have tried to bring out specific principles that can be applied to the interpretation of stories not discussed here.

What about men who write about animals within a feminist politic? I am not aware of many of these. One exception might be Timothy Findley, whose novel *Not Wanted on the Voyage* (Harmondsworth: Penguin, 1984) is a scathing attack upon Judeo-Christian patriarchy. Findley's is an extraordinary novel, although an event occurs at its heart which, I would guess, would never happen in a woman's story about animals. The ugliest event in the novel is what can only be described as the rape of an eleven-year-old girl with the horn of a unicorn (the unicorn dies from having his horn nearly torn from his head). Granted, the episode reveals the full depth of violence in patriarchy, for it is the chief patriarch who has performed this act. Yet as valuable as revelations like Findley's are, it appears that the sympathy for animals one finds in stories such as those described in the section on victimization simply disallows the presentation of gross violence. Findley does not accord power to "others"; in one concentrated image he articulates instead the full horror of treating the animal and the woman as victims and nothing but victims.

The principles that seem to divide men's work on animals from women's where identity is concerned is the naturalness of the animal and the sense of the person as a person. I have found little tendency in women's writing to convert the animal into a symbol or an abstraction. Granted, it would be difficult to surpass Franz Kafka, for example, on the score of destabilizing identity by means of the animal. In my own reading of Kafka, I find he has that strength of literalness that is more consistently evident in women's writing. Others, of course, find his work allegorical and busily translate his animals and his people into figurative entities. Women's writing about animals and identity is not, I would suggest, as amenable to such translation as are Kafka's animal stories.

It is on the third count, the matter of community, that women writers stand far ahead of men. I know of no male writer whose utopia gives full status to both animals and humans. Indeed, William Kotzwinkle's *Doctor Rat* (New York: Knopf, 1976) is informative: Kotzwinkle imagines a world in which all the animals come together in peace, but men come along with their tanks and bombs and simply wipe them all out. Again, as with the violence in Findley's work, this degree of aggression and pessimism might be very true to male-dominated society. But it is to be hoped, as women's stories hope, that male domination will not last forever.

All in all, I believe that the title and theme of this essay sums up the distinctiveness of women's stories about animals. As a rule, women recognize the redemptive power of otherness in animal. When they are working well with animals, men (again, as a rule) expose the evils of human society by pointing to the abuse of the "other" or, as with Plutarch and Swift, shaming humankind with animal superiority.

5. I have examined representations of animal victims at length in *Animal Victims in Modern Fiction: From Sanctity to Sacrifice* (Scholtmeijer 1993).

6. For an extensive treatment of Webb's novel and that strange phenomenon of yoking libido with the lust to kill animals, see chapter 5 of my book *Animal Victims* (1993).

7. This analysis draws upon the literal surface of "Attack at Dawn." A figurative reading of the story (observed and astutely examined by members of a class I conducted on animals in fiction), which would work with phallic, vaginal, and rape imagery, yields a fascinating interpretation but fails to address, and in fact runs contrary to, the reality of hostility between humans and animals vividly invoked in this story. I do not claim that the literal reading is the correct one, only that it works just as well as the figurative reading, which might receive greater favor with literary critics.

8. For discussion of "The Birds" in a different context, see my article "The Animal at the Door: Modern Works of Horror and the Natural Animal," in *State of the Fantastic: Studies in the Theory and Practice of the Fantastic in Literature and Film*, ed. Nicholas Ruddick (Westport, Conn.: Greenwood Press, 1992).

9. For further discussion of Mansfield's "The Fly," see *Animal Victims* (Scholtmeijer 1993).

10. Several philosophers of animal rights could be cited here: Tom Regan, Peter Singer, Mary Midgley, Gary Francione, Michael Allen Fox—the names

are probably familiar to readers. One of the most recent books to argue for the moral extension of human status to animals is *The Great Ape Project: Equality Beyond Humanity*, ed. Paolo Cavalieri and Peter Singer (London: Fourth Estate, 1993). In this anthology, writers take a truly bold step and argue seriously that the great apes should be treated as persons.

11. A similar image, with similar import, occurs in the popular book *Women Who Run with the Wolves: Myths and Stories of the Wild Woman Archetype* by Clarissa Pinkola Estés 1993). In a highly effective description, Estés appeals directly to the wolf to articulate mischievous defiance of sober institutions:

> Like my kith and kin before me, I swagger-staggered on high-heels, and I wore a dress and hat to church. But my fabulous tail often fell below my hemline, and my ears twitched until my hat pitched, at the very least, down over both my eyes, and sometimes clear across the room. (5–6)

While Emshwiller is working in the domain of fantasy and Estés is speaking figuratively, both fuse woman and animal to give physical shape to the literal power of otherness in women. In a more accessible image, Mary Webb brings Foxy and Hazel's other animal companions into church to witness Hazel's wedding in *Gone to Earth*. All three writers correct the oppressive dullness of the institution by means of animals.

References

Corrigan, Theresa, and Stephanie Hoppe, eds. 1989. *With a Fly's Eye, Whale's Wit, and Woman's Heart: Animals and Women*. San Francisco: Cleis Press.

——. 1990. *And a Deer's Ear, Eagle's Song, and Bear's Grace: Animals and Women*. San Francisco: Cleis Press.

Donovan, Josephine. 1990. Animal Rights and Feminist Theory. *Signs: Journal of Women in Culture and Society* 15 (Winter):350–75.

Du Maurier, Daphne. 1976. The Birds. In *Echoes of the Macabre: Selected Stories*. London: Victor Gollancz. Story originally published 1952.

Emshwiller, Carol. 1990. *Carmen Dog*. San Francisco: Mercury House.

Estés, Clarissa Pinkola. 1993. *Women Who Run with the Wolves: Myths and Stories of the Wild Woman Archetype*. New York: Ballantine Books.

Gordimer, Nadine. 1952. *The Soft Voice of the Serpent and Other Stories*. New York: Simon and Schuster.

Grahn, Judy. 1988. *Mundane's World*. Freedom, Calif.: Crossing Press.

Hurston, Zora Neale. 1991. *Their Eyes Were Watching God*. Foreword by Ruby Dee, introduction by Sherley Anne Williams, illustrated by Jerry Pinkney. Chicago: University of Illinois Press. Originally published 1937.

Jackson, Rosemary. 1981. *Fantasy: The Literature of Subversion*. London: Methuen.

Johnson, Mary A. 1986. Animals in Folklore: A Cross-Cultural Study of Their Relation to the Status of Women. *Michigan Academician* 18 (Spring):175–83.

Lansbury, Coral. 1985. *The Old Brown Dog: Women, Workers, and Vivisection in Edwardian England.* Madison: University of Wisconsin Press.

Le Guin, Ursula. 1988. *Buffalo Gals and Other Animal Presences.* New York: New American Library.

Lessing, Doris. 1974. *The Temptation of Jack Orkney and Other Stories.* New York: Bantam.

Lispector, Clarice. 1985. *Family Ties.* Translated and with an afterword by Giovanni Pontiero. Manchester: Carcanet. Originally published 1960.

———. 1986. *The Foreign Legion: Stories and Chronicles.* Translated and with an afterword by Giovanni Pontiero. New York: New Directions. Originally published 1964.

———. 1989. *Soulstorm.* Translated and with an afterword by Alexis Levitin, introduction by Grace Paley. New York: New Directions. Originally published 1974.

Mansfield, Katherine. 1967. The Fly. In *Selected Stories,* chosen and introduced by D. M. Davin. London: Oxford University Press.

Moises, Massaud. 1971. Clarice Lispector: Fiction and Cosmic Vision. *Studies in Short Fiction* 8 (Winter):268–81.

Munro, Alice. 1968. *Dance of the Happy Shades.* Foreword by Hugh Garner. Toronto: Ryerson Press.

Pitts, Deirdre Dwen. 1974. Discovering the Animal of a Thousand Faces. In *Children's Literature,* ed. F. Butler, vol. 3. Philadelphia: Temple University Press.

Scholtmeijer, Marian. 1993. *Animal Victims in Modern Fiction: From Sanctity to Sacrifice.* Toronto: University of Toronto Press.

Walker, Alice. 1989. *The Temple of My Familiar.* New York: Pocket Books.

Webb, Mary. 1982. *Gone to Earth.* Introduction by Erika Duncan. Toronto: Lester & Orpen Dennys. Originally published 1917.

Wilson, Harriet E. 1984. *Our Nig; or Sketches from the Life of a Free Black.* Introduction by Henry Louis Gates. London: Allen & Busby. Originally published 1859.

11
Reginald Abbott

irds Don't Sing in Greek:
Virginia Woolf and
"The Plumage Bill"

MY DEAR GODPAPA HAVE YOU BEEN TO THE ADIRONDACKS AND HAVE
YOU SEEN LOTS OF WILD BEASTS AND A LOT OF BIRDS IN THEIR NESTS
YOU ARE A NAUGHTY MAN NOT TO COME HERE GOOD BYE

YOUR AFFECT[e]
VIRGINIA

From Virginia Stephen, age six, to her "godfather" James Russell
Lowell, 20 August 1888—Woolf's first surviving letter (*Letters of
Virginia Woolf*, 1:2)

[Virginia] heard voices urging her to acts of folly; she believed that
they came from overeating and that she must starve herself. . . .
[Violet Dickinson] took Virginia to her house at Burnham Wood and
it was there that she made her first attempt to commit suicide. She
threw herself from a window, which, however, was not high enough

from the ground to cause her serious harm. It was here too that she lay in bed, listening to the birds singing in Greek.

(from Quentin Bell's *Virginia Woolf: A Biography*, 1:89– 90)

On 10 July 1920, H. W. Massingham (1860–1924),[1] writing under the nom de plume of "Wayfarer," made the following comments concerning the failure of the 1920 Plumage Bill in the House of Commons:

> Now that the Plumage Bill has been smothered the massacre of the innocents will continue. Nature puts an end to birds and the trade together. Her veto will be final, and as science declares that six years without birds means the end of her animate system, the end of the Plumage Trade may possibly coincide with the end of *us*. . . . What does one expect? They have to be shot in parenthood for child-bearing women to flaunt the symbols of it, and, as Mr. [William H.] Hudson[2] says, one bird shot for its plumage means ten other deadly wounds and the starvation of the young. But what do women care? Look at Regent Street this morning! (quoted in "The Plumage Bill," Woolf, *Essays*, 3:243–44, n.2; 241)

A maturing writer took Massingham at his word. Virginia Woolf, the thirty-eight-year-old author of two novels—*The Voyage Out* (1915) and *Night and Day* (1919)—and several dozen essays and book reviews, did look out onto Regent Street (at least figuratively) and decided in her own signed essay on the Plumage Bill of 1920 (originally published in Rachel [Ray] Strachey's [1887–1940] *The Woman's Leader*, 23 July 1920) that, given time and money, she *would wear* a plume, an egret plume to be exact.[3] As a rhetorical device, Woolf's declaration expressed both a sincere anger at a gender-biased anti-plumage argument and absolved a sincere anti-plumage writer (Woolf herself) of the "plumage guilt" that a real purchase would have incurred. Unfortunately, the rhetoric backfired on Woolf, as it was used by Massingham and others in their critical attacks on Woolf's essay. In a written response to these attacks, Woolf—in a gesture that can be characterized as ambivalent, ironic, and curiously apropos—promised to turn her fee for the article over to the anti-plumage Plumage Bill Group (*Essays*, 3:245, n.4). Thus, the story of Woolf's "earliest feminist polemic" ends just as her last feminist polemic, *Three Guineas* (1938), begins: with questions about the economic status of women, money, and a charitable cause.

Woolf's "The Plumage Bill" (see appendix) finds its small place—it hardly fills two full pages—in the third volume (1919–1924) of Woolf's collected essays (241–43). The length of the essay, about 1,000 words, belies its importance. In his introduction to this volume, Andrew McNeillie refers first to the "polemical panache" of the essay (xii) and later in the introduction states that "The Plumage Bill" stands as Woolf's "earliest feminist polemic" (xviii). That the essay has "punch" as well as "polemical panache" can hardly escape the reader of Woolf's collected essays. Throughout the first two volumes of Woolf's reviews and essays, one is presented with page after page of insightful and engaging commentary on books, people, things, and life. At no time in these calm essays, however, does Woolf become enthusiastic to the point of fever-pitch praise, or outraged to the point of condemnation.[4] Then the reader comes to "The Plumage Bill," Woolf's first exclamation as an essayist. This "panache" or unmistakable polemical tone alone would make "The Plumage Bill" an important essay for the Woolf scholar. McNeillie, however, points to an even more important feature of the essay: its place as the first public, controversial, feminist statement by the writer who was destined to become the author of A Room of One's Own (1929) and Three Guineas (1938)—arguably the two most important feminist polemics in English literature.

Indeed, I would suggest that this short essay is not just Woolf's "earliest feminist polemic" but the direct prototype of the longer, more developed works, not only in tone but also in the issues that it raises. But it is also important to note how Woolf frames her first public statement on the "woman question." Though Woolf has been labeled a "socialist, pacifist, feminist, and anti-fascist" (Marcus, "Introduction," xv), no one has to date taken Carol Adams's statements concerning an "historic alliance of feminism and vegetarianism in . . . suffrage movements and twentieth century pacifism" (The Sexual Politics of Meat, 167) and applied them to Woolf and her writings. Such an approach to Woolf appears ideal from the standpoint of the ostensible subject of "The Plumage Bill."

However, while "The Plumage Bill" does raise both the "woman question" and what might be called the "bird question," Woolf's answer clearly distinguishes the two concerns as separate, with the woman question the more important of the two. Woolf cannot be said to fit Adams's feminist-vegetarian (or feminist-animal rights) theory as a "major figure in women's literature" who "conjoined feminism and vegetarianism in ways announcing continuity, not discontinuity" (166). Still, it is undeniable that Woolf in "The Plumage Bill" put herself right in the middle of the controversy surrounding the bird preservation movement and conservationist concerns as they had developed throughout the nineteenth century and as they existed in 1920. In doing so, Woolf also hit upon other controversial issues—dress, gender distribution of wealth and political power, and the roles of women in society and art as producers and consumers— that she consistently addressed throughout her career.

Woolf's essay appeared just as a well-organized anti-plumage campaign was about to succeed in banning the importation of exotic feathers (Plumage Act of 1921) and, ironically, just as the huge demand for exotic plumage was about to end. That plumage was an essential part of Victorian and Edwardian fashion cannot be doubted. Robin W. Doughty in *Feather Fashions and Bird Preservation* presents a highly detailed chart of the feather fashions recorded in *Harper's Bazaar* for 1875–1900 (20–21). The uses were seemingly endless: turbans, neck ruches, boas, bonnets, bandeaus, capes, aigrettes, and innumerable styles of hats. The variety of plumage was also seemingly endless: herons, egrets, ostriches, grebes, pheasants, cocks, owls, parrots, ibis, marabou, peafowl, etc. Both domestic and wild fowl contributed to the trade. Technology developed to clean and dye feathers for extended use and retrimming as well as for the manufacture of artificial feathers—an ironic development as these processes would eventually enable domestic fowl feathers to imitate endangered wild species (Ginsburg, 92; Doughty, 67). Wings, bodies, heads, as well as tail plumage were all used; occasionally, different species were merged on one hat (Doughty, 22). A demand for the heads of South American hummingbirds for jewelry even flourished for a time (Bury, 619). Ostrich farming was established (in the Cape Colony in the mid-1860s) as a result of the demand for those sumptuous feathers (Doughty, 18; Ginsburg, 92), and, as the demand for egret plumes—the specific example used by both Massingham and Woolf in their respective essays—reached ever greater heights, egret farming was successfully achieved, albeit too late to benefit the plumage trade (Doughty, 75–79).

Obviously, feather fashions prompted an immense and highly profitable trade in the Victorian, Edwardian, and Georgian eras. At the height of feather fashions in this century, 1901–1910, 14,362,000 pounds of feathers were imported into the United Kingdom at a total valuation of £19,923,000 (Doughty, 26). What was the impetus or fashion motive behind this intense trade? Doughty is no fashion writer, but does suggest some of the utility and beauty of feather fashions: "Feathers upon enlarged hats and bonnets lent height to upper features and provided dignity and elegance. They were also necessary to soften and fill out body and dress contours and to highlight the face. Through an infinite variety of color and shape, plumage conveyed a novel attractiveness and individuality to head wear" (17). The traditional Freudian interpretation of the feather fashions of the nineteenth century is offered by Madeleine Ginsburg in her study of the hat:

> It [feather mania and a contemporary entomological mania] seems to have been a case of loving the animal world to death. Dr. C. Willett Cunnington, costume authority and Freudian, associated the craze for zoological decoration with the sublimation of sexual desire among women doomed to late marriage in a time of economic slump. Redirected affections are also credited with the philanthropic and conservationist movements which were also a feature of the age. The conservationist American Audubon Society was founded in 1886 and the English Royal Society for the Preservation of Birds in 1889. (92)

It would be impossible to provide a brief summary of the organizations, legislative proposals, and trade proposals involved in the plumage trade controversy of the late nineteenth century and early twentieth century.[5] Some mention must be made, however, of the men and women, especially the women, involved in anti-plumage activities. In "The Plumage Bill," Woolf mentions "a vow taken in childhood and hitherto religiously observed" concerning not wearing the plumage of wild, endangered birds (241).[6] Such a vow was part of membership in organizations like the Society for the Protection of Birds, founded by Mrs. Robert W. Williamson (Royal Society after 1904), and other groups led by Mrs. Edward Phillips and Mrs. Frank E. Lemon, as well as the Plumage League founded in 1885 (Doughty, 96; Haynes, 26). Other important women in the anti-plumage campaign included Baroness Burdett-Coutts, an intense advocate of the Royal Society for Prevention of Cruelty to Animals, and Winifred, Duchess of Portland, who was president of the Society of the Protection of Birds for sixty-three years and who encouraged Queen Alexandra to ban "osprey" feathers at court in 1906 (Doughty, 96, 116). As for the anti-plumage men, Lord Robert Cecil (1864–1958) introduced the first comprehensive plumage bill in the House of Commons in 1908. His wife, Lady Robert Cecil (1868–1956), was a close friend of Virginia Woolf.

All this anti-plumage activity cannot, however, be credited with the abandonment of feather fashions by the early 1920s. Although attention must be given to the effects of World War I in disrupting international trade in general, there was an unquestionable decline in the consumption of exotic feathers after 1910. Between 1911 and 1920, feather imports (excluding ostrich after 1912) were 7,397,000 pounds, roughly half of the amount for 1901–1910 (Doughty 26). Allan Haynes in his article "Murderous Millinery" also notes the decline and characterizes it as a "collapse" from 1,275,413 pounds of exotic feathers in 1913 to 35,877 pounds in 1920 (30). Imports from France fell from a high of "2.2. million pounds in 1913 to less than one-tenth that amount in 1920" (Doughty, 25). Doughty quotes a contemporary source who attributes the decline in feather fashions to the rise of the automobile and the need for simpler clothes capable of being defended from automotive dirt and dust (23, n.19). Aileen Ribeiro in *Dress and Morality* credits the decline of fashionable plumage to fashion itself:

> The campaign against fur coats is of fairly recent origin, but it follows in the footsteps of the Edwardian attacks on the "immorality" of using birds' plumage to decorate the vast hats which were in vogue; such "murderous millinery" was preached against in pulpits and derided in newspapers, but it was due *more to a change in fashion than to a change of heart* that women stopped wearing such styles in the second decade of this century. (14, emphasis added)

This change in fashion was almost a complete renunciation of plumage: "The opulent curves of the Edwardian lady, with her stately piled-high hair in art-nouveau curves and her huge hat covered in birds' plumage, were no longer required" (Ribeiro, 149).

Thus, the voluptuous Edwardian lady in plumes gave way to couturier Paul Poiret's (1879–1944) "Grecian" silhouette, aigretted turbans, and hobble skirts, all of which in turn gave way to the unmistakable look of the 1920s: short skirts, "boyish figures," and the unplumed, unaigretted cloche hat.[7] Of course, the genius of Poiret and Paris fashions were worlds away from the Victorian household of Sir Leslie Stephen (1832–1904), Woolf's father, and the geniuses and would-be geniuses of what would be called Bloomsbury. The Stephen family has come to represent for many the quintessential patriarchal Victorian household. It should not be surprising, therefore, to find that Woolf was fully inculcated in the Victorian concept of an ordered animal world governed by man—a concept described by Harriet Ritvo as the "animal estate":

> the animal-related discourse of nineteenth-century England was both enormous and diverse. It described a wide range of interactions, which might be inspired by primary motives as disparate as sentiment (petkeeping), economics (animal husbandry), and curiosity (natural history). (4)[8]

As heir to the Victorian "animal estate," young Woolf was aware of the details of the Muzzling of Dogs Act (1871) as it applied to the neighbors' dog (*Letters*, 1:2) and attempted to judge the "species" of a dog herself (*Letters*, 1:11). Woolf would later refer to the Muzzling of Dogs Act in her obituary to the Stephens' dog Shag ("On A Faithful Friend" [1905], *Essays*, 1:12–15) and recall concern over Shag's pedigree: "[Shag] came to us, however, with a pedigree that had all the elements of romance in it; he, when, in horror at his price, his would-be purchaser pointed to his collie head and collie body, but terribly Skye-terrier legs—he, we were assured, was no less a dog than the original Skye—a chieftain of the same importance as the O'Brien or the O'Connor Don in human aristocracy" (12–13). Woolf and her sister Vanessa witnessed a carriage running over a dog and, soon after, its owner setting off to the "Lost Dogs home to buy a new creature" (*Letters*, 1:12). The Stephens' own dogs were given to being put into "prison" for running wild through the town (*Letters*, 1:352, 354–55). In 1902, Woolf visited the zoo and wished to buy a green monkey (*Letters*, 1:60) to add to the Stephen household. In 1904, Woolf recalled looking at pictures of animals in the nursery even before being able to be read aloud to: "It is quite true that I still know all my beasts from their pictures in Bewick which we were shown before we could listen to reading aloud" (*Letters*, 1:165).

All of these examples illustrate aspects of the "animal estate" as presented by Ritvo. Indeed, Woolf's first exposure to books included one of the "most influential mediators" of period discourse about the physical aspects of animals and "their place in the natural order, and their relationship to people" (Ritvo, 6). Thomas Bewick's (1753–1828) *A General History of Quadrupeds* (1790) and *British Birds* (1797, 1804) were both immensely successful upon publication and throughout the nineteenth century:

Within approximately five hundred pages [*Quadrupeds*] offered entries ranging in length from a few sentences to many pages on what purported to be the entire range of known quadrupeds.... Almost every entry was illustrated by one of Bewick's appealing woodcuts. (Ritvo, 7)

These entries also expressed an order of nature especially appealing to the Victorian world: "Bewick presented the animal kingdom as rationally ordered and easily comprehensible, a perception that was itself strong evidence of the power of human intelligence" (14). This order was not only seen in illustrated books but also in the popular, highly ordered world of the Victorian zoo, an institution emblematic in Ritvo's view of the British imperial system (Ritvo, chap. 5: "Exotic Captives," 205–42).

As suggested above, the young Woolf also inherited the Victorian preoccupation with and intense love of dogs, even to the point of parodying the obsession: "I expect I shall leave all my fortune to a home for stray pug dogs, having become entirely maudlin in my old age" (*Letters*, 1:364).[9] One manifestation of the era's preoccupation with dogs were the various discourses on and attempts to control the spread of rabies (a subject also thoroughly chronicled by Ritvo [chap. 4: "Cave Canem," 167–202]). One of the successful legislative measures concerning rabies was the Muzzling of Dogs Act of 1871. Much later, Quentin Bell, Woolf's nephew and biographer, would use the trope of Victorian concerns over dog breeding, pedigree (see Ritvo, chap. 2: "Prize Pets," 82–121), and antivivisection to illustrate the caprice of fashion:

Dogs are the fashion because we can fashion them to our will.... The highly bred dog can have its whole frame twisted and distorted into shapes of the most astonishing kind and can in fact become an ornamental monster.... On being [informed] that the monstrosity fanciers are amongst the most resolute critics of vivisection, [an observer] would set them down as hypocrites. Such an accusation would however be unjust; the owners are genuinely devoted to their victims. Fashion ... has a morality of its own; and the cruelty involved in breeding deformed animals, like that involved in blood sports, is redeemed by the economic futility of the motive; that involved in scientific experiments is felt to be odious because of its unpardonable utility. (*On Human Finery*, 55–56)

It is fitting to turn to Quentin Bell's writing on fashion, as Bell's sartorial sense consistently chronicled his aunt's concerns over clothes and personal appearance as well as apprehending Woolf's struggle to fashion a "public" Woolf as polished and as self-confident as her prose.[10] This sartorial struggle, I suggest, offers a highly informative perspective on Woolf's concept of women in the public sphere and, in this instance, merges with the plumage controversy of the Victorian, Edwardian, and Georgian eras. The infant Woolf who was entertained by Bewick's ordered natural world of quadrupeds and birds, the six-year-old Woolf who wrote her godfather about the birds and beasts of North America,[11] the ten-year-old Woolf who vowed never to wear an egret plume, the twenty-two-year-old Woolf who madly imagined birds singing in Greek, all became the "thirtysomething" Woolf who had just barely managed to deal with milliners ("I dont [sic] like buying hats though: though I've conquered some part of the horror by learning how to look into the eyes of milliners, & make my demands boldly" [Diary, 1:6, 148–49]) and who, in her own exercise in "animal discourse," would "buy an egret plume, and stick it— is it in the back or the front of the hat?" ("The Plumage Bill," 241) as a rhetorical symbol of defiance at an assault on the integrity of her sex.

This outrage, this defiance, should not surprise the reader, for it is exactly how A Room of One's Own begins, as the essay's persona is first intercepted on the green by the beadle (6) and then by the "guardian angel" of the library who turns her away from the library's door (7–8). The persona's curse on the library follows, as does her meditation on the "unending stream of gold and silver" (9) needed to build a university, particularly the lack of money women had to donate to build a university for women (20–21). Money makes an earlier appearance in A Room of One's Own as part of the essay's thesis ("a woman must have money and a room of her own if she is to write fiction" [4]), and money gives Three Guineas its title, frame, and thesis. Money also begins "The Plumage Bill": "If I had the money and the time I should, after reading 'Wayfarer,' in the Nation of 10 July, go to Regent Street, [and] buy an egret plume" (241). "The Plumage Bill," therefore, introduces three themes that would always interest Woolf: women and money, women as consumers (egret plumes), and women as producers (writers).

From the beginning of the "The Plumage Bill," Woolf places herself in the role of female producer—a busy writer who earns her living by writing and really does not have the time or the money to shop on

Regent Street.[12] Thus, Woolf's egret plume must remain, for practical reasons alone, simply a rhetorical figure, a metaphor for her rage. Instead of visiting Regent Street, the author exercises her craft and produces a word picture of the shopping district:

One can look at Regent Street without leaving one's room. The lower half of the houses is composed of plate glass. One might string substantives and adjectives together for an hour without naming a tenth part of the dressing bags, silver baskets, boots, guns, flowers, dresses, bracelets and fur coats arrayed behind the glass. Men and women pass incessantly this way and that. Many loiter and perhaps desire, but few are in a position to enter the doors. Most of them merely steal a look and hurry on. (241)

Woolf's fascination with shopping and shopping districts found full expression in *Mrs. Dalloway* (1925) with Woolf's brilliant depiction—one could almost say characterization—of Bond Street. Unlike Bond Street, Regent Street had been created as part of an elegant, exclusive shopping district for men and women rather than developing as one (like Bond Street) over time (Adburgham, 98–100). The style of Woolf's prose picture of Regent Street in "The Plumage Bill"—the focus on plate glass windows full of desirable goods listed in detail—would appear again in *Mrs. Dalloway* and in Woolf's study of mass consumerism in the essay "Oxford Street Tide" (1932). What is important here is Woolf's emphasis on a marketplace appealing to both men and women. Save for the dresses and bracelets, all of the goods listed could be desired and used by both sexes, but even the dresses and bracelets could be purchased by men. In *Mrs. Dalloway*, two characters shop for their respective wives: Hugh Whitbread inspects jewelry for his wife (171–73) and Richard Dalloway buys flowers for his wife (174). Woolf's focus on Regent Street begins with this mass of men *and* women, of would-be consumers. This ungendered group quickly disappears amongst the various producers and consumers mentioned later in the essay, but their inability to consume the goods on display immediately highlights the entrance of the archetypal consumer—the lady of means:

And then there comes on foot, so that we may have a good look at her, a lady of a different class altogether. A silver bag swings from her wrist. Her gloves are white. Her shoes lustrous. She holds herself upright. As an object of beauty her figure is incomparably more delightful than any other object in street or window. It is her face that one must discount, for, though discreetly tinted and powdered, it is a stupid face, and the look she sweeps over the shop windows has something of the greedy petulance of a pug-dog's face at tea-time. (241–42)

It is at this point in the essay that Woolf's attention shifts from the female producer of goods (essays) to the female consumer as found by Massingham in his own essay to be "[a] child-bearing [woman]" willing to "flaunt" her child-bearing status with such things as egret plumes, thereby being guilty of a hard and heartless "carelessness" regarding the ecological consequences of the plumage trade. Woolf responds to Massingham's charge with the creation of "Lady So-and-So." Woolf's recourse to a fictional character to illustrate an argument would be used again in the character of "Shakespeare's sister" in *A Room of One's Own*—a memorable and effective rhetorical creation. Here, however, the reader may question the rhetorical soundness of Woolf's example. Woolf appears to have made her "actual" egret consumer into the very persona—vain, selfish, careless—condemned by Massingham.

But Lady So-and-So is more ambiguous than that. While Lady So-and-So is a creation of a patriarchal system of male production and wealth and a patriarchal aristocracy (it is doubtful that she is Lady So-and-So in her own right), she is also a reflection/product of patriarchal society as produced and consumed by women. Lady So-and-So's bag, gloves, shoes, and cosmetics were at least sold by if not designed and/or made by women.[13] Lady So-and-So's existence as a consumer, a flawlessly finished consumer icon at that, was at least partly the work of women producers of luxury goods or services. The "artfully arranged" egret plumes in the window ("flights of hats on little rods" [*The Years* (1937), 333]) that attract Lady So-and-So were probably arranged by female hands. The "lemon-coloured egret" was probably dyed by female hands. In 1889, 8,000 women were employed in Paris in the millinery trade (Ginsburg 100). The majority of the 83,000 people employed in New York City in 1900 in making and decorating hats were women (Doughty, 23).[14] The true milliner was an artist and generally, almost exclusively, a woman:

A true creative artist, the milliner was frequently "author" of "a masterpiece." She constantly invented new models of hats and revived earlier styles; and even when the basic substructure of the hat was simple, she decorated it artistically with ribbons, flowers, and feathers, creating a "harmonious ensemble." (Steele, 72–73; see also Doughty, 24)

At least one Parisian milliner, Caroline Reboux (1837–1927), gained an international reputation and is credited with inventing the "plumeless" cloche of the 1920s (O'Hara, 210–11). Woolf herself was later to create a maker of hats in the character of Rezia in *Mrs. Dalloway* (34, 131, 135).

Here, however, women as workers or artists who produce or create hats and millinery[15] is a point missed by the class-bound Woolf, or intentionally ignored so Woolf could focus on the "male producers" and "profiteers" in the plumage trade and in patriarchal society as a whole. This change of focus or rhetorical shift is quick and cutting. The word picture of Regent Street is subsumed by another picture, a picture of the jungle: egrets nesting and producing young, hunters fashioning decoys as artfully contrived as Lady-So-and-So's toilette, and the "opening and shutting" of "innumerable mouths" as egret young die of starvation (242). While Woolf does not ponder the position of women as producers of millinery or spokespersons for the plumage trade, she does pause to consider the "gender" of the plumage trade itself:

> But these hands—are they the hands of men or of women? The Plumage Bill supporters say that the hunters "are the very scum of mankind." We may assume that the newspapers would have let us know if any of the other sex had been concerned in it. We may fairly suppose then that the birds are killed by men, starved by men, and tortured by men—not vicariously, but with their own hands. (242)

In this passage, Woolf's direction in the essay is clearly established: male producers of plumage = female consumers of plumage. While Lady So-and-So is not to be absolved of all guilt when she opens her silver mesh bag and "disgorges I know not how many notes" (242) in the purchase of an egret plume, Woolf does not place primary blame in this act of trade with the female consumer. After all, Lady So-and-So is a success with the very tools of the only "profession" (marriage) Woolf acknowledged to be open to women before 1919 (*Three Guineas*, 20). It was Woolf's plea throughout her life that just enough economic power and independence ("Of the two—the vote and the money—the money, I own, seemed infinitely the more important." [*A Room of One's Own*, 37]) guaranteed women rooms of their own. This stance sets the stage for another production/consumption equation: male consumers of women = female producers of children. Woolf deftly takes Massingham's cry against "child-bearing women" who must flaunt that status in fashionable plumes and turns it away from questions concerning the feminine motivations and vicarious guilt of fashion to a critique of the structures of patriarchal capitalism as manifested in a male-dominated workplace. Woolf then extends this attack to include the patriarchal family structure and even male desire:

> But what is the nature of this compulsion? Well, men must make their livings, must earn their profits, and must beget children. For though some people say that they can control their passions, the majority maintain that they should be protected from them rather than condemned for them. In other words, it is one thing to desire a woman; quite another to desire an egret plume. (243)

In her reply to Massingham's 30 July 1920 attack on her article, Woolf freely acknowledges that her essay was "an outburst of sex antagonism." Woolf also acknowledges that she has used "animal discourse," here "bird discourse," to champion women:

> To torture birds is one thing, and to be unjust to women is another, and it was, I hope, plain to some of my readers that I was attacking the second of these crimes and not the first. . . . I reply that I am not writing as a bird, or even a champion of birds; but as a woman. (245, n.4)

Beyond the fashionable facade—beyond the objectification of Lady-So-and-So in the contexts of both patriarchal power and consumerism—is the woman herself. Lady So-and-So as "an object of beauty" is "incomparably more delightful than any other object in street or window." Although her desires may make her take on a "pug-dog" countenance, Lady So-and-So as a human being and, more importantly for Woolf's argument here, as a woman is, faults notwithstanding, of more importance socially, politically, and morally than Massingham's egrets.

Woolf as "naturalist" does not buy an egret plume; instead, in a Bewickian gesture of species/sex classification, she places the phallic egret plume, plumage developed by the male egret at breeding time to attract a female, as a decoration marking both men and the patriarchal institutions behind male power. As stated above, men make themselves "attractive" with the plumage trade and, as a result, breed, but in the larger spheres of education, religion, and, most especially, politics, men assume even greater power and appropriate badges of this power—the "tufts of fur" worn at the university in *A Room of One's Own* (8) and the other badges of office derided in *Three Guineas* (19, 21, 114). This power orders nature (Muzzling of Dogs Act, Plumage Bill) and extends power, grudgingly, to women (suffrage). In the best of all possible worlds, these men wear their badges of office with honor and without bias or self-interest in wielding power over other men, women, and even egrets:

> There remains, however, a body of honourable and disinterested men who are neither plume hunters, profiteers, nor women. It is their duty, as it is within their power, to end the murder and torture of the birds, and to make it impossible for a single egret to be robbed of a single plume. (243)

Of course, in 1920 as in 1908, these men (and one woman)[16] were found wanting:

> The House of Commons took the matter up. The Plumage Bill was sent to Standing Committee C. With one exception [Lady Astor] each of its sixty-seven members was a man. And on five occasions it was impossible to get a quorum of twenty to attend. The Plumage Bill is for all practical purposes dead. But what do men care? Look wherever you like this morning! (243)

On Woolf's July morning in 1920, egret plumes were still arranged for sale on Regent Street, and Lady So-and-So, with cash in hand and the power/freedom said cash delivers, had every right to buy the beautiful, complementary accessory for her opera ensemble—an accessory deemed by the fashion press to be worthy of both Lady So-and-So and the occasion: "Lady So-and-So was 'looking lovely with a lemon-coloured egret in her hair.'" After all, Lady So-and-So "of the stupid face and beautiful figure is going tonight to the opera; Clara Butt is singing Orpheus; Princess Mary will be present" (242). After all, an egret plume was something even a princess, because of her grandmother's own anti-plumage vow, could not wear.[17]

Woolf's attack on the overt misogyny of Massingham's comments on "child-bearing" women begins with anger, with a "sex antagonism" that would shatter these patriarchal institutions as swiftly as protesting suffragettes broke every shop window on Regent Street at four in the afternoon on 1 March 1912 (Adburgham, 176–77). Or, is it that intense? The reader will recall that Woolf, as a woman artist caught in the production/consumption binds of art and without the weapons—money and time—needed to combat patriarchal strictures, "soft pedals" her act of defiance against Massingham's anti-plumage misogyny with the conditional "if" ("If I had the money and the time . . ."). At the end of the essay, this "sex antagonism" has been diffused even more by the laughter of parody. In turning Massingham's words upside down, Woolf attempts with hyperbole to smooth down any potentially ruffled feathers in her audience:

> The Plumage Bill is for all practical purposes dead. But what do men care? Look wherever you like this morning! Still, one cannot imagine "Wayfarer" putting it like that. "They have to be shot for child-begetting men to flaunt the symbols of it. . . . But what do men care? Look at Regent Street this morning!" Such an outburst about a fishing-rod would be deemed sentimental in the extreme. Yet I suppose that salmon have their feelings. (243)

Woolf's "earliest feminist polemic" posed a special problem for Woolf: balancing her own anti-plumage position with controlled outrage at Massingham (see note 1) and Massingham's misogyny. In the face of Massingham's statements, Woolf had no recourse but to the "perfect" act of rhetorical defiance: "If I had the money and the time I should . . . go to Regent Street, [and] buy an egret plume." Well, it was almost perfect. The controversy sparked by Woolf's essay—Massingham's and Mrs. Meta Bradley's ("Does it matter in the least to the birds so foully slain whether the blame rests most with men or women?") replies of 30 July 1920 to *The Woman's Leader* and Woolf's 6 August 1920 response to both Massingham and Bradley (Woolf, "Letter to the Editor," 244–45, n.4)—highlighted the intense involvement of women in the anti-plumage campaign, the potential for conflict when women's rights conflicted with other agendas (vegetarianism, animals rights, conservationism),[18] and Woolf's own identity as an artist. As a maturing producer of essays who strove for a polemical tone without stridency, Woolf could miss her mark or be misunderstood.

Woolf found that the production/consumption equation is just not so simple for the female writer. Earlier, Woolf's anxiety about her own productions and their reception by consumers prompted her relapse into madness after the completion of *The Voyage Out* (Bell,

Virginia Woolf, 2:11–27). This anxiety was later validated in Woolf's mind by certain unfavorable critical responses, including Massingham's (see note 1), to her next novel, *Night and Day* (Bell, *Virginia Woolf*, 2:69),[19] and no doubt also by the controversy in *The Woman's Leader* over "The Plumage Bill." However, in "The Plumage Bill," the woman as artist is not a writer but a singer: Dame Clara Butt (1872–1936) who "sings" the lead role in Christoph Willibald Gluck's (1714–1787) *Orfeo ed Euridice* (1762) at Lady So-and-So's "visit" to the opera (242).[20] The irony in Woolf's reference to Dame Butt lies in the public portrayal of a male Greek hero by a woman; moreover, it is a role that depicts male sorrow and frailty, originally written for a castrated male (more irony) voice. This irony runs even deeper, for the Greek language and its literature were a male-dominated cultural preserve, a preserve invaded by Woolf in private Greek tutorials with Janet Case (see note 1) and through her friendship with the classicist and vegetarian Jane Harrison (see note 8). The language became for Woolf an ideal means of expression ("The Perfect Language" [1917], *Essays*, 2:114–19), and, later, in her madness, Woolf heard the birds singing in Greek. The same Woolf probably apprehended the appropriateness of such a manifestation as the myth tells that the "real" Orpheus taught Greek to the birds. Birds do not sing in Woolf's "perfect language." While Woolf did not see herself writing "as a bird," she *did* write as a "champion of birds." Thus, Woolf's career as a polemicist began with an attempt at anti-plumage rhetoric. As such, "The Plumage Bill" produced controversy, but its merger of anti-plumage argument with "an outburst of sex antagonism" stands as the first feminist statement of the early twentieth century's most eloquent and influential "champion of women."

Notes

1. Henry William Massingham was editor of *The Nation* from 1907 until his resignation in 1923. Virginia Woolf's relationship with Massingham could best be characterized as strained and unstable. As "Wayfarer," Massingham published an unflattering paragraph on Woolf's second novel *Night and Day* (1919) on 29 November 1919 in which he described Woolf's characters as "Four Impassioned Snails" (*Diary*, 1:316, n.2; 318). Woolf refers to this "cutting paragraph" (*Diary*, 1:316) several times in her letters (*Letters*, 2:399–400, 405, 515), but was reconciled to Massingham when he twice offered (5 May 1920) her husband Leonard Woolf (1880–1969) a job at *The Nation* (*Diary*, 2:34, n.3; 42), and even more so when *The Nation* published a flattering review (15 May 1920) by Robert Lynd (1879–1949) on *Night and Day*

(*Diary*, 2:38, n.14). Conflict was renewed, however, with Massingham's attack on Woolf's "The Plumage Bill" (23 July 1920) in his letter to the editor in *The Woman's Leader* (30 July 1920). Woolf responded: "I've a vendetta with Massingham, against whom my arrow was launched" (*Diary*, 2:58). The "arrow" was Woolf's reply to Massingham (*The Woman's Leader*, 6 August 1920). The following year (21 February 1921), Woolf was to score another point in the "vendetta" by declining Massingham's request to review Dorothy Richardson's (1873–1957) 1921 novel *Deadlock* (*Diary*, 2:93). All was well again by the end of the following year (13 November 1922) when Woolf again "forgave" Massingham after reading Massingham's public praise (*The Nation & Athenaeum*, 22 October 1922) of Leonard Woolf: "I like this, & forgive Massingham his abuse of me from this time forward" (*Diary*, 2:212). However, Woolf could not forget, at least not in a letter (20 March 1922) to her former Greek tutor and suffragist sponsor Janet Case (1862–1937): "Massingham says L[eonard] is the best writer on the Nation: But what did Massingham say of Night and Day?" (*Letters*, 2:515). Woolf's complex relationship with Massingham invites a psychological reading of "The Plumage Bill" as it relates to Woolf's rage at patriarchal critique, to her dealings with literary "father" figures (Massingham), to her relationship with Leonard Woolf, to Woolf's delusions during her 1904 breakdown, and to additional "bird hysteria" before Woolf's 1915 breakdown as recorded in a letter to Lytton Strachey (1880–1932) (*Letters*, 2:61; see note 17 below)—a letter that Nigel Nicolson characterizes as "malicious beyond the point of sanity" (xvi). (Note: Throughout the second volume of Woolf's letters, H. W. Massingham is misidentified as H. J. Massingham [1888–1952], H. W. Massingham's son and a noted naturalist in his own right.)

2. Robin W. Doughty describes William H. Hudson (1841–1922) as a "noted naturalist and author, [who] allied himself with the infant SPB [Society for the Protection of Birds] by contributing to its leaflet program, which alerted the public to the potential disaster to birds from feather fashions" (53, n.5). Woolf reviewed Hudson's *Far Away and Long Ago: A History of My Early Life* (1918) ("Mr. Hudson's Childhood," *Essays*, 2:298–303) and was particularly captivated by Hudson's descriptions of birds: "These are the birds of earliest childhood, and from them his [Hudson's] dreams spring and by them his images are coloured in later life. Riding at first seemed to him like flying. When he is first among a crowd of well-dressed people in Buenos Aires he compares them at once to a flock of military starlings. From watching birds comes his lifelong desire to fly—but it is a desire which no airship or balloon but the wings of a bird alone will satisfy" (301).

3. "Osprey," "egret," and "aigrette" were generally interchangeable terms during the Victorian, Edwardian, and Georgian eras. An "aigrette" may not necessarily be made of "egret" plumes, but "osprey" plumes are the same as "egret" plumes—tall, slim, stately feathers that are white in their natural state. In other words, "osprey" feathers and "egret" feathers are from the same species of heron. The *osprey*, however, is a brown, fish-eating hawk not used in millinery. "Aigrettes" were generally made of "egret" feathers since the principle behind an aigrette is to wear a tall, slim, stately feather(s)

on the head as part of a jewel or headpiece, or actually in the hair. Obviously, "aigrette" is derived from "egret."

Woolf herself was confused about the distinction, or lack of distinction, between "osprey" and "egret": "At the age of ten or thereabouts I signed a pledge never to wear one of the condemned feathers [egret], and have kept the vow so implicitly that I cannot distinguish osprey from egret" (*Essays*, 3:244, n.4). Another "feather controversy" of Woolf's era involved white feathers. During World War I, pro-war women branded men in civilian dress as cowards by handing them white feathers—an ironic gesture given that most plumage valued in millinery is produced by the male bird as a year-round sex indicator and/or for display during breeding season. In *Three Guineas*, Woolf condemned both the "white feather of cowardice" and public praise of wartime bravery, which Woolf symbolized in a reference to the French Legion of Honor as the "red feather of courage" (109).

On the subject of herons, the reader familiar with American literature may recall Sarah Orne Jewett's (1849–1909) short story "A White Heron" (1886) and Louis A. Renza's exhaustive study of this one short story—"A White Heron" and the Question of Minor Literature. Renza does mention the plumage issue, but dismisses it as not relevant to Jewett's story (127). However, Deborah Strom, in *Birdwatching with American Women: A Selection of Nature Writings*, does connect Jewett's story to the conservation movement (114). (My gratitude to the editors for pointing out Strom's comments.)

4. I refer, of course, to the essays themselves as they were published in Woolf's time and not to the revelatory endnotes provided by Andrew McNeillie to Woolf's letters, diaries, and other writings, which more often than not reveal Woolf's true feelings, always witty, often condemning, about her subjects. It should be noted that "The Plumage Bill" was reproduced earlier as Appendix 2 in the second volume (1920–1924) of Woolf's diary (337–38). It should also be noted that Woolf's letters (9 and 16 October 1920) to Sir Desmond McCarthy (1877–1952) in his position as literary editor of *The New Statesman* (collectively entitled "The Intellectual Status of Women") are generally regarded as Woolf's first feminist polemic. "The Intellectual Status of Women" is also reproduced in the second volume of the diary in Appendix 3 (339–40).

5. An attempt will be made. For Great Britain, laws pertaining to bird protection and plumage can be divided into two groups: native birds and nonnative birds. Native birds were protected under law by the Sea Birds Preservation Act of 1869, which was expanded in 1880. The Wild Birds Protection Act of 1887 regulated birds in India. The export of wild birds for millinery purposes was banned in British India in 1902. The first Plumage Bill to ban all exotic imports was proposed in 1908.

Doughty provides a chart of legislative efforts regarding plumage legislation from 1903 to the successful passage of the 1921 Plumage Act, implemented 1 April 1922 (118–20). The reader must also note the many, many distinctions made in all plumage discussions of the era. There were good (insect-eating) birds and bad (crop-eating or barnyard fowl–eating) birds, wild birds and ranched birds, and regional/cultural considerations (Why shouldn't a poor native of India profit from the carcass of a bird he would kill anyway to protect his crop? Why shouldn't an overpopulated species be put to some use? Why can't molted plumage be a profitable resource for native populations? What profit is there to England if a lucrative, tax-generating trade is abolished only to flourish elsewhere?).

Also, no anti-plumage society banned all plumage for millinery purposes. Domestic or ranched birds were acceptable. These included ostrich, eider, and all birds used as "articles of diet." Woolf herself states in her response to Massingham's attack on "The Plumage Bill" that: "Cocks, hens, parrots, and ostriches are the only birds whose feathers I recognise or wear" (Essays, 3:244, n.4). Legislative efforts varied from year to year as naturalists and conservationists researched and debated the status of specific species, the merits of specific species, and the methods of plumage gathering. The Plumage Bill of 1908 would have banned the importation and sale of exotic plumage. The successful Plumage Bill of 1921 banned the importation but not the sale of exotic plumage. It should also be mentioned that both the 1908 and 1921 bills exempted plumage worn by or carried with a traveler entering the country. In the United States, the 1914 Tariff Act banning exotic plumage made no such exemption. As a result, the public was outraged when women were detained at ports or followed by customs agents to their hotels in order to search for and/or confiscate banned plumage. An exemption for personal apparel was later added to the act (Doughty, 132).

6. In her response to Massingham's attack on "The Plumage Bill," Woolf recalls that her vow was probably made at the age of ten "or thereabouts" (see note 3 above).

7. This is not to imply that feather fashions completely disappeared from the fashion vocabulary. The reemergence of sophisticated millinery in the 1930s through the 1950s ensured some use of feathers. Recently, the Princess of Wales revived the ostrich-plumed toque. The exotic, sensual, and sensuous appearance of feathers, lots of feathers, also ensured continued use of plumage in theatrical settings. Gaby Deslys (1881–1920), Mistinguett (1875–1956) and Josephine Baker (1906–1975) all used costumes made entirely of feathers. The originator of this "feathered theater" was Deslys, whom Sir Cecil Beaton (1904–1980) referred to as "a human aviary" (Gardiner, 40). The accomplishments and trademarks of these entertainers, feathers prominently included, are preserved in musical revues around the world. A contemporary feathered performer of note—courtesy of innumerable turkey feathers dyed a bright canary yellow—is Sesame Street's Big Bird.

8. The Victorian world of the Stephen household—a world beautifully invoked by Quentin Bell in a passage on the family's favorite "blood sport" of butterfly/moth hunting (Virginia Woolf, 1:33)—was carried over into the world of Woolf's maturity and to a Bloomsbury filled with real animals, animal sports, "animalized" humans, and animal products. All of Woolf's brothers hunted birds—an activity enjoyed by young Jasper Ramsey in To the Lighthouse (1927) (26, 41, 123–24)—and/or foxes, or bird-watched (Letters, 1:130, 170, 172). Virginia and Leonard Woolf nearly always maintained

at least one dog in their household (Bell, *Virginia Woolf*, 2:175–76; see also Ritchie, xv–xvi). Leonard Woolf even owned a marmoset, which was said to resemble Josef Goebbels (Bell, *Virginia Woolf*, 2:189). Vanessa Stephen's (1879–1961) marriage to Clive Bell (1881–1962) in 1907 introduced Woolf to an unforgettable inkwell made of a hunter's hoof, as well as to life on a country estate: "The place was populated by stuffed animals and to a large extent by living ones; animals dominated the conversation" (Bell, *Virginia Woolf*, 1:103).

As for "human" animals in Bloomsbury, Woolf was always "Goat" to her sister Vanessa. Vanessa was sometimes "Sheepdog." Woolf adopted the nickname "Sparroy" when writing to her dear friend Violet Dickinson (1865–1948). Woolf would become "Mandrill" (!) to Leonard Woolf's "Mongoose." Vegetarianism appears to have been little known in early Bloomsbury. To Emma Vaughan (1874–1960; nicknamed "Toad"), Woolf wrote in August 1901 requesting a "long letter full of meat" (*Letters*, 1:44). To Lady Robert Cecil, Woolf wrote (January 1907) a beautiful appreciative note for a birthday gift of pheasants and furs: "Now the pheasants are long since gone, and I think they were specially nice pheasants, and I gave my solitary wing some special attention—considering it as a piece of tender meat, critically. Why is there nothing written about food—only so much thought? . . . I am fitted with a marvellous simplicity of nature so that to buy a fur is impossible to me, but to accept a fur is quite easy and pleasant" (*Letters*, 1:277–78). Clive Bell loved to criticize George Bernard Shaw (1856–1950), perhaps the most famous vegetarian of his time. Virginia quoted one Bellism on the subject in a letter to Lytton Strachey: " 'These vegetarians, my dear Virginia, always go at the top. [Shaw] needs Bullocks blood' " (*Letters*, 2:508). One writer on vegetarianism in Woolf's circle who certainly influenced Woolf's feminism was the Greek scholar Jane Harrison (1850–1928; see Adams, 171).

9. Of course, Woolf would turn to the "biography" of a dog in *Flush* (1933), a work that has not received its fair share of critical attention, particularly as Woolf reflects a tradition of Victorian animal discourse and "animal estate" fiction (e.g., Anna Sewell's [1820–1878] *Black Beauty* [1877]).

10. See Bell, *Virginia Woolf*, 1:73, 75, 146, 149; 2:37, 40, 60, 95, 96–97, 110–11, 117–18, 136–37, 144, 146.

11. James Russell Lowell (1819–1891), Woolf's "godfather" (the Stephen children were not baptized but were assigned "sponsors" [Bell, *Virginia Woolf*, 24–25]), also gave the young girl "a real, live bird in a cage, an incident that Virginia does not mention anywhere in her memoirs and yet caused Vanessa [Virginia's older sister] to recall more than fifty years later the 'evil passions' this preferential gift aroused in her" (Dunn, 31).

12. In his first endnote to the essay, McNeillie quotes Woolf's diaries regarding the writing of "The Plumage Bill": "Now for oh Reviewing!—Three weeks I think have passed without a word added to Jacob [*Jacob's Room*]. How is one to bring it through at this rate. Yet its [*sic*] all my fault . . . why take up the Plumage Bill for Ray [Strachey]? But after this week I do no more" (*Diary*, 2:53). Woolf was indeed too busy to go to Regent Street when

she began her essay on the Plumage Bill. Interestingly enough, one of the projects on Woolf's mind was her 1922 novel *Jacob's Room*, a passage from which Adams cites as a possible reference to a feminist-vegetarian perspective in Woolf's work (Adams, 188). Earlier (1907–1913), Woolf had created a failed vegetarian in the character of Mr. Ambrose in *The Voyage Out* (198).

13. Woolf would address the role of the female sale assistant in the short story "Mrs. Dalloway in Bond Street" (1923) and in the novel *Mrs. Dalloway* (15–19).

14. Woolf also does not acknowledge in the essay itself the participation of women as spokespersons for the plumage trade. In her reply to Massingham's critique of her essay ("Letter to the Editor," 244–45 n.4), Woolf does make a reference to E. Florence Yates, described by McNeillie as "a prominent campaigner on the part of the plumage trade" (245 n.4). (Miss E. Florence Yates should not be confused with the anti-plumage campaigner Colonel Sir Charles Yate [1849–1940], who introduced the 1920 Plumage Bill.)

15. The observant reader will note that Lady-So-and-So wears her egret plume in her hair and not in a hat. At the time, the word *millinery* applied to any decoration worn on the head. Hats and hair ornaments were sold in the same establishments.

16. The American-born Nancy Langhorn Astor, Viscountess Astor (1879–1964), was the first woman elected (1919) to Parliament. She was an active supporter of the Plumage Bill of 1920 (Doughty, 120).

17. Oddly enough, Haynes recounts that Queen Mary, Princess Mary's mother, did have one royal relapse into forbidden plumage in, of all years, 1920. Queen Mary wore an "osprey" at a royal garden party (30).

As for Woolf, in 1926 Vita Sackville-West (1892–1962) observed Woolf in an ensemble (matching dress and hat) featuring "a sort of top-hat made of straw, with two orange feathers like Mercury's wings" (quoted in Glendinning, 163). Jane Dunn, in her interpretation of Woolf's experiences in the ensemble (212–13), finds Woolf's attraction to the hat to be based on the ease with which it could be worn "because there could be absolutely no doubt as to which was the front and which the back" (Dunn quoting Sackville-West, 212). However, Sackville-West's pronoun references in the passage are vague. Sackville-West could be referring to the dress and/or hat.

Clive Bell, Virginia's sometime "lover" (Bell, *Virginia Woolf*, 1:132–33; 2:85–86) and the subject of a letter written just before Woolf's 1915 breakdown ("The thing is for us all to persuade [Clive] that the love of birds is the last word in Civilisation" [*Letters*, 2:61; see note 1]), ridiculed Woolf's hat and eventually the dress as well. Woolf felt that Bell, whom she once nicknamed "Parakeet" (Dunn, 97), and others attacked her on the occasion: "They pulled me down between them like a hare" (quoted in Dunn 213). What is interesting here is not only Woolf's choice of a plumed top-hat in 1926 (an anticipation of the 1930s, particularly the cross-dressing elements of European bohemia later popularized by Hollywood) but also the issues of Woolf's self-image and the animal/bird imagery used by Woolf to characterize herself and others.

18. An illustration of this is found in Adams's story of the "feminist vegetarian milliner" interrupting a 1907 National American Woman Suffrage Association meeting (172–73).

19. Jane Marcus, in her study of *Night and Day*, notes the presence of birds and bird imagery in the novel ("Enchanted Organ, Magic Bells: *Night and Day* as a Comic Opera," 26). The comic opera of Marcus's title is Mozart's (1756–1791) *The Magic Flute* (1791)—an opera featuring a bird-catcher.

20. McNeillie notes that Dame Butt "made her first professional appearance in opera" at Covent Garden on 1 July 1920 and that Princess Mary was in the audience (*Essays*, 3:244, n.3).

References

Adams, Carol J. *The Sexual Politics of Meat: A Feminist-Vegetarian Critical Theory*. New York: Continuum, 1990.

Adburgham, Alison. *Shopping in Style: London from the Restoration to Edwardian Elegance*. London: Thames and Hudson, 1979.

Bell, Quentin. *On Human Finery*. 1947. Reprint, New York: Schocken Books, 1978.

——. *Virginia Woolf: A Biography*. New York: Harcourt Brace Jovanovich, 1972.

Bradley, Mrs. Meta. "Letter to the Editor," *The Woman's Leader*, 30 July 1920. In *The Essays of Virginia Woolf, Volume Three: 1919–1924*, ed. Andrew McNeillie, 245 n.4. New York: Harcourt Brace Jovanovich, 1988. Partial citation by V. Woolf, "Letter to the Editor," *The Woman's Leader*, 6 August 1920.

Bury, Shirley. "Parisian Jewelry and American Patrons." *Antiques*, April 1992, 614–21.

Doughty, Robin W. *Feather Fashions and Bird Preservation: A Study in Nature Protection*. Berkeley: University of California Press, 1975.

Dunn, Jane. *A Very Close Conspiracy: Vanessa Bell and Virginia Woolf*. Boston: Little, Brown and Company, 1990.

Gardiner, James. *Gaby Deslys: A Fatal Attraction*. London: Sidgwick & Jackson, 1986.

Ginsburg, Madeleine. *The Hat: Trends and Traditions*. New York: Barrons' Educational Series, 1990.

Glendinning, Victoria. *Vita: The Life of Vita Sackville-West*. New York: Alfred A. Knopf, 1983.

Haynes, Alan. "Murderous Millinery." *History Today*. July 1983, 26–30.

Lynd, Robert. "A Tragic Comedienne" [Review of *Night and Day* by Virginia Woolf]. *The Nation*, 15 May 1920.

Marcus, Jane. "Enchanted Organ, Magic Bells: *Night and Day* as a Comic Opera." In *Virginia Woolf and the Languages of Patriarchy*, 18–35. Bloomington: Indiana University Press, 1987.

——. "Introduction." In *Virginia Woolf and the Languages of Patriarchy*, xi–xv. Bloomington: Indiana University Press, 1987.

Massingham, H. W. "Letter to the Editor," *The Woman's Leader*, 30 July 1920. *The Essays of Virginia Woolf, Volume Three: 1919–1924*, ed. Andrew McNeillie, 244 n.4 (partial citation). New York: Harcourt Brace Jovanovich, 1988.

——. "Wayfarer," *The Nation*, 29 November 1919.

——. "Wayfarer," *The Nation*, 10 July 1920.

——. "Wayfarer," *The Nation & Athenaeum*, 22 October 1922.

McNeillie, Andrew. "Introduction." In *The Essays of Virginia Woolf, Volume Three: 1919–1924*, xi–xxii. New York: Harcourt Brace Jovanovich, 1988.

Nicolson, Nigel. "Introduction." In *The Letters of Virginia Woolf, Volume Two: 1912–1922*, ed. Nigel Nicolson and Joanne Trautmann, xiii–xxiv. New York: Harcourt Brace Jovanovich, 1976.

O'Hara, Georgina. *The Encyclopaedia of Fashion*. New York: Harry N. Abrams, 1986.

Renza, Louis A. *"A White Heron" and the Question of Minor Literature*. Madison: University of Wisconsin Press, 1984.

Ribeiro, Aileen. *Dress and Morality*. New York: Holmes & Meier, 1986.

Ritchie, Trekkie. "Introduction." In *Flush*, Virginia Woolf, vii–xvii. 1933. Reprint, New York: Harcourt Brace Jovanovich, 1983.

Ritvo, Harriet. *The Animal Estate: The English and Other Creatures in the Victorian Age*. Cambridge: Harvard University Press, 1987.

Steele, Valerie. *Paris Fashion: A Cultural History*. New York: Oxford University Press, 1988.

Strom, Deborah. *Birdwatching with American Women: A Selection of Nature Writings*. New York: Norton, 1986.

"Wayfarer." [H. W. Massingham]. *The Nation*, 29 November 1919.

——. *The Nation*, 10 July 1920.

——. *The Nation & Athenaeum*, 22 October 1922.

Woolf, Virginia. *The Diary of Virginia Woolf, Volume One: 1915–1919*, ed. Anne Olivier Bell. New York: Harcourt Brace Jovanovich, 1978.

——. *The Diary of Virginia Woolf, Volume Two: 1920–1924*, ed. Anne Olivier Bell. New York: Harcourt Brace Jovanovich, 1978.

——. *The Essays of Virginia Woolf*, ed. Andrew McNeillie. 3 vols. to date. New York: Harcourt Brace Jovanovich, 1986– .

——. *Flush*. 1933. Reprint, New York: Harcourt Brace Jovanovich, 1983.

——. "The Intellectual Status of Women." 1920. In *The Diary of Virginia Woolf, Volume Two: 1920–1924*, ed. Anne Olivier Bell, 339–40. New York: Harcourt Brace Jovanovich, 1978.

——. *Jacob's Room*. 1922. Reprint, New York: Harcourt Brace Jovanovich, 1950.

——. "Letter to the Editor," *The Woman's Leader*, 6 August 1920. In *The Essays of Virginia Woolf, Volume Three: 1919–1924*, ed. Andrew McNeillie, 244–45 n.4. New York: Harcourt Brace Jovanovich, 1988.

——. *The Letters of Virginia Woolf, Volume One: 1888–1912*, ed. Nigel Nicolson and Joanne Trautmann. New York: Harcourt Brace Jovanovich, 1976.

——. *The Letters of Virginia Woolf, Volume Two: 1912–1922*, ed. Nigel Nicolson and Joanne Trautmann. New York: Harcourt Brace Jovanovich, 1976.

——. "Mr. Hudson's Childhood" [Review of *Far Away and Long Ago: A History of My Early Life* by William H. Hudson], 1918. In *The Essays of Virginia Woolf, Volume Two: 1912–1918*, ed. Andrew McNeillie, 298–303. New York: Harcourt Brace Jovanovich, 1988.

——. *Mrs. Dalloway.* 1925. Reprint, New York: Harcourt Brace Jovanovich, 1953.

——. "Mrs. Dalloway in Bond Street." 1923. In *The Complete Shorter Fiction of Virginia Woolf*, 1st ed., ed. Susan Dick, 146–53. New York: Harcourt Brace Jovanovich, 1985.

——. *Night and Day.* 1919. Reprint, New York: Harcourt Brace Jovanovich, 1948.

——. "On a Faithful Friend." 1905. In *The Essays of Virginia Woolf, Volume One: 1904–1912*, ed. Andrew McNeillie, 12–15. New York: Harcourt Brace Jovanovich, 1986.

——. "Oxford Street Tide." 1932. In *The London Scene: Five Essays by Virginia Woolf*, 16–22. New York: Frank Hallman, 1975.

——. "The Perfect Language." 1917. In *The Essays of Virginia Woolf, Volume Two: 1912–1918*, ed. Andrew McNeillie, 114–19. New York: Harcourt Brace Jovanovich, 1988.

——. "The Plumage Bill," *The Woman's Leader*, 23 July 1920. Reprinted in *The Diary of Virginia Woolf, Volume Two: 1920–1924*, ed. Anne Olivier Bell, 337–38. New York: Harcourt Brace Jovanovich, 1978. Also reprinted in *The Essays of Virginia Woolf, Volume Three: 1919–1924*, ed. Andrew McNeillie, 241–45. New York: Harcourt Brace Jovanovich, 1988.

——. *A Room of One's Own.* 1929. Reprint, New York: Harcourt Brace Jovanovich, 1957.

——. *Three Guineas.* 1938. Reprint, New York: Harcourt Brace Jovanovich, 1966.

——. *To the Lighthouse.* 1927. Reprint, New York: Harcourt Brace Jovanovich, 1955.

——. *The Voyage Out.* 1915. Reprint, New York: Harcourt Brace Jovanovich, 1948.

——. *The Years.* 1937. Reprint, New York: Harcourt Brace Jovanovich, 1965.

Appendix: "The Plumage Bill" by Virginia Woolf

(from *The Woman's Leader*, 23 July 1920)

If I had the money and the time I should, after reading 'Wayfarer', in the *Nation* of 10 July, go to Regent Street, buy an egret plume, and stick it—is it in the back or the front of the hat?—and this in spite of a vow taken in childhood and hitherto religiously observed. The Plumage Bill has been smothered; millions of birds are doomed not only to extinction but to torture; and 'Wayfarer's' comment is, "What does one expect? They have to be shot in parenthood for child-bearing women to flaunt the symbols of it, and, as Mr Hudson says, one bird shot for its plumage means ten other deadly wounds and the starvation of the young. But what do women care? Look at Regent Street this morning!" One can look at Regent Street without leaving one's room. The lower half of the houses is composed of plate glass. One might string substantives and adjectives together for an hour without naming a tenth part of the dressing bags, silver baskets, boots, guns, flowers, dresses, bracelets and fur coats arrayed behind the glass. Men and women pass incessantly this way and that. Many loiter and perhaps desire, but few are in a position to enter the doors. Most of them merely steal a look and hurry on. And then there comes on foot, so that we may have a good look at her, a lady of a different class altogether. A silver bag swings from her wrist. Her gloves are white. Her shoes lustrous. She holds herself upright. As an object of beauty her figure is incomparably more delightful than any other object in street or window. It is her face that one must discount, for, though discreetly tinted and powdered, it is a stupid face, and the look she sweeps over the shop windows has something of the greedy petulance of a pug-dog's face at tea-time. When she comes to the display of egret plumes, artfully arranged and centrally placed, she pauses. So do many women. For, after all, what can be more etherially and fantastically lovely? The plumes seem to be the natural adornment of spirited and fastidious life, the very symbols of pride and distinction. The lady of the stupid face and beautiful figure is going tonight to the opera; Clara Butt is singing Orpheus; Princess Mary will be present; a lemon-coloured egret is precisely what she wants to complete her toilet. In she goes; the silver bag disgorges I know not how many notes; and the fashion writers next day say that Lady So-and-So was "looking lovely with a lemon-coloured egret in her hair".

But since we are looking at pictures let us look at another which has the advantage of filling in certain blank spaces in our rough sketch of Regent Street in the morning. Let us imagine a blazing South American landscape. In the foreground a bird with a beautiful plume circles round and round as if lost or giddy. There are red holes in its head where there should be eyes. Another bird, tied to a stake, writhes incessantly, for red ants devour it. Both are decoys. The fact is that before "the childbearing woman can flaunt the symbols of parenthood" certain acts have to be devised, done, and paid for. It is in the nesting season that the plumes are brightest, So, if we wish to go on making pictures, we must imagine innumerable mouths opening and shutting, opening and shutting, until—as no parent bird comes to feed them—the young birds rot where they sit. Then there are the wounded birds, trailing leg or wing, as they flutter off to droop and falter in the dust. But perhaps the most unpleasant sight that we must make ourselves imagine is the sight of the bird tightly held in one hand while another hand pierces the eyeballs with a feather. But these hands—are they the hands of men or of women? The Plumage Bill supporters say that the hunters 'are the very scum of mankind.' We may assume that the newspapers would have let us know if any of the other sex had been concerned in it. We may fairly suppose then that the birds are killed by men, starved by men, and tortured by men—not vicariously, but with their own hands. "A small band of East End profiteers' supports the trade; and East End profiteers are apt also to be of the male sex. But now, as 'Wayfarer' says, the birds 'have to be shot in parenthood for child-bearing women to flaunt the symbols of it'.

But what is the nature of this compulsion? Well, men must make their livings, must earn their profits, and must beget children. For though some people say that they can control their passions, the majority maintain that they should be protected from them rather than condemned for them. In other words, it is one thing to desire a woman; quite another to desire an egret plume.

There remains, however, a body of honourable and disinterested men who are neither plume hunters, profiteers, nor women. It is their duty, as it is within their power, to end the murder and torture of the birds, and to make it impossible for a single egret to be robbed of a single plume. The House of Commons took the matter up. The Plumage Bill was sent to Standing Committee C. With one exception each of its sixty-seven members was a man. And on five occasions it was impossible to get a quorum of twenty to attend. The Plumage

Bill is for all practical purposes dead. But what do men care? Look wherever you like this morning! Still, one cannot imagine 'Wayfarer' putting it like that. 'They have to be shot for child-begetting men to flaunt the symbols of it. . . . But what do men care? Look at Regent Street this morning!' Such an outburst about a fishing-rod would be deemed sentimental in the extreme. Yet I suppose that salmon have their feelings.

So far as I know, the above, though much embittered by sex antagonism, is a perfectly true statement. But the interesting point is that in my ardour to confute 'Wayfarer', a journalist of admitted humanity, I have said more about his injustice to women than about the suffering of birds. Can it be that it is a graver sin to be unjust to women than to torture birds?

12

Brian Luke

*T*aming Ourselves
or Going Feral?
Toward a Nonpatriarchal Metaethic
of Animal Liberation

Animal liberationists oppose the institutionalized exploitation of animals in such industries as animal farming, animal vivisection, and sport hunting. *Ethically,* animal liberation involves recognizing the moral significance of the severe harms done to animals through these institutions. In this essay, I focus on the *metaethics* of animal liberation, that is, on the meaning of animal exploitation for people, the moral agents who sometimes support and sometimes oppose animal exploitation. The points made here are relevant to issues such as why people support animal exploitation and what this does to them; how people come to oppose animal exploitation; and how we might best understand the social function of animal liberationist ethics.

In particular, I extend here our developing realization of the limitations of patriarchal metaethics, a framework that structures many of the works written in support of animal liberation. By a patriarchal metaethic I mean a perspective that sees social control as the purpose of ethics and that incorporates elements of the ideology of male supremacy. The presumption of social control as the point of ethics fits into a pattern Sarah Hoagland has discerned:

> The focus and direction of traditional ethics, indeed its function, has not been individual integrity and agency (ability to make choices and act) but rather social organization and social control. (Hoagland 1988, 12)

The application of patriarchal metaethics to animal liberation takes the following form: a tacit acceptance of sexist derogations of female animal liberationists as overly sentimental or hysterical, leading to a distrust of emotion and an overemphasis on cold reason as the source of animal liberationism. The goal of animal liberationist ethics is then to delineate rational principles of conduct that control our putatively uncaring dispositions toward animals.

After highlighting the patriarchal elements of animal rights theory in the first section of this essay, I challenge a key belief motivating this metaethical perspective, namely the notion that humans' compassionate feelings for animals are undependable. Animal liberationists are not so much using reason to override some innate indifference to animals as we are overcoming institutionalized barriers to the expression of our deep connections with animals. This suggests an alternative metaethic, emphasizing not social control but the freeing of caring agency, a perspective that I sketch in the last section, "Going Feral." I see animal liberation as creative, not restrictive. It extends possibilities for action—in particular, possibilities for acting on our compassion for animals.

Patriarchal Animal Liberation

In this section I use the works of Tom Regan (author of *The Case for Animal Rights*) and Peter Singer (author of *Animal Liberation*) to exemplify elements of the patriarchal metaethics of animal liberation.[1] Within traditional nonfeminist ethics, utilitarianism and rights theory are often seen as the two primary moral alternatives. So with Singer's use of utilitarianism and Regan's adoption of a rights-based approach, it is understandable that the theories of Singer and Regan would often be viewed as the two opposing poles of philosophical support for animal liberation.[2] From a nonpatriarchal metaethical standpoint, however, Singer's and Regan's theoretical similarities are as significant as their differences. In particular, both Singer's utilitarian theory and Regan's rights approach are developed within a framework of patriarchal norms, which includes the subordination of emotion to reason, the privileging of abstract principles of conduct, the perception of ethical discussion as a battle between adversaries, and the presumption that ethics should function as a means of social control.

Reason

Both Regan and Singer characterize emotion as an unreliable basis for ethical decisions, and claim to have made no appeal to emotion in their arguments for animal liberation. Their emphatic subordination of emotion to reason has been much noted and criticized by feminist animal liberationists. For example, Deborah Slicer, among others, rejects the general privileging of reason over emotion, stating that "there is no pat formula for deciding when our affective responses have a place, or how much weight they should have" (Slicer 1991, 115). Regarding women's identification with animals, Andrée Collard writes that "we react to them in every fibre of our being. We can be moved to outrage without feeling a need to justify our emotions" (Collard, 1989, 96). And I have elsewhere described the primacy of direct sympathetic responsiveness in the motivations of many animal liberationists (Luke 1992, 102–4).

The point of such critiques is not to invert the traditional hierarchy—to instead place emotion over reason—but rather to suggest that in ethics reason and emotion work together, so that attempts to expunge emotion from theoretical ethics are artificial and self-defeating. Josephine Donovan has noticed that "despite his accent on rigorously rational inquiry, Regan throughout uses the term *counter-intuitive* as a kind of escape clause whenever deductive reason per se proves inadequate" (Donovan 1990, 353). Even the most "rigorous" argument must use some initial, unproven premises. At such points, Marti Kheel argues, the writers are implicitly relying on readers' common *feelings* to gain assent (Kheel 1985, 143).[3]

Since a dualism of reason over emotion makes so little sense theoretically, we might well wonder why academic defenders of animal liberation so often retain the rationalistic paradigm. Regan at times recognizes the motivational primacy of emotion, stating that "philosophy can lead the mind to water but only emotion can make it drink" (Regan 1986b, 40). His own experience confirms this, as he recounts in an autobiographical piece:

Reason demanded that I become a vegetarian. But it was the death of our dog that awakened my heart. It was the sense of irrecoverable loss that added the power of feeling to the requirements of logic. (Regan 1986a, 93)

Given this, it is all the more puzzling that Regan's primary exposition of animal rights theory, *The Case for Animal Rights*, is totally devoid of concrete references to feelings or experiences, and in fact is structured as an extended exposition on logical consistency.

The key to resolving this puzzle is recognizing that Regan and Singer have taken as one of their primary goals the establishment of the academic respectability of animal rights theory.[4] Certainly academic respectability conventionally requires the adoption of the reason-over-emotion paradigm, as Singer recognizes:

The portrayal of those who protest against cruelty to animals as sentimental, emotional "animal-lovers" has had the effect of excluding the entire issue of our treatment of nonhumans from serious political and moral discussion. (Singer 1990, iii)

But what this statement crucially obscures is the *gendered* nature of the derogation of emotion. A central patriarchal ideology is the elevation of the "rational/cultural" male over the "emotional/biological" female. Women's rage (labeled "sentiment," "hysteria," etc.) is thus divested of political significance by interpreting any female reaction against the established order not as a moral challenge to that order, but as a biosexual phenomenon to be ignored or subdued.

This is critical to understanding reactions against animal liberation; since animal liberationists have always been predominantly female, sexist stereotypes have been a favored technique for dismissing the movement.[5] So this may be the subtext to Singer's attempt to gain respectability through denial of emotion. Josephine Donovan suggests that his underlying concern is that "to associate the animal rights cause with 'womanish' sentiment is to trivialize it" (Donovan 1990, 351).[6] We male animal liberationists are additionally liable to respond to charges of sentimentality with hyperrationality; animal liberation implies vegetarianism, for many of us, but meat eating is strongly associated with masculinity (see Adams 1990, chap. 1), so the expunging of "female" emotion may be attractive as compensation for the loss of manly carnivorism.

In this context we can place the extreme sensitivity some male animal rights theorists have shown over the picture of animal liberationists as "little old ladies in tennis shoes." Regan, Singer, and Andrew Linzey all earnestly argue that by virtue of their rational discussions we may "safely put to rest" that stereotype.[7] The strategy is evidently designed to gain respectability for animal liberation by using formalistic male theorizing to distance the movement from the female objects of contempt. By seeing women/emotion as a public relations problem for animal liberation, this strategy tacitly accepts the patriarchal ideology behind the charges of "hysteria" and "sentiment," misrepresents animal liberationist morality by erasing its emotional elements, and disrespects the work of female animal liberationists (who are not only the majority of activists but comprise most of the movement's founders and leaders).

Of course, increasing the respectability of animal liberation is a worthwhile goal, but in pursuing this goal we need not defer to patriarchally constructed notions of respectability. Instead, we might directly rebut the sexism of the charges of female hysteria, as, for example, Carol Adams does by commending the women who were the first to perceive the injustice of animal exploitation, and by affirming that she *aspires* someday to be one such radical little old lady (Adams 1994, 199)! And, like nineteenth-century animal liberationist Anna Kingsford, we may reject the notion that emotion invalidates morality:

> They speak sneeringly of "sentiment". The outcry against vivisection is mere "sentiment". Why, in God's name, what is so great, so noble, as human sentiment! What is religion, what is morality, but sentiment? On what divine feeling are based the laws which bid men to respect the lives, the property, the feelings of their fellow men? Sentiment is but another name for that moral feeling which alone has made man the best that he is now, and which alone can make him better and purer in the future. (quoted in Vyvyan 1988, 121)

Principle

Within the dualistic paradigm of reason over emotion, "reason" typically means this: the derivation of highly abstract first principles which are then used to support more specific (but still quite general) rules of conduct. It is expected that one might have emotions and dispositions that contradict the rules of conduct, but that such unruly passions will be brought under control, overridden by one's commitment to the "rationally" established principles and rules. To be "rational," the rules of conduct must follow from the first principles through logical deduction, and the first principles must be established without reference to feelings or to traditions. Ideally, the principles are universal (binding all people) and general (applying in all situations). Regan and Singer both follow this model, with Regan basing his case for animal rights on a principle of respect (do not treat subjects as resources or as mere receptacles of good and bad experiences) and Singer grounding animal liberation in a principle of equal consideration (weigh the interests of all sentient beings equally). And both writers conclude their treatments with general rules of conduct, advocating universal vegetarianism and qualified antivivisectionism.

Feminist animal liberationists have questioned the wisdom of placing such general principles at the center of ethics. There are two points of abstraction that may be questioned: abstracting from the features of the moral agents, and abstracting from the features of those affected by our actions. In the latter case, the exclusive focus on the subjectivity and sentience of animals leaves out many morally relevant features (such as personal relationships and individual histories), thus "oversimplify[ing] our actual and potential relationships with and responses to animals, depriving us of opportunities to respond to and make responsible choices about" what we eat, the products we use, etc. (Slicer 1991, 114). There is also something artificial about reducing animal liberation to a principle of respect for sentience (or subjecthood), since we do not in fact respond to oppressed animals as *cases* of sentience or subjecthood, but as individuals who are in one way or another communicating their needs to us.

Deriving rules that apply to all agents in all situations also oversimplifies. Vegetarianism, to give one example, certainly carries quite different meanings and implications depending on one's class, gender, race, religion, culture, physiology, etc. For instance, Alice Walker, who in general aligns herself with those who feel that "eating meat is cannibalism" (Walker 1988, 172), still at times defers to cultural and situational factors:

> Since Bali, nearly a year ago, I have eaten several large pieces of Georgia ham (a cherished delicacy from my childhood, as is fried chicken; it is hard to consider oneself Southern without it!) and several pieces of chicken prepared by a long-lost African friend from twenty years ago who, while visiting, tired of my incessant

Taming Ourselves or Going Feral?

chopping of vegetables to stir-fry and eat over rice and therefore cooked a chicken and served it in protest. (Walker 1988, 172)

I do not know how those who defend vegetarianism on principle would respond to the above, whether they (or even Walker herself today) would see the situational factors that Walker describes as sufficient justification for eating flesh. But my point is that complexities based on our specific identities, histories, and relationships frequently arise to challenge preset formulas for behavior, and that often these complexities *are* more compelling than the formulas. In such cases, ethical theorists tend to qualify their formulas to allow for each "special case" as it arises. This suggests that universal principles are not primary in ethics, that the primary basis is ourselves in all our complex identities and relations to other people, other animals, and nature.

So we do not act as bare agents but as embodied individuals with personal histories, enmeshed in networks of gender, race, class, and familial relations. But abstracting from every feature but one (viz., rational agency) facilitates *control*, a point to which I return below.

Adversarial Relations

Academic ethicists see themselves as establishing their first principles *against* and *above* the principles of other theorists. Moral investigations are structured as battles between rivals:

> In academia, the Ethics Game is sometimes played to one-up the opposition. The goals include proving oneself right (about what is morally right) *and* proving the "opposition" wrong. Moral theories and arguments are used as weapons. Philosophical reputations are at stake: who can poke holes in the opponent's position and defend an alternative position against all objections—for all to see? (Warren 1989, 83–84)

This adversarial/territorial conception of ethical investigation is exemplified by the following passage, in which Regan indicates that his purpose in writing includes establishing the rationality of animal defenders in contradistinction to the irrationality of certain of our "opponents":

> *The Case for Animal Rights* was conceived by me to be, and I continue to hope that it will function as, an intellectual weapon

to be used in the cause of animal rights. I wanted to give the lie, once and for all, to all those opponents of animal rights who picture everyone in the movement as strange, silly, overly emotional, irrational, uninformed, and illogical. *The Case for Animal Rights* is my attempt to ram these accusations down the throats of the uninformed, illogical, careless, irrational, strange, silly, and overly emotional people who make them. (Regan 1986a, 94)

Singer also at times describes his arguments as weapons. For example, in a very ironic choice of metaphors for an animal liberationist, he characterizes his defense of his principle of equal consideration against a "competing" moral principle as using "heavy artillery to swat a fly" (Singer 1981, 107).

To a certain extent, this sense of competition is entailed once one has placed universal, general principles at the center of ethics. Different principles prescribe different behaviors, so when they are expected to apply to all people in all situations they cannot all be correct. But this is only a competition between *principles*, not people. We might still expect to discover the "one, true" principle through a cooperative, rather than mutually antagonistic investigation. The academic emphasis on doing battle *presumes* that truth emerges through conflict: "what truth (if any) this book contains can *only* be decided by how well it stands up under the heat of informed efforts to refute its claims" (Regan 1983, xii, emphasis added). But in an essay discussing feminist directions in medical ethics, Virginia Warren questions this presumption:

> It might be objected that the best way to get to the truth is for others to try their mightiest to slay one's arguments; an idea's survival is purported to be evidence of its truth. . . . Though schooled to accept the Gladiator Theory of Truth, I have never found it to be the only way to get to the truth. Moreover, I have often found it to distort truth and to crush creativity. (Warren 1989, 86)

Insofar as adversarial relations are not always truth-promoting, they are likely to be furthering some other end, such as the establishment of the victor's identity as rational, moral, or "pure." As many feminist theorists have noted, this type of identity formation—establishing the value of one's self through the devaluation of others—is particularly characteristic of masculine development under patri-

Taming Ourselves or Going Feral?

archy. Ethical discussion, including serious disagreement, need not be structured competitively, with one side achieving rationality only by proving the irrationality of the other. Alternatively, we may expect ethical discussion between those who disagree to further intellectual and moral development *mutually*, through a shared presumption of each others' rationality and goodness. So in response to those who defend animal exploitation, our focus shifts from salvaging our rationality by proving their irrationality, to asking how different people, all of whom are rational and good, can disagree about this issue. In the second section of this essay, "The Maintenance of Animal Exploitation," I present some results of applying this nonadversarial approach to the understanding of animal exploitation.

Social Control

The three structural elements of animal rights theory discussed above—reason/emotion dualism, adversarial approach, privileging of principles—are well suited for developing programs of social control: reason/emotion dualism includes the notion that reason should strive to control emotion, while the adversarial approach seeks to define a class of irrational others (the emotional ones needing to be controlled). And if one's object is to control the behavior of many people in many situations, then the use of general, universal principles of conduct immediately recommends itself. By abstracting from all but a few features of the people and the situations, the legislator is able to exert control (assuming the efficacy of the moral or legal hierarchy) over an indefinite number of people and situations through a very limited number of legislative acts.[8]

The tendency for animal rights theorists to structure their work in ways well suited to programs for social control becomes all the more significant given the institutional context of academic ethics. As academics, our theorizing takes place within an institution that is itself hierarchical and that often functions to further the economic and political hierarchies governing this society—for example, by developing authoritative legitimations for the suppression of dissent. Some recognize the power struggles between disputing academics, but suggest that this has no significant social implications:

Though philosophy is carried on as a coercive activity, the penalty philosophers wield is, after all, rather weak. If the other person is willing to bear the label of "irrational" or "having the worse arguments", he can skip away happily maintaining his previous belief. (Nozick 1981, 4)

The possibility of skipping happily away from charges of irrationality holds, at best, only between equals. But academic attributions of irrationality are made in a society of *unequals,* in which, as Kathryn Pyne Addelson puts it, "because of our social locations as researchers, educators, and policy advisors, we have, as a matter of fact, institutional warrant for making and dispersing knowledge" (Addelson 1991, 109–10). Addelson discusses the structural hierarchies that allow elite groups of leaders in government, the media, higher education, etc., to define "official points of view," which set the terms of debates, limit the range of acceptable positions, and determine the qualifications for participation in public discussions. The academic class exercises direct power over students, and influences the rest of society through access to publishers, the media, and government. The terms "rational" and "irrational" distinguish between positions worthy and unworthy of debate, and between people worthy and unworthy of being heard. Making and enforcing these distinctions is a substantial form of social control.

At stake in the struggle to define rationality is admission to or exclusion from the realm of public discourse, as well as access to professional credentials. For example, there are a multitude of cases, both past and ongoing, of biology departments, veterinary schools, wildlife management programs, and medical schools seeking to exclude those with an animal liberationist perspective. It is important to struggle against such exclusion, but on what terms do we engage this struggle? If we accept the present terms, then the task for animal liberationists is to establish our rationality by proving the irrationality of those who directly exploit animals, so that ultimately we become the authoritative gatekeepers. Before pursuing such a course it is worth examining the underpinnings of this system.

The nominal legitimation of the adversarial approach to ethics, including its exclusion of the "irrational," is this supposition: if the participants in the battle follow the rules and exhibit certain predetermined qualities, then truth will emerge. Addelson calls this the "enlightenment approach" to the problem of legitimating the educational hierarchy:

The enlightenment orientation, with its ideal of objectivity and the unity of mankind, gives a metaphysical and epistemological basis for [the warrant to make and disperse knowledge], not a political and institutional one: If we develop our methods properly, we will discover neutral fact and make neutral theory. On the enlightenment approach, the methods and metaphysics that we develop internally justify the authority that we exercise externally. The social, political, and moral questions about our cognitive authority in the society become moot. (Addelson 1991, 110)

Ideologically, an academic's differential power to determine knowledge is legitimate since the academy only promotes those whose methods reveal truth. This approach risks circularity, however, insofar as the political authority of the group is justified through its adherence to "truth-discovering" methods, while the list of methods that qualify as "truth-discovering" (such as the adversarial approach) is developed by the group itself and enforced by use of its political authority.

So the enlightenment pursuit of objective truth through disputation ultimately instantiates itself as a struggle for relative status within hierarchical power structures. To uncritically develop animal rights theories within this framework, especially when those theories are structurally well suited to programs of social control, is to move, intentionally or not, toward a situation in which animal liberationist goals are hierarchically imposed.[9] This raises the critical question of whether animal liberation requires or is even well served by programs of social control.

Taming Ourselves

The patriarchal elements of animal rights theory—including the hierarchy of reason over emotion, the delineation of "irrational" classes, the perception of ethical discussion as a battle, and the willingness to impose controls—all fit perfectly well within the conventional norms of academic ethics. But as I indicated above, these elements also work together to constitute the ideological underpinnings for programs of social control. Hierarchical social control is never neutral, it demands legitimation. Prototypically, this legitimation comes from the supposition that people need to be controlled, that we are fundamentally antisocial (as in Thomas Hobbes's theory, in which our supposed innate antisocial tendencies legitimate the erection of an all-powerful sovereign). The patriarchal aspects of animal rights theory can be similarly legitimated (or at least made coherent and superficially sensible) by holding that people are naturally antisocial toward animals: if we are motivationally disposed to support animal exploitation, then we need to be prodded toward animal liberation by a rational elite.

Within animal rights theories, the antisociality needed to legitimate the patriarchal approach takes the form of a denial of any reliable human capacity to sympathize with animals. For Regan, human sympathies in general are "chancy," but especially so with respect to animals: "The plain fact is, most people do not care very much about what happens to [nonhuman animals], or, if they do care, their care seems to be highly selective" (Regan 1991, 95–96). Singer insists his argument makes no "appeal to the reader's emotions where they cannot be supported by reason," because "reason is more universal and more compelling in its appeal" than "kind feelings and sentiments" (Singer 1990, iii, 243).

Singer goes beyond Regan's brief statement that humans lack concern for animals, devoting a whole book to explaining our supposed sympathetic deficiency. In *The Expanding Circle*, Singer argues that kin, reciprocal, and "possibly a little" group altruism are *biologically based*, by showing how tendencies to assist close relatives, those who assist us, and members of our group are adaptive and thus would be selected over time. Singer calls these dispositions to help those close to us our "genetically-based" social "impulses" or "instincts." This sociobiological theory does not account for consideration shown to those outside relations of kinship, reciprocation, and group membership. To explain altruistic behavior toward these "outsiders" (including most animals and many people), Singer argues that *reason*, in particular the practice of defending one's behavior to others, is intrinsically impartial, ultimately possessing "a logic of its own which leads to its extension beyond the bounds of the group" (Singer 1981, 114). Thus even though our genetically based altruistic dispositions apply only to a narrow circle, reason inexorably impels expansion of our consideration, ultimately to encompass all sentient beings.

While Singer admits, on the one hand, that all altruistic behaviors result from environmental as well as genetic factors, and on the other hand, that reasoning behavior is biologically as well as culturally supported, he retains throughout *The Expanding Circle* an extreme hierarchical dualism of reason over biology. At the level of individual motivation, Singer takes the relation between impartial reason and

Taming Ourselves or Going Feral?

partial social instincts to be a struggle between "the desire to avoid inconsistency" and "our self-centered desires (including our desires for our kin and close friends)" (144–46). Theoretical pictures of noble reason valiantly struggling to control base instinct lend themselves to the support of programs of social control—the group seeking control over others simply associates itself with reason and the others with instinct. This connection between theory and politics is highlighted by Singer's consistent use of the rhetoric of control, domination, and warfare in his sociobiological theorizing. Singer feels that we have hitherto been "slaves" (173) under the "unchallenged control of our genes" (94), but that as reasoning beings we can "rebel" (169), since "reason can master our genes" (131), reasoning being "inherently expansionistic," continually acquiring "territory" until "crushed by countervailing forces" (99).

The idea that our sympathies for animals are fundamentally unreliable, even genetically preempted, supports the view that the extensive cruelty of institutionalized animal exploitation—in vivisection, factory farming, and sport hunting—is a mere expression of an instinctively exploitative creature at the core of all or many of us. Animal liberation is thus seen as a process of *taming* ourselves and others (indeed, "Tame Yourself" is the title of the second animal rights record album produced by People for the Ethical Treatment of Animals [PETA]). So long as we remain committed to animal liberation, yet also see the direct sympathetic responsiveness of individual humans to animal suffering as undependable, we will be drawn toward authoritarian structures that promise this taming, through the domination of emotion by reason, selfishness by patriarchal ethics, and people by political authorities and their philosophical advisors. Before committing ourselves in this direction it is crucial to fully examine the premise supporting social control. In the following section, I suggest that the supposition of human antisociality toward animals is very dubious. In fact, institutionalized animal exploitation does not so much result from a lack of human sympathies for animals, as it continues in opposition to and despite these sympathies.

The Maintenance of Animal Exploitation

Suppose, as do James Serpell and Andrée Collard, that compassion for animals is a natural, normal, and healthy part of human life (Serpell 1986, 170; Collard 1989, 70). We would then expect institutions of animal exploitation to protect themselves from compassionate human opposition through an array of unnatural, abnormal, and unhealthy mechanisms. This is exactly what we find. In the following section, focusing particularly on animal farming and animal vivisection, I detail both highly developed mechanisms for *forestalling* the development of sympathies for exploited animals as well as powerful mechanisms for *overriding* (i.e., preventing us from acting on) any sympathies that might remain.

Forestalling Sympathetic Opposition to Animal Exploitation

The awareness *I am causing harm to an animal* is normally accompanied by hesitation, uneasiness, guilt, even anguish. Potential opposition to animal exploitation arising from such inhibitions can be forestalled by blocking one or more of the three parts of this awareness: personal responsibility (*I am causing*), damage due to hurting or killing (*harm*), and the presence of another subject (*to an animal*).[10]

Denying personal responsibility.
One tactic for expiating the guilt of animal exploitation is discussed by James Serpell under the heading of "blame-shifting":

> It was ultimately the gods who were to blame [for ancient animal sacrifice], since it was they who demanded the sacrifice in the first place. This is not merely speculation. According to an ancient Babylonian text, the head priest actually bent down to the ear of the slaughtered victim and whispered, "this deed was done by all the gods; I did not do it." (Serpell 1986, 167–68)

Following ancient precedent, the human responsibility for eating flesh is also deferred in our culture by reference to biblical myths of divine permission such as God's covenant with Noah: "Every moving thing that lives shall be food for you; and as I gave you the green plants, I give you everything" (Genesis 9:3). More broadly, all forms of animal exploitation can be and often are excused in this culture by insisting on certain interpretations of biblical stories such as the following:

> Then God said, "Let us make man in our image, after our likeness; and let them have dominion over the fish of the sea, and over the birds of the air, and over the cattle, and over all the earth, and over every creeping thing that creeps upon the earth." (Genesis 1:26)

This theological blame-shifting has secular counterparts. Today farmers shift responsibility for their exploitation of animals to the general public, by speaking of "consumer demand" for meat as if this technical term referred to an inexorable mass insistence rather than the conditional fact that under present circumstances people will buy a certain amount of meat at a given price.[11] The individual meat-eater, conversely, may defer personal responsibility for animal slaughter by reasoning that a national market is insensitive to one individual's choices, so *my* becoming vegetarian will not in fact affect production levels—that is, the number of animals killed.[12] While the farmer is "only giving the people what they want," the meat-eater figures "they'll be slaughtered anyway," so no one is responsible.

Denying the harm done.
Our economic system renders production processes invisible at the point of consumption. This distance between people and production may be self-consciously sustained and increased by an industry when general awareness of that industry's production processes decreases demand for its products. Both the animal farming and the animal vivisection industries (as well as other animal exploitation industries not discussed here, such as fur production, pet sales, circuses, etc.) attempt to minimize awareness of the animal suffering behind their products.

Laboratories that experiment on animals are generally closed to the public, even when they are publicly funded. Tours of research facilities typically are restricted to the holding facilities, omitting observation of any ongoing experiments. It is not uncommon for vivisectors using dogs to remove their vocal chords, thereby preventing tortured howling, which might arouse sympathies among outsiders or the vivisectors themselves. Verbal cover-ups of the harms inflicted on laboratory animals are universal: "sacrifice" instead of "kill," "aversive behavior" instead of "pain" or "fear," etc. I have noticed that scientists always stick to the term "animal experimentation," even (or especially) when discussing the ethics of their profession—"vivisection" has connotations of harm being done to the experimental subject, while "animal experimentation" does not.

The attempts to conceal the insides of animal labs are organized and thorough. For example, a planned episode of the television show *Quantum Leap* dealing with experiments on primates was opposed by pro-vivisection lobby groups (Aldhous 1991). The fact that this opposition was registered prior to production, without having seen a script, and despite the producer's reassurances ("I've asked [the writer] to show the necessity of using animals for medical research [*sic*]... We like to lay out both sides and let our audience decide what to think" [Beck 1991]), reveals that the concern was not with *how* animal vivisection would be treated, positively or negatively, but simply with the fact that experiments on primates would be re-created for television. A similar attitude against laying out both sides is exemplified in National Institutes of Health (NIH) director Bernadine Healy's public "worrying" over "the success of [animal] rights groups in getting their films and magazines into public libraries and schools" (NIH is a major funder of animal vivisection; see Culliton 1991).

And there are false assurances, as when Thomas Langfitt, who for years made a living smashing the heads of baboons, claimed, after his research program came under scrutiny, that he and the vivisectors under his supervision "treat the baboon the way we would treat humans" (*Philadelphia Inquirer*, 31 May 1984). (We might *hope* that this is a lie, for the sake of the people around Langfitt.)

Animal farmers also lie about the harms they inflict. Frank Perdue, who keeps tens of thousands of unhealthy, overstressed, debeaked chickens in a single 150-yard-long building, and whose mass destruction system kills 6.8 million birds a week, states that these chickens "lead such a soft life" (Singer 1990, 105). This falsehood is just one element of an industrywide effort to dim our awareness of the suffering behind animal farming. Advertisements consistently show animals perfectly content to be confined, striving to be hooked, happy to become commodities. The meat, egg, and dairy industries distribute bogus "educational" materials to thousands of schools. One pamphlet shows a grinning steer transported to the "meat packing company." Slaughter is not shown, and the text merely states that "at the packing plant, the 'beef crew' turned beef on the hoof into meat for the store" (Robbins 1987, 128). Killing and dismembering are never mentioned. A coloring book labeled a "factual story approved by The American Egg Board" erases the reality of laying chickens crowded into filthy battery cages by showing a hen standing proudly on a large straw bed with two chicks (Robbins 1987, 127).

As in vivisection, language is managed by the animal farming industry to remove unsavory associations, since "the meat business depends on our repressing the unpleasant awareness that we are devouring dead bodies" (Robbins 1987, 133). Animals are not killed or slaughtered, they are "processed" or "packed"; nor are they butchered, they are "dressed" or "disassembled." This verbal manipulation is carried out self-consciously; Serpell notes that:

> A recent edition of the British *Meat Trades Journal* recommended a change in terminology designed to "conjure up an image of meat divorced from the act of slaughter." Suggestions included getting rid of the words "butcher" and "slaughterhouse" and replacing them with the American euphemisms "meat plant" and "meat factory." (Serpell 1986, 158–59)

The denial of the harm done to exploited animals can become culturally entrenched. For example, the Ainu people of Japan hold that they are actually helping the bears they kill, since these bears want to return to the spirit world from which they came, while the Nuer people of the Sudan justify their consumption of cattle blood by claiming that periodic bleeding is beneficial to an animal's health (Serpell 1986, 148, 153). These expiatory beliefs find a parallel in the contemporary American myth that sport hunting benefits "game" animals who would otherwise starve. This ideology is refuted by Ron Baker (1985) and others who show that the American sport hunting system is more a cause of the overpopulation "problem" than a remedy. And now with the increasing popularity of cruel and ultra-phallic bow-hunting comes the promotion of the theory that "target" animals need not suffer because:

> if a bullet or broadhead [arrow] damages a vital organ, hemorrhagic shock will send a deer to a swift, painless and peaceful demise. If the general public was aware of this knowledge, *their minds could be set at ease* and a major argument against hunting would fall by the wayside. (*Deer & Deer Hunting*, October 1991, 51, emphasis added)[13]

Denying animal subjectivity.

The ability to harm animals on a daily basis without overwhelming distress requires an empathic curtailment which must be carefully inculcated. Arnold Arluke, in his studies of the sociology of animal experimentation, has found that the novice vivisector's typical initial response to laboratory animals includes affectionate attention and personal name-giving. Arluke remarks that these young researchers "have not yet learned to define laboratory animals as objects" (Arluke 1990, 198). This changes quickly:

The emotional costs are high when one has a long-term and complex pet relationship with animals that are sacrificed. In such cases, laboratory staff often feel as though they have to kill a friend. A critical phase of the socialization of animal experimenters is going through at least one such relationship. Because of the grief entailed in the death of these pets, people learn through emotional "burns" that some degree of detachment is necessary. After experiencing such a loss or observing others go through it, people may attempt to restrict the extent to which they become involved with animals. (Arluke 1990, 201)

The perception of laboratory animals as data-generating objects soon becomes automatic. An episode of the CBS news show *48 Hours* contains the following interview with Oscar Marino, a toxicologist who accepts money for placing chemicals in the eyes, on the skin, and into the stomachs of rabbits and mice:

> *Marino:* Sometimes, you know, I'll be riding along the road and if a rabbit comes out, I'll practically kill myself to avoid hitting the rabbit. But, out here, you know, it's kind of different. There's no feeling for these animals here in the laboratory. You know, they're a tool, and that's about it. . . .
>
> *Reporter:* Does it concern you in any way that an animal would be put to some discomfort, sometimes even in pain, so that a woman can have a perfume? That for reasons of vanity [*sic*] animals must suffer—does that bother you?
>
> *Marino:* Well, you do worry about it. But as I said, you know, when I come in here in the laboratory it doesn't bother me any more.

Similarly, an employee of Biosearch, a Philadelphia laboratory at which people expose caged animals to noxious chemicals and record the results, reports that "once you've been here a few days, you lose respect for all living things" (PETA videotape, "Inside Biosearch").

Vivisectors' psychological need to deny the subjectivity of their victims has been philosophically dressed up as the theory of animal automatism. In Descartes's original version, all mental properties adhere in an immaterial soul, which nonhumans lack—animals are mere machines, very complex, but completely unfeeling. Descartes's theory was a boon to seventeenth-century vivisectors, who could tell themselves and others that the howling of the dogs they cut into did not indicate suffering but was merely analogous to the squeaking of a

Taming Ourselves or Going Feral?

rusty clock. Though theoretically rejected by some scientists today, the practical implications of Cartesian automatism are universally retained within scientific circles through a strict adherence to operational behaviorism. Under behaviorist methodology, serious scientists must talk as if nonhuman animals have no thoughts, feelings, or purposes. The employment of a discourse purged of intentional vocabulary has the same guilt-easing effect as explicit adherence to animal automatism, but without the difficulty of maintaining a preposterous theory.

Farmers have traditionally recognized animal subjectivity (naturally enough, since managing individual animals well typically requires some understanding of their mental states). But with the recent development of factory farming (i.e., large-scale systems in which many animals are closely confined for long periods of time) the ideology of animal automatism has been imported from vivisection into farming:

> The modern layer is, after all, only a very efficient converting machine, changing the raw material—feed-stuffs—into the finished product—the egg—less, of course, maintenance requirements. (*Farmer and Stockbreeder*, 30 January 1962; quoted in Mason and Singer 1980, 1)

> Forget the pig is an animal. Treat him just like a machine in a factory. Schedule treatments like you would lubrication. Breeding season like the first step in an assembly line. And marketing like the delivery of finished goods. (*Hog Farm Management*, September 1976; quoted in Mason and Singer 1980, 1)

Modern factory farming systems require treating animals as machines, so workers naturally begin to think of the farmed animals as unfeeling machines. But this extreme denial of animal subjectivity could well also be a psychologically necessary response to the extra burden of guilt modern farmers bear—unlike traditional farming practices, today's factory farms entail the *unremitting* suffering of the confined chickens, pigs, and cows.

Overriding Sympathies for Exploited Animals

There are times at which the comforting denials detailed above cannot be sustained. In particular, those who directly inflict the harms may be too close to the situation for the usual denial mechanisms to work; and those newly exposed to animal exploitation may not yet have had a chance to internalize the ways of thinking and seeing that forestall the pangs of conscience. When denial is not possible, some mechanism for overriding inhibitions against causing harm is necessary. One example involves laboratory technicians who, for eight-hour shifts, observed pigs with implanted ventricular assist pumps:

> Each pig was observed for approximately three months, and then sacrificed. These "pig-sitters," as they were informally labeled, typically developed strong if not profound attachments to their pigs. . . . At the end of the observational period, one of the sitters had to sacrifice the pig. This was emotionally too difficult for a technician to do alone, so several sitters would do it as a group after first getting drunk in a bar across the street from the laboratory. (Arluke 1990, 197)

Those who cannot or have not yet detached themselves from "game," "livestock," or "laboratory animals" are still expected to play their roles as producers or consumers in the animal exploitation system. Structures of sanctions encourage or force us to find ways to act against our sympathies.

One of the most obnoxious of these structures is the practice of forcing children to eat meat. Children often refuse to eat meat when they discover its origin (the crucial fact that meat is the flesh of slaughtered animals is systematically withheld from them). Rarely is this moral stand supported, usually the power of parental authority is somehow brought to bear against the incipient vegetarianism. For example:

> [M]y son's first moral action . . . occurred at age four. At that time, he joined the pacifist and vegetarian movement, and refused to eat meat, because as he said, "it's bad to kill animals." In spite of lengthy Hawk argumentation by his parents about the difference between justified and unjustified killing, he remained a vegetarian for six months. (Kohlberg 1971, 191; cited in Singer 1990, 305)

Economic sanctions are used to get people to do the revolting work of animal slaughter. On the one hand, the dire economic situation of the dispossessed is exploited to recruit slaughterers: "IBP [Iowa Beef Packers, the nation's largest 'beef processor'] and its competitors seized upon the rural poor and the new immigrant groups flooding into the country from Mexico, Central and South America, and Southeast Asia, building corporate empires on the backs of a cheap pool of largely unorganized workers" (Rifkin 1992, 129). On the other hand, workers from the primary labor pool (i.e., the better paid, less transitory workers) are retained through what William Thompson calls the "financial trap": though the slaughterhouse employees hate every minute of the job, they stay because they must to pay off debts accrued through conspicuous consumption (Thompson 1983). In a vicious circle, this consumption is apparently an attempt to compensate for the low social status of slaughterhouse work, a status undoubtedly tied to the work's repellent nature.

Similarly, the need to keep their jobs presumably motivates lab technicians to override their aversion to harming animals. For the principal investigators, however, the motivation to vivisect may be less economic need and more the lure of professional rewards. Desire for professional status leads the aspiring vivisector to interpret her or his inhibitions as obstacles to be overcome rather than as reasons to oppose vivisection. Although the career vivisector learns generally to avoid situations, behaviors, and ways of seeing that cause uneasiness, such uneasiness, when it does occur (either unavoidably at the beginning of a career or accidentally later on), is seen as a test of one's scientific mettle:

> As a graduate student at Berkeley, I had many different kinds of experiences with animals. During my first year, traditionally a time of *having one's strengths tested by faculty*, a famous scientist whose ideas I had studied and greatly admired asked me to work on a project with him. . . .
>
> The scientist suggested that we start with some dissections. . . . It was harder than I anticipated to dismember and dissect those animals. *I remember feeling tested, feeling that I would show the great man I was capable of being a scientist.*
>
> *I wanted to succeed* and make important discoveries about primate social behavior and human evolution. I left the basement laboratory that afternoon in a state of emotional turmoil; my head ached and my stomach felt queasy. . . . The weight of the guinea pig corpses lay heavily on me, and *I felt a kind of primitive fear that I had committed a transgression.* (Sperling 1988, 5–8, emphasis added)

Sperling's revulsion at the physical manipulation of animals was eventually reconciled with her desire to succeed and to "make important discoveries"—she came to specialize in primate maternal deprivation, a field that requires "only" the psychological and social manipulation of monkeys, not dissection or brain ablation. Sperling's story exemplifies the process by which a young vivisector discovers which situations are personally repellent or bothersome, and then learns how to avoid these situations or mitigate their effects, while continuing her or his climb up the academic ladder. The motivation for this effort is plain in Sperling's account: professional success and status, and the permission and opportunity to address "interesting" and "important" questions such as, "Would the infant langurs become despondent when separated from the mother? Would they exhibit the behavioral and physiological 'depression' that Harlow had observed in his famous studies of separated rhesus macaque infants?" (Sperling 1988, 12).

Finally, people are generally capable of acting against their sympathies when they believe their lives or the lives of their families depend on it. The animal agriculture and animal research industries exploit this human capacity by propagating the myth that their products are necessary for human health and well-being. For instance, the meat and dairy industries developed the notion of four essential food groups, with meat and dairy as two of them (Robbins 1987, 171). With this false theory taught in elementary schools, generations are indoctrinated into the myth that we must eat animal flesh or animal products to be healthy. Of course, lobbyists for animal vivisection are constantly suggesting that we owe our lives to animal research. Such statements obscure three crucial points: increases in life expectancy in the industrialized West over the last century are not due primarily to animal experimentation (or even to medicine) but to improvements in public health, such as cleaner air and water, better sewage removal, improved nutrition and working conditions (Sharpe 1988); though some people have been helped by the medicines developed through animal vivisection, others have been harmed; and we cannot know whether the decision to invest in vivisection-based medicine while simultaneously repressing the nonviolent healing philosophies has had an overall beneficial effect on the health of our society. What healing opportunities have been lost by channeling funding exclusively into medical research rather than developing the so-called alternative therapies?

Going Feral

The development of such a diversity of mechanisms for forestalling and overriding sympathetic opposition to harming animals shows that human resistance is always a potential threat to the continuation of the animal exploitation industries. So the supposition that a natural human indifference to animal well-being is the problem to be solved is unfounded. But this supposition is the linchpin of the patriarchal approach to animal liberationist ethics. Recognizing compassion and an unwillingness to harm as normal human responses to animals undermines each element of the patriarchal approach. The subordination of emotion to reason is justified by describing sympathies for animals as undependable. In fact, sympathies for animals are so dependable that every institution of animal exploitation develops some means of undercutting them. So rather than focusing exclusively on logic and considerations of formal consistency, we might better remember our feeling connections to animals, while challenging ourselves and others to overthrow the unnatural obstacles to the further development of these feelings. This process of reconnecting with animals is essentially concrete, involving relations with healthy, free animals, as well as direct perceptions of the abuses suffered by animals on farms and in laboratories. Thus the patriarchal privileging of abstract principle is put into question. And the construction of ethical discussion as a battle to separate the rational from the irrational now loses its grip. *All* of us, whether vivisector or vegan, have been subject to mechanisms undercutting sympathy for animals. How long and to what extent we submit to these mechanisms is not a matter of rationality: to cut off our feelings and support animal exploitation *is* rational, given societal expectations and sanctions; but to assert our feelings and oppose animal exploitation is also rational, given the pain involved in losing our natural bonds with animals. So our task is not to pass judgment on others' rationality, but to speak honestly of the loneliness and isolation of anthropocentric society, and of the damage done to every person expected to hurt animals.

The patriarchal perspective views ethics as a means of social control, and animal liberation as a matter of taming our "naturally" exploitative dispositions toward animals. This view ignores the taming of compassion and outrage that proceeds every day as part of the business of exploiting animals. In this society people are domesticated, trained through external rewards and punishments, through myths and lies, through instilled fear and ignorance, to disconnect from animals, especially from those animals designated "game," "livestock," or "guinea pigs." So animal liberation is not so much a taming of ourselves as it is a refusal to be tamed into supporting anthropocentrism. For most of us in the West, animal liberation involves coming to reject a previous domestication into meat-eating, dependence on modern medicine, human chauvinism, etc. By reasserting and expanding our officially circumscribed compassion for animals, we are in the position of feral animals, formerly domesticated but now occupying a semiwild state on the boundaries of hierarchical civilization.

Thus animal liberation is not furthered by *imposing* controls ("reason" over "natural" indifference), but by *breaking through* the controls on human-animal connection to which we are subject. Since those controls are limitations on our integrated agency, animal liberation can be seen, metaethically, as a process of human moral development, an extension (often a reclamation) of our capacities as agents.

Animal liberation enhances our agency in two ways: through our increased autonomy, and through our development as caring beings. First, most of the devices for continuing animal exploitation violate important formal conditions for autonomous action—such as knowledge, integrity, and moral self-determination. The promulgation of falsehoods—"animal exploitation is necessary," "exploited animals are not harmed," "animals are mindless," etc.—obviously decreases our capacity to base decisions concerning animal exploitation on full, relevant knowledge. The sanctioned expectation that individuals (especially farmers and vivisectors) will find ways to act against their sympathies for animals undermines integrity, that is, the ability to live with one's most significant desires in mutual harmony.[14] And some mechanisms for continuing animal exploitation—such as forced meat-eating, compulsory inoculations, and mandatory dissection in schools—blatantly oppose autonomy by blocking moral self-determination. By debunking the ideological legitimations of animal exploitation and creating communal support for nonexploitative practices (such as vegetarianism and nonmedical healing practices), the animal liberation movement develops individual knowledge, integrity, power, and other conditions of autonomy.

Second, many of us understand caring as intrinsic to our moral agency. For example, Carol Gilligan discusses the approach to morality in which "responsibility signifies response, an extension rather than a limitation of action. Thus it connotes an act of care rather than the restraint of aggression" (Gilligan 1982, 38). The caring approach to morality is neither exclusively nor universally adopted by women. Many men besides myself support animal liberation at least

Taming Ourselves or Going Feral?

in part as an extension of caring agency; examples include Roong-tham Sujithammaraksa (1987), Steve Sapontzis (1987), and John Robbins (1987).[15] Though one could argue that the adoption of a caring morality does not logically entail animal liberation (if one can be a caring person without caring for nonhumans), it is still true that animal liberation is one way to extend our capacities as caring agents.[16]

Animal liberation involves overcoming institutionalized barriers to our compassionate connections with animals. But beyond challenging the desensitizing ideologies and distancing mechanisms, the existence of a healthy animal liberation movement also helps us take our empathies for animals more seriously as a basis for action. For example, years ago when I was living in St. Louis, a friend returned from a visit to the East Coast, bringing with her a live lobster at my request. Though I had eaten lobsters in restaurants, I had never cooked one. My friend did not eat lobsters herself but she was familiar with the cooking procedures. She told me that you must drop the live lobster into boiling water. I asked her whether this hurt the lobster. She said she was not sure, but she had heard that the lobsters let out a high-pitched scream for some time after being dropped into the water. I found this extremely distressing, and wondered whether I would be able to carry out the procedure. I kept imagining being boiled alive. I went through the cooking preparations, and when the time came to boil the lobster, I gingerly picked him up, lifted the lid off the large pot, dropped him in, and then ran from the room with my hands over my ears, frantically determined not to hear the screaming. I returned later, finished the cooking and then ate the lobster.

I now see this as a paradigmatic failure of authentic agency, an incapacity to act: especially the willful self-deception and blocking of perception, but also the fragmentation of a person who does not recognize his sympathies as a potential basis for action. It is not that I considered sparing the lobster but decided against it, rather, *the possibility never occurred to me,* even though I sweated and agonized over the suffering I expected to inflict. An animal liberationist perspective would have made freeing the lobster a salient option, and thus would have opened up greater possibilities for action.[17]

Sarah Hoagland writes:

In my opinion, the heart of ethical focus, the function of ethics, and what will promote lesbian connection, is enabling and developing individual integrity and agency within community. I have always regarded morality, ideally, as a system whose aim is, not to control individuals, but to *make possible,* to encourage and enable, individual development. (Hoagland 1988, 285)

Similarly, animal liberation does not limit action through control of self and others, it develops the individual's capacity for a broader range of action. It is creative, not restrictive. Patriarchal support for restrictions and controls, based on a pernicious elevation of reason over emotion and on a distorted view of human sympathetic tendencies, is a threatened impairment of autonomous individuals living in community with humans and nonhuman animals. Fortunately, we need not choose between patriarchal animal rights theory and support for the continuation of animal exploitation. A nonpatriarchal understanding of morality, in which, as Kathryn Pyne Addelson puts it, "the whole human being is the basis of ethics" (Addelson 1991, 151), fits animal liberation very well.

Notes

1. This section has benefited from the comments of Carol Adams, Paul Benson, and several anonymous reviewers.

2. Singer and Regan themselves see the differences between their approaches as "fundamental" (Singer 1987, 3; Regan 1986a, 94), while Charles Magel, bibliographer of animal liberationist literature, takes Regan and Singer jointly to define the terms of debate:
   > If a student interested in animal rights were to ask what to study, my advice would be: first, read all the works by Regan and Singer; then read all the responses to their works; and then read whatever you wish. (Magel 1989, xiii)

3. Alternatively, the rationalistic writers may be unwittingly dependent on convention or authority to gain assent to their initial intuitions (see below for an instance of deference to authority). In any case, at these points reason has run out. For a fuller explanation of how the purely rationalistic arguments for animal liberation fail, see Luke 1992, 100–102.

4. Regan begins his book with the quote "every great movement must experience three stages: ridicule, discussion, adoption," and he often adverts to the "growing intellectual respectability of exploring the moral status of animals" (Regan 1982, 113).

5. For example, this nineteenth-century dismissal:
   > Is it necessary to repeat that women—or rather, old maids, form the most numerous contingent of this group [i.e., antivivisectionists]? Let my adversaries contradict me, if they can show among the leaders of the agitation one girl, rich, beautiful, and loved, or some young wife who has found in her home the full satisfactions of her affections. (Quoted in Kalechofsky 1992, 62)

And recently at an antihunting demonstration I heard hunters call some female activists "dykes" and advise others that "someday, when they had children" they would understand. Both today and a century ago women's feelings for exploited animals are derogated as the misplaced affections a proper woman would direct only to her husband and children.

6. And Andrée Collard (1989, 97) links Singer's insistence that he does not love animals (Singer 1990, ii) with a "fear of appearing too 'soft.' "

7. Linzey stated in 1990, "we are no longer a movement of little old ladies in tennis shoes: ours is a movement of intellectual muscle" (quoted in Kheel 1993, 262). Regan has used similar metaphors, calling his animal rights theory "tough-minded" (Regan 1986a, 95), and concluding elsewhere that through the "forceful" editorship of anthologies on animal rights and other such efforts "we may safely put to rest the stereotypical picture of 'little old ladies in tennis shoes' " (Regan 1982, 113). Singer has argued that the perception of animal welfare as "a matter for old ladies in tennis shoes to worry about" is an unfounded prejudice (Singer 1979, 48). Significantly, in a later version of the same book, Singer replaced the phrase "old ladies in tennis shoes" with "people who are dotty about dogs and cats" (Singer 1993, 55).

8. The Greek root *arche*—appearing in "patriarchy," "hierarchy," etc.— means both *rule* and *principle,* thus highlighting the close connection between ruling and the use of principles. This point was brought to my attention by Jennifer Whiting.

9. The present essay differs from the works under discussion in that it (1) promotes a metaethical framework that is not structurally suited for programs of social control and (2) critically examines the hierarchical academic structure of which it is a part. Even so, the fact that this essay, authored by an assistant professor and appearing in an academic press, is clearly part of the hierarchical institution under examination raises questions about its consistency. This is one case of the common political problem of determining when criticizing an institution from within is more valuable than separatism. For me, the present case is unresolved, and, though I fully intend and hope to further animal liberation through the academic publication of this essay, I am still open to the possibility that animal liberation is best served by deemphasizing academic theorizing altogether.

10. This can be compared to Stanley Milgram's research on the conditions under which individuals accept a scientific authority's commands to apply electric shock to another person. He found that the willingness to follow such commands correlated with the breakdown of what he called "the structure of a meaningful act—*I am hurting a man*" (Milgram 1965, 64).

11. "The most commonly reported justification for slaughtering, mentioned by 9 of the 19 interviewees, was that people eat meat, so that slaughtering must be done by someone" (Herzog and McGee 1983, 130).

12. This reasoning is formalized and defended by philosophers Peter Wenz (1979, 424), Michael Martin (1976, 27), and R. G. Frey (1983).

13. Even apart from its prima facie implausibility, this theory ignores the fact that bow-hunting for deer has a 50 percent wounding rate (i.e., for every

deer "bagged" by a bowhunter, one is hit but not retrieved) (Boydston and Gore 1986).

14. Integrity is evidently more an ideal of autonomy than a condition, since we are still agents when we act with internal conflict.

15. Here I pass over an issue that is critical for a full development of a feminist metaethic of animal liberation, namely, the gendered politics of caring—how caring by men and caring by women are structured so differently in our society.

16. Nel Noddings's argument that the "true ethical sentiment" of caring requires the reciprocity of mutual recognition and affection (and thus does not arise vis-à-vis unknown farmed and vivisected animals) seems to me to involve an unnecessarily restricted notion of moral caring (see Noddings 1984, 148–59; also Noddings and Donovan 1991).

17. Even if liberating a lobster in St. Louis presents serious practical difficulties, surely there is some fate better than being boiled alive that caring intentions could discover.

References

Adams, Carol. 1990. *The Sexual Politics of Meat: A Feminist-Vegetarian Critical Theory.* New York: Continuum.

———. 1994. *Neither Man nor Beast: Feminism and the Defense of Animals.* New York: Continuum.

Addelson, Kathryn Pyne. 1991. *Impure Thoughts: Essays on Philosophy, Feminism, and Ethics.* Philadelphia: Temple University Press.

Aldhous, Peter. 1991. A Leap Into Controversy. *Nature* 352:463.

Arluke, Arnold. 1990. Moral Elevation in Medical Research. *Advances in Medical Sociology* 1:189–204.

Baker, Ron. 1985. *The American Hunting Myth.* New York: Vantage Press.

Beck, Marilyn. 1991. Scott Bakula Goes Ape on NBC's *Quantum Leap. TV Guide* 39(29):17.

Boydston, Glenn, and Horace Gore. 1986. Archery Wounding Loss in Texas. Internal study, Texas Parks and Wildlife Dept., Austin, Texas.

Collard, Andrée, with Joyce Contrucci. 1989. *Rape of the Wild: Man's Violence against Animals and the Earth.* Bloomington: Indiana University Press.

Culliton, Barbara. 1991. Can Reason Defeat Unreason? *Nature* 351:517.

Donovan, Josephine. 1990. Animal Rights and Feminist Theory. *Signs* 15:350–75.

Frey, R. G. 1983. *Rights, Killing, and Suffering: Moral Vegetarianism and Applied Ethics.* Oxford, England: Basil Blackwell.

Gilligan, Carol. 1982. *In a Different Voice: Psychological Theory and Women's Development.* Cambridge: Harvard University Press.

Herzog, Harold A., Jr., and Sandy McGee. 1983. Psychological Aspects of Slaughter: Reactions of College Students to Killing and Butchering Cattle and Hogs. *International Journal for the Study of Animal Problems* 4:124–32.

Hoagland, Sarah Lucia. 1988. *Lesbian Ethics: Toward New Value.* Palo Alto, Calif.: Institute of Lesbian Studies.

Kalechofsky, Roberta. 1992. Dedicated to Descartes' Niece: The Women's Movement in the Nineteenth Century and Anti-vivisection. *Between the Species* 8 (2):61–71.

Kheel, Marti. 1985. The Liberation of Nature: A Circular Affair. *Environmental Ethics* 7 (2):135–49.

———. 1993. From Heroic to Holistic Ethics: The Ecofeminist Challenge. In *Ecofeminism: Women, Animals, Nature,* ed. Greta Gaard, 243–71. Philadelphia: Temple University Press.

Kohlberg, Lawrence. 1971. From Is to Ought. In *Cognitive Development and Epistemology,* ed. Theodore Mischel, 151–235. New York: Academic Press.

Luke, Brian. 1992. Justice, Caring, and Animal Liberation. *Between the Species* 8 (2):100–108.

Magel, Charles. 1989. *Keyguide to Information Sources in Animal Rights.* Jefferson, N.C.: McFarland & Company.

Martin, Michael. 1976. A Critique of Moral Vegetarianism. *Reason Papers* 3:13–43.

Mason, Jim, and Peter Singer. 1980. *Animal Factories.* New York: Harmony Books.

Milgram, Stanley. 1965. Some Conditions of Obedience and Disobedience to Authority. *Human Relations* 18:57–76.

Noddings, Nel. 1984. *Caring: A Feminine Approach to Ethics & Moral Education.* Berkeley: University of California Press.

Noddings, Nel, and Josephine Donovan. 1991. Comment and Reply. *Signs* 16 (2):418–25.

Nozick, Robert. 1981. *Philosophical Explanations.* Cambridge, Mass.: Belknap Press.

Regan, Tom. 1982. *All That Dwell Therein: Essays on Animal Rights and Environmental Ethics.* Berkeley: University of California Press.

———. 1983. *The Case for Animal Rights.* Berkeley: University of California Press.

———. 1986a. The Bird in the Cage: A Glimpse of My Life. *Between the Species* 2:42–49, 90–99.

———. 1986b. The Search for a New Global Ethic. *The Animals' Agenda* 6 (December):4–6, 40–41.

———. 1991. *The Thee Generation: Reflections on the Coming Revolution.* Philadelphia: Temple University Press.

Rifkin, Jeremy. 1992. *Beyond Beef: The Rise and Fall of the Cattle Culture.* New York: Dutton.

Robbins, John. 1987. *Diet for a New America.* Walpole, N.H.: Stillpoint Publishing.

Sapontzis, S. F. 1987. *Morals, Reason, and Animals.* Philadelphia: Temple University Press.

Serpell, James. 1986. *In the Company of Animals: A Study of Human-Animal Relationships.* New York: Basil Blackwell.

Sharpe, Robert. 1988. *The Cruel Deception: The Use of Animals in Medical Research.* Wellingborough, England: Thorsons Publishing Group.

Singer, Peter. 1979. *Practical Ethics.* Cambridge: Cambridge University Press.

———. 1981. *The Expanding Circle: Ethics and Sociobiology.* New York: Farrar, Straus & Giroux.

———. 1987. Animal Liberation or Animal Rights? *Monist* 70:3–14.

———. 1990. *Animal Liberation.* 2d ed. New York: New York Review.

———. 1993. *Practical Ethics.* 2d ed. Cambridge: Cambridge University Press.

Slicer, Deborah. 1991. Your Daughter or Your Dog? *Hypatia* 6 (1):108–24.

Sperling, Susan. 1988. *Animal Liberators: Research & Morality.* Berkeley: University of California Press.

Sujithammaraksa, Roongtham. 1987. *Agent-Based Morality in the Ethics of our Treatment of Animals.* Doctoral dissertation, University of California, Santa Barbara.

Thompson, William. 1983. Hanging Tongues: A Sociological Encounter with the Assembly Line. *Qualitative Sociology* 6:215–37.

Vyvyan, John. 1988. *In Pity and in Anger: A Study of the Use of Animals in Science.* Marblehead, Mass.: Micah Publications.

Walker, Alice. 1988. *Living by the Word.* San Diego: Harcourt Brace Jovanovich.

Warren, Virginia. 1989. Feminist Directions in Medical Ethics. *Hypatia* 4:73–87.

Wenz, Peter. 1979. Act-Utilitarianism and Animal Liberation. *Personalist* 60:423–28.

13

Susanne Kappeler

Speciesism, Racism, Nationalism . . . or the Power of Scientific Subjectivity

The importance of the groundbreaking work of feminists who have politicized animal oppression cannot be overestimated. Not only does it make a much needed feminist intervention in (masculinist) theories of animal rights or animal liberation, revealing the sexism as well as other masculinist structures of thought underlying those theories. In pointing out the fundamental speciesism that underlies much of our own work, it has also contributed significantly to feminism. For many of us feminists, too, have worked with the apparently "natural" distinction between the oppression of humans (women) and the oppression of animals. As Carol Adams has pointed out in *The Sexual Politics of Meat,*[1] expressing our outrage at the treatment of women through metaphoric comparisons to the treatment of animals—that a violent man treats a woman like a dog, or pornography treats women as meat, etc.—actually validates the oppression of animals, implying that while these things should not be done to women, they *may* be done to animals: that dogs may be treated "like dogs" or animals be herded into cages "like animals," that animals may be "slaughtered like animals" and treated as meat. Not only do we thus tacitly recognize this form of oppression and exploitation as "acceptable," we are also missing an important link in the critique and understanding of oppression itself. As feminists we have argued that we need to oppose *all* forms of oppression, that we must question power and violence on principle, not just on given occasions; that we need to challenge power even where it is an apparently benevolent use of power, or where it is conceptual power, as Brian Luke, for instance, has challenged it in his contribution to this volume.

Victimism and Protectionism

We know that the naming of violence after its victims—as the sexual violence against women, the sexual abuse of children, the enslavement of black people, the present-day racism against black people and the people of the Third World, the anti-Semitism directed at the Jews, and also the oppression and exploitation of animals and of nature—may all too easily lead us to compartmentalize oppressions and conceive of them as separate phenomena, thus setting up a competition between oppressions, or between different groups of the oppressed, as to which are more or less important than others. It may lead us to adopt one particular oppression as our special "cause" and to champion these particular "victims," calling for their special consideration if not their protection. Instead of challenging the power relationships and interests that institutionalize these oppressions, it may lead us with the best intentions to victimize the oppressed, in the practice of victimism as Kathleen Barry has defined it: treating them *as* victims and trying to speak and act on their behalf.[2] This is all the more likely where we are dealing with a form of violence and oppression of which we are not ourselves the principal sufferers and where, as in the case of animals, the victims have no power or possibility to represent themselves—so that if *we* do not act as their champions, who will? Yet it is a feature common to all those oppressed that they lack the power to assert their interests, especially vis-à-vis their oppressors, and less a special feature of animals who do not speak human language. And it is the very strength of feminist politics to have developed a practice of supporting survivors, which significantly differs from the championing of victims: a politics that challenges the structures of oppression without revictimizing the oppressed, that is, without making them the clientele of our benevolent protection and representation.

We may feel, of course, that there is little support to be given to animals and animal survivors when millions of animals are being killed and tortured every day—that is, when many of them do indeed become victims and not survivors. This is a different question, however, and again not one limited to animals alone. It is the question whether in the face of immediate death or, as it usually presents itself, the immediate extinction of entire species, protection may not after all be justified. Yet to see ourselves faced with a choice between extinction or protection is to assume the viewpoint of the murderers. It is to overlook that we no more have the power to protect than we have the power to prevent the murderous aggression having led to this point of impending extinction in the first place. Or conversely, if we do have the power to move the aggressor to let us intervene with our protection, we have the power to stop the aggressor altogether. If we do have this power, however, and still bid for protection only, we are making a pact with the aggressors, guarding their interest in aggression and merely negotiating a respite for the victims.

More likely, however, we do not have this power. If we nevertheless opt for protectionism, we are actually (ab)using the threat of death and extinction—in a situation where we have no power to stop it (and no power to protect the victims)—in the interest of "allowing" ourselves an attitude of protectionism (and consequent victimization of the oppressed) in the situation of our personal political activity, far from the scene of the crime we invoke. That is to say, we do not protect those actually being killed, we exploit their victimization to "protect" and patronize those surviving and within our reach. It means not only to abuse and instrumentalize those victimized, but to abandon the victims and what it means that there are victims in favor of a politics in the world of the living—ourselves and the actual survivors. It is a conceptual practice of "divide and rule" that relegates the dead to the scrapheap of history. A politics that is serious about challenging violence and oppression must defend the interests of victims as well as survivors, else we equate those killed with the nonexistent. Precisely because we do not have the power to protect all and everyone from the violence that threatens them, our political work of challenging oppression and victimization (including the oppression and victimization of animals) is all the more important—challenging it in every situation and context within our power. And with a conceptual framework that does not in practice dismiss or revictimize victims on the basis that they are "past help."

All the more important, in other words, is our theoretical understanding of the way in which animal oppression interconnects with all other forms of oppression, including victimism that "extends the terrorism of the act of . . . violence" (again in Barry's words).[3] Compartmentalizing violence and oppressions according to their objects misleads us to focus on particular groups of the oppressed—(victim) identities that are created *through* that oppression. Instead, we need to look at the common factors of power that not only connect these different oppressions but which through their intersection point to an accumulation of power in the hands of those whose interests are being served by all forms of oppression: the principal beneficiaries of all power and exploitation, the elites and corporations of (principally) white, Western, capitalist, educated adult men. This is not to say that other people do not profit from the oppression of others—most of us do in different ways and to varying degrees. For example, whites in general—including women and even children, and including workers exploited by capitalism—benefit from the racism in their own countries, from Eurocentrism, and from the international imbalance of power—that is, the exploitation of the South by the North. Humans in general profit, however differentially, from the exploitation of animals; adults in general benefit from the lack of rights of children; the educated in general benefit from the lack of education of others; and so forth. It is precisely this possibility—the possibility that most oppressed groups have of sharing (however unequally) in the profits from the oppression of others—that is designed to break the solidarity between different oppressed groups and to corrupt our will to join in resistance against all oppression. Our focus should be less on the groups who are oppressed by or benefit from various singularized forms of oppression than on how the different oppressions operate, differentially coopting us, and how the multiple systems of oppression intersect to concentrate cumulative power in veritable centers of power, combining the benefit of every single form of oppression.

As feminists, we have challenged the Western ideological tradition—which constructs a diverse, yet interrelated, set of "others," each on a different axis of a dualistic opposition and one at a time— as the construction of a hierarchy between the superior norm and the deviant "other": man/woman, white/black, adult/child, First World/Third World, national/foreign, human/animal, (human) culture/nature, heterosexual/homosexual, Aryan/Jew, Christian/Jew, Christian/Muslim, healthy/sick, abled/disabled, civilized/primitive, and so forth. And we have been arguing for a form of resistance that resists these divisions while recognizing the different material realities they are creating. More than ever we need to understand that the struggle against oppression is more than the struggle of women against men, of blacks against whites, of the disabled against the able-bodied, of workers against capitalists, or of animals (or humans on behalf of animals) against humans and so forth—more, in other words, than a struggle over "difference." We need to understand how masculinity, capitalism, white supremacy, speciesism, Western nationalisms and Western internationalism, science, professionalism, educationalism and culturalism, eugenics, reproductive technology and population control, etc. combine to build a formidable power pyramid, a megapower system of interlocking forms of oppression and exploitation, which requires our combined resistance if we really mean to dismantle it rather than just reshuffle a few positions for some on the oppression ladder. We must resist the embracing of single causes and challenge an identity politics that makes each struggle a single struggle and the responsibility of a particular "lobby."

Conservationism

As war tears the Balkans apart, and nationalism and racism resurge all over Western and Eastern Europe, the connections and continuities in Western thinking about animals and about humans become apparent in new and startling form. When Western media began reporting the mass violence against women in the wars in Croatia and Bosnia-Hercegovina, feminists in the West mobilized large-scale protest. Over two decades of feminist politics against sexual violence seemed to have predestined Western feminists to make a major intervention in the public international arena, challenging the specific ways in which women are victimized in war and how international politics deals with such violence. Yet, rather than seeing a feminist analysis challenging mainstream patriarchal ideology, what we saw was a feminist analysis that seemed to be slowly giving way to an analysis in conventional categories, succumbing to and integrating itself into the dominant understanding of "rape in war."

While feminist analysis defines rape as a crime against *women*, Western media and war propagandists in the Balkans agree in seeing rape in war as a crime against *men and their nation*. Consequently, the emphasis shifts from gender to nationality, from an analysis of sexual violence to an analysis of crimes against the nation—in which women function as the reproducers of the nation. While first reports had cited some 50,000 women raped, of whom 30,000 were also pregnant, subsequent reports put the number at 20,000 Bosnian Muslim women raped. In an article in *Ms.*, Alexandra Stiglmayer and Laura Pitter explain the apparent discrepancy in these figures:

> A team of European Community (E.C.) investigators estimated in a January [1993] report that 20,000 Bosnian Muslim women have been raped by Serb soldiers; at the end of October [1992], the Bosnian Ministry for Interior Affairs put the number at 50,000, which also includes Croatian women who have been raped by Serbs.[4]

In other words, the total number of women who had been raped (by Serbian men) stays the same, but the new figure quoted in subsequent reports was the figure of 20,000 Bosnian Muslim women raped. Proving a crime of *genocide* rather than rape in war required *sorting out* the Bosnian Muslim women from the total number of women who have been raped, and *sorting out* the Bosnian Muslim people from the entire population of Bosnia-Hercegovina—because only they qualify for a genocide in international terms. Because even if the Croatian and Serbian population of Bosnia-Hercegovina were massacred by a war that continued unabatedly, we apparently do not need to worry about the massacre of civilian populations—since there will continue to be Croats in Croatia and Serbs in Serbia. It is an argument about the preservation of endangered "human species," whom we begin to protect only when they are threatened with extinction.

Following the construction of new nation states in the Balkans on ethnicist principles—Slovenia and Croatia—and a nationalist war in the name of a "Greater Serbia" aiming to unite all "Serbian" people on a common Serbian territory, Western public argument actively joined in the nationalist logic, constructing a new "ethnic nationality" of Bosnian Muslims and separating the Bosnian community into its alleged component national species of Serbs, Croats, and Muslims[5] (there is rarely talk of the Jews, Rom, and other ethnicities living in Bosnian communities). Public protest was carefully mobilized, not to take a principled stand against war (and nationalism)—the cause of the suffering of civilians of all nationalities—but to favor the protection of a people threatened by extinction, if need be by means of further war. Publicizing rape thus became part of a campaign to ethnicize the war and to gain support for its management by international power. Women's particular contribution consisted in supporting the reinterpretation of rape as a crime not against women themselves, but against "their" men and "their" national people—"a message from man to man: your woman is now also my possession."[6]

To speak of "mass rape," as the media have done, is to imply that mass rape is fundamentally different from single-incident rape, however high the total number. The very concept of "mass" is a signifier of speciesist thinking, which in the context of defining genocide becomes ethnicist or nationalist thinking, reflecting an internationalist concern regarding the protection of ethnic species: only once a people or ethnic community as a whole is seriously threatened in its numbers does it deserve our international protection—like a threatened animal species may incur our protection shortly before its extinction. This simultaneously implies that if the ethnic community is not so threatened in its numbers, everything is not so bad. "Mass" signifies less a very large number—like, say, the very large number of rapes in the United States, or the 30,000 rapes of Croatian women, or the high number of rapes of women of all nationalities in this and any other war—than a large number conceived as a percentage in relation to another total, the sum total of the ethnic population.

The language of international law, of the conventions on war crimes and the prevention of genocide, is the language of power and dominance. Be the aim the protection of endangered peoples or the protection of endangered species, the fundamental presupposition remains that a moderate, "lawful" amount of killing may take place. Thus there may be a temporary international moratorium on the killing of whales, not because there is a fundamental objection to the murdering of whales, but so as to give endangered species a chance to reproduce and regenerate themselves. The aim is not to put an end to the slaughtering, the aim is moderate slaughtering, slaughtering "within limits": permitted murder of individuals within a prohibition to exterminate the entire species. The species shall survive, not through its individual members remaining alive, but through the species' reproduction. Survive it shall for *our* benefit—for some of us, so that there may continue to be whales to slaughter; for others, because the whales' extinction would constitute a loss to us, an impoverishment of the multitude of life forms on this planet for those of us continuing to live on it. Self-interest is the motive in both cases, for the slaughterers as well as the protectors, an interest that the survival of the *species* guarantees and to which the interests of *individuals* are being sacrificed.

In the same way, any measures for the protection of civilian populations during war—the so-called "rules of humanitarian warfare"[7]— remain within the framework of an axiomatic right to war. Their aim is self-imposed restraint in the manner of war conduct—in other words, murder and destruction "within limits," murder that keeps to agreed rules and limitations. It is what military experts—including now women experts—consider "clean" warfare, as for instance Ruth Seifert, who speaks of "dirty" wars that do not keep to "the common 'rules of war.' "[8] And we all know what a clinically clean, surgical war looks like since the Allies' war against Iraq.

Zoology and the "Human Sciences"

As Lynda Birke writes elsewhere in this volume, "there is a reciprocal relationship between the two knowledges, of humans and of animals: each structures the other." That is, any similarity depends less on a postulated similarity between the objects—humans and animals, or women and animals/nature—than on the common structure of thought and knowledge—be it science or politics—that is making them its objects. Thus Birke emphasizes, quoting Donna Haraway, that "primatology is 'politics by other means.' " As we could equally well say, politics is primatology by other means, or more generally, zoology by other means. Politics heavily relies on so-called scientific knowledge, while the construction of scientific knowledge is heavily political.

Western theories of racism attained proper "scientific" status in the nineteenth and twentieth centuries in the guise of medicine, psychiatry, eugenics, anthropology, demography, and so forth. They stand in direct continuity with the theories that categorize non-human animals into species, and living beings into humans, animals, and plants—categories modeled on the paradigms of the natural sciences. These included attempts to establish classifications of "kinds" of people based on "typical" data—be it measurements of bodies and body parts, genetic data, or behavioral features. Nor have they been overcome in the present: modern dictionaries continue to explain the term "race" as signifying a "set" or "kind" of people, animals, or plants of common descent or origin, "a limited group of persons descended from a common ancestor; a house, a family,

Speciesism, Racism, Nationalism

kindred . . . a tribe, nation or people regarded as common stock . . . a group of tribes or peoples, forming a distinct ethnical stock . . . a breed or stock of animals; a particular variety of a species," and so on.[9]

In particular, the idea of a diachronic history of evolution was translated into the synchronic hierarchy of species. Just as the animal world was said to reflect an historical evolution in the simultaneity of the different species, so the multitude of "peoples" (today we would say "cultures") is said to reflect the history of humankind, from its "primitive" beginnings to its "most advanced development," a "natural" hierarchy of "indigenous" or "aboriginal" peoples through to the "highly developed" peoples of the West. That is, the notion of a natural evolution translates into a conception of the political history of humanity as a steady progression toward increased "civilization" or "higher development." Thus history or histories, the social and political conditions of life, are turned into quasi-biological features, said to be manifest in the different "species" or "races."

Since the Holocaust and the reign of German Fascism, which made the breeding of a "pure race" of humans or "the most highly developed Aryans" its explicit goal, ending in the murder of millions of European Jews as well as of other people designated as inferior, we have become cautious, at least superficially, about using a (traditional) racist vocabulary in relation to humans. Yet no such caution seems to apply when it comes to animals, or indeed to our self-differentiation from the animals: we still do talk of the human race. The German word for a pedigreed animal (i.e., a dog, horse, cat, etc. of "pure" race or breeding) also is "race" (*Rasse*), and the same word is used to denote the different breeds. The practice of breeding seems uncontested when those bred to standard or discarded as substandard are animals (or plants). That is to say, we are on our guard against race ideology and its practices only on the basis of the object groups to whom they might be applied (humans); we do not seem to object to the ideological structures and functions of racism and breeding themselves. Thus we continue the tradition of race ideology, which simply redraws the lines from time to time between "us," we *who do*, and the "others," the races or kinds *to whom it is permissible to do*— between the "master race" and the "sub-human," between humans and nonhumans.

Hence we are becoming alarmed at the doings of genetic engineers—whose ideological, not to mention in some cases personal, provenance from the "scientific research" of Nazi Germany is well documented[10]—only when they propose to apply their technology to ourselves, the human "race," as, for example, in the recent case of the cloning of a human embryo in a U.S. laboratory. However, knowingly or not, we have long been consuming the products of their labor in the form of genetically manipulated medicines, fruit, vegetables, dairy products, and—for those eating meat—manipulated animals, benefiting from their experiments moreover in the form of an increasingly polluted and poisoned environment.[11] That is, we have had little problem with the principle of breeding and genetic experimentation so long as it has not apparently been applied to humans— although "eugenic" abortion of fetuses with suspected "disability," a mechanism of breeding "healthy" people—has already widely gained acceptability. Similarly, it is becoming increasingly obvious that the experiments we have tolerated in relation to animals and plants have also been the testing ground for techniques to "improve" the human race[12]—to breed more efficient, more resistant, and more useful human beings—say, workers resistant to the perilous and poisonous conditions at work[13] or babies made to measure,[14] not to mention the promise of eliminating the "genes" of homosexuality or violence. In other words, we continue to make "biological" categories the basis for political decisions, from the acceptance of genetic manipulation in the case of animals and plants to the demand that the "biological" no longer be allowed to have political significance in the sphere of human society—that is, the decision to relegate the political significance of biology to the world of animals or "nature."

As Lynda Birke argues elsewhere in this volume, the animal world now seems to be the epitome of the biological: "Everything about animals—including their behavior—is [seen as] biological." With regard to animals, in other words, humans continue to feel justified not only in making typologies based on biological differences, but in making "biologist" arguments in relation to issues that are in fact political and social issues—as, for instance, the social behavior of animals under human observation and manipulation, that is to say, in conditions of human dominance and rule. Thus the "animal world" of science is the "legitimate" sphere where biologist thinking—behaviorism, sociobiology, etc.—continues to be developed, ready to be reimported into the "human sphere" as the "scientific" basis of apparently "human" sciences such as sociology, politics, and psychology. The primary ideological function of the significance of "animal," as of "biological," is to designate the "natural." But while there has been considerable critique of the ideological meaning and function of the concept of "nature," "biology" not only continues to fulfill the same function but enjoys the additional significance of being accepted as the scientific and objective truth about nature.

From Human Rights to Species Rights

Political critiques of racism and sexism have insisted that physiological differences among humans must be regarded as insignificant as far as political rights are concerned, emphasizing, like the definition of human rights, that no factors of sex or skin color or body structure nor any other factors of physiology or biology must be used to discriminate between humans. All humans shall be equal in their rights—whatever their diversity as humans. While in terms of human politics this constitutes a major ethical (even if mainly theoretical) advance, animal liberationists point out that it has been achieved at the cost of all other animals and living nature: through the shoring up of the dichotomy between humans and other animals or nature as a whole.

As Lynda Birke points out, in the dichotomy between humans and animals, the term "animals" is used in a universalizing way, as if all animals were the same. Yet we know this to be a feature of all dichotomous and hierarchical oppositions, affecting the subordinate category: under the perspective of sexism, all women are "the same," exemplars of the sex and interchangeable; under the perspective of racism all black people are "the same" and exchangeable. The very point of categorization is to create discriminating *identities*, "types" of people allegedly sharing the same (typical) feature(s), thus to justify their social and political roles—in this case their usefulness to men or whites, respectively—and to invalidate their rights as individuals. Hence the use of the generic form—sexist discourse speaking of "Woman" or "the Sex," racist discourse of "the Black man" [*sic*]. And as Birke and others have shown, speciesism speaks not only of "the lion" and "the fox," but generally of "the animal(s)."

However, to me the problem seems less that feminist or animal rights approaches that implicitly rely on speciesism universalize, generalize, or stereotype animals, than that the basis on which they wish to secure the rights of women and now of animals *is no different from that on which they were previously denied.* That is to say, the same hierarchy of categories is presupposed, only the boundary of those included in the group with rights is extended "downward"

along the ladder, shoring up a different dichotomy as the crucial—
that is, exclusionary—boundary. The idea of the ladder of categories—of the "objective" classification of given, "natural" species—
remains unquestioned and unchallenged, in the interest of those
who see the chance of being adopted into the top class. Equally
unchallenged is the power of the original group that sees itself at the
uncontested top of the ladder, arrogating to itself the right to classify
and to decide over the rights of others—the epitome of the speciesist
paradigm.

Thus white men, in their endeavor to buttress white male supremacy, used to draw the line defining "human"—and thus "rights"—
between (among others) whites and blacks as well as between men
and women, on the basis of an alleged natural and evolutionary
hierarchy that placed both the race of black people and the sex of
women on a stage of development below that of white men and
hence closer to "the animals." In turn, the struggles for the emancipation of black people and of women in the U.S. in the nineteenth
century led to various proposals of how the crucial boundary should
be reshuffled: should it run between whites and blacks, including
white men and women and excluding blacks (men and women), or
between men and women, including white and black men and excluding (black and white) women?[15] Both black men and white
women had something to gain (though it never was equality) depending on how the line was drawn; but white men's membership and
their power to classify and to grant rights was unaffected either way,
as was the certain exclusion of black women, their assured position
below any boundary. The eventual emancipation of both black people (men and women) and women (black and white) in Western
societies may have led to their inclusion in the category of humans,
even of citizens, yet without either group having become equal to the
white men who previously occupied that category exclusively. The
boundary of inclusion/exclusion has been shifted "downward," yet
the idea of a hierarchy of categories and the supremacy of the group at
the top has been left unshaken. The ladder of categorization (and
subcategorization) continues to exist, both within the category "human" and outside of it.

Hence to speak of "humans and the other animals" so as to signal
the inclusion of humans among the animals—in the interest of promoting animals into the class of those deserving rights—equally
leaves the hierarchy intact, shoring up instead the dichotomy between animals and nonanimals. As we know, the boundary between

what we consider to be animal life on the one hand and plant life on the other is less "natural" and less clear-cut than we would like to think and these categories tend to imply, as is the dividing line between living and so-called dead matter. But we need not even go that far "down" the ladder to see that what is at stake is not equality, that the crucial boundary still exists, and the question simply is at what precise point it shall for now be fixed.

The zoological—and archetypally speciesist—subdivision of animals into different species has led animal rights advocates to do with animals what on the level of humans we are trying to overcome: to affirm and maintain an evolutionary hierarky and to grant rights to some and not others on the basis of zoological differences—say, to primates but not to worms. Or to wild animals, perceived as "natural" animals, but not to farm and domestic animals, seen as "subanimals" (see Karen Davis's article in this volume). The zoological classification, however, is less biological than biologist, including factors concerning the animals' lifestyles, habitats, and political history—that is, criteria concerning the sociopolitical coexistence of animals and humans. Although the perspective of classification masquerades as the "objectivity" of no standpoint at all,[16] it reflects the human-subjective—that is, speciesist—standpoint: crucial principles of evaluation and hierarchizing are the animal species' alleged similarity with or difference *from humans* (the evolutionary order), their usefulness *to humans*, complemented by traditional *human* (male, white, etc.) sympathies (or antipathies) for particular species (see Diane Antonio on wolves in this volume). That is to say, the subjective norm of valuation is incorporated within the very objects being constituted, even as the scientific subject disappears from its object-science.

The specific criteria by which it has been proposed that rights should be granted or withheld are either the animals' ability to feel pain (sentience) or to lead a life "worth living"[17]—both being judged by a jury of self-appointed, white, human, scientific experts. Not only is sentience more likely to be perceived the more the animals' expression resembles human expression, but such expression tends to be tested in response to human infliction of pain, thus revealing the real objective behind the withholding of rights from animals, namely that humans may abuse animals. Similarly, assessing whether another's life is worth living involves recognizing factors dear to the judges: consciousness (long considered to be *the* defining characteristic distinguishing humans from animals), intelligence (ditto), and moral agency, extended by Tom Regan to include the passive experience of so-called "moral patients."[18] The proposal that rights should continue to be withheld from domesticated or farm animals shows up the fundamental cynicism behind "scientific" rights discourse: the disastrously violating—"inhuman"(!)—conditions that humans impose on farm animals are acknowledged not in order to change them, but in order to disqualify the animals from rights, as though these conditions were objective factors of biological capacity—the kind of life of which these animals are capable.

As is well known among critics of Peter Singer and Helga Kuhse, the latters' consideration of "the differences" among animals (and humans) as well as of their alleged capacity to lead lives "worth living"—also measured as "objective" capacities of the "objects," while excluding the social and political construction of living conditions—has led them to reshuffle the ladder of rights at the bottom line: not just so as to include some animals but so as to exclude simultaneously some humans—be it at the level of eugenic breeding (selective aborting) or "euthanatic" killing.[19] What masquerades as an antispeciesist defense of (some) animals in fact is a form of super-speciesism, redefining a superrace of the "healthy" and "whole" with lives "worth living."

Similarly, the pseudo-objective "classes" (or "races" or "species") of people whose rights were up for discussion in the "civil societies" of the West over the last few centuries were classes of "domesticated"—farm, factory farm, factory, plantation, and domestic—people: slaves (having been literally factory farmed and bred), peasants, domestic servants, workers, women, and black people (former slaves). Similarly, in Western European societies today, it is migrant workers, however settled, whose political rights are still being debated—that is, whether they should be granted any or continue to be deprived of them. In other words, "species" or "kinds" of people are not only defined by those at the top of the human hierarchy, but defined specifically in terms of their usefulness to and usability by them. Who shall be considered for rights at all, and hence by what criteria rights are to be granted or withheld, was and still is defined by white, male, property-owning, expert citizens, who also judge the candidates' ability to fulfill these criteria—be it women's or black people's ability to think politically and to hold political office, or migrants' ability to assimilate sufficiently and embrace the national political and cultural concerns of the country.[20] What we consider to be the speciesist paradigm has never been the simple binary opposition between "humans" and "animals," but the complex interaction of speciesism, racism, sexism, classism, nationalism, etc., which crystallizes a narrow yet historically changing group of masters who give themselves the name "human." The zoological (including the racist) continuum of classification blends with the classist instrumentalization of those classified, with the sexist division thrown in as and when required.

Whether the criterion for animal rights now be *sentience*—judged not only from a human point of view, but from that of white Western scientific experts—or *a life worth living*, judged by a similar self-appointed assembly of human experts, these approaches to animal rights or animal liberation have nothing to do with challenging the power hierarchy: they simply aim to adjust some positions in the middle, leaving the hierarchy as such intact, above all leaving the position of judgment unchallenged. It is not speciesism that is being challenged, but merely the content of the categories constituted by speciesism. Even the most radical animal rights position, which would grant rights to all species of animals, is no different in theory from that which denies such rights: not only does it need the crucial boundary shored up between animals and nonanimals (or animals that qualify and those who do not), but it continues to arrogate to itself the right to grant rights. Neither does it help if we speak of *intrinsic value:* value is a fundamentally relational category, which implies the possibility of a lack of value as well as a subject defining and recognizing that value. The very project of granting and extending rights is fundamentally speciesist, exempting the human agent and judge into the category of subject ruling over an object world.

Speciesism, or the Constitution of Power

In the political context of the behavior of humans on this planet (not to say in the universe), the question is not so much who else, apart from humans, shall have what are considered to be rights: the question is how the massive abuse of power by (specific groups of) humans, their exploitation and destruction of the lives of others (human and nonhuman) and of the so-called environment, can be stopped. Talking of rights and the extension of rights to other groups and species masks that what humans (differentially privileged according to the human species ladder) have been exercising are not any rights to life and survival, but the power and privilege to dominate, exploit, and destroy others—to rob others of their lives and existence (and on given occasions to grant it). Not only do these specific humans require no protection of their own "rights," they are the very reason why protecting (the rights of) the majority of people and animals and nature becomes a necessity. In particular, the rhetoric of rights and groups of "objects" in line as candidates for rights disguises that the position of the subject—of this discourse of rights and its classification—is itself a crucial position of power, based on the same power structures that enable the exploitation that "rights" are to grant protection from: power over others, over those it makes the objects of its discourse and classification. The shared "scientific" perspective, the common focus on *objects*, be it objects of exploitation or of rights, lets the subject disappear from view—and with it the human agency necessitating (and on choice occasions granting) human rights, animal rights, and protection of the environment. Power, as well as the human agency of exploitation and violence, are implicitly legitimated and affirmed, as an axiomatic ("natural"?) force in need of regulation.

The question is, rather, why such an abuse of power and such a will to dominance—constituted in white, male, Western, adult, expert supremacy, but exercised in the name of humanity—continues to be seen and defined as a *right*. What does it mean if rather than exposing it, we are trying to *extend* such a right, making it the implicit standard of rights? Power cannot be democratically extended to all, since it requires others over whom it is exercised, privilege being an excess of rights at the cost and to the detriment of others and their rights. If we really want freedom for all to live and exist—to live free from violation by the powerful—power and privilege must not be more widely shared, they must be radically dismantled. What masquerades as an extension of rights down the ladder in fact is a degree of protection extended to groups previously exploited—granted by the very exploiters now playing protectors, and passing exploitation "down" the ladder. Not only does the inclusion of groups as worthy of protection legitimate the continued exploitation of all and everything "below" that boundary; the mandate to protect moreover consolidates power in those entrusted with it, requiring power over the most powerful from whom protection is to be granted.

A radical critique of speciesism—at least as feminists have made it—would lead us to question why what are called "universal human rights" should be confined to humans at all, who grants and defines them in whose interest, and why they are necessary at all. As a radical critique of power and exploitation it would imply the neces-

Speciesism, Racism, Nationalism

sity of abolishing power and violence rather than affirming a select "right to freedom"—a concept developed by the leading culture of power and violence, European "civilization," in recognition of the unfreedom it creates (for others).[21] What is required is a fundamentally different human attitude toward reality,[22] and thus a radically different conception of the human self, rather than a legal charter that defines what we can safely continue to destroy. What is required is an attitude that is not premised on the human subject in relation to an object world and the consequent human interest, let alone "right," to dominate, exploit, and destroy, which is axiomatic to Western human ideology. Violation of the "object world"—be it of groups of humans, animals, or nature—cannot be rectified by adjustments in the object world—a wider "zoning" of protection. It can be stopped only by stopping the violators' violating, that is, by a fundamental reconception of human subjectivity.

Hence we need a radical political struggle not only against the so-called "rights" of the powerful, but equally against the legitimations of power and dominance—the conviction that the human interest in exploitation and dominance is "natural" and the abuse of power a matter of course. Neither is significantly curbed nor even challenged by an extension of human or animal rights. On the basis of current political practice, the definition of rights not only defines nonrights— that is to say, the (legitimate) abuse of power and the (lawful) exploitation of all and everything which falls beyond the crucial boundary of rights—it simultaneously creates and maintains power and privilege above the rights so defined: the right to legislate and to define these "rights."

Identity Politics or Cultural Biologism

Current trends in cultural politics, however, seem to be going in the opposite direction. Not only is there confusion as regards the uses and abuses of universalism and notions of equality, but since the triumphant advent of academic theories of difference there also seems to be increasing confusion about the significance of differences. Political movements challenging the "differences" in the rights and treatment, that is, the social and political inequality of specific groups in our societies—of black people in white society, of women in patriarchal society, of lesbians and gay men in heterosexist society, of disabled people in ablist society, of prostitutes in a hypocritical society, etc.—have used the concept of political identity to underline the systematic, collective political histories of oppression of these groups. We have called ourselves blacks, women, lesbians, gays, whores, cripples, etc., not to define who we "really are," but as an act of political resistance. Naming the identities these oppressions create has been a means of the political struggle to dismantle these forms of oppression and eventually to overcome these discriminatory identities.

Yet what originally was a political instrument of resistance and liberation, challenging existing power structures, is in the process of becoming an end in itself, a classification of "object" groups. Political—or increasingly now "cultural"—identities are being celebrated as the true identity found, a means of insisting on personal and group difference. Cultural differences are being fetishized and used to construct new typologies of circumscribed groups—under the guise, as one critic puts it, "of the irreproachable concept of 'culture.' "[23] "Multiculturalism" has become the catch phrase of Western liberalism, signifying a multitude of different cultural identities existing "side by side." As a mere pluralism of objectified cultures it seems to hold the democratic offer of an identity for everyone, replacing any notion of political inequalities that require political struggles for equality.

In other words, we have reverted to a human zoology of cultures. We seem to think that in emphasizing cultural differences and constructing cultural identities—a classification of cultural species—we are pointing to something more defensible and harmless, indeed "positive," as compared to so-called biological differences. We seem to think that the harm in racism lies in the use of *biological* criteria of classification. Yet we know that even the racist theories of the past, including those of the Nazi regime and its scientific "race theorists," never were exclusively biological, just as the so-called "biological" distinctions of zoology are not exclusively biological. The problem of racist ideology lies less in the fact that "biological" criteria are being used than in the use they are being put to: constructing typologies of *kinds* of people in the interest of social and political discrimination and instrumentalization. Biology has had the role of signifying the natural, the given, the innate, the unchangeable, and thus the "objective" grounds on which to construct classes, races, and sexes, thus to justify a classist, racist, and sexist political order. The critique of biologism is not that there are no biological differences between people—which is a platitude of the first order—but that the science of biology, like all sciences, is political. An

Speciesism, Racism, Nationalism

arbitrary selection of biological features constructs as "biological types" what are in fact identities/classes/groups created through social practices of dominance and exploitation. Typology systematizes (scientifically rationalizes and generalizes) political and social roles, thus enabling them to be politically institutionalized as structural inequality based on "difference."

Classification is neither neutral, being put to political use only "thereafter," nor is it objective: it is itself an act of social and political discrimination and thus the expression of the subjectivity of power. What is said to be a quality of the object is in fact a difference construed in relation to an implicit norm constituted in the classifying subject. Racism and sexism as political practices construct *another* race and *another* sex, a race of "others" and a sex of "others." The "objective" biological features—the objective grounds for classification said to reside in the object—are said by a social, political, and ideological subject class to reside in a social, political, and ideological object class, thus to justify the subject class's systematic practices of dominance and exploitation.

The racist—and invariably nationalist—ideologues in Europe today do not argue predominantly on biological grounds; they argue on cultural grounds with a vengeance. Capitalizing on the acceptability of the concept of multiculturalism, the extreme Right in Europe has made "ethnopluralism" its own catch phrase, albeit with a different (but equally unspoken) attitude as to the spacial organization of this pluralism and a different political program concerning the multicultural or ethnopluralist societies of the West.[24] Cultural differences that have grown historically and politically are used to define and circumscribe communities or ethnicities—to argue for their hermetic preservation according to the logic of multiculturalism, or for their incompatibility with other communities and their lifestyles according to the nationalist logic of ethnopluralism. It is the cooking habits, the language, the music habits, the religious practices, and the social codes of migrants, refugees, or Rom that are said to be incompatible with the national lifestyles of Europeans and to create unmanageable social tensions for which the only solution lies in separate living spaces for each community. Culture, seen as rooted in history and grown over centuries, is as good as biology to signify the "objective," the virtually unchangeable and quasi-innate.[25] Cultural differences are made out to be as specific to each community, and as intolerable by virtue of being "other" to any other community, as are the differences between species in popular mythology: like "cats and dogs," they cannot live together in peace (although we know that cats and dogs can).

Neither is the "evolutionary" aspect missing: cultures too are hierarchized synchronically to reflect a fictional diachrony of progression, an alleged evolution of human culture from primitive to civilized, from ahistorical to historic, from native and traditional to modern and dynamic, where "modern" is synonymous with "Western" and "advanced," signifying a contemporariness that simultaneously boasts historic tradition.

In the same way, the "emergence" of the modern European nation-states was represented by their architects and advocates in the nineteenth century as an evolutionary step forward, an "adaptation" to the global conditions of the modern worldscape for which the crumbling multiethnic empires were no longer adequate: the drama of the survival of the fittest fulfilling itself in the political realm, with the most "advanced" European cultures or nations "naturally" leading the way into modernity and survival in modern times, and modernity "naturally" meaning "most advanced."[26] Yet the new global conditions that required adapting to were not climatic conditions in the environment, but the economic and global-political conditions created by an expanding world capitalism: free-trade liberalism or those "component national units in the developed world" that constituted it, such as British industry, the American economy, German capitalism, etc.[27] To "survive" did not mean to survive as a nation among nations, but as one contemporary put it, "to ascertain the means by which any community has attained the eminence among nations."[28] That is to say, to maintain an already achieved position of supremacy and superiority over, rather than coexistence with, other nations—"national advantage" in a race among "nations."[29]

Thus one of the three criteria that according to historian Eric Hobsbawm were necessary to qualify as a nation—besides an historic association with a current or recent state and an old cultural elite possessing a written national literary and administrative vernacular—was the "proven capacity for conquest."[30] As Hobsbawm comments, "nothing like being an imperial people to make a population conscious of its collective existence as such . . . Besides, for the nineteenth century conquest provided the Darwinian proof of evolutionary success as a social species."[31] In other words, behind the positivist, scientific claim of the formula "state = nation = people" stood a politics of expansion, exploitation, and conquest diametrically opposed to the formula's democratic appearance.

Speciesism, Racism, Nationalism

The political argumentation that we have called biologist explicitly focuses on the quasi-scientific description of biological, cultural, national, ethnic, etc. differences—much aided by identity politics and multiculturalism—as the allegedly neutral and pre-political starting point, with the political conclusions to be drawn remaining the tacit assumption. Nationalism and the nationalist idea—also developed by leading intellectuals in eighteenth- and nineteenth-century Western Europe—combines with the typology of different cultures to form a political theory that demands exclusive "living space" for each community as a "natural" consequence of their difference. Although the construction of European nation-states—be it through revolution, as in France, or from "above"—politically unified disparate communities under one government, these communities have since been educated to develop a sense of "national identity." Theories of national history and culture as well as the imposition of a national language combine to constitute a concerted program of national inculturation, which make national borders seem "natural," the communities within them "homogeneous." Many Europeans today indeed believe that France, England, Germany, Italy, Sweden, Norway, etc. are "natural" homogeneous communities, unified by a language, a common history, and a common will to belong together—despite even present-day evidence to the contrary, not to mention the evidence of history.

More importantly, the idea that apparently homogeneous national communities have a right to an exclusive territory, to exclusive living space in which to realize their national identity, has become the uncontested "natural" assumption of modernity. The reunification of Germany, as the apparently "natural" consequence of the GDR's liberation from its communist dictatorship, has reaffirmed the national-ethnic principle—"Germany to the Germans" having become a slogan again which politicians frame into policy and national extremists murderously act out in the streets. Territorial conquests by Serbian forces in Croatia and Bosnia-Hercegovina are accompanied not only by what is known as "ethnic cleansing"—that is, the murder and dispersion of non-Serbian (and oppositional Serbian) inhabitants—but by international "peace talks" honoring such conquest by proposals for the ethnic division of the Bosnian state (Vance-Owen plan). Ethnic self-definition and constitution are what the West chooses to see in the outbreak of war in the territories of Eastern Europe and the former Soviet Union after the collapse of the colonial Soviet empire, as it chooses to see in the strife in the territories of its own former colonies in the Third World.

The claim to an exclusive national territory—apartheid on a world scale—is structurally continuous with that "horrendous refusal to share the world with another 'race,'" which Finkielkraut sees at the root of the crime against humanity we call genocide.[32] Nationalism today—in contrast to the history of the emergence or construction of modern nation-states—signifies *both* the so-called "naturalness" of a community (like a species) *and* its apparent will to self-determination on an exclusive territory of its own. The hegemony of this ideology of nationalism within the political reality of today's international "community of nations" thus seems to oblige any oppressed community, be it a statistical minority within a nation-state or a statistical majority that is a political minority, to assert its rights and its survival by seeking to obtain the status of a nation on a territory of its own. Governments as well as individuals, whether conservative or progressive, support (select) national liberation struggles the world over, as seemingly the only means for oppressed communities below nation status of achieving freedom and rights. Not only do we thereby legitimate nationalism and the racist idea of "pure" nation-states, we also undermine any political resistance struggles within given societies: struggles for equality, political autonomy, and self-determination within heterogeneous communities and the understanding of community *as* heterogeneous.

Hence resistance struggles—like, for example, those of the Indigenous Peoples of the Americas—that do not aim at establishing a separate nation, but challenge the abuse of power by and within the nation-state, tend to fall outside the ideological framework of nationalism and internationalism and fail to get effective support from the "international community." They remain the "internal" affair of the respective nation-states, which the international community respects as the state respects an individual man's privacy within his family. That is, it is considered not as an international issue but as a national issue of dissent within a state—so to speak, a family quarrel. (Hence the discussion among Indigenous Peoples increasingly turns around the key question: independent nation-state or justice within existing states?) In the same way, it remains the right—that is, the internal affair of any Western state—whether to see itself as a so-called "immigration state," to regulate immigration as it sees fit, and to deny political rights to immigrants within its borders. International law and the ideology of internationalism guarantee the state's internal sovereignty, its power over "its" inhabitants.

The International Zoo of Nations

The idea of an international community of nations is akin to that of a zoo, with species separated into their respective territories—be they cages or reservations. It is a measure that has its appeal at a point where so many species (and communities) are indeed threatened by extinction, so that a cage in a zoo appears like the last protection from final aggression. Yet the zoo has been established and is being maintained precisely by those responsible for the extinction of species in the first place. The naive visitor to the zoo may be under the misapprehension that cages are protecting animals from each other, that without fences and walls they would eat each other up—that is, that the threat to the animals' survival is coming from other animals. Similarly, apologetes of the nationalist and internationalist idea in the modern era will argue that national borders and the international order protect neighboring communities from each other. So, for instance, it was in the case of Croatia, where the German government argued for the quick recognition of Croatia's independence as a means of stopping the war campaign by their Serbian neighbors, and for the quick recognition of Bosnia's independence as a means of preventing such a war.

The nationalist idea however, like the idea of the animal zoo and of national parks and reservations, was developed by intellectuals and statesmen of the leading European powers, at a time when the European conquest of the world's territories and resources had reached its unprecedented peak with the colonial empires. These conquests and the accompanying practices of slavery, colonialism, and exploitation had imposed a reign of terror, a rule of violent domination and a scarcity of resources (or of access to them) on the vast majority of the people of the world, fostering indeed strife for survival also among nearest neighbors. But if neighboring communities (or their leaders) today do fight each other for resources and living space, the fact that they have to survive in conditions of poverty and scarcity and in the circumscribed territories of the political and economic order in the "South" and the "East," is of European (Northern/Western) making—just as the circumscribed territory of a zoo and the restricted conditions of animals' habitats in the world are of human making.

The establishment of the modern international order of nation-states, apparently superseding the European colonial world empires, has neither diminished nor dismantled the power of the leading European nations. Rather, it has been the unquestionable starting point, the power base from which a semblance of "rights" is eventually passed down the ladder to other "nations." In particular, the methods that had built the modern European nation-states and former empires—war, territorial conquest, genocide, slavery, colonialism, militarism, the exploitation of humans, animals, and natural resources—have neither been ended nor even put into question; they are now simply being regulated by international conventions. Just as the extension of "human" rights to black people and women within national frameworks—their so-called emancipation—has not managed to shake the superior power of white men, so the "emancipation" of nations in the Third World or now in Eastern Europe and the former Soviet Union does not challenge or seriously put into question the superior power of the former imperialist and colonial empires.

The architects of the international community of nations, like the directors of the zoo, have first of all secured their own vast and overabundant territories, their continued ruling power over other species or communities, their continued "right" of access to and exploitation of the territories and resources (including the inhabitants themselves) of other communities. Only once the European world powers were securely established and European political and economic hegemony unchallengeable, did they begin to carve up the rest of the land (and seas) into apparently similar nation-states and to grant so-called "nation status" to newly emerging nations, thus exporting and imposing the ideology of nationalism and internationalism on the "rest" of the world. Whether a prospective nation qualifies as a nation and is granted independence is still the decision of the directors of the international community of nations. The principle of self-determination to the contrary, a community can no more establish (or dissolve) borders without international consent than a group of animals could erect or tear down a fence in the zoo without the consent of the managers of the zoo. Thus Slovenia, Croatia, and later Bosnia-Hercegovina were granted recognition as independent nation-states, while Macedonia, for example, has been denied it. Many other aspirants to nation status, or "national ethnicities," especially but not only in Europe, have been denied it. The Irish remain divided; the Basques are struggling in vain for independence;

the Sami constitute minorities in a number of northern nation-states without a country called Samiland or Lapland.

Where a human species is seriously threatened but the international community does not consider it in its interest to grant it independent nation status, the community establishes "natural reserves" or reservations and protection zones, as for instance in the case of the Kurdish people in Iraq after the war of 1991 or at present in parts of Bosnia. The notion has already acquired notoriety with the installation of Indian reservations in the United States. The cause of the threat—the will to war, destruction, and exploitation on the part of the aggressors—is left untouched and unchallenged: the "international community" simply extends protection where war and destruction have reached a degree that it finds excessive.

Just as the directors of the zoo and their "human race" are not just another species among species with its designated space in the zoo, but command the entire natural space including the zoo, eat the meat of other animals, and live off the large-scale exploitation of animals and their habitats, so the directors of the internationalized globe preserve their right of access to and exploitation of the entire globe, and in particular their right to organize the zoo. Western capital and Western multinationals exploit the natural and human resources of the entire globe, while Western-dominated, "international" military forces secure their access to them (impressively demonstrated, for example, during the Gulf war of 1991). Similarly, members of Western nations are roaming every corner of the world as their rightful recreational living space, while the borders of their own countries are increasingly becoming sealed to people from outside the Western world. Through the successful exportation of the nationalist idea, including its principles of national power based on militarism and war, Western nations moreover have secured the vital support of the governments of other nations for the maintenance of the international order and for their own hegemony within it.

Sexism and Reproduction

Sexism—the construction of the female sex on the basis of its reproductive function—is the sine qua non of speciesism and the zoological paradigm, including all its derivatives. Even if the category of *women* at particular points in history seemed to stand in competition with, say, *blacks* or *workers* as vying for a superior position on the evolutionary ladder, it never was the category of women or females, but a speciesist, racist, or classist subdivision of it. No race, class, species, or ethnicity makes any sense without its "own" constituency of females guaranteeing the group's reproduction. Sexism is so central to zoology as to have become truly "naturalized" or biologized.

Feminism has challenged this zoological definition of women, at least on the level of human society. We need to challenge it on every level, including the level of animal species definition. From the practice of breeding through to the protection of endangered species, the reproductive use of females is central and axiomatic. We have seen both breeding and "species protection" seamlessly being applied to plants, animals, and "human species"—by a master race of humans, of scientific classifiers, technologists, legislators, politicians. If more "kinds" of humans and specifically some women in the West have been allowed to join the master race, this does not mean the dissolution of the zoologist paradigm or the sexism at its center. It is the very point of speciesism—what we might also call scientific subjectivity—to exempt the subject of all the determinants it applies to its object categories and to emerge as the polymorphous norm from which all else is defined as other.

Thus many Western intellectuals today support or assess nationalist endeavors the world over (while regarding the legitimacy of their own nations and nationalities as beyond doubt or question), using the same arguments as do governments shoring up for war and international institutions pretending to mediate. Westerners see themselves, if not personally as the directors of the international zoo, at least as part of the scientific community of zoologists acting as umpires between rivaling claims, granting recognition to new nations here or there, not granting it somewhere else, but never questioning the logic of the zoo. Western feminists can be heard musing along with the General Secretary of the United Nations or the President of the United States about whether to launch an international military intervention to "end the rapes of Bosnian women" or whether the Bosnian Muslims should after all be allowed to arm themselves.[33] Ethnic species of Croats, Serbs, or Bosnian Muslims are being constructed by the now-familiar scientific means, the selective use of "relevant" features which construct people living today not only as the same among themselves but as the same as their historical antecedents.

Women and their reproductive function are the necessary factor constructing a plurality of individuals as the singularity of a collective entity. Thus one feminist from Zagreb protesting against the rape of women in the war in Bosnia highlights women's reproductive function:

> These are young girls and young women who are being held in the rape camps, the most reproductive part of the Bosnian population. There they are being systematically destroyed. Even if they escape alive, you don't seriously think that they will ever have normal relationships. It is part of the genocide of the Bosnian people.[34]

The chosen focus is on women with reproductive capacity—"the most reproductive part of the Bosnian population"—although we know women of all ages have been sexually violated and tortured. Yet this does not seem to "matter" in the same way, just as the survival or death of a woman apparently does not really matter—the focus being on her function as reproducer. While to each individual woman it does indeed matter whether she is killed or escapes a camp alive, it apparently does not matter to "us," we who define the problem and assess the damage. The damage we focus on is the damage to the reproductive future of the people; for even if the women return from the camps alive, if their reproductive capacity or willingness has been destroyed, they are apparently as good as dead as far as their people is concerned (or as far as we, as that people's assessors, are concerned). Women surviving, Bosnian Muslim women continuing to *live*, are not apparently part of the Bosnian Muslim people surviving, they are a *loss* to that people, a loss to its future reproduction as a people. They do not seem to have lives worth living in their own right, but only as the reproductive members of their own "species." Individual women count as being alive only if they reproduce, just as their destruction—that is, the impact of the violence against them—is measured not in terms of its consequences for them, but in terms of its contribution to the destruction of their ethnic community. If the women live without fulfilling their reproductive function, they are part of "their" people's threatening extinction—"it is part of the genocide of the Moslem people."

Hence it is the *reproductive consequences* of rape that also weigh particularly severely in the eyes of the onlooking experts, namely "the forcible impregnation of non-Serbian women."[35] "The purpose is to produce what Serbs regard as 'chetnik' babies to populate the 'Greater Serbian' state."[36] What the warring rapists think and intend obviously is also what the experts think, and what many Western women also seem to think. So, for instance, in *Off Our Backs:* "The heinous genocidal rape campaign may have left her [the Bosnian woman who was raped] with the child of her aggressor; a 'Chetnik' baby she is forced to deliver."[37] Or as a woman journalist on German television put it in a question to the Muslim leader of the SDA party: "What does it mean for the future also of this people? The point is that these women will now gradually give birth to children—that this people will be adulterated/decomposed [*zersetzt*]. Or how do you judge it when now these children will be born by women impregnated by Serbs?"[38]

Thus the principal problem of rape does not seem to lie in the violence against the woman, but in the nationality of her rapist, and the nationality of the fetus with which she may have become pregnant. It implies that these women do not want these children because they are Serbian or Chetnik babies, rather than because the women are pregnant as a consequence of rape. It moreover supports a nationality principle whereby the child's nationality is strictly determined by the biological father—they are "Serbian babies," not children of Bosnian women. (That the child fathered by a Serbian Chetnik will also be a male child, moreover with a Chetnik political future, is even less in question than the child's nationality.) It is a view that not only makes it more difficult for those women for whom it is too late to have an abortion, but also for those—however few they may be—who have decided to keep the baby, to see the child as their own child and to assert this vis-à-vis their community. As one woman testifying put it: "This child may be a bastard, but whoever is the father, I am the mother. I will do everything within my power for this child and for my other daughter. I will make no concessions to my husband; if he doesn't accept it, I will take a flat of my own and raise the children conscientiously. If need be, I'll go begging in order to feed them."[39] Putting the emphasis on the nationality of the fetus shifts the focus from the women's problems of having to deal with a pregnancy as a consequence of rape to the problem these children may constitute for their people.

The nationalist analysis reproduces the violators' perspective, and indeed the perspective of most men of any nationality, as well as of the nation-state, all of whom continue to regard women as men's individual and national-collective possession. The rape of women becomes an assault on the masculinity and nationality of the men "owning" these women, and on the state or the "nation" that similarly owns them. The perspective of the victims is sacrificed in favor

Speciesism, Racism, Nationalism

of a "universalistic scientific" perspective, the subjectivity of power and dominance.

Reproduction, the sexist instrumentalization of women as reproducers of their "kind," is the pivot of all speciesism, racism, ethnicism, and nationalism—the construction of collective entities at the cost of the rights and interests of individuals. This is true not only in the context of genocide and the threat of collective extinction, but equally in the context of the "positive" construction of nations, peoples, and ethnicities, in whose interest women are instrumentalized as reproducers and women's reproductive choices are regarded not as their individual right, but as an interest of the state or the community. What was intended as a defense of women raped in war—the protesting of rape as an instrument of genocide—implicitly reaffirms the position of women as the nations' reproducers, whose duty is not only to reproduce but to reproduce within her own "kind"—a definition few women in the West would accept for themselves. The emphasis lies on the violation of the nation's reproduction, rather than the violation of the women.

Life vs. Life

Species, nations, and ethnic communities are not just "communities" constituted through the self-determined choice of their individual members: they are collective entities requiring men and women (males and females) to serve that entity's reproduction. Neither are they historical communities determined by their actual members; they are transhistorical entities, constructs of the mind, endowed (by that mind) with a life that supersedes the lives of their individual members. Affirming the life of the collective entity means to affirm the instrumentalization of individuals as reproducers, sacrificing their lives and their right to life in the interest of the collective entity's survival. Reproduction becomes an interest on the meta-level of the collective, a positive expectation of individual members' reproductive activity. Reproductive choice thus ceases to be the right of individuals, their choice *against* reproduction becoming a threat to the species' survival.

Focusing on the preservation of peoples, of species, of collective entities in the interest of maintaining for "the world" the rich multiplicity of life-forms is equally to advocate species' survival through reproduction, at the cost not only of the lives of individuals, but of the dignity of their living. This perspective is already so "natu-

ralized" in the "scientific" Western perspective that environmentalists as well as scientists foreground the preservation of the multiplicity of life-forms and of the planet's genetic pool. Hence California
scientists may propose to archivize and explore the genetic information of the "Bushmen" of South Africa, the "Hill People" of New
Guinea, African "Pygmies," the Yanomami of the Amazon, and the
Basque people of Spain before they finally become extinct.[40] The
dying out of these peoples is calmly presumed, but genetics and
reproductive technologies will preserve the survival of the genetic
wealth of humanity. Instead of a political struggle in favor of securing
living conditions for people in this world, we—the certain survivors
continuing to live on this planet—invest in a scientific struggle to
engineer "their" genetic survival—at the cost of the dignity of living
people and for our own benefit after the people themselves may have
died.

In this way the focus on species survival and extinction deflects
attention from the need for political action on behalf of the oppressed
where their survival as a "species" is assured through reproduction
or, indeed, breeding. The necessity for support for Croatian and all
other women raped receded behind the need to protect the Bosnian
Muslim people. People in the Third World may be oppressed, with
thousands dying of poverty and hunger, yet the Western world's
political focus is not on the elimination of the causes of this oppression, but on the contrary, on controlling their reproduction.[41] Similarly, factory animals produced for human consumption, scientific
experimentation, and pet keeping—who therefore are in no danger of
collective extinction, human breeding ensuring their "survival"—do
not have the support of animal conservationists to end violence
against them.[42] While there is no suggested analogy between the
groups of "objects"—people in oppressed conditions and animals in
oppressed conditions—there is a similarity in the subjectivity producing that oppression, a similarity in the doing.

"Breeding" is the answer of human science to the threat of extinction, with a technology developed side by side with the technology
for the industrial mass destruction of people and life on the planet.
The two technologies are two sides of the same intent: the engineered destruction of people, other living beings and life-forms, and
the artificial "production of life" under the control of the superrace,
the exterminators of all else. Behind the science of an "object world"
is a scientific human subject with the desire to have complete power
over that world.

Notes

1. Carol J. Adams, *The Sexual Politics of Meat* (New York: Continuum, 1990).

2. Kathleen Barry, *Female Sexual Slavery* (New York and London: New York University Press, 1979), 43–46.

3. Ibid., 45.

4. Laura Pitter and Alexandra Stiglmayer, "Will the World Remember? Can the Women Forget?" *Ms.* 3, no. 5 (March/April 1993):20.

5. Melanie Beyer, "Interventionsstrategien und feministische Politik," in *Vergewaltigung, Krieg, Nationalismus: Eine feministische Kritik*, ed. Susanne Kappeler, Mira Renka, and Melanie Beyer (Munich: Frauenoffensive, 1994), 81.

6. Nihada Kadić, cited in Alexandra Stiglmayer, "Die totale Degradierung der Frau zu einer Ware," *Weltwoche* 45, 5 November 1992, 9; also in Alexandra Stiglmayer, "Massenvergewaltigungen in Bosnien-Herzegowina," *Blattgold* 1 (January 1993), 3 (my translation). This became the dominant interpretation in the German media and for many women's groups; see Susanne Kappeler, "Massenverrat an Frauen im ehemaligen Jugoslawien," in *Vergewaltigung, Krieg, Nationalismus*, ed. Susanne Kappeler et al.

7. Helga Wullweber, "Kriegsverbrechen Vergewaltigung," in *Massenvergewaltigung: Krieg gegen Frauen*, ed. Alexandra Stiglmayer (Freiburg im Breisgau: Kore Verlag, 1993), 248.

8. Ruth Seifert in an interview in the German daily *taz* (17 February 1993); see also Ruth Seifert, "Krieg und Vergewaltigung: Ansätze zu einer Analyse," in *Massenvergewaltigung: Krieg gegen Frauen*, ed. Alexandra Stiglmayer, 96–98.

9. *Shorter Oxford English Dictionary* (Oxford: Oxford University Press, 1973, rev., 1978).

10. Jutta Ditfurth, *Feuer in die Herzen: Plädoyer für eine ökologische linke Opposition* (Hamburg: Carlson Verlag, 1992), 30–32, 62.

11. Ibid., esp. 37–42.

12. Gena Corea, *The Mother Machine: Reproductive Technologies from Artificial Insemination to Artificial Wombs* (London: The Women's Press, 1988).

13. Jutta Ditfurth, *Feuer in die Herzen*, 42–47.

14. Janice Raymond, *Women as Wombs: Reproductive Technologies and The Battle Over Women's Freedom* (San Francisco: HarperSanFrancisco, 1993); Theresia Degener and Swantje Köbsell, *"Hauptsache, es ist gesund"? Weibliche Selbstbestimmung unter humangenetischer Kontrolle* (Hamburg: Konkret Verlag, 1992).

15. bell hooks, *Ain't I a Woman: Black Women and Feminism* (London: Pluto Press, 1981), 90, 127.

16. See Catharine A. MacKinnon on *aperspectivity* in "Feminism, Marxism, Method, and the State: An Agenda for Theory," *Signs: Journal of Women in*

Culture and Society, vol. 7, no. 3 (1982), 537–38; and Catharine A. MacKinnon, *Towards a Feminist Theory of the State* (Cambridge, Mass.: Harvard University Press, 1989), 97, 121.

17. See Josephine Donovan, "Animal Rights and Feminist Theory," *Signs: Journal of Women in Culture and Society*, vol. 15, no. 2 (1990), 355–56.

18. Ibid., 354.

19. Theresia Degener and Swantje Köbsell, *"Hauptsache, es ist gesund"?*, 21–22, 62–63; *Tödliche Ethik: Beiträge gegen Eugenik und "Euthanasie,"* ed. Theo Bruns, Ulla Penselin, and Udo Sierck (Hamburg: Verlag Libertäre Assoziation, 1990), passim.

20. Thus a professor of aesthetics, Bazon Brock of the University of Wuppertal in Germany, writes: "Every fourth person in Frankfurt is a foreigner . . . I cannot see how someone from the Third World should be able to develop an interest in our architectural facades . . . You cannot teach a Persian painter here how we see our paintings. Our imagery is not intelligible to him." Cited in Jutta Ditfurth, *Feuer in die Herzen*, 159 (my translation).

21. Toni Morrison, *Playing in the Dark: Whiteness and the Literary Imagination—The William E. Massey Sr. Lectures in the History of American Civilization, 1990* (London: Picador, 1993), 34.

22. Cf. Paula Gunn Allen's introduction to *Spider Woman's Granddaughters: Traditional Tales and Contemporary Writing by Native American Women*, ed. Paula Gunn Allen (London: The Women's Press, 1990), 6, 8f. See also Paula Gunn Allen, cited in Josephine Donovan, "Animal Rights and Feminist Theory," 370.

23. Alain Finkielkraut, *The Undoing of Thought*, translated from French by Dennis O'Keefe (London: The Claridge Press, 1988), 79.

24. Hanspeter Siegfried, "Kulturrevolution von rechts? Zur Ideologie der Neuen Rechten," in *Widerspruch* 21 (June 1991), 77–78; Matthias von Hellfeld, *Die Nation erwacht* (Cologne: PapyRossa Verlag, 1993), 46–47.

25. Paul Gilroy, *"There Ain't No Black in the Union Jack": The Cultural Politics of Race and Nation* (London: Unwin Hyman, 1987; London: Routledge, 1992), 60–61. (Page references to 1992 edition.) See also note 24.

26. Eric Hobsbawm, *Nations and Nationalism Since 1780* (Cambridge: Cambridge University Press, 1990), 35, 41.

27. Ibid., 25.

28. George Richard Porter, cited in Hobsbawm, *Nations and Nationalism*, 28.

29. Ibid., 27.

30. Ibid., 37–38.

31. Ibid., 38.

32. Alain Finkielkraut, *Remembering in Vain: The Klaus Barbie Trial and the Crimes Against Humanity*, translated from French by Roxanne Lapidus with Sima Godfrey (New York and Oxford: New York University Press, 1992), 47.

33. E.g., Susan Jeffords, "Fantastic Conquests in U.S. Military History, Only Some Rapes Count," *Village Voice,* 13 July 1993, 22, 24, 29. Leading women activists like former peace activist and now German Euro-MP Eva Quistorp (Greens), the journalist and author Alexandra Stiglmayer, and Amelija Janovic of Mothers For Peace all argued for military intervention on the television debating program *Einspruch* (SAT.1, 12 January 1993), a demand taken over by many women's groups in Germany. See also Melanie Beyer, "Interventionsstrategien und feministische Politik," in *Vergewaltigung, Krieg, Nationalismus,* ed. Susanne Kappeler et al., 76–77 and note 3.

34. Nihada Kadić, cited in Alexandra Stiglmayer, "Die totale Degradierung der Frau zu einer Ware," 9 (my translation).

35. "Women Express Concern Over Tour," by Kareta Feminist Group et al., *Off Our Backs* (May 1993), special pull-out section "Serbia's War Against Bosnia and Croatia," 10.

36. Ibid.

37. "More on Madre," by Aimee Wielchowski, Women's Action Coalition-Chicago et al., *Off Our Backs* (May 1993), special pull-out section "Serbia's War Against Bosnia and Croatia," 11.

38. Sibylle Bassler on *Mona Lisa* (ZDF, 15 November 1992).

39. On the German television program *Panorama* (ARD, 15 February 1993).

40. Jutta Ditfurth, *Feuer in die Herzen,* 33–34.

41. Janice Raymond, *Women As Wombs,* esp. chap. 1.

42. Thanks to Carol Adams for her suggestion that vegetarianism has so little support as a political strategy against animal oppression because animals produced for "meat" consumption are not endangered by collective extinction (personal communication, 1993).

Carol J. Adams and Josephine Donovan

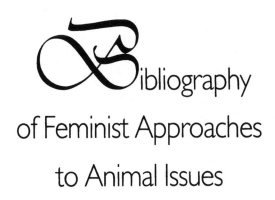

ibliography
of Feminist Approaches
to Animal Issues

This bibliography is an attempt at a comprehensive listing of works that deal specifically with women and animals and/or feminism and animal defense theory.

Abbott, Sally. 1990. The Origins of God in the Blood of the Lamb. In *Reweaving the World: The Emergence of Ecofeminism*, ed. Irene Diamond and Gloria Feman Orenstein, 35–40. San Francisco: Sierra Club Books.

Adams, Carol J. 1975. The Oedible Complex: Feminism and Vegetarianism. In *The Lesbian Reader*, ed. Gina Covina and Laurel Galana, 145–52. Oakland, Calif.: Amazon.

——. 1976. The Inedible Complex: The Political Implications of Vegetarianism. *The Second Wave: A Magazine of the New Feminism* 4 (1):36–42.

——. 1987. The Sexual Politics of Meat. *Heresies* 21:51–55.

——. 1989a. Antifur . . . Antiwoman? *Animals' Voice* 2 (6):56.

——. 1989b. The Arrogant Eye and Animal Experimentation. In *With a Fly's Eye, Whale's Wit and Woman's Heart: Relationships between Animals and*

Women, ed. Theresa Corrigan and Stephanie Hoppe, 204–21. Pittsburgh, Pa.: Cleis Press.

———. 1990a. Cat's/I. *Animal's Voice* 3 (2):68.

———. 1990b. "Deena"—the World's Only Stripping Chimp. *Animals' Voice* 3 (1):72.

———. 1990c. On the Fallacy of Germaine Greer. *Newsletter of the International Association Against Painful Experiments on Animals* (Fall):6–7.

———. 1990d. *The Sexual Politics of Meat: A Feminist-Vegetarian Critical Theory*. New York: Continuum.

———. 1990e. Speech on feminism and animal rights. Presented at the March for the Animals, Washington, D.C., 10 June 1990. Reprinted in *Feminists for Animal Rights Newsletter* 5 (3–4):3.

———. 1991a. Abortion Rights and Animal Rights. *Feminists for Animal Rights Newsletter* 6(1):1, 14–15. Expanded version in *Between the Species* 7 (4):181–89.

———. 1991b. Anima, Animus, Animal. *Ms.* (May/June):62–63.

———. 1991c. Developing Courses that Integrate Animal Rights and Feminism. *American Philosophical Association Newsletter on Feminism and Philosophy*, Special Issue on the Environment:135–43.

———. 1991d. Ecofeminism and the Eating of Animals. *Hypatia* 6 (1):125–45.

———. 1993a. Feeding on Grace: Institutional Violence, Christianity, and Vegetarianism. In *Good News for Animals? Contemporary Christian Approaches to Animal Well-Being*, ed. Jay McDaniel and Charles Pinches, 142–57. Maryknoll, N.Y.: Orbis.

———. 1993b. The Feminist Traffic in Animals. In *Ecofeminism: Women, Animals, Nature*, ed. Greta Gaard, 195–218. Philadelphia: Temple University Press.

———. 1994a. Bringing Peace Home: A Feminist Philosophical Perspective on the Abuse of Women, Children, and Pet Animals. *Hypatia: A Journal of Feminist Philosophy* (Special Issue on Feminism and Peace) 9 (2):63–84.

———. 1994b. *Neither Man nor Beast: Feminism and the Defense of Animals*. New York: Continuum.

———. 1994c. PETA and a Pornographic Culture: A Feminist Analysis of "I'd Rather Go Naked than Wear Fur." *Feminists for Animal Rights Newsletter* 8 (3–4):1, 8.

———. 1994d. Sheltering the Companion Animals of Battered Women. *Feminists for Animal Rights Newsletter* 8 (1–2):1, 8.

———. 1995. Comment on Kathryn Paxton George's "Should Feminists be Vegetarians?" *Signs: Journal of Women in Culture and Society* 21 (1).

Adams, Carol J., with Marjorie Procter-Smith. 1993. Taking Life or Taking on Life: Table Talk and Animals. In *Ecofeminism and the Sacred*, ed. Carol J. Adams. New York: Continuum.

Albino, Donna. 1988. C.E.A.S.E.: Building Animal Consciousness. An Interview with Jane Lidsky. *Woman of Power* 9:64–66.

Anderson, Lorraine, ed. 1991. *Sisters of the Earth.* New York: Vintage.

Aylon, Helene. 1990. The Projection of Patriarchal Values onto Animals. *Feminists for Animal Rights Newsletter* 5 (3–4):15.

Bartlett, Kim. 1990. Editorial: A Patriarchal World. *Animals' Agenda* 10 (8):2.

Bauman, Batya. 1989. Flesh or No Flesh [letter]. *Womanews* (September).

———. 1990a. Ecofeminist Statement. In *Vegan Street: Cruelty-Free and Environmentally Safe Products,* 17. Rockville, Md.: Vegan Street.

———. 1990b. What Is Loving Animals All About? *Feminists for Animal Rights Newsletter* 5 (3–4):1, 12.

Benney, Norma. 1983. All of One Flesh: The Rights of Animals. In *Reclaim the Earth: Women Speak out for Life on Earth,* ed. Léonie Caldecott and Stephanie Leland, 141–51. London: Women's Press.

Birke, Lynda. 1984. They're Worse than Animals: Animals in Biological Research. In *More than the Parts: Biology and Politics,* ed. Lynda Birke and Jonathan Silvertown, 219–35. London: Pluto Press.

———. 1991a. Science, Feminism, and Animal Natures I: Extending the Boundaries. *Women's Studies International Forum* 14 (5):443–50.

———. 1991b. Science, Feminism, and Animal Natures II: Feminist Critiques and the Place of Animals in Science. *Women's Studies International Forum* 14 (5):451–58.

———. 1994. *Feminism, Animals, and Science: The Naming of the Shrew.* Buckingham, England; Philadelphia: Open University Press.

Bloodroot Collective. 1980. *The Political Palate: A Feminist Vegetarian Cookbook.* Bridgeport, Conn.: Sanguinaria.

———. 1984. *The Second Seasonal Political Palate: A Feminist Vegetarian Cookbook.* Bridgeport, Conn.: Sanguinaria.

———. 1993. *The Perennial Political Palate: The Third Feminist Vegetarian Cookbook.* Bridgeport, Conn.: Sanguinaria.

Bring, Ellen. 1988. Moving Towards Coexistence: An Interview with Alice Walker. *Animals' Agenda* 8 (April): 6–9.

Cantor, Aviva. 1980. The Club, the Yoke, and the Leash: What We Can Learn from the Way a Culture Treats Animals. *Ms.* (August):27–29.

Clift, Elayne. 1990. Advocate Battles for Safety in Mines and Poultry Plants. *New Directions for Women* (May/June):3.

Clifton, Merritt. 1990. Killing the Female: The Psychology of the Hunt. *Animals' Agenda* 10 (7):26–30, 57.

Collard, Andrée. 1983. Rape of the Wild. *Trivia* 2:64–86.

———. 1987. Freeing of the Animals. *Trivia* 10:6–23.

Collard, Andrée, with Joyce Contrucci. 1988. *Rape of the Wild: Man's Violence against Animals and the Earth.* London: Women's Press; Bloomington: Indiana University Press.

Comninou, Maria. 1991. Pornography and Hunting. *Feminists for Animal Rights Newsletter* 6 (1–2):1, 18.

Corea, Gena. 1985. *The Mother Machine: Reproductive Technologies from Artificial Insemination to Artificial Wombs.* New York: Harper & Row.

Corea, Genoveffa. 1984. Dominance and Control: How Our Culture Sees Women, Nature, and Animals. *Animals' Agenda* 4 (May/June):37.

Corrigan, Theresa. 1990. A Woman Is a Horse Is a Dog Is a Rat: An Interview with Ingrid Newkirk. In *And a Deer's Ear, Eagle's Song, and Bear's Grace: Animals and Women,* ed. Theresa Corrigan and Stephanie Hoppe, 162–80. Pittsburgh, Pa.: Cleis Press.

Curtin, Deane. 1991. Toward an Ecological Ethic of Care. *Hypatia* 6 (1):60–74. Reprinted in *Beyond Animal Rights: A Feminist Caring Ethic for the Treatment of Animals,* ed. Josephine Donovan and Carol J. Adams (New York: Continuum, 1996).

Dagilis, Andrew. 1980. Feminism: Our Sister Movement. *Agenda,* no. 4 (October):9–10.

Davis, Karen. 1988a. Farm Animals and the Feminine Connection. *Animals' Agenda* 8 (Jan/Feb):38–39.

———. 1988b. Farm Animal Feminism [letter]. *Animals' Agenda* 8 (June):4.

Donovan, Josephine. 1990. Animal Rights and Feminist Theory. *Signs* 15 (2):350–75. Reprinted in *Ecofeminism: Women, Animals, Nature,* ed. Greta Gaard (Philadelphia: Temple University Press, 1993), and *Beyond Animal Rights: A Feminist Caring Ethic for the Treatment of Animals,* ed. Josephine Donovan and Carol J. Adams (New York: Continuum, 1996).

———. 1991. Response to Nel Noddings. *Signs* 16 (2):422–25.

———. 1995. Comment on Kathryn Paxton George's "Should Feminists be Vegetarians?" *Signs: Journal of Women in Culture and Society* 21 (1).

———. 1996. Attention to Suffering: A Feminist Caring Ethic for the Treatment of Animals. *Journal of Social Philosophy* (forthcoming). Also in *Beyond Animal Rights: A Feminist Caring Ethic for the Treatment of Animals.* New York: Continuum.

Donovan, Josephine, and Carol J. Adams, eds. 1996. *Beyond Animal Rights: A Feminist Caring Ethic for the Treatment of Animals.* New York: Continuum.

Dwyer, Helene L. 1991. Women, Animals, and Sentimentality. *Women Wise* 14(3):7–8.

Elston, Mary Ann. 1987. Women and Anti-vivisection in Victorian England, 1870–1900. In *Vivisection in Historical Perspective,* ed. Nicolaas Rupke. London: Croom Helm.

Estés, Clarissa Pinkola. 1992. *Women Who Run With Wolves: Myths and Stories of the Wild Woman Archetype.* New York: Ballantine.

Feminists for Animal Rights. 1991. Statement of Opposition to the Gulf War. *Feminists for Animal Rights Newsletter* 6 (1–2):1.

Forbes, Dana. 1992. Liberating the Killing Fields. *Ms.* 2 (4):84–85.

Frantz, Pollyanne. 1991. Shame on the Furriers, or Will the Real Sexist Stand Up? *Feminists for Animal Rights Newsletter* 6 (1–2):9.

Gaard, Greta, ed. 1993. *Ecofeminism: Women, Animals, Nature.* Philadelphia: Temple University Press.

——. 1994. Mothering, Caring, and Animal Liberation. *Feminist for Animal Rights Newsletter* 8 (3–4):5, 12.

Gaard, Greta, and Lori Gruen. 1993. Ecofeminism: Toward Global Justice and Planetary Health. *Society and Nature* 4:1–35.

Goodyear, Carmen. 1977. Man Kind? *Country Women* (December):7–9.

Griffin, Susan. 1978. *Woman and Nature: The Roaring Inside Her.* New York: Harper & Row.

Grosshut, Sina. 1976. The Politics of Cruelty: Impressions of a Psychology Class on My Soul (Dedicated to the Victims of Vivisection). *Majority Report* (7–21 August):8–9.

Gruen, Lori. 1990. Gendered Knowledge? Examining Influences on Scientific and Ethological Inquiries. In *Interpretation and Explanation in the Study of Animal Behavior*, Vol. 1, ed. Marc Bekoff and Dale Jamieson, 56–73. Boulder, Colo.: Westview Press.

——. 1991. Review of Judith Plant, ed., *Healing the Wounds*, and Andrée Collard, *Rape of the Wild. Hypatia* 6 (1):198–206.

——. 1992a. Exclusion and Difference: Reflections on Women, Nature, and Animals. *American Philosophical Association. Newsletter on Feminism and Philosophy* (Spring):78–82.

——. 1992b. Review of Janet Biehl, *Rethinking Ecofeminist Politics. Environment Values* 1, 1:90–92. Longer version in *Hypatia* 7 (3):216–20.

——. 1993a. Dismantling Oppression: An Analysis of the Connection between Women and Animals. In *Ecofeminism: Women, Animals, Nature,* ed. Greta Gaard. Philadelphia: Temple University Press.

——. 1993b. Another Bridge to Cross [review of Carol Adams' *The Sexual Politics of Meat*]. *Between the Species* 9 (2):98–101.

Gruen, Lori, and Greta Gaard. 1995. Comment on Kathryn Paxton George's "Should Feminists be Vegetarians?" *Signs: Journal of Women in Culture and Society,* 21 (1).

Halpin, Zuleyma Tang. 1989. Scientific Objectivity and the Concept of the Other. *Women's Studies International Forum* 12 (3):285–94.

Haraway, Donna. 1989. *Primate Visions: Gender, Race, and Nature in the World of Modern Science.* London: Routledge.

——. 1992. Otherworldly Conversations: Terran Topics, Local Terms [review of Barbara Noske's book *Humans and Other Animals*]. *Science as Culture* 3 (1), no. 14.

Hoffman, Merle. 1990. Editorial [on the connection between women's liberation and animal liberation]. *On the Issues* 16 (Fall):2–3, 40–41.

Holford, Tricia. 1992. Snake Oppression. *Feminists for Animal Rights Newsletter* 6 (3–4):7.

Hoppe, Stephanie, and Theresa Corrigan. 1990. Paper into Flesh into. . . . In *And a Deer's Ear, Eagle's Song, and Bear's Grace: Animals and Women,* ed. Theresa Corrigan and Stephanie Hoppe, 190–217. Pittsburgh, Pa.: Cleis Press.

Johnson, Mary A. 1986. Animals in Folklore: A Cross-Cultural Study of Their Relation to the Status of Women. *Michigan Academician* 18 (Spring):175–83.

Kalechofsky, Roberta. 1988. Metaphors of Nature: Vivisection and Pornography—The Manichean Machine. *Between the Species* 4(3). 179–85.

———. 1991. Dedicated to Descartes' Niece: The Women's Movement and Anti-Vivisection in the Nineteenth Century. In *Autobiography of a Revolutionary: Essays on Animal and Human Rights,* 97–122. Marblehead, Mass.: Micah Press. Also in *Between the Species: A Journal of Ethics* 8, no. 2 (1992):61–71.

Kevles, Bettyann. 1990. Meat, Morality, and Masculinity. *Women's Review of Books* (May):11–12.

Kheel, Marti. 1983. Animal Rights Is a Feminist Issue. *Matrix* (March):1, 8–9. Revised version in *New Catalyst* (Winter 1987/88):8–9.

———. 1985a. An/Aesthetics: The Representation of Women and Animals. *Between the Species* 1 (Spring):37–45.

———. 1985b. The Conference on "Animals: Their Souls and Ours"—A Mixed Blessing. *Feminists for Animal Rights Newsletter* 1 (4):1, 6.

———. 1985c. A Feminist View of the Mobilization for Animals. *Feminists for Animal Rights Newsletter* 1 (1):2.

———. 1985d. The Liberation of Nature: A Circular Affair. *Environmental Ethics* 7 (2):135–49. Reprinted in *Beyond Animal Rights: A Feminist Caring Ethic for the Treatment of Animals,* ed. Josephine Donovan and Carol J. Adams (New York: Continuum, 1996).

———. 1985e. Speaking the Unspeakable: Sexism in the Animal Rights Movement. *Feminists for Animal Rights Newsletter* 2 (1):4–7.

———. 1987a. Befriending the Beast. *Creation* (September/October):11–12.

———. 1987b. The Conference on Culture, Nature, and Theory: Ecofeminist Perspectives. *Feminists for Animal Rights Newsletter* 3 (1–2):10–13, 15.

———. 1989. From Healing Herbs to Deadly Drugs: Western Medicine's War Against the Natural World. In *Healing the Wounds: The Promise of Ecofeminism,* ed. Judith Plant, 96–111. Philadelphia, Pa.: New Society Publishers.

———. 1990a. Ecofeminism and Deep Ecology: Reflections on Identity and Difference. In *Reweaving the World: The Emergence of Ecofeminism,* ed.

Irene Diamond and Gloria Feman Orenstein, 128–37. San Francisco: Sierra Club Books. Expanded edition in *Covenant for a New Creation,* ed. Carol S. Robb and Carl J. Caseboalt (Maryknoll, N.Y.: Orbis, 1991).

——. 1990b. Finding a Niche for Animals within the Greens. *Feminists for Animal Rights Newsletter* 5 (1–2):1, 5–6.

——. 1990c. If Women and Nature Were Heard. *Feminists for Animal Rights Newsletter* 5 (3–4):5, 7–8.

——. 1991. Of Wimps, Wars, and Biocide. *Feminists for Animal Rights Newsletter* 6 (1–2):5–7.

Kitzinger, Celia. 1991. Sex, Beauty, and Beasts. *New Internationalist* (January):18, 19.

Lansbury, Coral. 1985. *The Old Brown Dog: Women, Workers, and Vivisection in Edwardian England.* Madison: University of Wisconsin Press.

Leaps Forward: Postpatriarchal Eating. 1990. *Ms.* (July/August):59.

Luke, Brian. 1992. Justice, Caring, and Animal Liberation. *Between the Species* 8 (2):100–108. Reprinted in *Beyond Animal Rights: A Feminist Caring Ethic for the Treatment of Animals,* ed. Josephine Donovan and Carol J. Adams (New York: Continuum, 1996).

Macauley, David J. 1991. On Women, Animals, and Nature: An Interview with Eco-Feminist Susan Griffin. *American Philosophical Association Newsletter on Feminism and Philosophy* 90 (3):116–26.

Manning, Rita. 1992. Caring for Animals. *Speaking from the Heart: A Feminist Ethics.* Lanham, Md.: Rowman and Littlefield.

Mason, Jim. 1992. Malepractice & Animal Rights. *Animals' Voice* 5 (3):49.

——. 1993. *An Unnatural Order: Uncovering the Roots of Our Domination of Nature and Each Other.* New York: Simon and Schuster.

McDaniel, Jay B. 1989. *Of Gods and Pelicans: A Theology of Reverence for Life.* Louisville, Ky.: Westminster/John Knox Press.

McGuire, Cathleen. 1992. The Silencing of Women and Animals. *Feminists for Animal Rights Newsletter* 6 (3–4):1, 7.

McGuire, Cathleen, and Colleen McGuire. 1994. PETA and a Pornographic Culture: A Feminist Analysis of "I'd Rather Go Naked than Wear Fur." *Feminists for Animal Rights Newsletter* 8 (3–4):1, 9.

McKay, Nellie. 1992. Animal Rights and Me. *Feminists for Animal Rights Newsletter* 6 (3–4):5.

Merchant, Carolyn. 1984. Women of the Progressive Environment Movement: 1900–1916. *Environmental Review* 8 (1):57–85.

Meyerding, Jane. 1982. Feminist Criticism and Cultural Imperialism. *Agenda* 2 (6):14–15, 22–23.

Midgley, Mary. 1983. Women and Other Problems. In *Animals and Why They Matter: A Journey Around the Species Barrier.* New York: Penguin Books.

Moran, Victoria. 1988. Learning Love at an Early Age: Teaching Children Compassion for Animals. *Woman of Power* 9:54–56.

Newkirk, Ingrid. 1981. Animal Rights and the Feminist Connection. *Agenda* 1 (January):15–16.

Newkirk, Ingrid, with C. Burnett. 1988. Animal Rights and the Feminist Connection. *Woman of Power* 9:67–69.

Noddings, Nel. 1991. Response to Josephine Donovan. *Signs* 16 (2):418–22.

Noske, Barbara. 1989. *Humans and Other Animals.* London: Pluto Press.

Piggin, Julia R. 1988. Speciesism/Sexism: Exploitation in the 20th Century. *NAVS* [National Anti-Vivisection Society] *Bulletin* 2.

Polonko, Isle. 1991. Editorial on N.O.W.'s agenda and animal rights. *Feminists for Animal Rights Newsletter* 6 (1–2):8.

Prescott, Heidi. 1994. Hunting the Hunters: Women Hunt Saboteurs. *Feminists for Animal Rights Newsletter* 8 (3–4):5, 12.

Regan, Tom. 1991. Feminism and Vivisection. In *The Thee Generation.* Philadelphia: Temple University Press.

Reiter, Christine. 1990. We Are All Connected. *Feminists for Animal Rights Newsletter* 5 (3–4):17.

Ruether, Rosemary. 1992. Men, Women, and Beasts: Relations to Animals in Western Culture. *Between the Species* 8 (3):136–41. Reprinted in *Good News for Animals? Contemporary Christian Approaches to Animal Well-Being,* ed. Jay McDaniel and Charles Pinches (Maryknoll, N.Y.: Orbis, 1993).

Salamone, Connie. 1973. Feminist as Rapist in the Modern Male Hunter Culture. *Majority Report* (October).

——. 1982. The Prevalence of the Natural Law Within Women: Women & Animal Rights. In *Reweaving the Web of Life: Feminism and Nonviolence,* ed. Pam McAllister, 364–75. Philadelphia: New Society Publishers.

——. 1988. The Knowing. *Woman of Power* 9:53.

Scholtmeijer, Marian. 1993. *Animal Victims in Modern Fiction: From Sanctity to Sacrifice.* Toronto: University of Toronto Press.

Shapiro, Kenneth. 1994. The Caring Sleuth: Portrait of an Animal Rights Activist. *Society and Animals* 2 (2):145–65. Reprinted in *Beyond Animal Rights: A Feminist Caring Ethic for the Treatment of Animals,* ed. Josephine Donovan and Carol J. Adams (New York: Continuum, 1996).

Slicer, Deborah. 1991. Your Daughter or Your Dog? A Feminist Assessment of the Animal Research Issue. *Hypatia* 6 (1):108–24.

Smedley, Julia J. 1990. The Fathers Speak. *Feminists for Animal Rights Newsletter* 5 (1–2):4.

Smedley, Lauren. 1990a. Further than F.A.R.: In Search of a New Name. *Feminists for Animal Rights Newsletter* 5 (3–4):1, 12.

——. 1990b. Hunting Rabbits, Squirrels, and Little Girls. *Feminists for Animal Rights Newsletter* 5 (1–2):9.

Spangler, Luita. [1991]. A Woman's Task of Universal Respect. *Woman Wise* 14 (3):7–8.

Strom, Deborah, ed. 1986. *Birdwatching with American Women*. New York: Norton.

Sweeney, Noel. 1990. Animalkind and Human Cruelty: Racism, Sexism and Speciesism. *The Vegan* (Autumn).

Taksel, Rebecca. 1992. Feminists in the Making: Women Activists in the Animal Rights Movement. *Feminists for Animal Rights Newsletter* 6 (3–4):4–5.

Wagner, Sally Roesch. 1989. Animal Liberation. In *With a Fly's Eye, Whale's Wit, and Woman's Heart: Relationships between Animals and Women*, ed. Theresa Corrigan and Stephanie Hoppe, 222–30. Pittsburgh, Pa.: Cleis Press.

Walker, Alice. 1986. Am I Blue? *Ms.* (July). Reprinted in *Living by the Word: Selected Writings, 1973–1987* (San Diego, Calif.: Harcourt Brace Jovanovich, 1989).

———. 1988. Why Did the Balinese Chicken Cross the Road? *Woman of Power* 9:50. Reprinted in *Living by the Word: Selected Writings, 1973–1987* (San Diego, Calif.: Harcourt Brace Jovanovich, 1989).

———. 1988. Not Only Will Your Teachers Appear, They Will Cook New Foods for You. In *Living by the Word: Selected Writings, 1973–1987*, 134–38. San Diego Calif.: Harcourt Brace Jovanovich, 1989.

Weil, Zoe. 1990. Feminism and Animal Rights. *Labyrinth: The Philadelphia Women's Newspaper* (February):1–2.

———. 1993. Ecofeminist Education: Adolescence, Activism, and Spirituality. In *Ecofeminism and the Sacred*, ed. Carol J. Adams. New York: Continuum.

Westra, Laura. 1988. Animal Ethics, Biocentric Environmental Ethics, and Feminism. Response to Roberta Kalechofsky. *Between the Species* 4 (3):186–90.

Woman Wise. 1991. Animal Rights issue, 14 (3).

Notes on Contributors

Reginald Abbott recently received his doctorate in English from Vanderbilt University. His writing has appeared in *Modern Fiction Studies, Mosaic, The Henry James Review,* and *The Southern Quarterly.* He recently completed *Purple Prejudices: The Selected Criticism of Frances Newman.*

Carol J. Adams is the author of *The Sexual Politics of Meat: A Feminist-Vegetarian Critical Theory,* which will soon appear in German and Japanese editions, and *Neither Man nor Beast: Feminism and the Defense of Animals.* She edited *Ecofeminism and the Sacred* and has written the book *Woman-Battering,* part of Fortress Press's Creative Pastoral Care and Counseling Series. With Josephine Donovan, she coedited *Beyond Animal Rights: A Feminist Caring Ethic for the Treatment of Animals* (1996).

Diane Antonio, an animal conservationist, is an instructor at SUNY Stony Brook, where she is pursuing a doctorate in philosophy.

Lynda I. A. Birke is a biologist; she lectures in continuing education at the University of Warwick, where she also teaches Women's Studies (particularly feminism and science). Her books include *Feminism, Animals, and Science: The Naming of the Shrew; Women, Feminism, and Biology;* and *Tomorrow's Child: Reproductive Technologies in the 90s,* with Susan Himmelweit and Gail Vines. She coedited *More Than the Parts: Biology and Politics* and is currently editing a book with Ruth Hubbard, *Reinventing Biology: Respect for Life and the Creation of Knowledge.*

Maria Comninou is a professor of mechanical engineering and applied mechanics at the University of Michigan, Ann Arbor. Since 1986 she has been an animal rights activist, having founded a local nonprofit organization (ARARAT/WCAR) and served as an officer in various capacities for many years. Since writing this article, she has enrolled in the J.D. program at the University of Michigan Law School while holding a half-time academic appointment in engineering.

Karen Davis, Ph.D., is the founder, president, and director of United Poultry Concerns, Inc., which addresses the treatment of domestic fowl in food production, science, education, entertainment, and human companionship situations. Her articles have appeared in *Between the Species: A Journal of Ethics, Journal of English and Germanic Philology, Humane Innovations and Alternatives,* and many other professional journals and newspapers. She is the author of *Instead of Chicken, Instead of Turkey: A Poultryless "Poultry" Potpourri* and *Why Birds Don't Have Feathers: A Candid Look at the Poultry and Egg Industry.*

Josephine Donovan is the author of articles on the intersections between feminism and animal defense theory, as well as numerous works in feminist theory and women's literature, including *Feminist Theory: The Intellectual Traditions of American Feminism* (rev. ed., 1992). With Carol Adams, she coedited *Beyond Animal Rights: A Feminist Caring Ethic for the Treatment of Animals* (1996). She is Professor of English at the University of Maine.

Joan Dunayer is a freelance writer specializing in animal rights issues. Her publications include articles on such topics as stockyard cruelty to animals too disabled to walk, genetic disorders in "purebred" dogs, the sensitivity and human-inflicted suffering of fish, and academia's censorship of faculty members who oppose vivisection. A graduate of Princeton University, where she was among the school's first women undergraduates, she has master's degrees in English literature, English education, and psychology. Currently she is completing a book on speciesist language.

Gary L. Francione is professor of law and Nicholas deB. Katzenbach Scholar of Law at Rutgers University Law School, where he teaches criminal law, torts, and animal rights. Professor Francione is also codirector (with Anna Charlton) of the Rutgers Animal Rights Law Center. He is the author of *Animals, Property, and the Law* (intro. by William Kunstler; forthcoming from Temple University Press) and *Animal Rights and the Law* (forthcoming from Duke University Press).

Susanne Kappeler is a feminist activist and theorist who has taught feminist studies in universities and in other contexts. Based at the University of East Anglia's Centre for Creative and Performing Arts, she works as a freelance teacher and writer in England and Germany. She is the author of *The Pornography of Representation*.

Marti Kheel is a writer and activist in the areas of ecofeminism and animal liberation. Her articles have appeared in numerous journals and anthologies, including *Environmental Ethics, Between the Species, Woman of Power, Healing the Wounds: The Promise of Ecofeminism, Reweaving the World: The Challenge of Ecofeminism, Ecofeminism: Women, Animals, and Nature,* and *Animal Rights and Human Obligations.* She is cofounder of Feminists for Animal Rights (FAR) and creator of the FAR slide show, "Women, Animals, and Nature Through an Ecofeminist Lens."

Brian Luke grew up in Wisconsin and now lives in Dayton, Ohio, where he teaches philosophy at the University of Dayton and is coparenting two sons. He is very active in grassroots animal liberationist activism.

Marian Scholtmeijer is a freelance academic teaching English when employment is available and working independently on cultural representations of nonhuman animals. She has taught at several Canadian universities. Her book *Animal Victims in Modern Fiction: From Sanctity to Sacrifice* (University of Toronto Press, 1993) analyzes the intensive thought that fiction-writers have given to animal suffering since evolutionary theory demonstrated human connectedness to other animals.

Linda Vance is a professor at the California Institute of Integral Studies in San Francisco, where her focus is studies in self, society, and ecology. She has published and lectured widely on ecofeminism. In the summers, she works as a wilderness ranger for the San Juan/ Rio Grande National Forest in Durango, Colorado. She maintains a small private practice as an attorney representing environmental, women's, and peace organizations.

Index

Animal liberation (*cont.*)
168, 171–173, 290; nonpatriarchal metaethics of, 311–315; patriarchal metaethics of, 290–302, 312–313, 334; reason and, 291–296, 301–302, 312; social control and, 300–302, 312–313. *See also* Animal rights; Animal rights theory

Animal Liberation (Singer), 152, 291

"Animal nature," 37, 38

Animal research. *See* Vivisection

Animal rights: abortion and, 149–159; activists as "Bambi lovers" or terrorists, 144 n.19; environmentalism and, 98, 111, 115 n.223, 119 n.42, 202, 204, 210 n.9; politics of, 49; temperance movement and, 7; women and, 5, 34, 293–294. *See also* Animal liberation; Animal rights theory

Animal rights theory: academic respectability of, 293–294, 299; antisociality and, 300–312; emotion and, 291–295, 301–311, 312–314; ethical narrative of, 168, 171–173; feminist theory and, 49–50, 109, 175–185, 213–214, 217–219, 232, 233–234, 295, 322–324; holist philosophy vs., 98; individuals and, 172, 202, 295; patriarchal elements of, 291–302, 312–313, 334; reason and, 291–296, 301–302, 312; sentience and, 152–154, 295, 332, 334; social control and, 300–302, 312–313; speciesism in, 332–333, 334; subject-of-a-life concept and, 153–154, 332–333, 334; universalizing "other animals" and, 38–39; women absent in, 80; women's caring traditions and, 5–6. *See also* Animal liberation; Animal rights

Animals: altruism in, 23; as automatons, 221, 307–308; biological determinism and, 39, 50 n.4; biology and, 37, 39, 329–330; breeding of, 328–329, 345, 349; care respect for (*see* Caring); caring by, 217–218, 219; commodification of, 7–8; commonsense view of, 35, 41, 42; consciousness of, 40; defined, 25 n.17; denial of exploitation of, 303–308; emotional distance

from, 18, 19, 43–44, 45, 46, 303–311, 312; feminizing of, 5, 6, 12–13, 80; fixity of, 39, 50 n.3; genetic engineering and, 328–329, 349; giving voice to, 183, 185; human-animal connection (*see* Human-animal connection); humans as, 19, 23, 26 n.22; humans as superior to, 3–5, 11, 18, 19–23, 26 n.21, 35, 36–39; human suffering vs., 3–4; inferiority of women and, 1–2, 11, 16, 35; as irrelevant to women, 3–4, 35, 47; language and (*see* Language); legal rights of, 20, 127–128, 135, 156, 168–169, 196, 207, 261 n.10; legal standing of, 127–128, 135, 143 n.4; life history of, 182–183; lying by, 41; massive exploitation and abuse of, 16; minds of, 40–41; moral sense of, 40; objectification of, 7–8, 41, 67, 78–79, 106, 110, 168, 183, 306–308; as property, 156, 168, 169, 207; rationality in, 23; social constructionism and, 39, 42, 48, 163–189, 234; somatophobia and, 2; subjectivity of, 7, 41, 306–308; universalizing "other animals," 37–39, 46, 49, 106, 182, 231–235, 330; as victims, 234–241, 321–324; woman-animal connection (*see* Woman-animal connection); women as unlike, 1–2, 32, 49. *See also* Animal abuse; Domestic animals; Eating animals; Ethical narratives about animals; Fictional portrayals of animals; Slaughter of animals; Vivisection; Wild animals; *specific animals*

Animal sacrifice (religious), 128, 129, 144 n.11, 13, 303

Animal Welfare Act, 127, 143 n.5

Animal welfarists, 152–153, 195

Anthropocentric utilitarianism. *See* Utilitarianism

Anthropocentrism, 3–5, 23, 232–233, 234, 256

Anthropomorphism, 40, 241, 244, 252

Anti-Semitism, 321

Antisociality, 300–312

Antivivisection movement. *See* Vivisection

Apes. *See* Primates (nonhuman)

Children: forcing to eat meat, 309; somatophobia and, 2
Chimpanzees. *See* Primates (non-human)
Chodorow, Nancy, 105
Christianity. *See* Religion
Citadel, 75
Classification: power and, 336–342
Classism, 333–334, 337–338
Cobb, John, 206, 207
Cockfighting, 223
Coercion: methods of, 69–71
Cognitive ethology, 40–41
Collard, Andrée, 16, 22, 171, 292, 302
Commodification of animals, 7–8
Communal virtue, 218–219
Communication: human vs. non-human forms of, 21–22, 26 n.20
Community: as construct, 348–349; fictional human-animal, 235, 252–256, 259 n.4, 260 n.4; international, 341–344, 345; otherness and, 235, 252–256
"Companion animals": use of term, 81 n.2. *See also* Animal abuse; Domestic animals; *entries beginning with* Pet
Compassion. *See* Caring; Emotion
Consciousness of animals, 40
Consequentialism, 152–153, 158 n.3. *See also* Utilitarianism
Conservationism, 324–327
Constructionism. *See* Social constructionism
Contrucci, Joyce, 16, 22
Cooperation: by wild animals, 6
Cosmetics testing, 34, 41, 45
Cows: factory farming of, 13–14, 24 nn.6, 7, 8, 9, 192–193, 308; pejorative metaphors and, 13–14, 15; veal calves, 207; women and, 13, 14, 15, 196. *See also* Domestic animals
Creativity: animal liberation and, 314–315
Croatia. *See* Bosnian/Serbian war
Cronon, William, 166–167, 179
Culling, 44–45
Cultural biologism, 336–342
Cultural constructionism. *See* Social constructionism

Cultural feminism. *See* Feminism: radical cultural
Culturalism, 324, 337–339

Dairy industry. *See* Cows
D'Eaubonne, Françoise, 229 n.1
Declension narratives about animals, 166–167, 168, 170–174, 179, 182
Deep ecology: domestic animals and, 6, 195–197, 198; ecofeminism and, 6, 195–197, 198, 229 n.3; ethical narrative of, 168, 173–174, 181; experience and, 86; hunting and, 101, 108, 196–197; identification with nature and, 100–101, 108; macho mystique of, 196–197, 201. *See also* Environmentalism; Land ethic; Leopold, Aldo
Democracy, 339
Denial of animal exploitation, 303–308
Deontologism, 153–154, 159 n.3. *See also* Rights theories
Descartes, René, 221, 307–308
Devall, Bill, 101, 174
Dialectic narratives about animals, 166–167, 169–170, 177–178, 179
Dillon, Robin S., 217
Dinnerstein, Dorothy, 105
Dissection, 313
Dodos, 18
Dogs: breeding of, 14, 24 nn.10, 11, 42; child abuse and abuse of, 75, 76, 77; in fiction, 249; forced sex between women and, 66–67, 68; harassment and abuse of, 78; pejorative metaphors and, 12, 14, 15; Victorian preoccupation with, 270; woman-battering and abuse of, 60, 61, 62, 63, 66–67, 68, 73, 78; women and, 12, 14, 15, 249
Dolphins, 23, 207
Domestic animals, 192–210; animal conservationists and, 195, 349; Downed Animal Act, 127; environmentalism and, 6, 193–194, 195–197, 198–209; feminism and, 81 n.2, 195–197, 198; feminizing of, 5, 6, 12–13, 80; giving voice to, 194–195, 197, 198–209; holistic

ethics and, 173, 174; liberation in fiction, 238–239; moral status of, 173, 174, 193–194, 195–197, 198–209, 333; sexism and, 23 n.2; as slaves, 207, 249, 258 n.3; speciesism and, 15; women and, 5, 6, 7, 12–15, 196. *See also* Factory farming; Slaughter of animals

Domestic violence. *See* Woman-battering

Dominance. *See* Ethical narratives about animals; Male dominance

Donovan, Josephine, 5, 109, 217, 292, 293

Doughty, Robin W., 266, 267, 268

Downed Animal Act, 127

Dualism, 2, 3, 233, 292–293, 323–324

Dworkin, Andrea, 130, 132

Eating animals: animal welfarists and, 195; autonomy opposed by, 313; biblical justification for, 303; as communion, 103, 107; denial of harm done by, 304, 305–306; denial of personal responsibility for, 303–304; eating vegetables vs., 109; environmentalism and, 111, 119 n.42, 210 n.7; ethical narratives and, 185; forcing children to eat meat, 309; holistic ethics and, 173; hunters and, 103–104, 107, 136, 141, 178; male aggression and, 250; "necessity" for, 311; as sexual, 103–104; utilitarian arguments against, 169, 187 n.4. *See also* Vegetarianism

Eaton, Randall, 90, 100, 141

Ecofeminism: caring and, 111, 181, 183–185, 213–219; deep ecology and, 6, 195–197, 198, 229 n.3; defined, 229 n.1; domestic animals and, 6, 195–197; ethical narratives and, 168, 175–185, 188 n.12; experience and, 86; humanist/rationalist tradition and, 35; hunting and, 88, 104–111, 112 n.2; violence and, 111; wolves and, 214–216, 217, 218–219, 226, 228; woman-animal connection and, 35; woman-nature connection and, 233–234, 258 n.3

Educationalism, 324

Egg industry. *See* Chickens: factory farming of

Emotion: animal liberation and, 291–295, 301–311, 312–314; distancing from animals, 18, 19, 43–44, 45, 46, 108, 303–311, 312; ethics and, 291–294, 301–314; gender issues and, 292–294; primacy of, 312–313; psychological battering and, 63–65; reason vs., 291–295, 312; reliability of, 312; science's denial of, 43–44, 45, 46, 306–308; undercutting, 303–311; unreliability of, 292, 301, 302, 312. *See also* Caring

Empathy. *See* Caring; Emotion

Emshwiller, Carol, 253, 254–256, 261 n.11

Endangered species, 326–327, 345

Enlightenment orientation, 299–300

Environmentalism: animal rights and, 98, 111, 115 n.23, 119 n.42, 202, 204, 210 n.9; anthropocentrism and, 5; biological diversity and, 349; domestic vs. wild animals and, 6, 193–194, 195–197, 198–209; eating animals and, 111, 119 n.42, 210 n.7; ethical narratives and, 166–174, 176–185, 197–198; holism of, 171, 173–174, 177–178, 197–198, 199, 202–203, 210 n.7; hunting and, 86–88, 92–101, 102–104, 108, 109–110, 111, 114 n.16, 17, 115 nn.18–23, 119 n.42, 196–197; macho mystique of, 196–197, 201. *See also* Deep ecology; Ecofeminism; Leopold, Aldo

Estés, Clarissa Pinkola, 227, 261 n.11

Ethical narratives about animals, 163–189; conscious and appropriate, 176–177, 178–185; declension (anti-anthropocentric), 166–167, 168, 170–174, 179, 182; dialectic (anthropocentric utilitarian), 166–167, 169–170, 177–178, 179; ecofeminism and, 168, 175–185, 188 n.12; environmentalism and, 166–174, 176–185, 197–198; facts vs. values and, 180–181; progress (dominationist), 166–167, 179, 182, 232

Ethics: actions vs. state of mind and, 111; adversarial relations and, 296–298; classical theories of, 171–172; emotion and, 291–294, 301–314; feminism and, 111; holistic, 171, 173–174, 177–178, 197–198, 199, 202–203, 210 n.7; hunting and, 86–88, 92–104, 110, 111; moral sense of animals, 40; necrocentric, 107; nonpatriarchal metaethics of animal liberation, 311–315; patriarchal metaethics of animal liberation, 290–302, 312–313, 334; reason and, 291–296, 298–299, 301, 312; social control and, 290–291, 296, 298–302, 312–313; universal principles and, 294–297

Ethnic cleansing, 324–327, 340
Ethnicism, 340–344, 348–349
Ethnopluralism, 338–339
Ethology, 40–41
Eugenics, 324, 329, 333
Eurocentrism, 323
Europe: nationalism and, 338–339, 340–341, 342–343
Evolution, 22–23, 37, 328, 339
Exploitation of animals. *See* Animal abuse; Animal rights; Denial of animal exploitation; Factory farming; Vivisection
Extinction, 324–327, 348, 349

Factory farming: animal conservationists and, 349; antisociality and, 302; of chickens, 13, 24 nn.4–6, 200–202, 204–205, 206, 208–209, 305, 308; of cows, 13–14, 24 nn.7, 8, 9, 192–193, 308; denial of harm done, 304, 305–306, 308; fur "farming," 16; language and, 305–306; objectification and, 308; of pigs, 18, 25 nn.15, 16, 308. *See also* Domestic animals; Slaughter of animals
Fantasy: as subversive, 255–256, 258 n.2
Farnham, Alan, 133, 136, 141
Fascism: animal rights and, 49
Feelings. *See* Caring; Emotion
Femicide, 110
Feminism, 1–8; adversarial relations and, 297–298; ambivalence about

animals in, 35–36; animal rights politics and, 49; animal rights theory and, 49–50, 109, 175–185, 213–214, 217–219, 232, 233–234, 295, 322–324; anthropocentrism and, 3–5; attention and, 109, 111, 184, 215; biological determinism and, 34, 36, 37, 39, 49–50; caring and, 5–6, 108, 109, 111, 118 n.37, 151–152, 181, 183–185, 189 n.16, 213–219; commonsense view of animals and, 35; domestic animals and, 81 n.2, 195–197, 198; dualism and, 2, 3, 233, 323–324; ethical narratives and, 168, 175–185; evolutionary discontinuity and, 37; fictional portrayals of animals and, 234, 251–252, 256–257; future research needs, 6–7; human-animal connection and, 33–39, 49–50; hunting and, 104–111; interconnection of forms of oppression and, 321–324; irrelevance of animals to, 3–4, 35, 47; liberal, 1–3; otherness and, 45–46, 47, 48–49, 50, 257; pornography and, 129–130; power and, 321, 322–323; purpose of, 3; radical cultural, 3, 7; rape and, 324–325, 345–348; rights theories and, 151–152, 188 n.7; science and animals and, 32–39, 45–46, 47–50; sexism and, 345; silence about animals in, 3, 34; social constructionism and, 36–37, 38, 39, 234; somatophobia and, 2; speciesism and, 320–321, 335–336; universalizing "other animals" and, 37–39, 46, 49; utilitarian theories and, 188 n.7; victimism and protectionism and, 321–324; war and, 324–325, 345–348; woman-animal connection and, 1–8, 33–39, 233–235; woman-battering and animal abuse and, 73–80; woman-nature connection and, 2, 36, 213–214, 233–234, 258 n.3; women as unlike animals and, 1–2, 32, 36–37

Feminist Anti-Censorship Task Force, 130
Feminists for Animal Rights, 81 n.6
Feminizing: of domestic animals, 5,

Hunter harassment (*cont.*)
  nography and, 129, 131, 132–133,
  135–136, 140; sexual harassment
  and, 128, 137–140
Hunting, 85–119; absent referent
  concept and, 136, 139; actual experience of animals, 108–110,
  111; attention and, 109–110, 111;
  biocide and, 87, 88; birth and,
  107–108, 118 n.36; bow-hunting,
  306; death and, 103, 107–108, 182;
  denial of harm done, 306; eating
  animals killed, 103–104, 107, 136,
  141, 178; ecofeminism and, 88,
  104–111, 112 n.2; as elemental/
  instinctual, 89–90, 95, 105, 106–
  107, 110, 113 n.8, 119 n.40, 198,
  302; environmentalism and, 86–
  88, 92–101, 102–104, 108, 109–
  110, 111, 114 nn.16–17, 115
  nn.18–23, 119 n.42, 196–197; ethical codes of, 86–88, 92–104, 110,
  111; of foxes, 15–16; happy (recre-
  ational/sport) hunters, 87, 88, 89,
  92–95, 97, 98, 99, 104, 109–111,
  135; hired hunters, 87, 112 n.3;
  holist (objective) hunters, 87, 89,
  95–99, 104, 109–111, 174; holy
  hunters, 87, 88, 89, 99–104, 107–
  111; hostile hunters, 87, 112 n.3;
  hungry hunters, 87–88; identification with animals and, 100, 101,
  108–109, 141; identification with
  nature and, 89–90, 100–101, 102–
  103, 105, 106–108, 141; management of "game" and, 96–97, 115
  n.19, 178, 188 n.10, 223–224, 306;
  masculine self-identity and, 15,
  88, 94, 104–110, 112 n.4, 135,
  196–197; as mutual exchange,
  101–102, 104, 108–109, 110, 117
  n.30, 31; Native Americans and,
  86, 87–88, 101–102, 112 n.4, 116
  n.27, 177–178, 182, 225; natural
  predators vs., 96; objectification of
  animals and, 110; photography
  vs., 90, 91; pornography and, 128–
  137, 140; privacy rights and, 131–
  132, 134, 136, 140; rape and, 104,
  111, 136–137, 140–141; rites of
  passage and, 106, 135, 198; self-
  restraint and, 92, 94–95, 99, 104,
  115 n.18; sexual component of,

88, 90–92, 94, 97, 103–104, 110,
  113 n.4, 113 nn.8, 10, and 11, 114
  n.12; speciesism and, 15–16; as
  speech, 135, 140; types of hunters,
  87; utilitarian arguments against,
  169; violence and, 87, 88, 93, 98–
  99, 104, 106, 108, 110, 111;
  woman-animal connection and,
  15–16; women and, 88, 107, 113
  n.6, 140, 141, 142
Hurston, Zora Neale, 241–242, 245–
  247, 251

Identity: and fictional portrayals of
  animals, 235, 241–252, 259–260
  n.4
Identity politics, 336–342
Immigration, 341–342, 344
Indigenous peoples, 306, 341. *See
  also* Native Americans
Individualism: animal rights theories and, 172, 202, 295; conflict
  resolution and, 151–152, 173; defined, 171; holism vs., 171, 173–
  174, 197–198, 199, 202–203; reproduction and, 348–349
Inferiority of women: animals and,
  1–2, 11, 16, 35
Inherent value concept. *See* Rights
  theories; Subject-of-a-life concept
Initiation. *See* Rites of passage
Insects, 171, 243–244, 253
Instinct: hunting and, 89–90, 95,
  105, 106–107, 110, 113 n.8, 119
  n.40, 198, 302; reason vs., 301–302
Interconnection: feminizing and,
  108; of forms of oppression, 2, 3,
  4, 79, 321–324; of forms of violence, 79–80. *See also* Caring
International community of na-
  tions, 323, 341–344, 345
Internationalism, 324, 341–342, 343
Invertebrates, 171. *See also* Insects
Isolation, 70, 72, 235–236

Jackson, Mike, 74, 75, 82 n.15
Jones, Ann, 65, 67, 71
Judeo-Christian tradition. *See* Reli-
  gion
A Jury of Her Peers (Glaspell), 55–56

Kafka, Franz, 260 n.4
Kanzi, 21

Kelly, Liz, 77
Kheel, Marti, 141, 171, 172, 183, 292
Killing of animals. *See* Slaughter of animals
Kingsford, Anna, 294
Knowing: ways of, 23
Koko, 21, 26 n.20
Kotzwinkle, William, 260 n.4
Kuhse, Helga, 333

Laboratory research. *See* Vivisection
Land ethic, 95–96, 173, 193. *See also* Deep ecology; Leopold, Aldo
Language: animal indifference to, 255; chicken metaphors, 12–13; cow metaphors, 13–14; emotional distance from animals and, 18; factory farming and, 305–306; female pejoratives, 11–16; fox metaphors, 15–16; identity and, 248; male pejoratives, 16; nonhuman vs. human, 21–22, 26 n.20; oppression and, 17; patriarchy and, 19–22, 208; pornography and, 24 n.4; racism and, 16–17; science and, 43–45, 48, 51 n.10, 208; sexism and, 11–16, 18–21, 143 n.2; speciesism and, 11–26, 143 n.2; vivisection and, 304; wolves and, 17, 220, 222, 229 n.4
Lansbury, Coral, 232
Lardner, George Jr., and Kristin, 60–61
Left wing: animal rights and, 49
Legal rights: of animals, 20, 127–128, 135, 156, 168–169, 196, 207, 261 n.10
Legal standing: of animals, 127–128, 135, 143 n.4
Le Guin, Ursula, 221, 231, 241–242, 244–245, 247, 248, 251, 253, 255–256
Leopold, Aldo, 89–90, 94–96, 97, 98, 114 n.17, 115 nn.18–19, 141, 173, 193–194, 196, 199–200, 219
Lesbian battering: animal abuse and, 82 n.16
Lesbian pornography, 138
Lessing, Doris, 237–238
Lewis, Martin, 98
Liberal feminism. *See* Feminism: liberal
Lispector, Clarice, 241, 242–243, 247

Loneliness, 235–236, 312
Lopez, Barry, 100, 102, 218, 219, 222
Lorenz, Konrad, 62–63, 228
Lowe, Cecelia, 62, 63, 75
Lowe, Michael, 62, 63, 73, 75
Lying: by animals, 41
Lynch, M. E., 35, 44

MacKinnon, Catharine, 58, 126, 130, 132, 137
Mahoney, Martha R., 82 n.13
Male dominance: animal abuse and, 56, 59, 62, 63, 67, 69–75, 78, 79–82; construction of, 6–7, 11, 19–20, 21, 22, 23, 26 n.21; fictional portrayals of animals and women and, 235–241, 250–252, 254–255, 259–260 n.4; as "natural," 336; as a right, 334–335; woman-battering and, 56, 57–58, 59, 62, 63, 65, 67, 69–75, 78–82. *See also* Masculinity; Patriarchy; Sexism
"Man"/"mankind," 19–22
Marchiano, Linda, 66, 68
Marital rape. *See* Rape
Masculinity: cruelty toward animals and, 232; environmentalism and, 196–197, 201; hunting and, 15, 88, 94, 104–110, 112 n.4, 135, 196–197; interconnection with other forms of oppression, 324; of nature, 6–7; rape and, 347–348; wild animals and, 6–7, 196–197. *See also* Male dominance; Men; Patriarchy
Massingham, H. W., 264, 266, 273, 274–275, 276–277, 280–281 n.1
Maurier, Daphne du, 240–241
Mazza, Chris, 240, 241
Meat-eating. *See* Eating animals
Media: wilderness as masculine and, 6–7
Men: disidentification process of, 105–106; nature and, 105–106; speciesist language and, 16, 18–19. *See also* Male dominance; Masculinity; Patriarchy
Men's movement: initiation and, 117 n.34
Metaethics. *See* Ethics
Metaphors. *See* Language
Mice, 42, 78, 127
Minds of animals, 40–41

Morality. *See* Ethics
Mrs. Dalloway (Woolf), 272, 274
Mueller, Gene, 131
Mules, 18, 245, 246–247
Multiculturalism, 337, 338–339, 340
Multinational corporations, 344
Mumford, Lewis, 90
Mundane's World (Grahn), 253–254, 255–256
Munro, Alice, 238–239
Murdoch, Iris, 109
My Ántonia (Cather), 225–228
Mythmaking, 182, 183

Naess, Arne, 173–174. *See also* Deep ecology
Narratives. *See* Ethical narratives about animals; Fictional portrayals of animals
Nash, Roderick Frazier, 197–198
Nationalism, 324, 338–339, 340–344, 345, 347–349
Native Americans: conscious ethical narratives and, 177–178, 182; hunting and, 86, 87–88, 101–102, 112 n.4, 116 n.27, 116 n.27, 177–178, 182, 225; reservations of, 344; resistance struggles of, 341; wolves and, 225
Nature: biology and, 329–330; ethical narratives and, 165–189, 232; humans vs., 35; hunting and, 89–90, 100–101, 102–103, 105, 106–108, 141; as masculine, 6–7; men and, 105–106; science and, 43; somatophobia and, 2. *See also* Environmentalism; Woman-nature connection
Nazis, 328–329
Necrocentric ethic, 107
Nelson, Richard, 86, 89, 90, 101, 102, 109, 112 n.4
New World Order, 341–344
Nilsen, Alleen Pace, 12
Noddings, Nel, 317 n.16
Noske, Barbara, 32

Objectification: of animals, 7–8, 41, 67, 78–79, 106, 110, 168, 183, 306–308; science and, 335; of women, 67, 79, 105–106. *See also* Otherness; Subjectivity

Objectivity, 43
Object relations theory, 105, 117 n.33
Oppression: domestication of animals and, 23 n.2; identity politics and, 336–342; interconnection of forms of, 2, 3, 4, 79, 321–324; language and, 17; victimization and, 321–324
Ortega y Gassett, José, 89, 90–91, 103, 141
Otherness: care respect and, 217–219, 226; community and, 235, 252–256; feminism and, 45–46, 47, 48–49, 50, 257; fictional portrayals of animals and, 231–261, 257 n.2; identity and, 235, 241–252; power of, 233–235, 241, 251, 256, 257; science and, 45–46, 47, 48–49; technology and, 46; universalizing "other animals," 38–39, 46, 49, 106, 182, 231–235, 330; victimization and, 234–241; woman-animal connection and, 231–235, 257, 261 n.11; women as "other," 231–235, 257. *See also* Objectification
Our Nig (Wilson), 252

Paglia, Camille, 130–131
Pain, 171, 304, 332. *See also* Suffering
Parrots, 21, 25 n.19
Passive voice: science and, 43–44, 51 n.10
Patriarchy: animal rights theory and, 291–302, 312–313; human-animal relationship and, 2, 19; language and, 19–22, 208; metaethics of animal liberation and, 290–302, 312–313; "The Plumage Bill" (Woolf) and, 274–277; rights concept and, 151; speciesism and, 19–20, 330–334; violence and, 79–80, 82 n.16; wilderness as masculine and, 6–7. *See also* Male dominance; Masculinity; Sexism
"Peace talks," 340, 345
Pejoratives. *See* Language
Pepperberg, Irene, 25 n.19
Pet abuse: woman-battering and, 55–56, 58, 59–82. *See also* Animal abuse; Domestic animals

Pet death, 64, 65, 76–77
Pet keeping: animal conservationists and, 349
"Pets": use of term, 81 n.2
Pet shelters: for battered women's companion animals, 61–62, 81 n.6
Pigs, 17–19, 25 nn.15–16, 308. *See also* Domestic animals
Pitts, Deirdre Dwen, 241
"The Plumage Bill" (Woolf): analysis of, 6, 263–278, 280–286; text of, 287–289; themes of, 271
Plumwood, Val, 108, 174
Politics: biology and, 327–330, 336–342; feminism and animal rights and, 49; identity, 336–342; vegetarianism and, 352 n.42; wolf social organization and, 228
Population control, 324
Pornography: antipornography legislation and free speech and, 126–127, 128–129, 130, 132–134, 135–136, 138, 140, 142; feminism and, 129–130; harms theory and, 133–134, 138; human-animal sexual activity and, 66–67, 78; hunter harassment and, 129, 131, 132–133, 135–136, 140; hunting and, 128–137, 140; lesbian, 138; pejorative language and, 24 n.4; supporters of, 130–131; violence and, 130, 131, 133; vivisection and, 232; wildlife documentaries and, 6
Poultry. *See* Chickens
Power: abolishing, 335–336; abuse of, as "natural," 336; classification and, 336–342; feminism and, 321, 322–323; methods of coercion, 69–71; of otherness, 233, 234, 241, 251, 256, 257; rights vs., 334–336; speciesism and, 334–336; of woman-animal connection, 233–235
Primates (nonhuman): abstract thinking in, 193, 196; communication by, 21, 26 n.20; humans as apes, 26 n.22; rights of, 196, 207, 261 n.10; as subjects, 41; as superior to humans, 23; written vs. spoken scientific accounts of, 44
Primatology: politics of, 34, 36
Privacy rights: animal abuse and,

156; child abuse and, 155–156, 157, 159 n.7; hunting and, 131–132, 134, 136, 140; legal decisions protecting, 155; reproductive choice and, 126–127, 132, 134, 136, 155–157, 158
Procter-Smith, Marjorie, 208
Professionalism, 324
Progress narratives about animals, 166–167, 179, 182, 232
Property: animals as, 156, 168, 169, 207
Prostitution, 136
Protectionism: victimism and, 321–324, 335
Psychological battering, 59, 63–65, 68, 76, 81 n.11

Racism: benefiting from, 323; biology and, 337–338; changing targets of, 328–329; compartmentalizing, 321, 324; culture and, 337–339; nationalism and, 341; reproduction and, 348; science and, 327–328; speciesism and, 330, 331, 333–334; speciesist language and, 16–17. *See also* Slavery
Rape: "condom rape" trial, 78; feminism and, 324–325, 345–348; forced sex between women and animals, 58, 60, 65–69, 71, 77–78; hunting and, 104, 111, 136–137, 140–141; marital rape, 65–69, 139; masculinity and, 347–348; "mass," 326; nationalism and, 324–327, 345, 346–348, 349; as natural behavior, 140–141; reproductive consequences of, 346–347; in war, 324–326, 345–348, 349; woman-battering and, 58, 59, 60, 63, 65–69, 71, 77–78, 222–223, 321
Rationality. *See* Reason
Rats, 18, 25 n.13, 41, 42, 127
Reason: animal liberation and, 291–296, 301–302, 312; in animals vs. humans, 23; emotion vs., 291–295, 312; ethics and, 291–294, 298–299, 301, 312; liberal feminism and, 2, 35; moral community membership and, 1; somatophobia and, 2
Reductionism of science, 39–40

Regan, Tom, 116 n.27, 150, 153, 154, 171, 291–294, 295, 296–297, 301, 315 nn.2 and 4, 316 n.7, 333
Reiger, John, 93, 94
Religion: animal sacrifice, 128, 129, 143 n.11, 13, 303; eating animals and, 303; fall from grace, 172; freedom of, law and, 128; hunting and, 114 nn.14 and 15; nature and animals and, 43; wolves and, 216, 219–220. *See also* Bosnian/Serbian war; Holy hunters
Reproduction, 328–329, 344–349
Reproductive choice. *See* Abortion
Reproductive technology, 324, 349
Reservations: establishment of, 344
Respect: defined, 214–215. *See also* Caring
Rights theories: conflict and, 172; feminism and, 151–152, 188 n.7; fetal rights and, 153–154, 155, 159 n.5; inherent value and, 159 n.3; power vs., 334–336; Regan's, 150, 153, 171, 291–294, 295, 301; speciesism and, 334–336. *See also* Subject-of-a-life concept
Right wing: animal rights and, 49
Rites of passage, 106, 117 n.34, 135, 198
Ritvo, Harriet, 35–36, 269–270
Roe v. Wade, 155, 157, 159 n.6
Rolston, Holmes, 91, 98, 100, 103, 180
A Room of One's Own (Woolf), 265, 271, 273, 276
Roosters. *See* Chickens
Ruddick, Sara, 184
Ruether, Rosemary Radford, 2
Russell, Diana, 62, 69

Santeria religion, 128, 129, 144 nn.11 and 13
Schleifer, Harriet, 195
Science: ambivalence about animals, 44–45, 48–49; anthropomorphism and, 40; biological determinism vs. social constructionism and, 39, 48; compassion and caring and, 45–47; culling and, 44–45; denial of feelings, 43–44, 45, 46, 306–309, 310–311; denial of individual animals, 40; ethology, 40–41; feminism and

animals and, 32–39, 45–46, 47–50; feminist praxis in, 48; interconnection with other forms of oppression, 324; justifying use of animals in, 38, 302–305, 306–309, 310–311; minds of animals and, 40–41; naturalism vs. experimentalism in, 41; nature and, 43; objectification and, 335; objectivity and, 43; otherness and, 45–46, 47, 48–49; passive voice and, 43–44, 51 n.10; politics and, 327–330, 336–342; racism and, 327–328; reductionist approach of, 39–40; role of animals in, 36, 39–43, 48; sexism and, 34; spoken accounts of, 44, 45; subjectivity and, 345, 347–348, 349; women in, 45, 46–48; written accounts of, 43–45, 48, 51 n.10, 208; zoological classification and speciesism and, 332–333, 334, 344–348. *See also* Biology; Vivisection
Sentience, 152–154, 155, 295, 332, 334
Serbia. *See* Bosnian/Serbian war
Serpell, James, 302, 303, 306
Sessions, George, 89, 101, 174
Sessions, Robert, 229 n.3
Sexism: animal rights theory and, 292–294; biology and, 337–338, 344–348; defined, 344; feminism and, 345; language and, 11–16, 18–21, 143 n.2; reproduction and, 344–348; science and, 34; speciesism and, 5, 6, 11–16, 18–19, 22, 23 nn.1–3, 330, 331, 334, 344–348
Sexual abuse: of children, 78, 321; forced sex between women and animals, 58, 60, 65–69, 71, 77–78; woman-battering and, 58, 59. 60, 63, 65–69, 71, 222–223, 321. *See also* Rape
Sexual harassment: bestiality and, 78; defined, 137–138, 139, 146 n.33; free speech and, 126–127, 140, 142; gender-based norms and, 138; hunter harassment and, 128, 137–140
Sexuality: eating animals and, 103–104; hunting and, 88, 90–92, 94, 97, 103–104, 110, 113 n.4, 113 nn.8, 10, and 11, 114 n.12

Three Guineas (Woolf), 265, 271, 276, 282 n.3
Trapping, 15–16, 135
Tuan, Yi-Fu, 75, 81 n.2
Tulip, 197
Tuna, 207
Turtles, 23

United Poultry Concerns, 197
Universalizing "other animals," 37–39, 46, 49, 106, 182, 231–235, 330
Universal principles: ethics and, 294–297
Utilitarianism: anthropocentric, 169–170; conflict and, 172, 297; defined, 158 n.3; eating animals and, 169, 187 n.4; environmental, 181; feminism and, 188 n.7; hunting and, 169; moral issues and, 169; Singer's, 150, 152–153, 171, 291–292, 293–294, 295, 297, 333; vivisection and, 169

Veal calves, 207
Vegetables: eating animals vs. eating, 109
Vegetarianism: in fiction, 249–250; as political strategy, 352 n.42; reason and gender and, 293; universal principles and, 295–296; women and, 7, 249–250; Woolf and, 284 n.8, 285 n.12. *See also* Eating animals
Victimism: protectionism and, 321–324, 335
Victimization: in fictional portrayals of women and animals, 234–241, 259 n.4
Victorian "animal estate," 268–270, 283–284 n.8, 284 n.9
Violence: abolishing, 335–336; common characteristics of, 77; eco-feminism and, 111; fiction and, 234; genetic engineering and, 329; hunting and, 87, 88, 93, 98–99, 104, 106, 108, 110, 111; interconnection of forms of, 79–80; naming forms of, 110–111; as natural, 98–99, 335; patriarchy and, 79–80, 82 n.16; pleasure and, 93, 99; pornography and, 130, 131, 133; rites of passage and, 106; sexual component of, 58; spiritualization

of, 88 (*see also* Holy hunters); victimism and protectionism and, 321–324; in wildlife documentaries, 6–7. *See also* Animal abuse; Child abuse; Rape; Woman-battering
Viva, 194–195, 198, 209
Vivisection: abortion and, 154; animal conservationists and, 349; antisociality and, 302; antivivisection movement, 5, 7, 34, 41, 42; cosmetics testing, 34, 41, 45; culling and, 44–45; denial of harm done, 304–305, 306–308; dissection, 313; feminism and, 32–39, 45–46, 47–50; invisibility to public, 304–305; "laboratory animal" construction and, 42–43, 48, 51 nn.7 and 9; laboratory technicians, 45, 46–47, 309, 310; language and, 304; laws protecting, 127–128; "necessity" for, 311; number of animals used in, 47–48; objectification and, 7, 41, 306–308; overriding aversion to, 310–311; pain and suffering of animals, 47–48, 304; pornography and, 232; professional rewards of, 310–311; public opposition to, 41–42; role of animals in, 36, 39–43; utilitarian arguments against, 169; women and, 142. *See also* Science
Vixens: women as, 15
"Voice of the voiceless," 208

Walker, Alice, 199, 242, 248–252, 295–296
War, 324–326, 340–341, 344, 345–348, 349
Warren, Karen, 176, 177–178, 181, 182, 188 n.12
Washoe, 21
Webb, Mary, 236–237, 261 n.11
Werewolves, 216, 220, 222, 244–245
Whales, 195, 223, 326
Wild animals: environmentalism and, 6, 193–194, 195–197, 198; ethical narratives and, 179, 189 n.18; holistic ethics and, 173, 178; legal rights of, 135; masculinity and, 6–7, 196–197; violence in documentaries about, 6
Wilderness: as masculine, 6–7

Library of Congress Cataloging-in-Publication Data
Animals and women : feminist theoretical explorations / edited by
Carol J. Adams and Josephine Donovan.
Includes bibliographical references (p.   ) and index.
ISBN 0-8223-1655-2 (cl : alk. paper). —
ISBN 0-8223-1667-6 (pbk. : alk. paper)
1. Animal welfare.   2. Animal rights.   3. Feminist theory.
I. Adams, Carol J.   II. Donovan, Josephine, 1941–
HV4711.A59   1995
179'.3'082—dc20   95-17002 CIP